T0330362

Work, Employment and Flexibility

THE FUTURE OF WORK AND EMPLOYMENT

The future of work and employment has rarely been as opaque as it is now and never as speculated upon. This important series will explore the biggest issues facing the modern workforce, policy-makers and businesses today. Its books will include topics as diverse as the rise of the gig economy to the role of platform companies and an ageing workforce. Book proposals on topics such as employment (in)security, inclusivity, equity, remote teams, wellbeing, AI, digitalisation and voice will be welcomed. Books will be theoretically rigorous and empirically grounded but also will light the way for future research and debate in the field of employment relations.

For a full list of Edward Elgar published titles, including the titles in this series, visit our website at www.e-elgar.com.

Work, Employment and Flexibility

Innovation, Technology and the Changing
World of Work

Edited by

Peter Holland

*Professor of Human Resource Management, Swinburne
University of Technology, Melbourne, Australia*

Chris Brewster

*Professor of International Human Resource Management,
Henley Business School, University of Reading, UK*

Nadia K. Kougiannou

*Associate Professor of Work and Employment, Nottingham
Business School, Nottingham Trent University, UK*

THE FUTURE OF WORK AND EMPLOYMENT

Edward Elgar
PUBLISHING

Cheltenham, UK • Northampton, MA, USA

Published by
Edward Elgar Publishing Limited
The Lypiatts
15 Lansdown Road
Cheltenham
Glos GL50 2JA
UK

Edward Elgar Publishing, Inc.
William Pratt House
9 Dewey Court
Northampton
Massachusetts 01060
USA

A catalogue record for this book
is available from the British Library

Library of Congress Control Number: 2024934606

This book is available electronically in the **Elgar**online
Business subject collection
http://dx.doi.org/10.4337/9781035309368

MIX
Paper from
responsible sources
FSC
www.fsc.org   FSC® C013056

ISBN 978 1 0353 0935 1 (cased)
ISBN 978 1 0353 0936 8 (eBook)

Printed and bound in Great Britain by TJ Books Limited, Padstow, Cornwall

Contents

About the editors

Peter Holland is Professor of Human Resource Management and Director of the Executive MBA at Swinburne University of Technology, Melbourne, Australia. Peter has worked in the Australian Finance sector and consulted to the private and public sector in a variety of areas related to human resource management (HRM) and employee relations. His current research interests include employee voice and silence and workplace electronic monitoring and surveillance. He has authored/co-authored 15 books and over 150 journal articles, monographs and book chapters on a variety of human resource management and employee relations issues.

Chris Brewster has substantial industrial experience and got his doctorate from the London School of Economics before becoming an academic. He is now a part-time Professor of International Human Resource Management at Henley Business School, University of Reading in the UK, specialising in international and comparative HRM. He has been involved as author or editor in the publication of more than 30 books, including McNulty and Brewster, *Working Internationally: Expatriation, Migration and Other Global Work* (Edward Elgar, 2019) and Brewster, Mayrhofer, and Farndale, *A Handbook of Comparative Human Resource Management* (2nd edition. Edward Elgar, 2018).

Nadia K. Kougiannou is Associate Professor of Work and Employment at Nottingham Business School, Nottingham Trent University, UK, and an Academic Associate of the CIPD. Nadia has published in several high-ranking journals such as the *British Journal of Management, Human Resource Management Journal, British Journal of Industrial Relations, Industrial Relations: A Journal of Economy and Society* and *New Technology, Work and Employment* and has written and co-authored several book chapters on employee voice and silence. Nadia's research interests are employee voice and silence, trust, social justice, 'atypical' work such as the gig/platform economy and bridging the research-practice gap.

Contributors

Valerie Anderson is Emeritus Professor of HRD and Education at the University of Portsmouth, UK. Valerie is also Chair of the international grouping, the University Forum for HRD (UFHRD). She is an expert in learning, development and employability. She chairs the British Standards Institute (BSI) and the Technical Committee for Human Capital Standards (HCS/1) and is a member of the International Organization for Standardization (ISO) and the Technical Committee for Human Resource Management Standards (TC260). As a committed researcher-practitioner, she combines work on funded research projects with authoring of practitioner tools, webinars and reports.

Angel Belzunegui-Eraso works in the Department of History and History of Art (Sociology section) at the University Rovira I Virgili, Spain. Angel has researched two main fields: organisational transformations and, specifically, how teleworking impacts these changes, and social structures, social exclusion and poverty. He directed the Chair of Social Inclusion at the URV. His skills and experience are in quantitative social research, sociology of organisations, social capital, social exclusion and public health. He has been principal investigator in competitive projects at national and international level and director of the Jean Monnet module 'The challenges of the European Union in the social agenda: poverty, inequality, and social inclusion'.

Ilona Bučiūnienė is Professor and Dean of the Doctoral School at ISM University of Management and Economics, Lithuania. Ilona's research focuses on sustainable HRM and its outcomes, technological change, diversity management and well-being at work. Her research has been published in the *Academy of Management Journal, Academy of Management Discoveries, Journal of Vocational Behavior*. She is on the editorial boards of *Human Resource Management* (Wiley) and *Human Resource Management Review* (Elsevier), and serves as the Ambassador for Lithuania at the AOM HR Division. She has led and has been involved in international research initiatives and networks, and represents Lithuania in the Cranet International HRM Network.

Alyssa Chhim has completed a masters by research degree focusing on the work experiences of young people with disabilities. Alyssa has extensive industry experience working alongside providers to support people with disabilities to gain and maintain employment.

Amaya Erro-Garcés is Associate Professor at the Universidad Pública de Navarra, Spain. Amaya received a PhD in Economy at Universidad Pública de Navarra. Her research is focused on open innovation, teleworking and digital transformation. Her articles have appeared in the *Human Resource Management Journal, International Journal of Manpower, Employee Relations, Journal of Cleaner Production, Journal of Higher Education Policy and Management* and *International Business Review,* among other outlets. She has served as the guest editor for two Special Issues in the *Production, Planning, and Control Journal* and the *International Journal of Manpower.*

Antonio Fernández García is Lecturer in Labour and Social Security Law at Universitat Oberta de Catalunya (UOC), Barcelona, Spain (since 2017). Antonio has a PhD in Law (2012), a Masters degree in Business and Contractual Law (2009) and a Bachelor's degree (2008) in Labour Sciences (all from Universitat Rovira i Virgili). His research interests are: employment policies, digital recruitment, new forms of employment and self-employment, equality and non-discrimination.

Anthony Forsyth is Distinguished Professor in the Graduate School of Business and Law at RMIT University in Melbourne, Australia. His research covers many aspects of employment and workplace law, including collective bargaining, trade unions, union education, labour hire, the gig economy, and the optimal legal and regulatory systems for building collective worker power. In 2015–16, Anthony was the independent Chair of the Victorian Government Inquiry into Labour Hire and Insecure Work. The recommendations in the Inquiry's Final Report formed the basis for the Labour Hire Licensing Act 2018 (Vic). He is the author of *The Future of Unions and Worker Representation – The Digital Picket Line* (Hart Publishing, 2022) and co-author of *Creighton & Stewart's Labour Law* (7th edition, The Federation Press, 2024).

Angela Garcia Calvo is Lecturer (Assistant Professor) at the Henley Business School, University of Reading in the UK. Her research focuses on comparative political economy, industrial transformation, business policy, globalisation and the intersection of these themes. Angela's academic work has been published by *Review of International Political Economy, Business and Public Policy* and the *Journal of Economic Policy Reform.* She has held visiting positions at the London School of Economics, Harvard University, UC San Diego, Yonsei University and the Collegio Carlo Alberto in Torino.

Debora Jeske is a work psychologist and L&D practitioner in Berlin, Germany. Debora is also Adjunct Senior Lecturer at University College Cork in Ireland where she supports a number of research projects. Debora completed her PhD in Industrial-Organizational Psychology in 2011 at Northern Illinois University. Her main area of interest pertains to the interaction of technology and psychology at work.

Rūta Kazlauskaitė is Professor at ISM University of Management and Economics, Lithuania. Rūta's research interests include occupational health and well-being, social well-being, work environment, corporate social responsibility, sustainability and comparative HRM. She has published her research in *Academy of Management Journal* and *International Journal of Management Reviews*. She is the editor-in-chief of the *Baltic Journal of Management* and editorial/review board member of the *International Journal of Human Resource Management* and *European Management Review*. She is a representative for Lithuania and Advisory group member in Cranet International HRM Network.

Clare Kelliher is Professor of Work and Organisation at Cranfield School of Management, Cranfield University, UK. Clare's research examines the organisation of work and the management of the employment relationship. In particular, she has developed a body of work focused on the implementation and outcomes of flexible working arrangements. She has published her research findings widely in academic journal articles, books, blogs and through media commentary. Her research has been used in the development of policy by governments, non-governmental organisations and think tanks and she has worked with many employers to shape their working practices.

Marius Kušlys is Senior Lecturer and a PhD student at ISM University of Management and Economics, Lithuania. Marius completed his undergraduate and postgraduate studies at ISM and has been working at ISM since 2016. In 2020, he participated in the Lithuanian Research Council funded research project 'Industry 4.0: Addressing Challenges for Productivity, Employment and Inclusive Growth', and presented the results of the research to politicians and business leaders. Marius has published two textbooks for students and several research articles in peer-reviewed journals. He teaches macroeconomics, mathematics and statistics.

Hannah Meacham is Senior Lecturer in the School of Management at RMIT University in Melbourne, Australia. Hannah's research focus is on the inclusion of workers with intellectual disabilities within mainstream workplaces, along with the workplace well-being of home care workers in the aged care sector. She has previous industry HR management experience in developing policy for disability inclusion. Hannah is currently an associate editor of the *Asia Pacific Journal of Human Resource Management* and *Journal of Business Research*.

Pedro Mendonça is Associate Professor of Work and Employment at Edinburgh Business School, Heriot-Watt University in Scotland, UK. His research interests lie in global and digital dynamics involving supply chain impacts on work and employment and in particular how new technologies are harnessed by companies to increase labour flexibility and productivity and at the same time decrease opportunities for worker voice and general working conditions. Pedro has published in journals including *Work, Employment and Society*, *British Journal of Industrial Relations*, *Industrial Relations: a Journal of Economy and Society* and *British Journal of Management*.

Tse Leng Tham is Researcher and Lecturer at the Chair of Organisation and Human Resource Management, ESCP Business School, Berlin, Germany. She has published scholarly work on workplace well-being and climate and has a particular focus on its intersection with challenges arising from the changing landscape of contemporary workplaces (e.g., technology, employee privacy, voice, burnout) in journals such as *Human Resource Management* and *International Journal of Human Resource Management*. Tse Leng's research interests include workplace well-being and climate, and future of work challenges, particularly within the frontline workforce. Her research projects are conducted often in collaboration with large industry partners such as the Police Association of Victoria and the Victorian Ambulance Union.

Daniel Wheatley is Reader in the Department of Management at the University of Birmingham, UK. Daniel's research focuses on work and well-being including job quality, work-life balance, flexible working, remote and hybrid work, spatial dimensions of work including work-related travel, leisure time and the household division of labour. He is author of *Well-being and the Quality of Working Lives and Time Well Spent: Subjective Well-being and the Organization of Time* (Rowman & Littlefield, 2017) and co-editor of the *Handbook of Research on Remote Work and Worker Well-being in the Post-COVID-19 Era* (with Irene Hardill and Sarah Buglass, IGI Global, 2021) and the *Handbook of Research Methods on the Quality of Working Lives* (Edward Elgar, 2019).

Tugce Yerlitas is a PhD student in Management at ISM University of Management and Economics, Lithuania. Her research focuses on human capital sustainability and sustainable human resource management. She also has a particular interest in emerging technologies in human resource management and is exploring the potential effects of artificial intelligence on ethical issues within the field of human resources. Tugce has presented her research results at various prestigious international conferences, such as the Annual Academy of Management Meetings, and has been involved in global research projects, such as the Global Alliance for Ethics and Impacts of Advanced Technologies.

PART I

Historical and evolutionary perspective

1. The changing nature of work, employment and flexibility

Peter Holland, Chris Brewster and Nadia K. Kougiannou

INTRODUCTION

We are witnessing a significant structural change in work and employment. The fact that this change has been evolving over several decades and evolves spasmodically should not blind us to what is happening. Work always evolves – driven by new markets, new technology, rapid developments in information and communications technology (ICT) and artificial intelligence (AI), and, of course, major events like the pandemic. As such, work is increasingly being done in new ways. Work is so fundamental to our societies that it inevitably interacts with other significant changes. In this book, we want to tease out and draw attention to some of the major changes that have been, and are going on in our societies and the world of work. We suggest that in many of the more developed countries, the 20th century saw an increasing 'standard-isation' of work and a growing reliance by society on 'employment'. Things change at different speeds in different countries, but we can take the end of the 20th century as the high point of that movement. Since then, our societies have been, incoherently and stutteringly, but unerringly, moving away from employment and standard working methods and developing ever more flexible forms of work (and terms and conditions). Little is 'new' in the 21st-century development of flexible working practices, varying working times, working places and working contracts – though technology enables different forms. In many respects, our approaches to work tend towards going 'back to the future' to replicate those patterns and practices that occurred at the beginning of the first industrial revolution. The end result has been the gradual separation of work from employment and the creation of ever more precarious work, self-employment epitomised and the rise of the 'gig' economy.

Arguably, employment has been a fundamental aspect of developed economies for approximately 300 years, contingent upon the specific societal context. In the world's wealthier nations, often referred to as Advanced Market

Economies (AMEs), these societies have been structured around employment, which, for a considerable duration, underwent a gradual (albeit uneven) standardisation process. Our living patterns, towns and cities, our transport systems, our health, social security and education systems, and our approaches to funding government all relied on a notion of standardised employment. Less importantly, but meaningfully for some of our readers, human resource management (HRM) has also been built on the concept of employment.

Standard (full-time) or regulated employment reached its peak, perhaps, towards the end of the economic boom of the late 1970s. Up to this point, there was a broad assumption that the steady development of employment towards a regulated, established 'jobs for life' pattern would continue and while economists, politicians, business leaders and trade unionists were cautious about any belief that the stable economic conditions would continue, they nevertheless tended to see the same pattern of employment continuing into the future. But things change.

Supporting this transition from the late 1970s onward was the rise of new economic ideologies, notably neoliberalism, which prompted a shift in economic paradigms across many AMEs towards embracing free markets and deregulation, significantly impacting the labour market (Harvey, 2007). At the macro government level, the deregulation of labour markets has filtered down to the meso organisational level, influencing work principles, policies and practices. This has manifested in the adoption of less stringent employment contracts at the micro or workplace level, often resulting in less job security or increased flexibility. At the heart of this change was a sense of strategic management of people within a philosophy of creating competitive advantage through what were seen as these increasingly key resources (Boxall, 2018) in an expanding and interconnected global economy. The underlying word here is resources, which actively commodified labour. From this focus, a strategic fit between all aspects of HRM and organisational strategy was developed (Sheehan et al., 2016). The use of these seemingly 'bland' terms overlooks the significant contextual shift in work and working life that has occurred, frequently disguised under the notion of flexibility. These changes are frequently perceived as predominantly benefiting the employer (Schultz et al., 2003). They illustrate a one-sided progression when observed within the context of rising job insecurity, heightened work intensity, extended work hours, and diminishing protective measures such as labour laws and representation (Brewster & Holland, 2020; Olafsen et al., 2017). This was further exacerbated (or entrenched) by the emergence of globalisation and technological advancements, which facilitated knowledge outsourcing and offshoring of white-collar work to emerging economies (Holland et al., 2008). These cost-cutting strategies, of course, were a logical extension of the commodification of labour.

Many of these changes in work patterns and practices have been instigated under the overarching concept of 'flexibility' and the removal of what management might perceive as constraining work structures and practices. The diminishing influence of trade unions has often facilitated this shift, ironically a result of restructuring, offshoring and governmental support through legislation that has been unfavourable towards trade unions, notably prevalent in Anglo-American countries.

By the end of the 20th century, several academic commentators, such as Legge (1998) and Sennett (1998), recognised the effect and impact of flexibility in hollowing out the workplace jobs, occupations and professions and, ultimately, the narrative of people's working lives. This is an important time to note these commentaries as this was at the cusp of what many have described as the 4th industrial revolution (Holland et al., 2021). While there is nothing new about the commentators for each industrial revolution hailing a fundamental change in work and employment, we would argue what we are experiencing now is akin to a transformation in work and employment not seen since the first industrial revolution (Schwab, 2016). So, what are the differences? In a traditional sense, old jobs and sectors are being replaced by new ones, for example, social media managers. However, what is significant in the 4th industrial revolution is that robots and AI can increasingly perform both old and new kinds of work. Put differently, the groundwork is being laid for the substitution of work and employment by advancing technology – a cycle where technology itself will eventually replace the existing technological advancements (Holland et al., 2021). This, coupled with the growingly unregulated 'gig' economy where individuals work independently without a specific employer and lack the safety net of established terms and conditions, draws parallels to the dynamics of the first industrial revolution. During this period, the emphasis shifted towards seeking work rather than formal employment within the work system. Reflecting on this gives an insight into the potential future of work and employment as we currently understand it.

What we suggest is that today's revolution is different in kind from that of previous technological revolutions, and in the following sections of this chapter, we explore the nature of the current revolution, its impact on employment in developed societies, and the implications for those of us who study work and employment. This potential scenario might represent a dystopian future for individuals seeking stability in traditional employment relationships. This may be best encapsulated in Lyons's commentary on Silicon Valley's work culture, arguably one of the most modern work environments worldwide, which begins with a somewhat ironic introduction – welcome to your job.

First, you are lucky to be here. Also, we do not care about you. We offer no job security. This is not a career. You are serving a short-term tour of duty. We provide no training or career development. If possible, we will make you a contractor rather than an actual employee, so we don't have to provide you with any benefits or a pension plan. We will pay you as little as possible. Our goal is to burn you out and churn you out. (Lyons, 2019: 1)

This may be the fulfilment of Legge's (1998) and Sennett's (1998) argument regarding the erosion of meaningful employment and the eventual attainment of absolute flexibility, where labour is ultimately, or in modern terms, 'strategically' reduced to a commodified cost factor.

While we grapple with these transformations in AMEs, it is crucial to recognise that these changes remain an ongoing challenge for developed societies. In many less developed economies, employment was always available to only a minority of people, with most working in 'informal employment' – or what we will refer to as non-employed work. For many countries, such work remains the source of income for a huge majority of the working population. Similar working patterns have been slowly, inconsistently, but steadily returning to developed societies since the first stages of labour market deregulation in the early 1980s.

Recent 'shocks' to the system have accelerated these changes and given them a higher profile – though we accept Grint's (2022) point that there never was a mythical period of calm when people felt that they were not living through major change. The accelerated use of flexible patterns of work became an essential part of the economies of most developed societies as a result of the global economic crisis that began in 2008. Similarly, the election of populist leaders in some developed countries encouraged businesses to increase their use of flexibility. Using the internet to work from home (or from anywhere) had been possible for decades but was hugely accelerated by COVID-19. And, in the UK specifically, Brexit has been associated with greater pressures to move away from standard working. We emphasise our point, though, that these changes have been developing over several decades. Recent shocks have served to underscore the ongoing transformations, and while technology has facilitated some shifts in work practices, it may be more appropriate to see it as having accelerated the pace or scale of change. However, the trajectory of these changes has been evident for many years. Regardless of the specific causes or circumstances in each country or case, the data is evident, leaving no doubt that flexibility in employment has been increasing while standard employment patterns have been declining. Now, more people have work (rather than employment) that involves 'atypical' and increasingly virtual work relationships than have 'typical' employment patterns. Our thesis is that the implications of these changes for our societies, economic success, people and scholarship are enormous and considerably more substantial than our current understandings suggest.

Next, we set the changes in a historical context, outline some of the key features of these changes and draw out some of the important implications of the growth in flexibility in working patterns for all the stakeholders.

HISTORICAL PERSPECTIVE

The evolution of work, shaped by successive industrial revolutions, reached its apex during the era of 'standard employment' from around 1945 to the 1980s. This period marked a significant upsurge in job security, heightened employment rates, and the establishment of a comprehensive regulatory framework governing work practices. Characterised by enduring, secure employment featuring defined hours and extensive benefits, it set the benchmark for job stability. Yet, a noticeable shift unfolded in the 1980s, witnessing a decline in traditional secure job models. This transformation was instigated by technological leaps, globalisation, and shifts towards neoliberal economic ideologies. These alterations steered a departure from conventional employment norms, fostering greater acceptance of flexible work setups, a surge in temporary and part-time roles, and a waning sense of job security that had long defined previous decades. This shift away from the prevailing standard employment model has continued to expand, marking a significant departure from mid-20th-century employment structures.

The profound impact of technological advancements has wielded a pivotal influence in reshaping the global employment landscape. Alongside this, government interventions, spanning regulation and deregulation, have significantly steered the evolution of work structures. The departure from the once-dominant 'standard' employment model has evolved gradually, heralding the rise of the gig economy. This international transformation arises from various drivers, including the pressing need for employer cost-efficiency. However, the ethos of neoliberalism, stressing market deregulation and economic efficiency, has accentuated a singular focus on cost reduction within the employment domain. This paradigm shift has revamped employer-employee dynamics, championing flexibility and often placing cost-efficiency above broader concerns of job security and stability. The ascendance and growing prevalence of the gig economy epitomises this transformation, characterised by transient arrangements such as short-term contracts, freelance work and on-demand labour. Consequently, conventional employment norms are yielding to more adaptable and flexible work structures on a global scale.

EVOLUTION OF FLEXIBLE PATTERNS OF WORK

The evolution of flexible work patterns represents a pivotal chapter in the narrative of employment transformation. It embodies a departure from the conventional work norms, tracing its roots to diverse forms such as flexible working, zero-hour contracts, and temporary work arrangements that gained prominence over the years. However, the most emblematic shift has been witnessed in the proliferation of gig and platform-based working models. These frameworks encompass various independent, short-term engagements where individuals operate on a task-to-task basis facilitated through digital platforms. The gig economy, characterised by its flexibility and transient nature, has reshaped labour markets, offering opportunities and challenges to workers and industries.

Moreover, the concept of flexible organisations, epitomised by the 'Flexible Firm' model, has emerged as a paradigm shift in organisational structures. These entities exhibit adaptability in responding to market changes by employing a mix of permanent and temporary staff, allowing for nimble adjustments in workforce composition based on demand fluctuations.

The pandemic outbreak has indeed magnified the criticality of flexible work arrangements. Remote work swiftly emerged as a norm, illustrating the paramount significance of adaptable locations in reshaping the conventional workplace landscape. Across numerous industries, organisations promptly pivoted, enabling employees to operate from diverse locations, effectively erasing the boundaries between the home and office spheres. This shift underscores the profound interconnection between flexible work patterns and the transformative nature of work amidst external disruptions. However, it is crucial to acknowledge that while remote work has become feasible and prevalent in numerous sectors, there remain industries where such flexibility remains limited. In certain sectors, the nature of work and operational requirements necessitates physical presence, making remote work impractical. This disparity in the feasibility of remote work highlights the nuanced landscape across industries, emphasising the selective adaptability of flexible work arrangements in specific sectors.

IMPLICATIONS

The rise of flexible work patterns, intertwined with the tenets of neoliberalism, bears significant implications that intersect with broader socio-economic dynamics. The shift towards flexible arrangements is intricately linked with the framework of 'predatory capitalism', characterised by the relentless pursuit of profit at the expense of societal well-being. The widening gap in wealth distribution, a hallmark of this era, has been fuelled by the selling off of state assets to often unaccountable private interests, exacerbating inequality on a global scale. Furthermore, the expansion of government reliance on management consultancies has narrowed political discourse, relegating crucial societal concerns – particularly those of the marginalised and impoverished – to the periphery of public debate.

As we glimpse into the future, a growing segment of the workforce finds themselves situated at the bottom rungs, engaged in highly flexible work arrangements. This trend mirrors an alarming increase in societal inequality, with the privileged seeking to fortify their positions at the expense of the disadvantaged. These disparities manifest both nationally and internationally, raising critical questions about the sustainability of such a paradigm. The societal ramifications are profound, fracturing communities and exacerbating social stratification. This trajectory of growing inequality and entrenched privilege challenges the sustainability of this model in the long term.

Moreover, it is imperative to recognise the profound reliance of governments and societies on traditional employment structures. Government revenue streams heavily depend on employment metrics, while historical union agendas have been largely centred on employment rather than broader conceptions of work. The decline of unions, inextricably linked with the rise of flexible working and the erosion of 'employment', further reinforces this systemic shift. Even in the 1980s, prescient voices warned of the implications of increased work flexibility, underscoring the urgency of addressing the evolving dynamics of work and their far-reaching consequences (Brewster & Connock, 1985). This evolution not only impacts economic landscapes but fundamentally reshapes the social fabric, demanding a re-evaluation of policies and priorities to mitigate the adverse effects of this paradigm shift.

CONTRIBUTIONS

The first part of this book explores the historical and evolutionary perspective of work, employment and flexibility. In providing context to this change, Kougiannou and Mendonça explore the impact of technology. They emphasise that work stands as a dominant element in contemporary society. However, the definition and practice of work are undergoing a transformation due to heightened competition and technological advancements. From this standpoint, they question traditional assumptions regarding the time, place and space in which work takes place, as well as the nature of work. While highlighting the impact of the COVID-19 pandemic on work patterns and practices, they stress that this should be perceived within the context of accelerating work patterns rather than accepting a 'new normal', as the post-pandemic discourse on work tends to imply. What they do emphasise, though, is the issue of the technological impact on work, fundamentally altering how workers undertake their tasks. To highlight this, they point to the rise of the gig economy workforce, which is estimated to have increased from 43 million in 2018 to 78 million in 2023 (Alfes et al., 2022). As a result, the traditional concepts of work and employment are becoming increasingly disassociated for many. The most notable issue for the worker is the loss of benefits such as workplace security, safety and income guaranteed by their employers. Kougiannou and Mendonça note that the emergence of work without formal employment agreements has prompted discussions regarding the future of workers' rights and well-being. Moreover, with the apparent decline of employment and the potential loss of even gig economy work to those who can offer a lower cost, there is increasing uncertainty about worker rights in this race to the bottom. As such, they call for the exploration of regulatory frameworks tailored to address the unique challenges posed by these evolving work practices to ensure the well-being and rights of workers in non-traditional employment arrangements.

In exploring these issues advanced above, the experts in their fields have been asked to provide a contemporary perspective on how they see aspects of this work and employment changing. In investigating the evolution of work, Kelliher thoroughly examines various forms of new working arrangements broadly categorised as flexible working. Specifically, the author scrutinises the diverse aspects of where, when and what defines work, alongside exploring the nature of work within employment relationships. As with this book's focus, Kelliher notes that the emergence of these working arrangements challenges standardised contemporary notions of the work, workplace and working day. In undertaking this approach, Kelliher explores the factors that have influenced the development and growth of particularly flexible work patterns. From this, the author explores the impact of these working arrangements on individual workers as well as the consequences of these developments and implications for future working patterns.

The second part of the book focuses on work patterns and flexibility, commencing with Wheatley's chapter. This chapter explores the evolution of working time, particularly examining the perceived rise in flexibility over recent decades. It discusses the associated issues concerning the temporal, spatial and locational aspects of work across various occupations and industries. However, the central theme is the tensions between worker autonomy and managerial control and the imposition of managerial control systems associated with the concept of 'productivity paranoia' – where management doesn't trust a workforce they can't actively see, to be productive. This reminds us of the ongoing autonomy-control paradox debate where 19th-century monitoring surveillance is veiled over 21st-century work practices, which have implications for job satisfaction, performance and improved work-life balance (seen as crucial aspects of a productive workforce). Such paranoia can actively limit genuine flexibility and can be captured in the 'faux flexibility' moniker.

Following Wheatley's focus on time, Bučiūnienė, Kazlauskaitė, Yerlitas and Kušlys focus on place of work as an emerging issue through the support of technology and the growing demand for flexibility. Focusing on telework, which has attracted increasing attention on a variety of levels, Bučiūnienė et al. explore the optimistic perspective, which is mainly achieved in AMEs, compared to the limited forms in less developed countries, highlighting multiple barriers and constraints to these work arrangements. The key point is that while the pandemic was a catalyst for this change, it is likely to be uneven and sporadic in its evolution across regions and countries. While calling for more research on this phenomenon, Bučiūnienė et al. explore the trends and development of this work in the post-COVID period and the challenges associated with them.

In the following chapter, Calvo examines the evolving nature of work and flexibility within the platform or 'gig' economy. Specifically, the discussion revolves around the contrast between the reality and rhetoric of platform work. The chapter emphasises the platform work's potential to create a substantial volume of jobs that may lack excellence in quality, conceivably reinforcing current societal inequalities. In addressing platform work, the author adopts a broad perspective of platforms to highlight tensions between existing institutional arrangements and three key areas of work: management power and work processes, social protection and labour rights, and skills and career prospects. This is important as these areas have received little attention from scholars and policymakers. In this part's final chapter, Garcés, Belzunegui-Eraso and Fernández García brings this part to a conclusion by combining several of the key features addressed above focusing on ICTs, as a key theme in organisations ability to control (platform work), the time worked (platform work, job sharing), the duration of the contractual relationship (casual work, interim management) and remuneration (voucher-based work). She notes that characteristics of these forms of employment do not lie so much in their novelty but in their spread. While remote platforms or teleworking from home had been developing to a different extent and intensity in Europe, it was only after the catalyst of the pandemic that has accelerated these forms of flexibility.

The third part of the book explores disruption, continuity and change in aspects of work post-pandemic. Kougiannou and Holland explore the changing dynamics of employee voice and communication. They argue that the pandemic has hastened the development of hybrid and remote work and assert that the redefining of the contemporary work environment has significant and often unintended effects on workplace relationships. They argue this decentralisation (and isolation) of the workforce can make it challenging for employees to interact effectively with each other and with management, fragmentating traditional voice mechanisms and systems. If voice/communication breaks down, effective decision-making will likely suffer. Amidst an environment growing more volatile and unpredictable, it becomes imperative to contemplate these facets that constitute the workplace fabric within this evolving landscape. The chapter delves into several emerging issues and the consequences of unchecked or unchallenged flexible work on employee voice and the power dynamics in the workplace.

An area also impacted by the changing nature of work through and after the pandemic is electronic monitoring and surveillance, or EMS. Tham, Holland and Jeske highlight the pandemic's role in accelerating and reshaping the where, when and how of work, amplifying flexibility and autonomy. However, for managers grappling with the challenges of overseeing work outside their direct supervision, the 'productivity paranoia' was met with a surge in electronic tracking, monitoring and surveillance tools. This returns us to the theme of the flexibility paradox, wherein higher levels of autonomy and flexibility beget greater and wider forms of control. The chapter also explores the repercussions of the blurring boundaries between work and home within remote and flexible work setups. It also examines the growing prevalence of AI in processing data gathered through EMS devices and its potential ramifications on privacy, discrimination, ethics and trust within the employment relationship. These issues have far-reaching consequences and must be more fully understood as remote and flexible work become part of our new normal.

This part concludes with a challenging assessment of the role of the trade union movement in all this change. Forsyth explores the future of trade unions through a mix of theoretical frameworks and case studies. While highlighting a series of high-profile successes in hostile environments, Forsyth's general view is pessimistic based upon the ongoing decline of trade union membership and the rise of insecure work – a key point he raises is the need to reverse in many AMEs the decades of hostile union legislation.

The final part of the book explores some often-overlooked aspects of work, technology and flexibility in this era of dynamic change. The first chapter in this part explores issues associated with learning, development and employability and disadvantaged and marginalised workers. Anderson discusses the skill and employability implications arising from the changing nature of work and employment. By illustrating changes in the labour market over decades, Anderson highlights the proliferation of different forms of non-standard, virtual, remote and precarious work arrangements, highlighting questions about whether traditional approaches to vocational training and employability remain appropriate. This leads the author to assess what learning, training, education and employability policy and practice responses will be necessary to address the consequences of these changes.

Meacham and Chhim explore flexibility from the perspective of those potentially more disadvantaged in society. They point out that over the decades, flexible work patterns have become attractive to disadvantaged and underprivileged workers, enabling them to gain and maintain a foothold in the labour market. However, the research identifies that while flexible work patterns may appear to open up opportunities for disadvantaged workers, they may, in fact, open them up to greater prejudice in the workplace and social isolation, work-family conflict and exclusion from promotion and training opportunities. This, they point out, is important as the workforce becomes more diverse through care responsibilities, younger workers combining work and study, older workers staying in the workforce longer, and more workers with disabilities attempting to enter the mainstream workforce. The issue of flexibility as a stigma for women in the workplace and voluntary and involuntary flexibility within the white-collar workforce is also examined. The chapter concludes with a discussion on mental health concerns and the needs of people with disabilities. In the final chapter, another area impacting the world of work brought to the fore by recent events is supply chains and e-supply chains and how they have affected the flexibilisation of work and employment. A significant aspect of the globalisation of trade is supply chains, which have emerged as the dominant form of industrial organisation worldwide. Mendonça critically examines the influence of supply chains on the diffusion of flexible work, employment practices and terms and conditions across workplaces and the resulting tension and conflict they have created. The chapter takes us back to an early point that this symbol of globalised workplaces highlights the commodification of labour as part of the production process. This chapter also highlights an under-discussed aspect of how contemporary e-supply chains facilitate the decline in working conditions and formalisation of work arrangements.

REFERENCES

Alfes, K., Avgoustaki, A., Beauregard, T.A., Cañibano, A. & Muratbekova-Touron, M. (2022). New ways of working and the implications for employees: A systematic framework and suggestions for future research. *International Journal of Human Resource Management*, 33(22): 4361–85.

Boxall, P. (2018). The development of strategic HRM: Reflections on a 30-year journey. *Labour & Industry: A Journal of the Social and Economic Relations of Work*, 28(1): 21–30.

Brewster, C. & Connock, S.L. (1985). *Industrial Relations: Cost-Effective Strategies*, London: Hutchinson Business Books.

Brewster, C. & Holland, P. (2020). Work 'or' Employment in the 21st century? In Wilkinson, A. and Barry, M. *The Research Agenda for the Future of Work*, pp. 19–32. Cheltenham, UK and Northampton, MA, USA: Edward Elgar.

Grint, P. (2022). Wicked problems in an age of uncertainty. *Human Relations*, 75(8): 1518–32.

Harvey, D. (2007). *A Brief History of Neoliberalism*. New York: Oxford University Press.

Holland, P., Pyman, A. & Hecker, R. (2008). Services offshoring: Reflections and new directions. *European Journal of Management*, 8(2): 56–67.

Holland, P., Brewster, C. & Kougiannou, N. (2021). Employment, work, and industrial revolutions: A Faustian deal. In *Identifying and Managing Risk at Work*, pp. 112–25. London: Routledge.

Legge, K. (1998). The morality of HRM. *Human Resource Management: Critical Perspectives on Business and Management*, 3: 357–73.

Lyons, D. (2019). *Lab Rats:Why Modern Orks Makes Us Miserable*. London: Atlantic Books.

Olafsen, A.H., Niemiec, C.P., Halvari, H., Deci, E.L. & Williams, G.C. (2017). On the dark side of work: A longitudinal analysis using self-determination theory. *European Journal of Work and Organizational Psychology*, 26(20): 275–85.

Schultz, K.L., McClain, J.O. & Thomas, L.J. (2003). Overcoming the dark side of worker flexibility. *Journal of Operations Management*, 21(1): 81–92.

Schwab, K. (2016). *The Fourth Industrial Revolution*. London: Penguin Random House.

Sennett, R. (1998). *The Corrosion of Character: The Personal Consequences of Work in the New Capitalism*. New York: W.W. Norton & Company.

Sheehan, C., De Cieri, H., Cooper, B. & Shea, T. (2016). Strategic implications of HR role management in a dynamic environment. *Personnel Review*, 45(2): 353–73.

2. Exploring the shifting landscape of work and employment: the interplay between technology, flexibility, and regulation

Nadia K. Kougiannou and Pedro Mendonça

INTRODUCTION

In contemporary society, work is considered an indispensable element, and its definition and practice are being transformed by intensified competition, globalisation and technological advancements (Kelliher & Richardson, 2012). This change leads to questioning traditional assumptions regarding the location, mode, performance and nature of work. COVID-19 accelerated these ongoing changes, exemplified by the surge in remote work, automation and skill gaps, leading to a growing number of non-traditional work arrangements (Alfes et al., 2022). For example, consultancy figures estimate that approximately 20–25 per cent of employees in developed economies can perform their job duties remotely (McKinsey, 2021). This trend is further reinforced by the estimation that nearly 60 per cent of job tasks in most occupations could be automated, fundamentally altering how workers undertake their tasks (McKinsey, 2017). The gig workforce increase has been projected to increase from 43 million in 2018 to 78 million in 2023 (Alfes et al., 2022). As a result, the traditional concepts of work and employment are becoming increasingly disassociated.

Furthermore, the contemporary era has witnessed a substantial surge in individuals engaging in self-employment without formal employment arrangements. Most of these workers lack access to capital and opportunities for building their reputation and typically carry out their daily work for algorithms. Consequently, they are bereft of employment entitlements such as minimum wage, insurance, sick pay and holiday pay.

Employment arrangements have both positive and negative implications for both employees and employers. Notably, employees enjoy the benefits of workplace security, safety and well-being guaranteed by their employers.

However, the emergence of work without formal employment agreements has prompted discussions regarding the future of workers' rights and well-being. Moreover, with the apparent decline of employment and the potential loss of even gig economy work, there is increasing uncertainty about worker security, health and safety.

Studies have attempted to identify the dimensions of contemporary workplace transformations, aiming to comprehend the causes and effects of evolving work practices, and have focused on particular aspects of new work arrangements. For example, some authors have concentrated on the timing and location of work, analysing employees who have been given greater flexibility in choosing when and where they work (Kossek & Lautsch, 2018). Others have examined who performs the work, observing the rise and diversity of adaptable contractual arrangements such as agency work, crowdwork or freelancing (Cappelli & Keller, 2013; Katz & Krueger, 2019). A third strand has been concerned with how work is organised in a more agile, participative and automated manner and the outcomes of such an organisation (Cappelli &Tavis, 2018; McIver et al., 2018).

Previous research has explored the potential advantages and drawbacks of new work arrangements for organisational-level outcomes; however, there exists a paucity of knowledge regarding their effects on employees, particularly those in lower-status/skill positions (Alfes et al., 2022), which several of the chapters in this book attempt to address. This research gap is noteworthy since modern enterprises are increasingly embracing new work models, which have the potential to modify how employees experience work, thereby bearing significant implications for the nature of their work, their attitudes, performance, competencies, career development and well-being (Chen & Fulmer, 2018; De Menezes & Kelliher, 2017; Shifrin & Michel, 2022). For instance, whether employees in lower-status occupations derive advantages from contemporary work arrangements, such as flexible work schedules, is ambiguous (Kossek & Lautsch, 2018). Consequently, it is rather startling that the role of new work arrangements in shaping employee outcomes remains inadequately understood (Alfes et al., 2022; Gerards et al., 2018; 2021). Therefore, the exploration of regulatory frameworks tailored to address the unique challenges posed by these evolving work practices becomes imperative to ensure the well-being and rights of workers in non-traditional employment arrangements. This chapter critically appraises these issues.

THE IMPACT OF TECHNOLOGICAL CHANGE AND FLEXIBILITY ON TRADITIONAL EMPLOYMENT

The present times are marked by disruption, with levels of change unparalleled in the lived experience of those currently in work or employment (Friedman,

2016). The proliferation of technological advancements, particularly in the field of artificial intelligence (AI) and globalisation, has led to substantial upheaval in traditional models of work, employment and business across various sectors such as fast food, transport, publishing and hotels (Evans & Wurster, 2000; Friedman, 2016). The changing nature of work, including the emergence of the gig or platform economy, has been at the forefront of a paradigm shift in work and employment that can be likened to the first industrial revolution (Holland et al., 2021). Many types of work, including new jobs created to replace those displaced by automation, could ultimately be performed by robots and AI. These machines progressively acquire human-like sensing, reasoning, comprehension and learning capabilities.

Some proponents of AI and the gig economy argue that these innovations have given workers greater autonomy and flexibility (Shibata, 2020). Gig economy organisations claim to offer workers increased independence and flexibility in choosing when and where to work and what tasks to undertake. However, this perceived freedom comes at a cost: workers have little to no input on the labour market, and algorithms can unfairly advantage or disadvantage them (Leonardi & Treem, 2020). Furthermore, as employers increasingly rely on AI to manage their workforce, workers remain subject to technological domination and control.

Research has cast doubt on the idea that gig work gives workers genuine autonomy and freedom (Wood et al., 2019). Claims that workers can choose when to work and which tasks to accept are often a myth due to algorithmic management techniques that obstruct workers' independence to decide when to work, what tasks to perform or how fast they work (Mendonça & Kougiannou, 2023). Therefore, the discourse promoted by gig organisations that gig work represents a new form of autonomous employment is questionable.

Algorithmic management creates an 'always on' form of control that allows gig economy organisations to minutely monitor workers' activity and performance (Gandini, 2019). Platforms and algorithms use GPS systems and performance control through rankings and ratings to monitor workers. Once a worker logs into an app, control and monitoring immediately begin. GPS systems monitor the speed and position of individuals, enabling the platform to compare and control individuals' movements. Platforms allow app users to evaluate gig workers' performance based on metrics gathered by the algorithm resulting from customers' subjective feedback and reviews after completing a task (Duggan et al., 2020). Businesses also use AI to scrutinise staff behaviour for evaluation purposes, which can undermine workers' freedom (Booth, 2019).

Similar observations of the impact of technological change can be made regarding flexible work. Indeed, the proliferation of information and communication technologies (ICTs) ushered in a new era of work characterised by unprecedented flexibility and dynamism, a phenomenon that can be traced back to the emergence of teleworking (which is discussed in depth later in this book). In this regard, scholars have observed that the rise of teleworking in the 1980s was a direct consequence of the remarkable advancements in ICTs, which allowed workers to work remotely and independently of traditional office environments (Caza et al., 2022; McPhail et al., 2024). Since then, there has been a gradual yet persistent increase in the number of individuals engaged in remote work and non-traditional working hours. In the European Union (EU), the proportion of the workforce engaged in teleworking increased by four percentage points between 2009 and 2019 (Ballario, 2020). The UK's CIPD (2019) reports an 80 per cent surge in the practice of working from home over the last two decades in the UK. Similarly, the USA witnessed a 115 per cent increase in teleworking from 2005 to 2015 (Dey et al., 2020). COVID-19 has brought these trends to a whole new level, rapidly accelerating the adoption of teleworking across various industries and nations. It has now become commonplace for a significant section of the workforce rather than being limited to a select few.

Despite the commonly held belief that teleworking is advantageous for permanent employees, the existing literature remains inconclusive (Song & Gao, 2020) and highlights the contradictory nature of flexibility (Cañibano, 2019; Putnam et al., 2014), especially in terms of its effects on traditional employment practices and individuals. On the one hand, teleworkers experience heightened job autonomy owing to the flexibility they enjoy in terms of their work location and schedule (Gajendran & Harrison, 2007). They also exhibit greater job satisfaction and commitment levels than their office-based counterparts (Kelliher & Anderson, 2010; Wheatley, 2012).

On the other hand, several studies have reported insignificant outcomes or adverse effects of the practice (Kossek & Lautsch, 2018). For instance, teleworking has been found to have little impact on self-rated performance and the quality of relationships between teleworkers and their co-workers (Gajendran & Harrison, 2007). In addition, recent research indicates that compared to office-based work, teleworking during weekdays, weekends and holidays may lead to increased rather than reduced stress levels (Song & Gao, 2020). Earlier studies comparing the experiences of high-intensity teleworkers and office-based workers found that the former often struggled with disconnecting outside working hours (Alfes et al., 2022). Prior research has also linked teleworking to intensified workloads (Avgoustaki & Bessa, 2019; Bathini & Kandathil, 2019) and increased work exhaustion (Golden, 2012).

Additionally, particularly in light of the increasing integration of smart machines, the development of work content has generated questions concerning workers' autonomy and ability to shape performance expectations and privacy – see Tham et al.'s chapter on this issue (Alfes et al., 2022; Bhave et al.,

2020). Scholars have invoked Bentham's 'panopticon' metaphor to examine these issues (e.g., Leclercq-Vandelannoitte, 2021; Leclercq-Vandelannoitte et al., 2014; Muratbekova-Touron & Leon, 2023). The panopticon, a circular institutional structure with a guard in the centre and prisoners in cells around the circumference, pertains to a control system in which the guard monitors all prisoners without them knowing whether or when they are being watched. The prisoners are thereby compelled to self-regulate their behaviour. Scholars not only highlight the surveillance concerns associated with the change of work but also workers' adherence to norms of constant availability, placing them in a position of 'permitted subjection' and rendering them subjects of 'free control' (Leclercq-Vandelannoitte et al., 2014). In this way, the employment relationship and the labour process acquire a new geometry. While organisations concede a level of autonomy over some aspects of the labour process (such as working time and pay), they retain and concentrate increasing power by implementing new surveillance and monitoring technologies, such as algorithmic management and AI (Vallas and Schor, 2020). What will be discussed further in this book as faux flexibility and the autonomous-flexibility paradox.

THE INCREASING MOVE AWAY FROM 'STANDARD' EMPLOYMENT TO MORE FLEXIBLE ARRANGEMENTS

The employment contract, which establishes the fundamental bond between individuals and their organisation by specifying their responsibilities and remuneration (Marsden, 2004), is experiencing a gradual decline (Alfes et al., 2022). Numerous studies point to a noticeable decline in the significance of 'standard' employment as a means of organising work, given the escalating popularity of alternative avenues such as temporary help agency workers, crowd workers, freelancers, contract workers, gig workers or service workers (Huws et al., 2018; Katz & Krueger, 2019). For example, in the USA, the share of workers involved in alternative work arrangements grew by five percentage points between 2005 and 2015, with half a per cent of the entire US workforce already engaged in crowdwork through platforms by that time (Katz & Krueger, 2019). In the UK, nine per cent of the population has participated in some form of crowdwork (Huws et al., 2018), while in 14 European countries, crowdwork constitutes the main occupation for two per cent of the entire workforce (Alfes et al., 2022).

From an HRM perspective, gig work represents a notable deviation from conventional forms of labour and the customary employer-employee relationships (Duggan et al., 2023). This is primarily due to the involvement of multiple parties within the HRM ecosystem, which are necessary to successfully operate a decentralised work arrangement such as one found within the gig economy (McDonnell et al., 2021; Meijerink & Keegan, 2019). For example, in traditional work setups, customer feedback may have some impact on the evaluation of employee performance. However, in gig work, the role of customers and third-party suppliers offering their services through platform organisations is especially significant. The considerable involvement of these non-organisational entities in shaping HRM activities that centrally control both work and workers (Waldkirch et al., 2021) renders the conventional conceptualisation of employer-employee relationships incompatible with the intricacies of gig work.

Research has investigated the individual consequences of gig employment, revealing that although gig workers can offer labour flexibility to organisations, they often do not receive the same benefits and protections as traditional employees, such as healthcare and a minimum wage (Duggan et al., 2020; Gleim et al., 2019). Gig workers can adjust their work schedule, the amount of work they undertake, and the number of employers they work for, completing tasks on demand. Yet, similar to teleworking, current research highlights a discrepancy between how individuals perceive gig employment opportunities and the actual effects of such opportunities on them (Gleim et al., 2019). The discussion around gig work has highlighted its different forms and their positive aspects, such as flexible schedules and higher remuneration levels, while simultaneously pointing out the substandard employment conditions and inadequate regulation associated with this type of work arrangement (Hall & Krueger, 2018; Mendonça et al., 2023; Racabi, 2021).

Various forms of gig employment opportunities exist, including the sharing economy, which entails platforms that digitally connect workers, and direct selling, where consumers act as direct sellers (Alfes et al., 2022). According to Hall and Krueger (2018), who compared Uber drivers with traditional taxi drivers, the former earn comparable compensation or even more than the latter. Chen et al. (2019) corroborated these findings by demonstrating that participating in gig jobs such as Uber driving allows workers to earn more than they would in traditional arrangements. However, not all gig jobs are created equal, as Gleim et al. (2019) found that worker perceptions and outcomes are more favourable for direct sales workers than for those in the sharing economy. This is because direct sellers experience greater self-congruence, resulting in improved job satisfaction due to better alignment between the brand and the worker's personality.

Notwithstanding the recent attention and popularity of gig work, existing literature posits that gig workers often hold insecure positions and experience an absence of social and job security compared to their traditional employee counterparts (Van Den Groenendaal et al., 2023). Specifically, on-call workers, independent contractors and freelancers earn notably less per week than regular employees with similar characteristics and occupations (Katz & Krueger, 2019). Moreover, freelancers are inclined to work irregularly and experience conflicts between their work and private commitments while also feeling compelled to remain perpetually available for work to maintain positive relationships with clients (Gold & Mustafa, 2013). In addition, gig workers often encounter job insecurity as they are responsible for finding their own work (Murgia & Pulignano, 2021).

In gig employment opportunities, various work arrangements utilise algorithmic processes embedded within digital platforms to match labour supply with demand, monitor worker performance and exert control (Duggan et al., 2020). Such algorithm-based jobs are characterised by pervasive surveillance, strict regulation and the absence of personal interaction with management, resulting in workers' perceptions of unfair treatment (Gandini, 2019; Pichault & McKeown, 2019). Furthermore, workers' experiences are shaped by technology and impersonal customer evaluations, which can erode trust and confidence and negatively impact their well-being (Duggan et al., 2020; Pichault & McKeown, 2019). This shift towards algorithm-based work has also transformed careers from stable, linear paths to more fluid and uncertain ones. Although some evidence suggests that freelancers may view their careers as successful (Lo Presti et al., 2018), the literature challenges such findings, revealing that gig workers often struggle to make sense of their work, have limited opportunities for career development, and experience little upward mobility within their organisations without sufficient support (Kost et al., 2020).

THE ROLE OF REGULATION

If regulatory constraints impede employers' implementation of desired employment practices in developed nations, technology presents an increasingly attractive avenue for work without employment (Blanchflower, 2019). Some argue that certain immediate and hands-on occupations, such as health and care work, cannot be entirely supplanted by automated systems. Nevertheless, an economic impetus exists towards deregulation in these areas, resulting in decreased job security and diminished working conditions. Despite arguments advocating for a collaborative combination of employees and AI, the policies of neoliberalism and labour practices observed in several developed countries suggest that other fields, where robots and computers are capable of executing progressively intricate tasks, may experience similar consequences (Holland et al., 2021). The pressure to deregulate, which finds support from employers, economists and politicians, is frequently rationalised as a means of eliminating cumbersome regulations and bureaucracy. While certain proponents argue for a 'high-road' approach to incorporating AI in the workplace, the prevailing trend seems to favour a 'low-road' approach prioritising profits over worker welfare (Holland et al., 2021). To clarify, in the context of integrating AI into the workplace, the 'high-road' approach refers to a strategy that emphasises the responsible and ethical use of AI, focusing on enhancing worker well-being, job quality and long-term benefits for both employees and the organisation. This approach seeks to harness AI technology to improve working conditions, promote employee skills development, and create a positive work environment while maintaining profitability. On the other hand, the 'low-road' approach is typically associated with practices that involve reducing labour costs by automating jobs, using AI to replace workers, or cutting corners on labour-related benefits and protections. This strategy may lead to increased productivity and profitability for the organisation in the short term, but it can also result in negative consequences for workers, such as job insecurity, stressful working conditions and reduced job quality.

The regulatory framework national institutions adopt can significantly influence organisations' business and employment models. Changing and shaping does not necessarily lead to the absence of regulation. Instead, it allows for a shift in regulatory practices, which can either benefit or disadvantage different stakeholders (MacKenzie & Martínez Lucio, 2005, 2014). Academic debate and inconsistent case law demonstrate how platform-based food delivery organisations gain a competitive advantage by exploiting this regulatory shift. For instance, the UK Supreme Court endorsed Deliveroo's argument that couriers are self-employed contractors and not workers, allowing them to avoid providing basic benefits such as hourly minimum wage, holiday pay or sick pay (The Independent Workers Union of Great Britain v. Roofoods Ltd., 2021). By allowing gig workers to use substitutes and work flexibly, platform organisations can adopt a low-road approach to maintain a competitive advantage and reduce labour costs. Platform businesses leverage this regulatory framework to redefine and control the management of on-demand gig work, often categorising gig workers as independent contractors (Aloisi & De Stefano, 2022). Platform organisations often externalise the responsibilities and costs to independent contractors. To participate in the labour process, these contractors must have specific work requirements, such as health insurance, working gear and transportation (bikes, mopeds, cars) (Goods et al., 2019; Veen et al., 2020).

By legitimately categorising workers as independent contractors, platform managers can further transform the regulatory space in some parts of the labour market. For instance, in a recent study of the food delivery sector in the UK, Mendonça et al. (2023) show that the gig economy has fundamentally transformed labour relations by introducing new forms of work and employment characterised by outsourcing to independent contractors and informal subcontracting practices. The study demonstrates that work is often outsourced to individuals who, in turn, may employ other (sometimes undocumented) workers or teams on wages or informalised subcontract fees. The opportunity to use informal subcontracted workers represents the creation of an arms-length and transactional relationship for platform organisations, which is key within a digital platform-based business and supply chain model (Veen et al., 2020). Platform organisations can use and dispose of this workforce without costs and regulatory consequences. This informalised employment relationship is characterised by hyper-flexible and precarious conditions, where informalised workers face labour market marginalisation with no access to a formal employment relationship, fair pay, effective voice mechanisms and health and safety protections (Kougiannou and Mendonça, 2021; Mendonça et al., 2023). Framing and shaping employment in these ways ends up breaking down capitalist production (and social) relations, allowing platform organisations to access an ultra-flexible and always-available workforce while simultaneously arguing that they are not bound by business practice regulations, such as payment of business rates, appropriate licensing arrangements, and employment regulations including minimum wage payments and associated terms (Mendonça et al., 2023).

Informalisation is an emergent business practice in contemporary capitalism where new forms of workflow, from formal macro-level deregulation by the state to meso-level deregulation of business practice standards, result in flexible, innovative alternative forms of worker engagement (Sassen, 2009). Informal work practices associated with self-employment represent a particular form of labour market deregulation, privatisation and associated flexibility in economic restructuring. The increasing informalisation of formal employment is highlighted in neoliberalised and ultra-flexible labour markets (Mendonça et al., 2023). In the case of Mendonça et al.'s (2023) study, technology and flexible permissive labour markets facilitate a reshaping of interactions between formalised employers and contractors to illustrate how the former colonises and shapes regulatory practice, giving rise to informal app subcontracting. This restructuring of labour relations has created a fragmented, ultra-flexible and unequal labour market in which platform organisations exert significant control over working conditions and worker protections. The study emphasises the role of platform organisations' regulatory practices, in tandem with the national regulatory void, in shaping the working conditions of gig workers.

THE INTERNATIONAL CONTEXT OF EMPLOYMENT REGULATION AND THE GIG ECONOMY

Europe and the rest of the Global North are undergoing a period of profound transition due to various structural changes, including technological advancements. These changes pose significant challenges to national economic and social policies. The rise of the platform economy has been argued to have altered the relationship between capital and labour. This is achievable because platform organisations leverage flexible national and supra-national legal structures to misclassify workers as self-employed (De Stefano, 2015; Johnston et al., 2023). Scholars and labour advocates identify the misclassification of platform workers as self-employed as the principal driver of labour degradation and precariousness (Dubal, 2017). The prominence of this discourse has garnered considerable attention because the legal classification of workers determines who bears the burdens and risks of employment. It is also perceived as a remedy for the exploitative practices of platform organisations (Van Doorn et al., 2023). If gig workers are categorised as self-employed, the responsibility of employment and associated costs are transferred from the organisation to the workers and the state (Aloisi & De Stefano, 2022).

Policy and legal debates often overlook the adaptability of corporations. For example, Dubal (2017) illustrates how FedEx evaded court decisions to redefine workers' status, rendering them more vulnerable than previously. The same study demonstrates that platform organisations can replicate such tactics. Scholars have proposed two main theoretical perspectives to explain how platform organisation legitimise their self-employment and minimum business risk model in the context of national and supranational institutional regulatory frameworks. The first perspective is based on institutional exceptionalism (Van Doorn, 2020), where platform organisation are seen as unique business entities entitled to tailor-made regulatory contexts. By taking advantage of this perspective, platform organisation can effectively circumvent regulatory frameworks and shirk their obligations towards workers, consequently attaining a competitive edge over other regulatory-compliant businesses. However, this perspective fails to acknowledge the control platforms exert over how their services are produced, valued and monetised: they can shape economic and labour markets by establishing hegemonic contractual arrangements, transforming them into an ultra-precarious employment system.

The second perspective is based on the idea that platform organisations are 'institutional chameleons' whose nature, meaning and impact are shaped by the institutional environment in which they operate. The institutional chameleon argument holds that there is nothing inherent in platform work that generates fixed or determined hazards for employment and working conditions. If platform organisations are given adequate institutional guidance, they can provide mechanisms for better working conditions and employment inclusion rather than increasing precariousness (Vallas & Schor, 2020). In addition, this perspective also acknowledges that some platform organisations rely on loopholes or ill-developed regulatory frameworks to maintain their competitive advantage, colonising and shaping the employment relationship. For instance, Van Doorn et al. (2023) argue that platform organisations use selective formalisation. In other words, platforms formalise some work and employment practices while enabling precarity and informalisation of other practices, such as relaxed formal entry requirements and renting account credentials. This selective approach has been documented to disproportionately affect undocumented migrants (Altenried, 2021; Mendonça et al., 2023).

While this perspective highlights the institutional contingencies that shape platform technology, it risks neglecting the common features that platforms exhibit, such as their rigid business models and organisational structures (Duggan et al., 2023). These features stem from platform organisations relying on rationalised lean operations to maintain profitability and gain competitive advantage. For instance, the variation in regulation across the globe can be so significant that some platform organisation have decided to exit certain national markets altogether (Taylor, 2022) as the necessary changes to adapt to the regulatory framework were deemed unattainable from a business perspective (Altenried, 2021; Griswold, 2019). This implies that although platform organisations are willing to adjust their business and employment models to a specific national institutional framework, they will only do so to a certain extent.

In this sense, what is then the regulatory solution for the gig platform economy? Considering the above theoretical assumptions, two approaches to regulation can be drawn. The first approach, which is informed by the exceptionalism perspective (Van Doorn, 2020), suggests that regulatory authorities need to limit the ability of platform organisations to engage in regulatory arbitrage. This can be achieved by enforcing existing labour laws and regulations more strictly and extending the scope of such regulations to include platform workers. It may also involve creating new regulations that explicitly address the unique features of platform work, such as the lack of bargaining power and the non-standard employment relationship. By doing so, regulatory authorities can prevent platform organisations from avoiding responsibility for their workers and ensure that the platforms are held accountable for their actions. Additionally, regulations that mandate a minimum wage, maximum working hours and adequate social security coverage could improve the working conditions of platform workers. Similarly, this approach may result in platform organisations choosing to exit the market as they may see the new regulatory framework as unattainable from a business perspective, as evidenced in the cases of Germany, the Netherlands and Australia (Altenried, 2021; Griswold, 2019; Reuters, 2022a, 2022b; Taylor, 2022).

This takes the debate to another approach to regulation, which is informed by the institutional chameleon perspective (Vallas & Schor, 2020). This perspective suggests that regulatory authorities must create a supportive institutional environment that facilitates better working conditions for platform workers. A supportive institutional environment may involve adopting a more flexible regulatory framework that allows experimentation with different work organisation models. For instance, policymakers could introduce a legal framework that enables platform workers to form and join unions, collectively bargain for better wages and working conditions and participate in decision-making processes related to their work. This would provide a level of protection for platform workers while also acknowledging the unique features of platform work. A recent case in Spain illustrates this approach. The Spanish Ley Rider (*Real Decreto* 9/2021) is a piece of legislation enacted in May 2021 aimed at improving the working conditions of delivery workers in the gig economy within the Spanish context. The law requires organisations to hire riders as employees rather than as self-employed contractors and grants them access to social security benefits such as sick leave, vacation time and retirement benefits. The employment outcomes and workers' experiences of this newly enacted law are yet to be reported and studied.

These approaches imply that regulatory solutions must be tailored to the specific institutional context in which platform organisations operate. Policymakers recognise that the gig economy, particularly platform work, is a complex and dynamic phenomenon that requires careful consideration of its various factors (Aloisi & De Stefano, 2022). For instance, at the supra-national level, the European Commission has proposed a directive (European Commission, 2021) to improve platform workers' working conditions in the EU. The directive has three core components: ensuring that the employment status of people working through platforms is correctly classified, increasing the transparency of algorithms, and setting reporting requirements for digital labour platforms. The employment status of platform workers is one of the key provisions of the directive and aims to ensure that platform organisations do not misclassify workers as independent contractors even though they are in a relationship of employment dependence. The legal presumption of an employment relationship applies if at least two of five criteria of dependence are present: control of remuneration; setting the entry/exit rules into the labour process; conduct or performance of work; supervision of performance; and restriction of the freedom to organise work and/or the possibility independently to build a client base. Transparency also sits at the core of the directive. This transparency concerns the right of workers to have access to clear and detailed information about the terms and conditions of their work, including information on the type of work they will be doing, their working hours, payment and deductions and any fees or charges they may incur. It also considers monitoring requirements for algorithmic management and introduces reporting requirements for platform organisations. The directive would also establish the right of platform workers to be represented by a trade union or other collective body and to engage in collective bargaining with platform operators (De Stefano et al., 2021).

Examining institutional exceptionalism and the chameleonic behaviour exhibited by platform organisations propounds a nuanced perspective on the presumed efficacy of legal frameworks in resolving the challenges posed by these entities. We believe that relying solely on employment reclassification may not effectively address the precarisation in platform work. With their adaptable nature, platform organisations can employ new control mechanisms to maintain exploitative conditions and capture surplus value. This ability perpetuates precarious working conditions through innovative means (Van Doorn et al., 2023). The prevailing notion that rectifying legislation can singularly address the multifaceted issues inherent in the gig economy and platform work oversimplifies the intricate dynamics at play, including algorithmic management. The assertion that introducing new laws is the panacea encounters scepticism when contextualised within the backdrop of platforms' chameleonic behaviour, where they often navigate legal frameworks adeptly (Dubal, 2017; Johnston et al., 2023). The declining influence of unions further diminishes the practicality of regulatory remedies, such as permitting union formation in situations where logistical barriers impede meaningful collective action (Woodcock & Cant, 2022). Likewise, advocating for transparency confronts inherent limitations, given the opaqueness characterising certain aspects of platform operations (Aloisi and De Stefano, 2022). Therefore, several questions arise.

The first underlying question extends beyond the mere formulation of new legislation to the critical dimension of enforcement. The inadequacy of dedicating commensurate attention to enforcement mechanisms is understated by current literature, as the impact of extant laws is contingent on their effective implementation. Consequently, the discourse surrounding regulatory interventions necessitates a recalibration, emphasising the articulation of new legal frameworks, the establishment of robust enforcement mechanisms, and a comprehensive understanding of the intricate dynamics shaping the gig economy and platform work landscape. Addressing the 'how' and 'by whom' in the enforcement context emerges as a pivotal consideration in navigating the evolving forms of platform-based employment.

Moreover, a second underlying question lies in how the contemporary landscape of labour markets prompts a critical reflection on the efficacy of traditional regulations in light of 21st-century technological advancements. The question arises as to whether drafting regulatory frameworks similar to those seen previously, for example, the EU directive (European Commission, 2021), remain relevant in the face of the transformative impact of present-day technology. The extant body of research primarily focuses on conventional sectors such as formalised food delivery and taxi services (Piasna & Drahokoupil, 2021; Rosenblat, 2018), which offer a semblance of regulatory manageability. However, a noteworthy proportion of gig economy and platform work activities is characterised by individual workers operating from their residential spaces (Wood et al., 2019), a phenomenon that diverges significantly from the structured environments of traditional workplaces.

This observation underscores the imperative of re-evaluating established regulatory paradigms. Perhaps, to address the nuances of contemporary gig work, innovative 21st-century systems driven by workers and their representatives, potentially computer or algorithm-controlled, or ingenious financial instruments, may be requisite. Such systems could serve the dual purpose of ensuring prompt remuneration for workers and capturing a fair share of business profits for their benefit. The intricate nature of this evolving landscape necessitates a departure from antiquated models, emphasising the need for pioneering solutions to navigate the complexities posed by the intersection of labour and technology. Despite the current lack of a concrete blueprint, it is incumbent upon policymakers and scholars to engage in exploratory discourse aimed at devising adaptive mechanisms tailored to the exigencies of the modern labour paradigm.

CONCLUSION

The current landscape of work and employment is undergoing significant changes due to increased competition, globalisation and technological advancements. These changes challenge traditional assumptions about the location, mode, performance and nature of work. COVID-19 has further accelerated these changes, leading to a rise in remote work, automation and non-traditional work arrangements. For example, a significant portion of employees in developed economies can potentially work remotely, and a substantial number of job tasks across various occupations could be automated. The gig workforce is expected to grow significantly. As a result, the traditional concepts of work and employment are becoming increasingly disconnected. Moreover, there has been a notable increase in self-employment without formal arrangements.

The gig economy, specifically, challenges the traditional dynamics of the employer-employee relationship, primarily due to the involvement of multiple parties and the substantial influence exerted by customers and third-party suppliers. While gig work offers flexibility, research consistently demonstrates that gig workers often lack the benefits and protections afforded to traditional employees, such as healthcare coverage and a minimum wage. This discrepancy between the perceived advantages of gig work and its actual impact on workers raises concerns regarding substandard working conditions and inadequate regulation. Various forms of gig employment exist, yielding diverse outcomes and worker perceptions. Generally, gig workers encounter job and social insecurity, often grappling with conflicts between work and personal commitments. Additionally, algorithmic processes in gig work introduce surveillance mechanisms and impersonal evaluations, which contribute to perceptions of unfair treatment and negatively affect overall well-being. Moreover, career paths in the gig economy tend to be uncertain, with limited opportunities for professional development and upward mobility unless accompanied by adequate support.

Under neoliberal policies and labour practices, the pursuit of profit takes precedence over the welfare of workers, leading to business approaches that exploit workers and diminish labour costs. Within this environment, the rise of technology has offered alternatives to conventional employment practices and has prompted a shift in regulatory practices, resulting in diminished job security and deteriorating working conditions. This shift allows platform-based organisations to redefine labour relationships and classify gig workers as independent contractors, evading their obligation to provide fundamental benefits and shifting responsibilities and costs onto the workers. Consequently, this creates hyper-flexible and precarious conditions for workers, leaving them bereft of formal employment rights and protections. In addition, the prevalence of informal subcontracting practices further exacerbates the marginalisation of labour within the job market, perpetuating an unequal and fragmented labour landscape. At a supra-national level, notable transformations of work and employment are ongoing, propelled by demographic shifts and technological advancements. Within this context, the emergence of the gig platform economy has created regulatory loopholes that platform organisations exploit by classifying gig workers as independent contractors.

Establishing regulations in the platform economy is crucial while upholding flexibility and safeguarding employment rights. However, the full implications of regulatory initiatives in diverse contexts are still to be comprehensively understood. For example, regulatory solutions may encompass various approaches, including stricter enforcement of existing labour laws, extending regulatory coverage to encompass platform workers, and introducing new regulations tailored to address the distinctive features of platform work. Alternatively, a flexible regulatory framework can allow for experimentation in work organisation and worker representation, such as enabling platform workers to form unions and engage in collective bargaining. Both approaches necessitate customising regulations to suit the specific institutional context while acknowledging the intricate nature of the gig economy.

The pervasive influence of technology on work and employment has become an inescapable reality in contemporary society. We argue that while the technological impact is undeniable, the consequential outcomes are contingent upon the approach adopted by various social actors. Will corporations and policymakers persist in their pursuit and insistence on implementing a cost-effective strategy rooted in free market ideology, which solely prioritises the interests of businesses and ultimately proves detrimental to workers' skills, wages and overall well-being? Alternatively, will these entities collaborate with trade unions, workers and society to foster social justice through activities such as upskilling, higher wages and improved worker well-being? A social justice-oriented approach acknowledges the inherent value of labour and emphasises achieving equitable outcomes rather than simply prioritising cost-effectiveness. Such an approach empowers workers to adapt to the evolving landscape, mitigating the risks associated with deskilling and preserving decent, sustainable employment opportunities. The various issues addressed in this chapter explore in depth the effective regulation of technology and aspects of flexibility in the workplace and underscore the challenges faced when attempting to enhance working and living conditions in the digital era. However, the current state of affairs clearly indicates that regulatory efforts must catch up with the diverse realities encountered by workers on the ground – such as platform work, AI and robotics – to progress towards labour markets that are more inclusive, skilled and sustainable.

REFERENCES

Alfes, K., Avgoustaki, A., Beauregard, T. ., Cañibano, A., & Muratbekova-Touron, M. (2022). New ways of working and the implications for employees: A systematic framework and suggestions for future research. *International Journal of Human Resource Management*, 33(22), 4361–85.

Aloisi, A., & De Stefano, V. (2022). *Your Boss Is an Algorithm: Artificial Intelligence, Platform Work and Labour*. Oxford: Bloomsbury Publishing.

Altenried, M. (2021). Mobile workers, contingent labour: Migration, the gig economy and the multiplication of labour, *Environment and Planning A: Economy and Space*, p.0308518X211054846.

Avgoustaki, A., & Bessa, I. (2019). Examining the link between flexible working arrangement bundles and employee work effort. *Human Resource Management*, 58(4), 431–49

Ballario, M. (2020). Telework in the EU before and after the covid-19: Where we were, where we head to. European Institute for Gender Equality. Accessed on 1 September 2023. https://policycommons.net/artifacts/1950578/telework-in-the-eu-before-and-after-the-covid-19/2702347/.

Bathini, D.R., & Kandathil, G.M. (2019). An orchestrated negotiated exchange: Trading home-based telework for intensified work. *Journal of Business Ethics*, 154(2), 411–23.

Bhave, D.P., Teo, L.H., & Dalal, R.S. (2020). Privacy at work: A review and a research agenda for a contested terrain. *Journal of Management*, 46(1), 127–64.

Blanchflower, D.G. (2019). *Not Working: Where Have All the Jobs Gone?* Princeton, NJ: Princeton University Press.

Booth R. (2019). UK businesses using artificial intelligence to monitor staff activity. Accessed on 6 September 2023. https://www.theguardian.com/technology/2019/apr/07/uk-businesses-using-artificialintelligence-to-monitor-staff-activity.

Cañibano, A. (2019). Workplace flexibility as a paradoxical phenomenon: Exploring employee experiences. *Human Relations*, 72(2), 444–70.

Cappelli, P., & Keller, J.R. (2013). Classifying work in the new economy. *Academy of Management Review*, 38(4), 575–96.

Cappelli, P., & Tavis, A. (2018). HR goes agile. *Harvard Business Review*, 96(2), 46–52.

Caza, B.B., Reid, E.M., Ashford, S.J., & Granger, S. (2022). Working on my own: The challenge of gig work *Human Relations*, 75(11), 2122–59.

Chen, M.K., Chevalier, J.A., Rossi, P.E., & Oehlsen, E. (2019). The value of flexible work: Evidence from Uber drivers. *Journal of Political Economy*, 127(6), 2735–94.

Chen, Y., & Fulmer, I.S. (2018). Fine-tuning what we know about employees' experience with flexible work arrangements and their job attitudes. *Human Resource Management*, 57(1), 381–95.

CIPD. (2019). *Megatrends report: Flexible working*. Accessed on 1 September 2023. https://www.cipd.co.uk/Images/megatrends-report-flexible-working-1_tcm18-52769.pdf.

De Menezes, L.M., & Kelliher, C. (2017). Flexible working, individual performance, and employee attitudes: Comparing formal and informal arrangements. *Human Resource Management*, 56(6), 1051–70.

De Stefano, V. (2015). The rise of the just-in-time workforce: On-demand work, crowdwork, and labour protection in the gig-economy. *Comparative Labor Law & Policy Journal*, 37(3), 471–504.

De Stefano, V., Durri, I., Stylogiannis, C., & Wouters, M. (2021). Platform work and the employment relationship (No. 27). Geneva: ILO Working Paper.

Dey, M., Frazis, H., Loewenstein, M.A., & Sun, H. (2020). Ability to work from home: Evidence from two surveys and implications for the labor market in the covid-19 pandemic. *Monthly Labor Review*, June, 1–21.

Dubal, V.B. (2017). Wage slave or entrepreneur?: Contesting the dualism of legal worker identities. *California Law Review*, 65–123. Accessed on 12 March 2024. https://repository.uclawsf.edu/cgi/viewcontent.cgi?article=2595&context=faculty_scholarship.

Duggan, J., Sherman, U., Carbery, R., & McDonnell, A. (2020). Algorithmic management and app-work in the gig economy: A research agenda for employment relations and HRM. *Human Resource Management Journal*, 30(1), 114–32.

Duggan, J., Carbery, R., McDonnell, A., & Sherman, U. (2023). Algorithmic HRM control in the gig economy: The app-worker perspective. *Human Resource Management*, 62(6), 883–99.

European Commission. (2021). *Proposal for a directive of the European Parliament and of the Council on improving working conditions in platform work*. Accessed on 1 September 2023. https://www.consilium.europa.eu/en/press/press-releases/2019/06/13/new-forms-of-work-council-conclusions/.

Evans, P., & Wurster, T. (2000). *Blown to Bits: How New Economics of Information Transforms Strategy*. Cambridge, MA: Harvard University Press.

Friedman, T. (2016). *Thank You for Being Late*. London: Penguin.

Gajendran, R.S., & Harrison, D.A. (2007). The good, the bad, and the unknown about telecommuting: Meta-analysis of psychological mediators and individual consequences. *Journal of Applied Psychology*, 92(6), 1524–41.

Gandini, A. (2019). Labour process theory and the gig economy. *Human Relations*, 72(6), 1039–56. Gerards, R., De Grip, A., & Baudewijns, C. (2018). Do new ways of working increase work engagement? *Personnel Review*, 47(2), 517–34.

Gerards, R., van Wetten, S., & van Sambeek, C. (2021). New ways of working and intrapreneurial behaviour: The mediating role of transformational leadership and social interaction. *Review of Managerial Science*, 15(7), 2075–110.

Gleim, M.R., Johnson, C.M., & Lawson, S.J. (2019). Sharers and sellers: A multi-group examination of gig economy workers' perceptions. *Journal of Business Research*, 98, 142–52.

Gold, M., & Mustafa, M. (2013). 'Work always wins': Client colonisation, time management and the anxieties of connected freelancers. *New Technology, Work and Employment*, 28(3), 197–211.

Golden, T.D. (2012). Altering the effects of work and family conflict on exhaustion: Telework during traditional and non-traditional work hours. *Journal of Business and Psychology*, 27(3), 255–69.

Goods, C., Veen, A., & Barratt, T. (2019). 'Is your gig any good?' Analysing job quality in the Australian platform-based food-delivery sector. *Journal of Industrial Relations*, 61(4), 502–27.

Griswold, A. (2019). Food-delivery giant Deliveroo is pulling out of Germany. *Quartz at Work*. Accessed on 12 August 2023. https:// qz .com/ 1685962/ food -delivery -startup-deliveroo-exitsgermany

Hall, J.V., & Krueger, A.B. (2018). An analysis of the labor market for Uber's driver-partners in the United States. *ILR Review*, 71(3), 705–32.

Holland, P., Brewster, C., & Kougiannou, N. (2021). Employment, work, and industrial revolutions: A Faustian deal. In *Identifying and Managing Risk at Work*, pp. 112–25. London: Routledge.

Huws, U., Spencer, N.H., Syrdal, D.S., & Holts, K. (2018). Work in the European gig economy: Research results from the UK, Sweden, Germany, Austria, the Netherlands, Switzerland and Italy. Foundation for European Progressive Studies. Accessed on 12 August 2023. https://uhra.herts.ac.uk/bitstream/handle/2299/19922/ Huws_U._Spencer_N.H._Syrdal_D.S._Holt_K._2017_.pdf.

Johnston, H., Ergun, O., Schor, J., Chen, L. (2023). Employment status and the on-demand economy: A natural experiment on reclassification. *Socio-Economic Review*, mwad047.

Katz, L.F., & Krueger, A.B. (2019). The rise and nature of alternative work arrangements in the United States, 1995–2015. *ILR Review*, 72(2), 382–416.

Kelliher, C., & Anderson, D. (2010). Doing more with less? Flexible working practices and the intensification of work. *Human Relations*, 63(1), 83–106.

Kelliher, C., & Richardson, J. (2012). Recent development in new ways of organising work. In C. Kelliher & J. Richardson (Eds.), *New Ways of Organising Work: Developments, Perspectives and Experiences*, pp. 1–15. New York: Routledge.

Kossek, E.E., & Lautsch, B.A. (2018). Work–life flexibility for whom? Occupational status and work–life inequality in upper, middle, and lower level jobs. *Academy of Management Annals*, 12(1), 5–36.

Kost, D., Fieseler, C., & Wong, S.I. (2020). Boundaryless careers in the gig economy: An oxymoron? *Human Resource Management Journal*, 30(1), 100–13.

Kougiannou, N.K., & Mendonça, P. (2021). Breaking the managerial silencing of worker voice in platform capitalism: The rise of a food courier network. *British Journal of Management*, 32(3), 744–59.

Leclercq-Vandelannoitte, A. (2021). 'Seeing to be seen': The manager's political economy of visibility in new ways of working. *European Management Journal*, 39(5), 605–16.

Leclercq-Vandelannoitte, A., Isaac, H., & Kalika, M. (2014). Mobile information systems and organisational control: Beyond the panopticon metaphor? *European Journal of Information Systems*, 23(5), 543–57.

Leonardi, P.M., & Treem, J.W. (2020). Behavioral visibility: A new paradigm for organisation studies in the age of digitisation, digitalisation, and datafication. *Organization Studies*, 41(12): 1601–25.

Lo Presti, A., Pluviano, S., & Briscoe, J.P. (2018). Are freelancers a breed apart? The role of protean and boundaryless career attitudes in employability and career success. *Human Resource Management Journal*, 28(3), 427–42.

MacKenzie, R., & Martínez Lucio, M. (2005). The realities of regulatory change: Beyond the fetish of deregulation. *Sociology*, 39(3), 499–517.

MacKenzie, R., & Martínez Lucio, M. (2014). The colonisation of employment regulation and industrial relations? Dynamics and developments over five decades of change. *Labor History*, 55(2), 189–207.

Marsden, D. (2004). The 'network economy' and models of the employment contract. *British Journal of Industrial Relations*, 42(4), 659–84.

McDonnell, A., Carbery, R., Burgess, J., & Sherman, U. (2021). Technologically mediated human resource management in the gig economy. *International Journal of Human Resource Management*, 32(19), 3995–4015.

McIver, D., Lengnick-Hall, M.L., & Lengnick-Hall, C.A. (2018). A strategic approach to workforce analytics: Integrating science and agility. *Business Horizons*, 61(3), 397–407.

McKinsey. (2017). Jobs lost, jobs gained: What the future of work will mean for jobs, skills, and wages. Accessed on 12 August 2023. https://www.mckinsey.com/featured-insights/future-of-work/jobs-lost-jobs-gained-what-the-future-of-work-will-mean-for-jobs-skills-and-wages.

McKinsey. (2021). The future of work after covid-19. Accessed on 12 August 2023. https://www.mckinsey.com/featured-insights/future-of-work/the-future-of-work-after-covid-19.

McPhail, R., Chan, X.W., May, R., & Wilkinson, A. (2024). Post-COVID remote working and its impact on people, productivity, and the planet: An exploratory scoping review. *The International Journal of Human Resource Management*, 35(1), 154–82.

Meijerink, J., & Keegan, A. (2019). Conceptualising human resource management in the gig economy: Toward a platform ecosystem perspective. *Journal of Managerial Psychology*, 34(4), 214–32.

Mendonça, P., & Kougiannou, N.K. (2023). Disconnecting labour: The impact of intraplatform algorithmic changes on the labour process and workers' capacity to organise collectively. *New Technology, Work and Employment*, 38(1). 1–20.

Mendonça, P., Kougiannou, N.K., & Clark, I. (2023). Informalization in gig food delivery in the UK: The case of hyper-flexible and precarious work. *Industrial Relations: A Journal of Economy and Society*, 62(1), 60–77.

Muratbekova-Touron, M., & Leon, E. (2023). 'Is there anybody out there?' using a telepresence robot to engage in face time at the office. *Information Technology & People*. 36(1), 48–65. https://doi.org/10.1108/ITP-01-2021-0080.

Murgia, A., & Pulignano, V. (2021). Neither precarious nor entrepreneur: The subjective experience of hybrid self-employed workers. *Economic and Industrial Democracy*, 42(4), 1351–77.

Piasna, A., & Drahokoupil, J. (2021). Flexibility unbound: understanding the heterogeneity of preferences among food delivery platform workers. *Socio-Economic Review*, 19(4), 1397–419.

Pichault, F., & McKeown, T. (2019). Autonomy at work in the gig economy: Analysing work status, work content and working conditions of independent professionals. *New Technology, Work and Employment*, 34(1), 59–72.

Putnam, L.L., Myers, K.K., & Gailliard, B.M. (2014). Examining the tensions in workplace flexibility and exploring options for new directions. *Human Relations*, 67(4), 413–40.

Racabi, G. (2021). Effects of city–state relations on labor relations: The case of Uber. *ILR Review*, 74(5), 1155–78.

Real Decreto (9/2021). *por el que se modifica el texto refundido de la Ley del Estatuto de los Trabajadores, aprobado por el Real Decreto Legislativo 2/2015, de 23 de octubre, para garantizar los derechos laborales de las personas dedicadas al reparto en el ámbito de plataformas digitales. Boletín Oficial del Estado*, 113, de 12 de mayo de 2021. Accessed on 23 March. https://www.boe.es/boe/dias/2021/05/12/pdfs/BOE-A-2021–7840.pdf.

Reuters (2022a). Deliveroo to exit Netherlands, loss widens in first-half. Accessed on 12 August 2023. https://www.reuters.com/world/uk/deliveroo-exit-netherlands-loss-widens-first-half-2022-08-10/.

Reuters (2022b). Britain's Deliveroo exits Australia, citing tough competition. Accessed on 12 August 2023. https://www.reuters.com/business/retail-consumer/britains-deliveroo-exits-australia-citing-tough-competition-2022-11-16/.

Rosenblat, A. (2018). *Uberland: How Algorithms Are Rewriting the Rules of Work*. Oakland, CA: University of California Press.

Sassen, S. (2009). Cities today: A new frontier for major developments. *Annals of the American Academy*, 626(1), 53–71.

Shibata, S. (2020). Gig work and the discourse of autonomy: Fictitious freedom in Japan's digital economy. *New Political Economy*, 25(4), 535–51.

Shifrin, N.V., & Michel, J.S. (2022). Flexible work arrangements and employee health: A meta-analytic review. *Work & Stress*, 36(1). 60–85.

Song, Y., & Gao, J. (2020). Does telework stress employees out? A study on working at home and subjective well-being for wage/salary workers. *Journal of Happiness Studies*, 21(7), 2649–68.

Taylor, J. (2022). Deliveroo quits Australia citing 'challenging economic conditions'. *Guardian*. Accessed on 12 September 2023. https://www.theguardian.com/business/2022/nov/16/deliveroo-quits-australia-citing-challenging-economic-conditions.

The Independent Workers Union of Great Britain v. Roofods Ltd. (2021) Court of Appeal, Civil Division, Neutral Citation Number: [2021] EWCA Civ 952. Accessed on 30 August 2023. https://www.bailii.org/ew/cases/EWCA/Civ/2021/952.pdf.

Vallas, S., & Schor, J.B. (2020). What do platforms do? Understanding the gig economy. *Annual Review of Sociology*, 46, 273–94.

Van den Groenendaal, S.M.E., Freese, C., Poell, R.F., & Kooij, D.T. (2023). Inclusive human resource management in freelancers' employment relationships: The role of organisational needs and freelancers' psychological contracts. *Human Resource Management Journal*, 33(1), 224–40.

Van Doorn, N. (2020). At what price? Labour politics and calculative power struggles in on-demand food delivery. *Work Organisation, Labour & Globalisation*, 14(1), 136–49.

Van Doorn, N., Ferrari, F., & Graham, M. (2023). Migration and migrant labour in the gig economy: An intervention. *Work, Employment and Society*, 37(4), 1099–111.

Veen, A., Barratt, T., & Goods, C. (2020). Platform-capital's 'app-etite' for control: A labour process analysis of food-delivery work in Australia. *Work, Employment and Society*, 34(3), 388–406.

Waldkirch, M., Bucher, E., Kalum Schou, P., & Grünwald, E. (2021). Controlled by the algorithm, coached by the crowd – how HRM activities take shape on digital work platforms in the gig economy. *International Journal of Human Resource Management*, 32(12), 2643–82.

Wheatley, D. (2012). Good to be home? Time-use and satisfaction levels among home-based teleworkers. *New Technology, Work and Employment*, 27(3), 224–41.

Wood, A.J., Graham, M., Lehdonvirta, V., & Hjorth, I. (2019). Good gig, bad gig: Autonomy and algorithmic control in the global gig economy. *Work, Employment and Society*, 33(1), 56–75.

Woodcock, J. & Cant, C. (2022). Platform worker organising at Deliveroo in the UK: From wildcat strikes to building power. *Journal of Labor and Society*, 1, 1–17. https://doi.org/10.1163/24714607-bja10050.

3. The evolution of flexible working patterns

Clare Kelliher

INTRODUCTION

Flexibility in organisations has emerged as a dominant discourse in recent decades, spawning multiple forms of new working arrangements loosely grouped under the term flexible working. These include, for example, variations to where, when and in what amounts work is done, and the nature of the relationship between the organisation and the individual worker, increasingly where work takes place outside of formal employment. The emergence of some of these working arrangements raises challenges for traditional notions of the workplace, the working day, what a job involves and who is an employer and an employee. Many of these arrangements have become increasingly common over this time period and have stimulated interest from governments and from employers. They have also been the subject of considerable attention from academic researchers and a significant body of evidence on their use and implementation has been built.

This chapter is concerned with examining the various working arrangements which have commonly grouped together as forms of flexible working. It looks first at their emergence and the factors that have influenced their development and growth. The discussion then moves to explore the evidence in relation to the outcomes of these working arrangements for individual workers and will assess more generally the consequences of these developments. Importantly, the use of some of these arrangements, most notably remote working, has been shaped in a major way by experiences during the Covid-19 pandemic. This will be considered and the implications for future working patterns discussed.

BACKGROUND

The discussion of flexibility in organisations has been wide ranging and rooted in a number of different perspectives, but the drive to achieve greater flexibility has been an undoubted force in shaping the way in which work is done

and the operation of labour markets in the last 40 years. These various perspectives on flexibility have included flexibility of labour markets (reflected
in a trend towards deregulation across many countries (Eurofound, 2023));
organisational flexibility (particularly a desire to be more agile and responsive
to changes in the external environment); and flexible working arrangements
and relationships. Flexible working arrangements and relationships will be the
primary focus of this chapter and will examine changes to the conduct of work
(e.g. location, scheduling, amount, stability) and the nature of the relationship
between the employing organisation and the worker. However, even within
this grouping a diverse set of arrangements and relationships exist (Lott et
al., 2022) and it is important to recognise that flexible working arrangements
can be introduced for a range of different reasons. These may broadly include
approaches designed to manage labour in more efficient ways (e.g. matching supply and demand more closely, or improving performance), to those
designed to be a more attractive employer in the labour market, by allowing
employees some degree of discretion over their working arrangements in order
to help them achieve a more satisfactory relationship between their work and
non-work lives. These different approaches have been referred to as flexibility
of and *for* the employee (Alis, 2006) and are classed as being primarily driven
by the interests of the employer or the employee and as such represent different
frames of reference (for a fuller discussion, see Bal & Izak, 2021). For some
employers assisting employees achieve a better work-life balance may also be
seen as a means to be a more responsible employer by, for example, supporting
families and communities.

Before examining these developments in more detail, it is worth reflecting
that the idea of work being an activity that is bounded by an agreed timeframe,
typically a set number of hours, which takes place at prescribed times and at
a specified location, is a comparatively recent phenomenon and reflective of
economic transition to greater industrialisation resulting in work being carried
out away from the home and at specified times. As such, what is considered
as 'normal' working arrangements is therefore often shaped by the economic
and social development of a country. For example, looking at working hours,
within the European Union (EU) there is variation across countries in relation
to the average number of hours in a collectively agreed working week and
the number of days of paid annual leave entitlement. Those countries whose
membership predates the EU enlargement in 2004 have lower average weekly
working hours and higher paid annual leave entitlements than the countries
that joined after this time (Eurofound, 2023).

Conventions relating to the number of hours worked, the scheduling of these
hours and the practice of work being done at a workplace have been pervasive
and as a result 'flexible working' is seen as a deviation from the Standard
Employment Relationship (SER) (Bosch, 2004), based on a conception of

work being continuous, full-time employment, with a single employer, taking place at a designated workplace and at prescribed, fixed working times.

In this chapter we examine the emergence of these different ways of working, both those which are designed to meet the needs for flexibility of the employer and the employee. Particular focus will be given to arrangements including flexible working arrangement (where there is discretion over when work takes place, where work takes place and the amount of work contracted for); the use of annual hours contracts, temporary work and gig/platform working contracted, outside of an employment relationship. The chapter will examine the evidence in relation to these arrangements and assess the extent to which they provide advantages and disadvantages for the individual employee. Where it is of most relevance, the chapter will examine the impact of the Covid-19 pandemic in facilitating (or constraining) these alternative ways of working.

EVOLUTION OF FLEXIBLE WORKING ARRANGEMENTS

Working arrangements normalised towards a model based on the SER over a long period of time and those which deviate from this have come to be labelled as 'flexible', even though in some cases there may be limited flexibility associated with them (e.g. part-time working, fixed-term or annual hours contracts). However, working arrangements which differ from the standard employment relationship have also emerged over a long period of time. In spite of the growing prominence of the flexibility debate and the proliferation of academic studies examining aspects of the implementation and outcomes of various flexible working arrangements and relationships since the turn of the 21st century, it is important to be aware that the emergence and use of these arrangements has a history which predates this time. Academic studies examining changes to both working times and place of work began emerging from the 1970s onwards (see for e.g. Dalton & Mesch, 1990; Dunham et al., 1987; Golembiewski et al., 1974; Kim & Campagna, 1981; Kraut, 1989; Kurland & Bailey, 1999; Latack & Foster, 1985; Orpen, 1981; Pierce & Newstrom, 1980; Schein et al., 1977; Shamir & Salomon, 1985; Trent et al.,1994). These changes in working arrangements and the need for greater flexibility on the part of employees reflected social changes, particularly in the developed world at this time (for an overview, see Kelliher & de Menezes, 2019). For example, part-time employment became more prevalent in response to greater participation of women, particularly mothers, in employment and early innovations in teleworking were in some cases prompted by the problems associated with transport congestion in urban areas.

Notwithstanding the above, the 21st century has seen more rapid expansion in working arrangements that differ from the SER in a greater range of countries across the globe. A number of factors can be identified as being influential in this shift, including developments in information and communications technology; changing workforce demographics; increasing global integration and competitive pressures (Kelliher & Richardson, 2019). The ongoing role of technological developments has acted as an important catalyst for a range of different types of working. Knowledge workers whose work could be connected via a computer and with an internet link were no longer tied to a particular work location or working times but were enabled to work in different places and at different times. Whilst this was of particular influence in relation to the development of flexibility over working time and place of work (Messenger & Gerschwind, 2016), technological advancements also enabled the development of different types of working relationships, notably the gig and platform economies, whereby those requiring work to be carried out could be connected with those willing to undertake work by the use of an algorithm.

Greater global integration has been an important driver of changes to working patterns. For example, in order to accommodate real-time communication and collaboration with others (co-workers, clients, suppliers etc.) located in different time zones, a more flexible approach to the scheduling of work is required. Flexibility over working time may be needed where the working day or working week does not overlap, to participate, for example, in meetings with co-workers outside of normal working hours, and this in turn may lead to flexibility over place of work to facilitate out of hours working. More flexible approaches to the timing and location of work also offers the opportunity for employers to recruit staff drawn from a wider labour market, rather than being confined to those who are able to attend a workplace and/or work at regulated times.

Other competitive pressures which have been a significant driver of the growth in flexibility include the need to contain costs. This may turn attention to more efficient ways of managing labour. Flexible approaches can reduce costs, for example, where staff are employed on short-term, temporary contracts, since they are only employed at the times when the employer expects them to be fully occupied. Likewise, contracting workers outside of a formal employment relationship, for example, as gig workers, or independent contractors offers the opportunity to reduce costs since organisations have fewer obligations to contractors without legal protection offered to employees. As a result, savings can be made on related employment costs such as making pension or other social insurance payments required for employees. An alternative approach to increasing efficiency can be through making flexible working available to employees in order to attract high-calibre staff. High calibre staff who perform effectively may allow for costs to be reduced if they are more efficient in what they do and at the same time may offer the potential for the organisation to compete on quality as well. Offering flexible working has been seen as an increasingly important tool in attracting staff in the post Covid-19 pandemic labour market since greater numbers of staff in a wider range of jobs experienced working remotely during mandated working from home during the pandemic, with evidence suggesting that whilst not favoured by all employees, the opportunity to work remotely for some of their working time is highly valued by many employees and has become an important consideration when choosing a job for many employees. Therefore, offering flexible working is likely to be important in the recruitment of staff, particularly for those with high levels of power in the labour market.

Changing demographics and attitudes to work have also contributed to growing demand for flexible working arrangements (Kelliher et al., 2019). Working parents may need flexibility over timing of work to balance childcare commitments with work, as do those with other caring and non-work commitments. Reference is often made to the value that younger workers place on work-life balance, rejecting the model of the so-called 'ideal worker' norm (Acker, 1990) and as a result seek flexible working arrangements, however, there is also evidence that other groups, such as older workers (Loretto & Vickerstaff, 2015) value being able to work in more flexible ways.

Changing attitudes and orientations towards work observed following the experience of the Covid-19 pandemic have also stimulated interest in flexible working as a means to achieve a better work-life balance. In some countries there is evidence that individuals, particularly those over 50 years old, want to reduce their work commitments and in some cases withdraw from the labour market. This trend, combined with the labour shortages experienced as economies recovered after the pandemic, prompted employers and sometimes governments to consider approaches to retain these workers in employment and to encourage those who had withdrawn from work to return. For example, the availability of part-time working opportunities may be attractive to those who want to remain in employment but with a reduced commitment, allowing them to pursue activities in their non-work lives. In addition to opportunities to reduce the number of hours they work, other forms of flexible working may be attractive to employees who wish to shift their focus towards their non-work life. For example, remote working may make work more attractive (by reducing the time and costs associated with commuting to work), and flexibility over when the working hours are scheduled can also facilitate a better fit of work and non-work commitments.

INDIVIDUAL-FOCUSED FLEXIBLE WORKING

Many of the early trends in different working arrangements and relationships that have emerged were based on the influential model of the flexible firm developed by John Atkinson (1985). This proposed how organisations could achieve greater flexibility by deploying staff in different ways (numerical, spatial and functional flexibility) and developing different types of relationships with those carrying out work of varying centrality to the organisation's purpose.

Since the publication of this model these arrangements have been the focus of extensive research. Below, consideration is given to the evidence which examines the implications of these different arrangements for employees, with a particular focus on employee discretion over the scheduling, location and contracted hours of work; employer-driven approaches that are sometimes termed precarious forms of work, such as short-term, temporary and zero hours contracts and freelance work contracted outside of employment; and arrangements that may combine elements of both such as annual hours contracts.

Allowing employees discretion over their working arrangements has been extensively researched, both in terms of the outcomes for employers and for employees (for an overview of research conducted in the pre Covid-19 pandemic, see Kelliher & de Menezes, 2019). Notwithstanding some of the challenges associated with assessing these findings as a body of evidence due to differences in the definitions of the various types of flexible working arrangements and the measures used in studies (e.g. availability, perceived availability, use) (Kelliher & de Menezes, 2019; Lott et al., 2022), overall the evidence points to a number of positive outcomes for employees, who, rather than other workers, have been the subject of most studies. These include mainly positive associations with job satisfaction (for a meta-analysis, see Kröll et al., 2017); employee well-being including stress, work-family conflict, work-life balance, physical and psychological health outcomes (for overviews, see Allen et al., 2013; Allen et al., 2015; Anderson et al., 2015; Bessa & Tomlinson, 2017; Kröll et al., 2017; Masuda et al., 2012); organisational commitment (Chen & Fulmer, 2018; de Menezes & Kelliher, 2017; Ross & Ali, 2017) and performance or related indicators (de Menezes & Kelliher, 2017; Kröll et al., 2017; Peretz et al., 2018). There is also evidence to show that the nature of the outcome is influenced by the nature of work, the types of flexible working arrangement and national context, amongst other factors.

In many ways it is not surprising that arrangements designed to assist employees should deliver positive outcomes for them. However, it is important to note there is also evidence of negative outcomes from employees. These include work intensification through working extended hours when working remotely (Kelliher & Anderson, 2010; Schöllbauer et al., 2023); flexibility stigmas associated with perceptions about the commitment and performance of flexible workers (Chung & van der Lippe, 2020; Leslie et al., 2012) and career penalties associated with lower visibility in the workplace (Gascoigne & Kelliher, 2018; Golden & Eddleston, 2020; Richardson & Kelliher, 2015). Those who work in different locations or at different times may also experience feelings of social exclusion and may find it harder to keep staff in touch with their team, especially where flexible working is less common. Similarly, employees who work at different times and locations may miss the opportunity for social interaction at work and may experience loneliness and isolation as was reported during the Covid-19 pandemic.

In addition to the above, researchers have identified what has been termed a flexibility or autonomy paradox (Cañibano, 2019; Chung, 2022; Mazmanian et al., 2013). This is where employees respond to the freedom afforded to them through flexible working by working longer hours, beyond the normal demands of the job and representing what may be a form of self-exploitation (Chung, 2022; Fleming, 2022). This occurrence has been explained in a number of ways including by reference to social exchange (Blau, 1964) and gift exchange (Akerlof, 1982) theories, where employees feel the need to respond to what has been made available to them with increased effort (de Menezes & Kelliher, 2017; Kelliher & Anderson, 2010).

Mandated working from home during the Covid-19 pandemic undoubtedly influenced the way in which flexible working, particularly remote working, is viewed. From previously having been largely restricted to professional knowledge workers, it rapidly became much more widespread and used in a more diverse range of jobs. This meant that not only did a more diverse range of workers experience flexible working, but many more managers gained experience of managing flexible workers. One outcome was to increase demand for flexible working and many employers responded to this by introducing hybrid working arrangements where employees can opt to split their working time between being present in the workplace and working remotely. It also provided managers with more insight into how remote working could work in practice and there is some evidence that the 'great working from home experiment' challenged staff who work remotely. However, at this point in time it is hard to assess what the longer-term impact of the pandemic will be for flexible working. It is important to reflect on the relevance of the experiences in the pandemic to future ways of working. Whilst there are lessons to be learned from remote working becoming more widespread that can inform the future design and management of work, particularly relating to aspects of physical remoteness, it is important to recognise that the relational aspects were very different (Anderson & Kelliher, 2020). Much of the extant research that shows positive outcomes of flexible working both for employers and for employees has been based on a situation where some degree of discretion over working arrangements was open to the employee. During the Covid-19 pandemic working from home was not as a result of the employee being able to exercise choice, but rather an intervention on the part of governments, and not a party to the employment relationship (Grant et al., 2023). This places limits in being able to translate the findings from studies conducted during this period of time into future remote working.

ORGANISATION-FOCUSED FLEXIBLE WORKING

Flexible working arrangements which fit in this category are generally designed to improve efficiency in the way in which labour is managed and enable organisational agility and the ability to respond to changes in the environment. Importantly also this approach to flexibility is sometimes operationalised outside of an employment relationship with the organisation contracting with freelance workers in a variety of ways including gig and platform working. At a general level it might be expected that since they are designed for organisational purposes, the outcomes would be negative for workers, or at least that any advantages for workers would be likely to be outweighed by the disadvantages for them. The insecurity of income associated with temporary employment and with arrangements such as zero hours contracts is a clear disadvantage, as is the lack of legal protection given to employees that those who are contracted to work outside of employment lack. However, on the other hand, these types of arrangements can also offer flexibility to employees, which may be valued by some and depending upon their individual circumstances (CIPD, 2015). For example, those on zero hours contracts are able, at least in theory, to accept or decline work. However, in practice, this may not represent a free choice if they believe that declining will influence whether they are offered work in the future. Similarly, temporary contracts may offer the opportunity to work at periods of time that suit the individual and not at times that do not. However, in order to be able to exercise this kind of choice the individual needs to be confident that work will be available when wanted.

The outcomes of these forms of flexible working have also been subject to investigation by researchers. Attention has been paid in particular to the consequences for health and well-being. In a review of evidence on the relationship between job insecurity and health, Green (2020) found a detrimental effect of job insecurity on both mental and physical health. Likewise, studies that examined specific forms of precarious employment have also found links to negative health outcomes. Temporary employment has been linked to negative mental health outcomes and that this is accentuated by a move from a permanent to a temporary contract (Moscone et al., 2016). Dawson et al. (2015), whilst noting that those in temporary employment have poorer mental health than those in permanent employment, argue that there may be an element of selection into temporary employment from those with poor mental health. Other forms of precarious employment such as zero hours contracts and health outcomes have also been investigated and show a link with long-term health conditions, particularly mental health conditions (Farina et al., 2023). They have also been found to be associated with lower pay (Koumenta & Williams, 2019).

Employees on annual hours contracts are also subject to variation in the number of hours they work, however, the total number of hours worked over a year is set in advance. As a result, they represent a situation where over the course of a year an employee will work an agreed number of hours, but the distribution of the hours will not be evenly spread throughout the year. Instead, employers will vary the time worked in line with business patterns. Normally an arrangement of this nature is operated in a framework which stipulates details such as the maximum number of hours that can be worked in a working day or week and minimum notice periods for any additional variations to working time. This type of arrangement is based on the premise that the employer's demand for labour is not stable but subject to fluctuations and that there will be times when they will want employees to work more hours than is normal in a contracted week, but that at other times the hours in a normal contracted week will be too much time for what is required. Being able to vary this and accommodate peaks and troughs in demand allows employers to use labour more efficiently and can reduce the need to pay overtime, or hire additional staff to cover peak periods. There are some differences in how these annual hours schemes operate. In some cases the annual working pattern is fixed in advance (Bailey et al., 2018), whereas in others changes to time worked may be scheduled throughout the year. As a result, employees on annual hours contracts do not face insecurity in relation to income, but ongoing variations to their working time may make planning their non-work lives more difficult.

The outcomes of working in this way are likely to differ for employees depending upon the way in which the scheme is set up. Times when a high number of hours are worked may result in fatigue and strain and be challenging for employees' overall well-being, particularly if it is sustained over a long period and where there is limited time for recovery between work periods. It is also likely to make achieving a satisfactory work-life balance problematic at these times. However, when employees are working fewer hours, this may allow for a better work-life balance to be achieved, particularly if these times fit well with employee's non-work commitments (e.g. school holiday for parents). UK research carried out for the Agile Futures Forum (Cannon, 2017) showed that employees used periods when they were not working to undertake a variety of non-work activities including travelling, concentrated focus on sport and leisure activities, home renovations, pursuing education and spending more time with family (more intensive parenting) and extended family. Although the pattern of annual hours arrangements may sometimes, at least on face value, seem to be unattractive, employees may judge these arrangements as more attractive and easier to manage with their non-working lives than more conventional working arrangements.

A notable feature of these types of arrangements is the focus on counting hours worked and linking this to effective management of labour. This is likely to work well in circumstances where the type of work lends itself to being measured in hours needed to perform a task, but may be more difficult to operate where there is variation in the amount of time taken to complete work tasks, determined by factors such as complexity of the issue being dealt with and differences in expectations from colleagues or customers in a service environment. In which case a focus only on hours worked may lead to staff having to work at a high level of intensity to complete the work.

With annual hours arrangements where there is regular variation to hours worked throughout the year, a further feature which may determine the nature of the outcomes for employees is whether they or the employer have discretion over when working hours can be reduced, or time off work taken to balance periods where a higher number of hours were work and the employee is 'in credit'. If employees are able to exercise discretion, or at least express preferences, this may have a positive impact on work-life balance and satisfaction.

CONCLUSIONS AND OBSERVATIONS

Flexible working arrangements have become increasingly prevalent in many countries over the past four decades, influenced by factors such as advancements in technology, greater global integration, more intense competitive pressures and changing workforce demographics and attitudes to work. A variety of different working arrangements have been grouped under this term, but they can be broadly grouped into those that are primarily designed to support employees achieve a better work-life balance and those that are driven by employers as a mean to manage labour more efficiently and allow organisations to be more agile and able to respond to changes in their environment. However, notably even within these groupings the range of practices is diverse.

The outcomes of these working arrangements for both employers and employees have been extensively studied by researchers. An appraisal of this research allows us to make an assessment of how beneficial specific arrangements have been for individual workers. For those that are designed to support employees there is good evidence of positive outcomes for employees. However, the 'darker side' of flexible working is also evident with flexible workers experiencing a number of penalties stemming from their working pattern. The requirement to work from home during the Covid-19 pandemic resulted in flexible working becoming much more widespread and, in some ways, served to normalise flexible working, particularly remote working. However, it is still too early to judge whether this will have helped ameliorate the darker side.

Overall, the outcomes for individual workers from employer-driven flexible working practices is less positive, largely due to the reduction in job and income security resulting from many of these practices. However, for workers in some circumstances the trading of security for flexibility may be one considered to be worthwhile. Furthermore, the diversity of arrangements in this grouping makes it hard to make general observations.

Given the developments in the past decades, it seems likely that the flexibility debate will remain a prominent one in organisations and that flexible working arrangements will continue to feature. Experiences during the pandemic are likely to continue to shape how workers and managers view flexible working and as such it will be important for researchers and policy makers to monitor these developments. A focus that is provided in the following chapters.

REFERENCES

Acker, J. (1990). Hierarchies, jobs, bodies: A theory of gendered organizations. *Gender & Society, 4*(2), 139–58.

Akerlof, G. (1982). Labor contracts as partial gift exchange. *The Quarterly Journal of Economics, 97*(4), 543–69.

Alis, D. (2006). From Gods to Goddesses: Horai management as an approach to coordinating working hours. *Time & Society, 15*(1), 81–104.

Allen, T.D., Johnson, R.C., Kiburz, K.M. & Shockley, K.M. (2013). Work-family conflict and flexible work arrangements. *Personnel Psychology, 66*(2), 345–76.

Allen, T.D., Golden, T.D. & Shockley, K.M. (2015). How effective is telecommuting? Assessing the status of our scientific findings. *Psychological Science in the Public Interest, 16*(2), 40–68.

Anderson, A.J., Kaplan, S.A. & Vega, R.P. (2015). The impact of telework on emotional experience: When, and for whom, does telework improve daily affective well-being? *European Journal of Work and Organizational Psychology, 24*(6), 882–97.

Anderson, D. & Kelliher, C. (2020). Enforced remote working and the work-life interface during lockdown. *Gender in Management, 35*(7/8), 677–83.

Atkinson, J. (1985). Flexibility: Planning for an uncertain future. *Manpower Policy and Practice, 1*, 26–9.

Bailey, C., Mankin, D., Kelliher, C. & Garavan, T. (2018). *Strategic Human Resource Management,* 2nd edn. Oxford: Oxford University Press.

Bal, P.M. & Izak, M. (2021). Paradigms of flexibility: A systematic review of research on workplace flexibility. *European Management Review, 18*(1), 37–50.

Bessa, I. & Tomlinson, J. (2017). Established, accelerated and emergent themes in flexible work research. *Journal of Industrial Relations, 59*(2), 153–69.

Blau, P.M. (1964). *Exchange and Power in Social Life.* New York: Wiley.

Bosch, G. (2004). Towards a new standard employment relationship in Western Europe. *British Journal of Industrial Relations, 42*(4), 617–36.

Cañibano, A. (2019). Workplace flexibility as a paradoxical phenomenon: Exploring employee experiences. *Human Relations*, *72*(2), 444–70.

Cannon, F. (2017). Agile futures. In F. Cannon (Ed.), *The Agility Mindset* (pp. 133–52). Cham, Switzerland: Springer International.

Chen, Y. & Fulmer, I.S. (2018). Fine-tuning what we know about employees' experience with flexible work arrangements and their job attitudes. *Human Resource Management*, *57*(1), 381–95. https://doi.org/10.1002/hrm.21849.

Chung, H. (2022). *The Flexibility Paradox*. Bristol: Policy Press.

Chung, H. & van der Lippe, T. (2020). Flexible working, work–life balance, and gender equality: Introduction. *Social Indicators Research*, *151*, 365–81.

CIPD (2015). *Zero hours and Short Hours Contracts in the UK. Employer and Employee Perspectives*. Wimbledon: CIPD.

Dalton, D. & Mesch, D. (1990). The impact of flexible scheduling on employee attendance and turnover. *Administrative Science Quarterly*, *35*, 370–87.

Dawson, C., Veliziotis, M., Pacheco, G. & Webber, D.J. (2015). Is temporary employment a cause or consequence of poor mental health? A panel data analysis. *Social Science & Medicine*, *134*, 50–8.

De Menezes, L. & Kelliher, C. (2017). Flexible working, individual performance and employee attitudes: Comparing formal and informal arrangements. *Human Resource Management*, *56*(6), 1051–70.

Dunham, R., Pierce, J. & Casaneda, M. (1987). Alternative work schedules: Two field quasi experiments. *Personnel Psychology*, *40*, 215–42.

Eurofound (2023), *Working Time in 2021–2022*. Luxembourg: Publications Office of the European Union.

Farina, E., Green, C. & McVicar, D. (2023). Zero hours contracts and self-reported (mental) health in the UK. *British Journal of Industrial Relations*, 1–22. https://doi.org/10.1111/bjir.12773.

Fleming, P. (2022). How biopower puts freedom to work: Conceptualizing 'pivoting mechanisms' in the neoliberal university. *Human Relations*, *75*(10), 1986–2007.

Gascoigne, C. & Kelliher, C. (2018). The transition to part-time: How professionals negotiate reduced time and workload i-deals and craft their jobs. *Human Relations*, *71*, 103–25.

Golden, T.D. & Eddleston, K.A. (2020). Is there a price telecommuters pay? Examining the relationship between telecommuting and objective career success. *Journal of Vocational Behavior*, *116*, 1–13.

Golembiewski, R., Hilles, R. & Kagno, M. (1974). A longitudinal study of flexi-time effects: Some consequences of an OD structural intervention. *Journal of Applied Behavioural Sciences*, *10*, 503–532.

Grant, K., McQueen, F., Osborn, S. & Holland, P. (2023). Re-configuring the jigsaw puzzle: Balancing time, pace, place and space of work in the Covid-19 era. *Economic and Industrial Democracy*, OnlineFirst, 0143831X231195686.

Green, F. (2020). Health effects of job insecurity. *IZA World of Labor 2020*, 212. doi:10.15185/izawol.212.v2.

Kelliher, C. & Anderson, D. (2010). Doing more with less? Flexible working practices and the intensification of work. *Human Relations*, *63*(1), 83–106.

Kelliher, C. and de Menezes, L.M. (2019). *Flexible Working in Organisations. A Research Overview*. Oxon: Routledge.

Kelliher, C. & Richardson, J. (2019) Work, working and work relationships in a changing world (pp. 1–14). In C. Kelliher & J. Richardson (Eds), *Work, Working and Work Relationships in a Changing World*. New York: Routledge.

Kelliher, C., Richardson, J. & Boiarintseva, G. (2019). All of work? All of life? Reconceptualising work-life balance for the 21st century. *Human Resource Management Journal*, *29*(2), 97–112.

Kim, J. & Campagna, A. (1981). Effects of flexitime on employee attendance and performance: A field experiment. *Academy of Management Journal*, *24*, 729–41.

Koumenta, M. & Williams, M. (2019). An anatomy of zero-hour contracts in the UK. *Industrial Relations Journal*, *50*(1), 20–40.

Kraut, R. (1989). Telecommuting: The trade off of homework. *Journal of Communication*, *39*, 19–47.

Kröll, C., Doebler, P. & Nüesch, S. (2017). Meta-analytic evidence of the effectiveness of stress management at work. *European Journal of Work and Organizational Psychology*, *26*(5), 677–93.

Kurland, N. & Bailey, D. (1999). Telework: The advantages of working here, there, anywhere and anytime. *Organizational Dynamics*, *28*, 53–68.

Latack, J. & Foster, L. (1985). Implementation of compressed work schedules: Participation and job redesign as critical factors for employee acceptance. *Personnel Psychology*, *38*, 75–92.

Leslie, L., Manchester, C., Park, T-Y. & Mehng, S.A. (2012). Flexible work practices: A source of career premiums or penalties? *Academy of Management Journals*, *55*(6), 1407–28.

Loretto, W. & Vickerstaff, S. (2015). Gender, age and flexible working in later life. *Work, Employment and Society*, *29*(2), 233–49.

Lott, Y., Kelliher, C. & Chung, H. (2022). Reflecting the changing nature of work? A critique of existing survey measures and a proposal for capturing new ways of working. *Transfer: European Review of Labour and Research*, *28*(4), 457–73.

Masuda, A.D., Poelmans, S.A.Y., Allen, T.D., Spector, P.E., Lapierre, L.M., Cooper, C.L., Abarca, N., Brough, P., Ferreiro, P., Fraile, G., Lu, L., Lu, C.-Q., Siu, O.L., O'Driscoll, M.P., Simoni, A.S., Shima, S. & Moreno-Velazquez, I. (2012). Flexible work arrangements availability and their relationship with work-to-family conflict, job satisfaction, and turnover intentions: A comparison of three country clusters. *Applied Psychology*, *61*(1), 1–29.

Mazmanian, M., Orlikowski, W.J., & Yates, J. (2013) The Autonomy Paradox: The implications of mobile email devices for knowledge professionals. *Organization Science*, *24*(5, 1337–57.

Messenger, J.C. & Gerschwind, L. (2016). Three generations of telework: New ICTs and the (r)evolution from home office to virtual office. *New Technology, Work and Employment*, *31*, 195–208.

Moscone, F., Tosetti, E. & Vittadini, G. (2016). The impact of precarious employment on mental health: The case of Italy. *Social Science & Medicine*, *158*, 86–95.

Orpen, C. (1981). Effect of flexible working hours on employee satisfaction and performance: A field experiment. *Journal of Applied Psychology*, *66*, 113–15.

Peretz, H., Fried, Y. & Levi, A. (2018). Flexible work arrangements, national culture, organisational characteristics, and organisational outcomes: A study across 21 countries. *Human Resource Management Journal*, *28*(1), 182–200.

Pierce, J.L. & Newstrom, J.W. (1980). Toward a conceptual clarification of employee responses to flexible working hours: A work adjustment approach. *Journal of Management*, *6*, 117–34.

Richardson, J. & Kelliher, C. (2015). Managing visibility for career sustainability: A study of remote workers (pp. 116–30). In B. van der Heijden & A. de Vos (Eds),

A Handbook of Sustainable Careers. Cheltenham, UK and Northampton, MA, USA: Edward Elgar.

Ross, P. & Ali, Y. (2017). Normative commitment in the ICT sector: Why professional commitment and flexible work practices matter. *International Journal of Employment Studies*, *25*(1), 44–62.

Schein, V., Maurer, E. & Novak, J. (1977). Impact of flexible working hours on productivity. *Journal of Applied Psychology*, *62*, 463–5.

Schöllbauer, J., Hartner-Tiefenthaler, M. & Kelliher, C. (2023). Strain, loss of time, or even gain? A systematic review of technology-based work extending and its ambiguous impact on wellbeing, considering its frequency and duration. *Frontiers in Psychology*. https://doi.org/10.3389/fpsyg.2023.1175641.

Shamir, B. & Salomon, I. (1985). Work at home and the quality of working life. *Academy of Management Review*, *10*, 455–64.

Trent, J., Smith, A. & Wood, D. (1994). Telecommuting: stress and social support. *Psychological Reports*, *74*, 1312–14.

PART II

Patterns of flexibility

4. Time: working any time

Daniel Wheatley

INTRODUCTION

This chapter explores the evolution of working time, in particular, debating the growth in flexibility in recent decades and associated tensions between worker autonomy and managerial control. Working time has expanded in its potential from historical routes based around hours of daylight to routines structured around standardised hours of work in co-located workplaces, for example, 9 am–5 pm, to contemporary fluidity in working time where work can, and does, take place at any time (Bienefeld, 1972; Felstead & Henseke, 2017; Wheatley, 2020). That said, there remain stark differences in the structure of working time between occupations, industries and other categories. For example, working time in a machine-operative role is subject to a level of spatial fixity and likely to follow shift patterns in a geographically specific workplace location as it has for much of the last two centuries (Felstead, 2022). Meanwhile, in knowledge occupations, including many managerial and professional roles, there has been a considerable expansion and flexibilisation of working time, with job performance increasingly measured with reference to the generation of outputs as opposed to only time spent working (Wheatley, 2022a). Distinct again are experiences in lower-wage service work including geographically mobile roles such as delivery and taxi drivers, where platform-driven technological developments have created new demands and opportunities in the structure of working time (Aloisi, 2016; van Doorn & Badger, 2020).

Within many occupations, flexibility has come to define recent developments in working time, yet there remains a tension between the projected image of worker autonomy and flexibility and the imposition of managerial control systems (Mazmanian et al., 2013; Putnam et al., 2014; de Vaujany et al., 2021). Autonomy and flexibility over the tasks, timing and location of work have been found to offer several benefits for workers and their organisations, including higher levels of job satisfaction, better performance and improved work-life balance (Glavin & Schieman, 2012; Wheatley, 2017a, 2017b). Meanwhile, greater choice over how to spend 'inactive' working time during breaks has been shown to be highly important to the ability of breaks to aid work recovery (Trougakos et al., 2014). The central supervisory function of management in extracting effort from workers gives managers considerable control over the levels of autonomy and flexibility experienced by workers (Findlay et al., 2017). The result is a complex interplay between autonomy and managerial control, which in some instances can act to limit realised levels of flexibility and can detract from, rather than increase, work-life balance, with this effect captured in the moniker 'faux flexibility' (Elliott et al., 2022, 68; Wheatley et al., 2023).

This chapter considers developments in working time, drawing on existing conceptual contributions and empirical evidence and trends in working time. The chapter begins with a discussion of the expansion of working time in a historical context. The chapter then considers the changing balance between the length and intensity of working time and what this means for a realised balance between work and life. The focus then moves to the expansion and growth in flexibility in working time. Reference here is given to the impacts of flexible working arrangements and flexibilisation of contracts, including the impacts of constant on-call, international time zones and virtual team working routines. The chapter then reflects on the tension between the image of flexibility in working time and realised levels of autonomy, drawing on debates surrounding the autonomy-control paradox. The chapter concludes by considering whether developments in working time more accurately represent a real growth in flexibility or the imposition of faux flexibility, and how flexibility can be used most effectively for the benefit of workers and organisations.

THE EXPANSION OF WORK TIME

Patterns and structures of working time have undergone significant change throughout history driven by a range of factors, including the growth of capitalism and advances in technology (see also Chapter 3). In medieval times, it was not uncommon to work from dawn until dusk, hours of work themselves varying in this case between 16 hours during the summer and eight hours in the winter. In hotter climates, substantive breaks taken in the middle part of the day also came to be the norm. Beginning in the 16th century, a period of reductions in working hours was recorded, driven by a large-scale scarcity of labour that acted to increase real wages (Bienefeld, 1972). However, the downward trend in hours was relatively short-lived as average working hours increased again towards the end of the century, and by the 17th century, further increases in working hours were recorded alongside the abolition of holidays by the Puritans. Longer working time during this period was associated with the Protestant Work Ethic, a term Max Weber used to describe Protestant values that emphasised hard work and wealth accumulation (Weber, 1976). During the 18th century, a combination of increases in real wages and reductions in working hours led to a normalisation of working time to a typical model of a ten-hour day from 6 am to 6 pm incorporating up to two hours of breaks (Bienefeld, 1972).

The Industrial Revolution witnessed further formalisation of working time under capitalism as technological advances, including the mechanical loom and steam engine, acted to centralise work, prompting considerable change in patterns of labour from individuals. Small-scale businesses that operated from the home (i.e., cottage industries) were replaced with large-scale movements of labour to centralised work locations in the growing urban centres, creating a separation between home and work (Bienefeld, 1972; Horrell & Humphries, 1995). Historical trends in working time, using the example of the UK, evidence a gradual decline from the mid-19th century in measures of both normal full-time hours from 1860 and average weekly hours from 1856 (see Wheatley, 2017c, 84). Working time decreased from around 60 hours per week in the mid-19th century to approximately 38 hours (normal full time) and 33 hours (average weekly) by 2015 (Wheatley, 2020). The downward trend in working hours during the 19th century was partly a response to the imposition of legislation restricting working hours. In the UK, for example, this began with the Factory Acts, a series of Acts focused on improving working conditions which, although initially limited in their impact, gradually acted to reduce overall hours of work. Reductions in working time continued during the 19th century, driven by the growth of organised trades and craft unions (Bienefeld, 1972). By the middle of the 19th century, reductions in working time prompted employers to turn their focus towards productivity increase (Hobsbawm, 1968).

During this period, workplace location was characterised by spatial fixity, that is, work taking place in a fixed geographical location such as a factory. Locating workers in one place in this manner offers employers several benefits associated with the concept of agglomeration, including enabling communications and coordination, knowledge sharing and mass production benefits, including economies of scale and scope (Shearmur, 2018; Zhu, 2013). It further offers employers the opportunity to exert considerable levels of managerial control over employees (Marglin, 1974). A key feature of the Industrial Revolution was mass production, which applied the division of labour concept, acknowledging the efficiency gains that could be generated through the application of labour in this way. The division of labour, a concept developed by Adam Smith (1776 [1981]), emphasised that by dividing tasks into their component parts, even complex tasks could be devolved into simple repetitive processes, offering efficiency gains as repetition enabled increasing speed and dexterity and associated reductions in errors. The subdivision of tasks in the division of labour further allowed the mechanisation of processes, replacing human labour with capital investment. These developments changed the nature of working time, increasing levels of repetition, reducing initiative and skill, and creating alienation from work (Spencer, 2009).

In the 20th century, key developments, including Scientific Management, a concept developed by Frederick Taylor and also termed Taylorism, altered the structure and nature of working time (Taylor, 1967). Taylorism emphasises the role of managerial control in realising productivity through standardisation and the application of systems that monitor and measure worker contribution and effort. As such, Taylorism argues for little initiative and autonomy on the part of the employee (Choi et al., 2008). The development of the rolling assembly line and automation of manufacturing processes associated with the innovations of Henry Ford, referred to as Fordism, further changed how work time was organised as standardisation and automation of processes further reduced levels of individual decision-making with the aim of increasing efficiency (Lipietz, 1997). Towards the end of the 20th century, changes in industrial structure across many developed nations, including the loss of traditional heavy industry, a concurrent growth of services, and eventual digitisation of both industrial and service work, have continued to alter the structure of working time. Further reductions in overall hours of work were recorded until towards the end of the 20th century when a relative stagnation of working time was reached (Wheatley, 2020). Further legislation, for example, across the European Union, the 1993 European Working Time Directive (Council Directive 94/103/EC) and its derivative legislation in member nations prompted the imposition of harder limits on working time in several economies, in this case, a maximum 48-hour working week (averaged over 17 weeks) although policy limiting hours even further was enacted in countries such as France where a 35-hour week was introduced (see LaJeunesse, 2009).

While overall trends and averages present a picture of shorter working time in relative terms, a distinguishing feature of the period from the late 20th century has been the de-standardisation of working time across sectors and occupations. Further advances in technology, including wireless internet, cloud computing, smartphones and the growth of digital platforms, have led to work becoming more location-independent in many occupations (Moos & Skaburskis, 2007). Since the beginning of the 21st century, there has been a recorded expansion of non-standard modes of work, including forms of self-employment such as gig working, e-lancing, and e-entrepreneurship (Carré & Heintz, 2013; Howcroft & Bergvall-Kåreborn, 2019), reduced and non-standard hours, for example, zero-hours contracts, and other types of flexible work that are characterised by greater fluidity in working time (Felstead & Henseke, 2017). Digital technologies have created a raft of new occupations, for example, content creation for social media. Work continues to evolve with further developments in highly flexibilised, digitally driven work, including a shift to forms of digital nomadism that have been captured in several monikers, including Bring Your Own Device (BYOD), Do It Yourself (DIY), Do It Together (DIT), holacracy (i.e., a system of self-management which can involve individuals taking on multiple functional roles), neo-craftmanship (i.e., traditional crafts using modern production techniques/tools), maker movements (i.e., technology-based creation of products/services) and open source (de Vaujany et al., 2021). These changes have prompted debates over working time, shifting further from traditional concerns around the length of working time and towards] the intensity of working time, the nature of flexibility, and the relative balance between individual autonomy and managerial control.

GROWTH IN THE INTENSITY OF WORK

The intensity of work has come to the fore in debates around paid work. Several decades of legislation, trade union bargaining and changes in the nature of work itself have prompted a refocusing towards the content of working time rather than solely the extent. Changes in the way work is organised, including a greater focus on output as opposed to time spent in work, have prompted associated changes in the structure of working time in many service-based, as well as other occupations, with evidence indicating an increase in levels of intensity in work (Felstead & Green, 2017; F. Green, 2006; A. Green, 2017; Kalleberg, 2012). While understanding of the extent of working time is well developed, including the distinction between paid and unpaid working time, overtime, on-call time and more, as a concept, the intensity of work is relatively under-developed. Work intensity has been conceptualised as reflecting how hard we work. This approach incorporates both a time component, that is, the length of working time, and a specific intensity component, that is, the pace and effort expended during the time worked (Burke et al., 2010). The literature on job demands also helps to elucidate the intensity of work as demands present in a job, such as time pressure, effort required and level of difficulty, directly influence the realised intensity experienced (see Bakker & Demerouti, 2007; Karasek, 1979). The work of Green is notable in this arena, as he has researched growth in the intensity of work extensively and refers to work intensity in reference to 'work effort', defining it here as the 'rate of physical and/or mental input to work tasks' (see F. Green 2001, 56).

Clear in conceptualisations of work intensity is that it is comprised of physical, mental and emotional demands at work (Felstead & Green, 2017). As such, the intensity of work presents difficulties in measurement and, in turn, the ability to accurately understand its impacts. Effort levels are likely to be uneven throughout any period of work, as there will be periods of paid working time which appear less productive but are used to think or network with others.

Time may equally appear inactive but be utilised for work recovery, that is, to rest and reduce fatigue and replenish personal resources (Sonnentag, 2001; Sonnentag & Fritz, 2007). These less productive periods, though, have an important function in enabling a worker to be more productive in subsequent periods of working time and potentially reduce the incidence of burnout and other negative well-being outcomes (Felstead & Green, 2017). Measuring the intensity of work in an objective manner, therefore, requires careful data collection, including through controlled experiments, to be accurate and reliable. Capturing the intensity of work using subjective self-reporting exercises, that is, asking a worker and/or their employer (line manager) about the level of intensity in their job, can present difficulties due to differences in subjective understanding of how hard someone is working and gaps between worker and employer thresholds or benchmarks of an acceptable or intense workload (Wheatley, 2022b).

While there remain difficulties with the conceptualisation and measurement of this concept, existing evidence emphasises the importance of the intensity of work to the quality of work and worker well-being. More intense working routines have been found to be associated with lower levels of work-related well-being (F. Green, 2008; F. Green et al., 2016) and incidence of overwork (Mazzetti et al., 2014). Role overload has been cited as a particular concern associated with intense working time. Role overload occurs when job demands surpass, or at least are perceived by the worker to surpass, the resources and time available and/or capabilities of the worker (Beehr et al., 1976, cited in Alfes et al., 2018). As such, role overload can negatively impact levels of work engagement and, through its negative impact on resources, result in burnout and increased turnover intention (Alfes et al., 2018; Crawford et al., 2010; Greenhaus et al., 2012; Montani & Dagenais-Desmarais, 2018, 758). The relevance of the intensity of work to experiences of working time is heightened by the behaviours of managers and leaders due to their considerable influence over the workplace culture within an organisation (McCarthy et al., 2010). Managers and leaders who impose, or do nothing to address, intensive and/ or extensive working time cultures enable a workplace environment which subjects workers to substantial work stressors, that is, stress-generating experiences in work (Greenhaus et al., 2012). Where managerial control is exerted over the structure of working time, which may, in principle, be flexible, work intensity is often greater with potentially negative consequences for workers and the organisation (Piasna, 2018). The result is a considerable tension between the length and intensity of working time and the ability of workers to realise potential levels of flexibility in paid work.

BALANCING WORK AND LIFE

Flexibility has come to characterise rhetoric surrounding developments in paid work since the beginning of the 21st century (Carré & Heintz, 2013; Felstead & Henseke, 2017; Mandl et al., 2015). Flexibility is present in many forms in contemporary work, with some dimensions of flexibility offering more widely evidenced benefits, for example, flexible working arrangements, while others remain more heavily debated, for example, flexible contracting (Glavin & Schieman, 2012; Kalleberg, 2012; Osnowitz & Henson, 2016; Wheatley, 2017a, 2017b). Core to the purpose of flexibility in paid work is the provision of greater choice for the worker and the ability to achieve a better balance or blend between work and the rest of life.

Work-life balance has been widely studied and debated in academic, policy and wider social spheres for several decades (Greenhaus et al., 2012), with contributions coining multiple variations of the concept, including work-family balance (Clark, 2000), work-life integration (Atkinson & Hall, 2009; Fagan et al., 2012) and work-life conflict with the latter refocusing the concept on the absence of work-life balance (Chang et al., 2010). As Clark described in her seminal work on work-life border theory, work-life balance refers to the ability to combine work with household and/or family responsibilities successfully or with minimum conflict (Clark, 2000). Work-life balance can be further disaggregated into a psychological and social perspective. The psychological component focuses on work-life balance as the relative satisfaction associated with achievement or otherwise of balance, while the social component centres on the accomplishment of work and family role-related expectations (Agosti et al., 2017). Work-life blending is a somewhat distinct concept, in which the focus is turned not to how to find an acceptable balance between what are conceptualised as two separate dimensions of time – work and the rest of life – but instead acknowledges how work and the rest of life can be blended together as one (Fetherston et al., 2021). Work-life blending, also referred to as work-life merge and work-life fusion, is connected to the concept of spillover (Carlson et al., 2014; Guest, 2002), as it emphasises the blurring of the boundary between work and the rest of life, with evidence indicative of both positive outcomes, for example, feelings of fulfilment and completeness, and negative outcomes, for example, difficulties in managing work and non-work demands (Clark, 2000). As a concept, work-life blending has become increasingly relevant as digital technologies and changes in the nature of work have increased the potential for work to take place anywhere and at any time. These changes have created an increasingly blurred reality of work, where work has been argued as 'not fully work anymore' (de Vaujany et al., 2021, 688).

Acknowledging the importance of the interaction between work and the rest of life, work-life or work-family policies have been put in place in many nations, including through regulations governing parental leave, rights for carers and formalised flexible working arrangements. In the UK, for example, the Shared Parental Leave Regulations 2014 provide rights for parents to share up to 50 weeks of leave, 37 weeks of which is paid, subject to meeting certain eligibility criteria. Meanwhile, the formalisation of flexible working occurred through the Flexible Working Regulations. Initially implemented in 2003, they offer the right to request a formal flexible working arrangement. The regulations were initially limited in their coverage, but following several expansions in 2014 the regulations extended to cover all workers following 26 weeks of service. A common feature of right to request policies, and one that is present in the UK, Australia and other cases, is that arrangements are subject to allowance decisions, that is, the request is considered relative to its impact on the organisation and policy often incorporates an option to reject requests on grounds of 'business need' or business impacts which can in practice be relatively arbitrary or vague in nature (Deakin & Morris, 2012; Poelmans & Beham, 2008). Policies in this regard have been criticised for being too employer-focused.

Policy in Australia is fairly consistent with that of the UK. The right to request a formal flexible working arrangement was introduced in 2009 through the Fair Work Act again with coverage initially limited to workers who met certain criteria. A paid parental leave scheme was also introduced from 2011 (Baird, 2011). Often cited as the most progressive societies with respect to flexible working and family-friendly policies are the Nordic countries, including Sweden, Finland and Norway. In Norway, for example, the Working Environment Act was introduced in 2006, providing the right to request a flexible working arrangement. Norway has put in place substantive paid parental leave entitlements of up to one year, much of which can be shared between parents (Brandth & Kvande, 2009; Rønsen & Kitterød, 2015). Alongside these legislative measures have been agendas promoting work-life balance and increased flexibility in work, with governments and non-profit organisations promoting positive dialogue between workers and their employers and organisation-level work-life balance policies. Further developments have included the trialling of a four-day working week in several nations, including Iceland and the UK, and developments across Europe on the right to disconnect, that is, a right to disengage from work, including emails, phone calls and other forms of communication outside of stated working time. In 2021, the European Parliament passed a resolution to begin work on a directive, while several states, including Ireland and Belgium, have already put in place right to disconnect policies and codes of practice, although not in all cases actual legislation.

At the organisational level, there are multiple layers of work-life balance policies, including flexible working arrangements; health and well-being programmes; childcare benefits and services; leave options, for example, maternity/paternity leave, career breaks, and organisational understanding and support (Zheng et al., 2015). The implementation of policy alone, though, is unlikely to engender a working environment that enables work and life to be successfully managed. Workplace culture is also key. It is highly relevant to the effectiveness of organisational work-life balance policy due to the impacts that local-level culture and behaviours can have on perceived availability and use of policies (Wheatley, 2017b). Evidence from a recent case study of a multi-national organisation conducted in the UK, for example, identified differences in the degree to which line managers embraced and, in turn, applied flexibility in their teams and local workplace norms, including working hours and work location cultures, as impacting both awareness and perceptions of the availability of flexible working policies (Wheatley et al., 2023).

FLEXIBILITY IN WORKING TIME AND LOCATION

Flexibility in work has been defined in several ways, including by Putnam et al. (2014) as the 'opportunity to adjust the where, when and how'. Flexibility comes in different forms, which can be usefully categorised into formal flexible working arrangements, informal flexibility and flexible contracting (details on the evolution of flexible patterns can be found in Chapter 2). Greater flexibility in paid work is purported to generate several benefits, including increased job satisfaction, better performance, and enhanced work-life balance through empowering workers to better manage work and other responsibilities (Laβ & Wooden, 2023; Lee & DeVoe, 2012; Wheatley, 2017b). The widely acknowledged potential benefits of flexibility have driven increased provision as workers are demanding flexibility, and organisations have recognised that the provision of flexibility can have significant positive impacts on the recruitment and retention of talent (Wheatley et al., 2023). Flexibility is not without difficulties, however, with evidence reporting concerns around the growth in the extent and intensity of working time due to flexibility resulting in availability pressures and always-on cultures (Taylor et al., 2021), associated blurring of work and life boundaries (Green & Riley, 2021; Laβ & Wooden, 2023), pay penalties for those making use of flexible working arrangements (Fuller & Hirsh, 2019), and isolation and loss of professional and social networks among remote workers (Bennett et al., 2021; Bentley et al., 2016). These difficulties are, in some cases, heavily connected to the nature of the flexibility provision and raise questions over whether the flexibility that is offered by organisations reflects authentic flexibility awarded to workers in an approach centred on responsible autonomy, that is, the provision of greater discretion and variety in work (Friedman, 1977), or faux flexibility that better reflects the imposition of employer-friendly forms of flexibility in ways which create an autonomy-control paradox (Mendonça et al., 2023; Putnam et al., 2014; de Vaujany et al., 2021).

Formal flexible working arrangements can be broadly split into three types: those that involve (1) the arrangement of working time, for example, flexi-time, compressed hours; (2) the reduction of working time, for example, part-time, job sharing; and (3) the location of work, for example, work from home (see Wheatley, 2017b). Formally arranged flexibility of this nature is governed by flexible working legislation and, as already noted in many cases, is subject to allowance decisions (Deakin & Morris, 2012). Relative use of such arrangements differs considerably, with some arrangements being much more common, including flexi-time, that is, flexible start and end times, sometimes around core hours, and part-time or reduced hours. Others, such as job share, that is, splitting a full-time job between two or more individuals, remain marginal in their use. A range of factors, both employer-driven, for example, difficulties in practical application or at least perception of difficulties by line managers, and employee-driven, for example, lack of awareness, are responsible for the content of the agreed arrangements, differences in relative levels of use, and realised levels of flexibility (Sweet et al., 2014; Wheatley, 2017b). As formal flexible working arrangements are subject to a formal agreement, they usually involve contract modifications which can be temporary or, in some cases, permanent. Also common is that formal flexible working arrangements tend to be structured and to a degree fixed, for example, an agreement to work from home every Monday and Friday or an agreement to work compressed hours over four days, Monday to Thursday, 9 am–6 pm. The structured nature of these agreements does raise a central concern regarding whether formal flexibility is authentically flexible or more accurately reflects the provision of flexibility within limits or faux flexibility (Elliott et al., 2022; Wheatley et al., 2023). In these cases, purported flexibility is actually subject to significant degrees of managerial control.

Informal flexibility refers to flexibility that occurs on a more ad hoc basis. By its nature, informal flexibility is free from the constraints of formal contractual agreements and can offer a greater degree of control to the individual. These more informal arrangements have been covered in several literatures including in contributions exploring the notion of flexibility idiosyncratic-deals or i-deals, which refers to personalised non-standard flexible working agreements negotiated between employee and employer (see, e.g., Erden Bayazit & Bayazit, 2019). Informal flexibility can take several forms, including flexibility over the timing of the working day and/or the ability to work from home or in other remote locations in many cases without this having to be agreed on a formal basis such as a rota. Informal flexibility may be used in combination with formal arrangements, but equally may be used as an alternative to a formal arrangement. Evidence is indicative of informal flexibility being of significant value to workers, as it provides a greater degree of control over the timing and location of work (Hall & Atkinson, 2006; Wheatley, 2021). However, it is subject to uncertainty as the informal nature of the agreements, often between workers and their line manager, leaves the worker potentially vulnerable where there is changing demand, for example, a change in business need or strategy or a change in line manager and associated preferences over how to manage their team. While informal flexibility may appear to offer greater control to the worker, the nature of these agreements can reflect the application of managerial control to flexibility over the timing and location of work.

Flexible contracting, sometimes referred to as flexibilisation, has re-generated increased interest in academic and policy spheres since the economic crisis of 2008–10 and prompted significant debate around its relative impacts (McCrate, 2012). At this time, there was a recorded increase in non-standard or contingent employment (Kalleberg, 2012) as organisations navigated through and out of the crisis. There was a notable expansion of alternative forms of contracting for employees, including zero-hours contracting, which refers to employment that is on-call with non-guaranteed hours (Mandl et al., 2015), as well as fixed-term, temporary and seasonal contracts. Increased flexibilisation has remained a feature of changes in paid work up to and since the Covid-19 pandemic, with a key area of expansion present in forms of self-employment, including the growth of workers classed as independent contractors, synonymous with work in the gig economy (Howcroft & Bergvall-Kåreborn, 2019; King, 2014). While there are documented benefits to these forms of work, including greater flexibility over when to work and the specific tasks that are taken on (Aloisi, 2016; Osnowitz & Henson, 2016), these are more often associated with higher-paid knowledge gig work, and several difficulties have been identified with flexibilisation including the on-call nature of some of this work acting to limit realised flexibility in working time, and in some cases limiting other labour market opportunities, for example, second job holding.

Research has shown, for example, a significant lengthening and fragmenting of working time among delivery-platform workers whose working time is determined by demand, which occurs at certain points throughout the day, that is, morning, middle of the day and evening (Badger, 2022). Workers face short-term concerns around levels of demand, prompting them to work whenever needed to reach their income goals, and the precarity of their position with the platform, including the potential impacts of poor ratings and risk of temporary deactivation by the platform, perpetuate a high degree of uncertainty (van Doorn & Badger, 2020). A key characteristic of much of the expanded flexibility in contracting is that it renders paid work precarious, creating a high degree of job insecurity and associated negative impacts, including uncertainty around the regularity of work and income and for worker well-being through work-related stress and burnout (Badger, 2022; Kalleberg, 2012; McCrate, 2012).

Technological progress has been a key driver of the gig economy as algorithm-based platforms act to provide a source of work method of completing work (Howcroft & Bergvall-Kåreborn, 2019), as well as enabling new forms of surveillance and control over workers (discussed in Chapter 3 and later in this chapter). Changes in technology have also prompted work to become less geographically bounded, adding a further dimension to flexibility (Shearmur, 2018). There has been a growth in work taking place across international time zones and in virtual teams. Working in this manner creates new opportunities, including expanding the labour market talent pool to provide access to required expertise and enabling 24/7 task progression (Dulebohn & Hoch, 2017). However, working in virtual teams results in fewer informal and emotional exchanges, creating difficulties including social distance between team members, that is, lack of emotional connection, that can result in relational problems including the presence of 'us' vs 'them' attitudes, in particular, in circumstances of status inequality between team members, and the potential for isolation and associated negative well-being impacts (Sander et al., 2021; Seshadri & Elangovan, 2021). Virtual working can also lead to the incidence of virtual presenteeism behaviours, including working while unwell, as the ease of connecting to work creates pressure to be available and creates difficulties in achieving cognitive separation from work.

In all cases, a consistent realisation is that flexibility is necessarily limited by the nature of the work being performed. Realised levels of flexibility can often practically be constrained by the content of a job, for example, a machine operator in a factory cannot practically complete their job from home (Felstead, 2022). As experienced by many workers during the Covid-19 pandemic, a lack of adequate space and physical resources (desk, chair, information and communications technology (ICT)) can also limit the potential for flexibility over workplace location, including working from home (Wheatley, 2022a). Job demands, such as the timing and/or location of meetings, deadlines and static workflows, further limit the flexibility that can be present (Putnam et al., 2014). Other practical considerations further impact whether flexibility can be manifest, for example, a worker needing to access limited car parking at a workplace reducing the potential for use of arrangements such as flexi-time as they are constrained to arrive at their workplace early to ensure that they are able to get a parking space (Wheatley, 2012). Flexibility at the individual level also has a potentially wider impact within the organisation, which has been conceptualised recently as the flexibility ripple effect (see Wheatley et al., 2023). The flexibility ripple effect is a phenomenon that occurs when the provision of flexibility at the individual level has knock-on effects within and between teams, across functions and potentially throughout the entire organisation. Through the study of a multi-national organisation, it was identified that these impacts are often unplanned and unexpected and can involve, for example, flexibility resulting in a lack of availability of required expertise, delays in workflows, problems with communication, conflation or duplication of effort, and associated well-being implications including feelings of frustration and resentment among colleagues. Navigating the application of flexibility to realise its true potential is certainly not straightforward and requires a commitment and buy-in on the part of the individual and organisation to the benefits of flexibility, as well as emphasising a key coordinating role of management in achieving successful integration of flexibility alongside other organisational systems and demands.

WORKING TIME AND THE AUTONOMY-CONTROL PARADOX

The imposition of managerial or organisational control in situations where flexibility is purported to be present is one of the most consistent characteristics of current applications of flexibility in working time and location. Historically, employer concerns around worker malfeasance and loss of control have acted to limit levels of flexibility and control in paid work (Felstead, 2022; Sato, 2019; Sweet et al., 2014). While greater flexibility has come to characterise developments in work in the last decade or so, scholars have recognised that the provision of greater flexibility and autonomy to the worker is often combined with the application of greater organisational control, albeit in forms that have evolved alongside the evolution of work itself. This phenomenon has been conceptualised as the autonomy-control paradox (Putnam et al., 2014). The paradox occurs due to greater employee autonomy being provided alongside methods of organisational control that are applied in 'unobtrusive' forms. For example, the provision of schedule flexibility can result in workers effectively being on call and working longer hours due to their connectedness to their organisation through ICT and mobile devices (Putnam et al., 2014). This issue of tensions between autonomy and managerial control has long been recognised, for example, in the work of Brannen (2005, 115), who noted that 'the more autonomy employees are given over organizing their time in work seems to mean that they are spending longer and longer at work or working'.

As noted at the beginning of this chapter, the imposition of control over workers has long been a central and distinguishing feature of management (Marglin, 1974). Managerial control refers to both the formal and informal actions taken by managers that can be used to motivate and/or discipline workers to direct or influence their actions (de Vaujany et al., 2021). The nature of this activity and mechanisms for enacting it have undergone considerable change as work has itself evolved. Traditional methods of control, such as physically walking around a workplace and checking in with workers, closely linked with other concerns around work, including presenteeism (Sewell & Taskin, 2015), have evolved into more covert surveillance conducted at a distance or even indirectly using algorithms that can monitor every aspect of a worker's engagement in their tasks of employment (Dayaram & Burgess, 2021). Managerial control in these instances is decentralised, with these technical control systems enabling unobtrusive surveillance over geographically and functionally dispersed workers, including those in precarious gig-type employment (Newlands, 2021). This is not to say that flexible forms of work are not subject to some more traditional forms of control. Indeed, flexible work can be subject to more traditional bureaucratic surveillance methods, including requiring workers to complete periodic reports, fill in timesheets, attend regular team meetings and report on progress and other such activities (Sewell & Taskin, 2015). Regardless of the exact mechanism of its operation, the core purpose of managerial control, to extract effort from workers, and the drivers of its enactment, including lack of trust in workers and lack of buy-in to the benefits of worker autonomy and flexibility, remain constant.

What characterises more recent developments in this sphere is that methods of enacting managerial control through surveillance have shifted to become unbounded and pervasive, and technological enhancements have enabled surveillance to increase in scope and reach (de Vaujany et al., 2021). Workers can be accessed at any time through mobile devices, and their activity monitored at the most micro level using technical control methods, that is, software that captures productivity data including through keystroke logging, application usage statistics, facial recognition and more (Dayaram & Burgess, 2021). This creates new tensions between worker autonomy and managerial control, as the application of new technologies to paid work has enabled and acted to heavily promote higher levels of flexibility in working time and location but concurrently provide organisations with new opportunities and methods of increasing control and surveillance including more covert forms (de Vaujany et al., 2021).

These control methods can engender specific behaviours in workers. For example, research by Hafermalz (2021) refers to the role of the fear of exile, defined as the fear of being left out, ignored or banished. The fear of exile is the result of workers being distant, geographically and/or relationally, from line managers and centres of organisational control, and acts to create competition between workers for exposure and recognition, mechanisms for which are embedded within digital technologies that are designed to control workers. Imposition of fear of exile managerial control can lead to several specific negative outcomes including heightened dependence on management, virtual presenteeism behaviours that create negative cultures, reduce productivity and disadvantage workers unable or unwilling to engage in this type of activity, and/or over-commitment and self-exploitation, resulting in overwork, stress and burnout (Hafermalz, 2021). In their study, Mazmanian et al. (2013) describe the impacts of new technologies as providing increased flexibility, peace of mind and control over short-term activity but resulting in an intensification of work due to raising expectations of availability and creating difficulties for workers in disconnecting from work, with potentially negative implications for work-life balance and worker well-being including increasing incidence of burnout, work-related stress and other impacts. The ability to work anywhere and at any time effectively results in work taking place everywhere and at all times.

The evolution of managerial control and its paradoxical relationship with worker autonomy and flexibility results in a further blurring of work, family and leisure, which is subject to significant spillover (de Vaujany et al., 2021). In their critical review, Putnam et al. (2014) identify three primary contradictions that are often present at the organisational level, specifically: (1) flexible working policies that are enacted through rigid criteria, for example, hybrid working with mandated numbers of days onsite each week; (2) simultaneously encouraging and discouraging use, including variations at different levels of management; and (3) creating universal policies that are limited in their availability to only certain subsets of workers resulting in inequity in real levels of provision. As Putnam et al. (2014) note, these tensions present between autonomy and control can be used in a positive manner, for example, through acknowledging, understanding and using tensions to develop creative alternatives. In practice, though, actual flexibility and autonomy over the timing, location and other aspects of work is often limited, resulting in the worker experiencing faux flexibility (Elliott et al., 2022; Wheatley et al., 2023).

As with any enactment of control on the part of the employer, workers respond in ways that afford them a level of resistance. Workers recognise these tensions and contradictions and will engage in some cases in resistance behaviours as a method of retaking some level of autonomy and flexibility, or at least reducing their exposure to control and surveillance of their activity. They may actively accept certain forms of surveillance where this affords them some benefits, for example, increased flexibility, efficiency or convenience (Sewell & Taskin, 2015). Meanwhile, workers will identify ways of resisting other forms of control. For example, research into platform food delivery driving identified limitations in algorithm-based organisational control that provided opportunities for workers to resist surveillance, including through temporarily switching off or swapping mobile devices, coordinating collective protests and other workarounds that exploit the limitations of the platform (Newlands, 2021). Other examples include remote workers engaging in behaviours such as mouse moving and asking others in their household to log into and navigate around monitored systems (Dayaram & Burgess, 2021). Hafermalz

(2021) further found that fear of exile can create an opportunity for resistance, somewhat contradictorily through workers fully embracing the need for exposure but focusing their efforts specifically on doing so for their own benefit. Equally, a worker may purposefully accept exile such that they can evade control and use their relative freedom to engage as and when they desire, albeit this latter case is acknowledged as reflecting an option open to workers with a higher degree of agency afforded by the possession of demanded skills and personal resources (Hafermalz, 2021).

The documented paradox between worker autonomy and managerial control is of significant relevance to our understanding of current patterns and the future of working time and flexibility in work. Tensions and contradictions exist between the potential for increased flexibility and autonomy arising from changes in the structures and content of paid work, including the application of digital technologies, and the mechanisms and apparent demand within hierarchies of organisations for the imposition of managerial control in new and pervasive ways. These tensions are important to recognise as they have the potential to restrict the benefits that can be realised from the growth of flexibility, with implications for job quality and worker well-being. Managerial control can create several negative well-being effects, including work-related stress, anxiety and uncertainty, and feelings of invasion of privacy and inequity (Choi et al., 2008; deVaujany et al., 2021; Putnam et al., 2014), well-being effects that existing evidence indicates can drive burnout, demotivation, lesser organisational commitment and increased turnover intention (Alfes et al., 2018; Choi et al., 2008; Hafermalz, 2021; Wheatley et al., 2023). Application of managerial control using more overt methods, such as requiring periodic reporting, creates unnecessary bureaucracy that can detract from a focus on the task at hand (Sewell & Taskin, 2015). Similarly, enacting control may also prompt resistance behaviours, and this should be a central consideration for organisations as resistance on the part of the worker could result in lowered productivity where time and effort are spent on the resistance activity rather than completing tasks of employment. Enacted poorly, managerial control could, therefore, reduce rather than increase performance levels while also negatively impacting job quality, worker well-being and internal and external perceptions of the organisation.

CONCLUSION: TOWARDS AUTHENTIC OR FAUX FLEXIBILITY

Working time continues to evolve in response to changes in industrial structure and the development and application of new technologies. It has expanded in its potential to go beyond the bounds of traditional norms and become more fluid in nature. Working time has become more fragmented and de-standardised across occupations. That said, working time does continue to follow norms, and many workers experience regular and standardised patterns of work including the 9 to 5 and formal shift patterns such as four-days-on-four-days-off. Flexibility cannot be enacted in the same way in all jobs. Indeed, some jobs do not fit well with current models and understanding of flexibility in work. Flexibility in these cases is often limited by the nature of the work itself, although in recent decades there have been observed legislative and social changes that have acted to drive increases in flexibility where it is possible. Flexibility in working time and location has increased, aided by technological advancements. The period 2020–21 of the Covid-19 pandemic acted as a catalyst for substantive increases in some forms of flexibility, including growth in the application of hybrid working routines, although the permanence of these developments remains unclear. Greater flexibility has become a feature in many service jobs, including in managerial and professional occupations where demands for knowledge and skills enable workers to bargain desired forms of flexibility, be that formal flexible working arrangements such as flexi-time or working from home, or more informal flexibility over working time and location. Meanwhile, uncertainty perhaps best captures the nature of working time in lower-paid flexibilised employment, including contingent employment such as zero-hours contracts and some forms of gig work.

These changes have created new tensions and contradictions between the potential for work to be characterised by worker autonomy and flexibility and the imposition of managerial control in new and pervasive forms. The imposition of control is a central and distinguishing feature of management, and the enactment of control has long been a source of conflict within organisations between workers and management. The growing flexibility and digitisation of work have prompted new methods of control being applied both overtly through adapting more traditional forms of control to new models of work, for example, submission of periodic progress reports to online systems, and covertly through monitoring and surveillance technical control systems that employ algorithms to monitor activity levels. The application of managerial control can result in an autonomy-control paradox, in which the apparent provision of autonomy and flexibility occurs in unison with forms of control that encourage and, in some cases, coerce workers to engage in more intense 'always-on' patterns of work. As such, managerial control can act to influence worker behaviours and diminish the potential for flexibility in work to generate benefits for workers and organisations. The ability to work anytime and anywhere in practice triggers work to take place all of the time and everywhere. Workers may also resist the efforts of the organisation to control them, creating tensions and conflict and potentially creating less favourable outcomes for both parties.

All is not lost, however, as flexibility can be enacted in a more successful manner that can enable it to fulfil its potential. This requires a refocusing away from high levels of managerial control at the micro level and towards measurement of performance based on the production of outputs and quality of work. To realise this requires the design of jobs to be revisited and preferably involve a level of co-production between workers and organisations, while organisational policies pertaining to flexibility over work tasks, time and location should be shaped by understanding of worker knowledge, skills, behaviours and preferences and in response to identified needs. It further requires the provision of adequate resources, including time and physical resources to support workers to fulfil their tasks of employment. To generate a positive outcome requires the organisation to put a level of trust and responsibility in workers, that is, responsible autonomy, while at the same time structuring work around milestones and deliverables that enable the organisation to be assured that their interests are being met. If potential benefits are to be realised, including for performance, recruitment and retention, and worker satisfaction and well-being, it is essential to avoid the provision of flexibility resulting in an autonomy-control paradox and to create an environment in which flexibility is authentic, and employees have agency over decisions regarding the tasks, timing and location of work. Faux flexibility is much like a string of faux pearls, at first glance effective but on close inspection a much weaker imitation that will eventually fail!

REFERENCES

Agosti, M.T., Bringsén, Å. & Andersson, I. (2017). The complexity of resources related to work-life balance and well-being – a survey among municipality employees in Sweden. *International Journal of Human Resource Management*, 28(16): 2351–74.

Alfes, K., Shantz, A.D. & Ritz, A. (2018). A multilevel examination of the relationship between role overload and employee subjective health: The buffering effect of support climates. *Human Resource Management*, 57(2): 659–73.

Aloisi, A. (2016). Commoditized workers: Case study research on labor law issues arising from a set of on-demand/gig economy platforms. *Comparative Labor Law and Policy Journal*, 37(3): 653–90.

Atkinson, C. & Hall, L. (2009). The role of gender in varying forms of flexible working. *Gender, Work and Organisation*, 16(6): 650–66.

Badger, A. (2022). Flexibility and work in the gig economy (Case Study). In Wheatley, D. (ed.), *Well-being and the Quality of Working Lives*. Cheltenham, UK and Northampton, MA, USA: Edward Elgar, 124–8.

Baird, M. (2011). The state, work and family in Australia. *International Journal of Human Resource Management*, 22(18): 3742–54.

Bakker, A.B. & Demerouti, E. (2007). The job demands-resources model: State of the art. *Journal of Managerial Psychology*, 22: 309–28.

Beehr, T.A., Walsh, J.T. & Taber, T.D. (1976). Relationships of stress to individually and organisationally valued states: Higher order needs as a moderator. *Journal of Applied Psychology*, 61(1): 41–7.

Bennett, A.A., Campion, E.D., Keeler, K.R. & Keener, S.K. (2021). Videoconference fatigue? Exploring changes in fatigue after videoconference meetings during COVID-19. *Journal of Applied Psychology*, 106(3), 330–44.

Bentley, T.A., Teo, S.T.T., McLeod, L., Tan, F., Bosua, R. & Gloet, M. (2016). The role of organisational support in teleworker wellbeing: A sociotechnical systems approach. *Applied Ergonomics*, 52: 207–15.

Bienefeld, M.A. (1972). *Working Hours in British Industry*. London: Weidenfeld and Nicolson.

Brandth, B. & Kvande, E. (2009). Norway: The making of the father's quota. In Kamerman, S. & Moss, P. (eds.), *The Politics of Parental Leave Policies: Children, Parenting, Gender and the Labour Market*. Bristol: Policy Press, 191–206.

Brannen, J. (2005). Time and the negotiation of work-family boundaries: autonomy or illusion? *Time & Society*, 14(1): 113–31.

Burke, R.J., Singh, P. & Fiksenbaum, L. (2010). Work intensity: potential antecedents and consequences. *Personnel Review*, 39(3): 347–60.

Carlson, D.S., Hunter, E.M., Ferguson, M. & Whitten, D. (2014). Work-family enrichment and satisfaction: mediating processes and relative impact of originating and receiving domains. *Journal of Management*, 40(3): 845–65.

Carré, F. & Heintz, J. (2013). Employment change and economic vulnerability in the US. In Parker, S. (ed.), *The Squeezed Middle: The Pressure on Ordinary Workers in America and Britain*. Bristol: Policy Press, 61–72.

Chang, A., McDonald, P. & Burton, P. (2010). Methodological choices in work-life balance research 1987 to 2006: A critical review. *International Journal of Human Resource Management*, 21(13): 2381–413.

Choi, S., Leiter, J. & Tomaskovic-Devey, D. (2008). Contingent autonomy technology, bureaucracy, and relative power in the labor process. *Work and Occupations*, 35(4): 422–55.

Clark, S.C. (2000). Work/family border theory: A new theory of work/family balance. *Human Relations*, 53(6): 747–70.

Crawford, E.R., LePine, J.A. & Rich, B.L. (2010). Linking job demands and resources to employee engagement and burnout: A theoretical extension and meta-analytic test. *Journal of Applied Psychology*, 95(5): 834–48.

Dayaram, K. and Burgess, J. (2021). Regulatory challenges facing remote working in Australia. In Wheatley, D., Hardill, I. & Buglass, S. (eds), *Handbook of Research on Remote Work and Worker Well-being in the Post-COVID-19 Era*. Hersey, PA: IGI Global, 202–19.

Deakin, S. & Morris, G. (2012). *Labour Law*, 6th edn. Oxford: Hart.

van Doorn, N. & Badger, A. (2020). Platform capitalism's hidden abode: Producing data assets in the gig economy. *Antipode*, 52(5): 1475–95.

Dulebohn, J.H. & Hoch, J.E. (2017). Virtual teams in organisations. *Human Resource Management Review*, 27(4): 569–74.

Elliott, B., Subramanian, S. & Kupp, H. (2022). *How the Future Works: Leading Flexible Teams to Do the Best Work of Their Lives*. Hoboken, NJ: John Wiley & Sons. ISBN: 978–1119870951.

Erden Bayazit, Z. & Bayazit, M. (2019). How do flexible work arrangements alleviate work-family-conflict? The roles of flexibility i-deals and family-supportive cultures. *International Journal of Human Resource Management*, 30(3): 405–35.

Fagan, C., Lyonette, C., Smith, M. & Saldaña-Tejeda, A. (2012). *The Influence of Working Time Arrangements on Work-Life Integration or 'Balance': A Review of the International Evidence*. Conditions of Work and Employment No. 32: International Labour Organization.

Felstead, A. (2022). *Remote Working: A Research Overview*. Routledge.

Felstead, A. & Green, F. (2017). Working longer and harder? A critical assessment of work effort in Britain in comparison to Europe. In Grimshaw, D., Fagan, C., Hebson, G. & Tavor, I. (eds), *Making Work More Equal: A New Labour Market Segmentation Approach*. Manchester: Manchester University Press, 188–207.

Felstead, A. & Henseke, G. (2017). Assessing the growth of remote working and its consequences for effort, well-being and work-life balance. *New Technology, Work and Employment*, 32(3): 195–212.

Fetherston, C., Fetherston, A., Batt, S., Sully, M. & Wei, R. (2021). Wellbeing and work-life merge in Australian and UK academics. *Studies in Higher Education*, 46(12): 2774–88.

Findlay, P., Warhurst, C., Keep, E. & Lloyd, C. (2017). Opportunity knocks? The possibilities and levers for improving job quality. *Work and Occupations*, 44(1): 3–22.

Friedman, A. (1977). Responsible autonomy versus direct control over the labour process. *Capital & Class*, 1(1): 43–57.

Fuller, S. & Hirsh, C.E. (2019). 'Family-friendly' jobs and motherhood pay penalties: The impact of flexible work arrangements across the educational spectrum. *Work and Occupations*, 46(1): 3–44.

Glavin, P. & Schieman, S. (2012). Work–family role blurring and work–family conflict: The moderating influence of job resources and job demands. *Work and Occupations*, 39(1): 71–98.

Green, A. (2017). Implications of technological change and austerity for employability in urban labour markets. *Urban Studies*, 54(7): 1638–54.

Green, A. & Riley, R. (2021). Implications for places of remote working. In Wheatley, D., Hardill, I. & Buglass, S. (eds), *Handbook of Research on Remote Work and Worker Well-being in the Post-COVID-19 Era*. Hersey, PA: IGI Global, 161–80.

Green, F. (2001). It's been a hard day's night: The concentration and intensification of work in late twentieth-century Britain. *British Journal of Industrial Relations*, 39(1): 53–80.

Green, F. (2006). *Demanding Work. The Paradox of Job Quality in the Affluent Society*. Princeton, NJ: Princeton University Press.

Green, F. (2008). Work effort and worker well-being in the age of affluence. In Cooper, C. & Burke, R. (eds), *The Long Work Hours Culture: Causes, Consequences and Choices*. Bingley: Emerald Group Publications, 115–36.

Green, F., Felstead, A., Gallie, D. & Inanc, H. (2016). Job-related well-being through the Great Recession. *Journal of Happiness Studies*, 17(1): 389–411.

Greenhaus, J.H., Ziegert, J.C. & Allen, T.D. (2012). When family-supportive supervision matters: Relations between multiple sources of support and work-family balance. *Journal of Vocational Behavior*, 80(2): 266–75.

Guest, D. (2002). Perspectives on the study of work-life balance. *Social Science Information*, 41(2): 255–79.

Hafermalz, E. (2021). Out of the panopticon and into exile: Visibility and control in distributed new culture organisations. *Organisation Studies*, 42(5): 697–717.

Hall, L. & Atkinson, C. (2006). Improving working lives: Flexible working and the role of employee control. *Employee Relations*, 28(4): 374–86.

Hobsbawm, E. (1968). *Labouring Men*. London: Weidenfeld and Nicolson.

Horrell, S. & Humphries, J. (1995). Women's labour force participation and the transition to the male breadwinner family, 1790–1865. *Economic History Review*, 48(1): 89–117.

Howcroft, D. & Bergvall-Kåreborn, B. (2019). A typology of crowdwork platforms. *Work, Employment and Society*, 33(1): 21–38.

Kalleberg, A.L. (2012). Job quality and precarious work: Clarifications, controversies, and challenges. *Work and Occupations*, 39(4): 427–48.

Karasek, R.A. (1979). Job demands, job decision latitude, and mental strain: Implications for job redesign. *Administrative Science Quarterly*, 24(2): 285–306.

King, M. (2014). Protecting and representing workers in the new gig economy: The case of the freelancers union. In Milkman, R. & Ott, E. (eds), *New Labor in New York: Precarious Workers and the Future of the Labour Movement*. Ithaca, NY: Cornell University Press, 150–70.

LaJeunesse, R. (2009). *Work-time Regulation as Sustainable Full Employment Strategy*. London: Routledge. ISBN: 978–0415460576.

Laß, I. & Wooden, M. (2023). Working from home and work-family conflict. *Work, Employment and Society*, 37(1): 176–95.

Lee, B. & DeVoe, S. (2012). Flextime and profitability. *Industrial Relations: A Journal of Economy and Society*, 51(2): 298–316.

Lipietz, A. (1997). The post-Fordist world: Labor relations, international hierarchy and global ecology. *Review of International Political Economy*, 4(1): 1–41.

Mandl, I., Curtarelli, M., Riso, S., Vargas, O. & Gerogiannis, E. (2015). *New Forms of Employment in Europe*. Dublin: Eurofound.

Marglin, S. (1974). What do bosses do? The origins and functions of hierarchy in capitalist production. *Review of Radical Political Economics*, 6(2): 60–112.

Mazzetti, G., Schaufeli, W.B. & Guglielmi, D. (2014). Are workaholics born or made? Relations of workaholism with person characteristics and overwork climate. *International Journal of Stress Management*, 21(3): 227–54.

Mazmanian, M., Orlikowski, W.J. & Yates, J. (2013). The autonomy paradox: The implications of mobile email devices for knowledge professionals. *Organisation Science*, 24(5): 1337–137.

McCarthy, A., Darcy, C. & Grady, G. (2010). Work-life balance policy and practice: Understanding line manager attitudes and behaviors. *Human Resource Management Review*, 20(2): 158–67.

McCrate, E. (2012). Flexibility for whom? Control over work schedule variability in the US. *Feminist Economics*, 18(1): 39–72.

Mendonça, P., Kougiannou, N.K. & Clark, I. (2023). Informalization in gig food delivery in the UK: The case of hyper-flexible and precarious work. *Industrial Relations: A Journal of Economy and Society*, 62(1): 60–77.

Montani, F. & Dagenais-Desmarais, V. (2018). Unravelling the relationship between role overload and organisational citizenship behaviour: A test of mediating and moderating effects. *European Management Journal*, 36(6): 757–68.

Moos, A. & Skaburskis, M. (2007). The characteristics and location of home workers in Montreal, Toronto and Vancouver. *Urban Studies*, 44(9): 1781–808.

Newlands, G. (2021). Algorithmic surveillance in the gig economy: The organisation of work through Lefebvrian conceived space. *Organisation Studies*, 42(5): 719–37.

Osnowitz, D. & Henson, K. (2016). Leveraging limits for contract professionals: Boundary work and control of working time. *Work and Occupations*, 43(3): 326–60.

Piasna, A. (2018). Scheduled to work hard: The relationship between non-standard working hours and work intensity among European workers (2005–2015). *Human Resource Management Journal*, 28(1): 167–81.

Poelmans, S. & Beham, B. (2008). The moment of truth: Conceptualizing managerial work–life policy allowance decisions. *Journal of Occupational and Organisational Psychology*, 81(3): 393–410.

Putnam, L.L., Myers, K.K. & Gailliard, B.M. (2014). Examining the tensions in workplace flexibility and exploring options for new directions. *Human Relations*, 67(4): 413–40.

Rønsen, M. & Kitterød, H. (2015). Gender-equalizing family policies and mothers' entry into paid work: Recent evidence from Norway. *Feminist Economics*, 21(1): 59–89.

Sander, E., Jordan, P.J. & Rafferty, A. (2021). The physical work environment of the home. In Wheatley, D., Buglass, S. & Hardill, I. (eds), *Handbook of Research on Remote Work and Worker Well-being in the Post-COVID-19 Era*. Hersey, PA: IGI Global.

Sato, A. (2019). Telework and its effects in Japan. In Messenger, J. (ed.), *Telework in the 21st Century: An Evolutionary Perspective*. Cheltenham, UK and Northampton, MA, USA: Edward Elgar, 76–127.

Seshadri, V. & Elangovan, N. (2021). Managing social distance in geographically distributed teams. In Wheatley, D., Hardill, I. & Buglass, S. (eds), *Handbook of Research on Remote Work and Worker Well-being in the Post-COVID-19 Era*. Hersey, PA: IGI Global, 286–307.

Sewell, G. & Taskin, L. (2015). Out of sight, out of mind in a new world of work? Autonomy, control, and spatiotemporal scaling in telework. *Organisation Studies*, 36(11): 1507–29.

Shearmur, R. (2018). The millennial urban space economy: Dissolving workplaces and the de-localization of economic value creation. In Moos, M., Pfeiffer, D. & Vinodrai, T. (eds), *The Millennial City: Trends, Implications, and Prospects for Urban Planning and Policy*. London: Routledge, 65–80.

Smith, A. (1776). Reprinted in 1981). *An Inquiry into the Nature and the Causes of the Wealth of Nations*. Indianapolis, IN: Liberty Fund, Book I, chapters 1–4.

Sonnentag, S. (2001). Work, recovery activities, and individual well-being: A diary study. *Journal of Occupational Health Psychology*, 6(3): 196–210.

Sonnentag, S. & Fritz, C. (2007). The recovery experience questionnaire: Development and validation of a measure for assessing recuperation and unwinding from work. *Journal of Occupational Health Psychology*, 12(3): 204–21.

Spencer, D.A. (2009). *The Political Economy of Work*. London: Routledge.

Sweet, S., Pitt-Catsouphes, M., Besen, E. & Golden, L. (2014). Explaining organisational variation in flexible work arrangements: Why the pattern and scale of availability matter. *Community, Work and Family*, 17(2): 115–41.

Taylor, F. (1967). *The Principles of Scientific Management*. London: Norton.

Taylor, P., Scholarios, D. & Howcroft, D. (2021). *Covid-19 and Working from Home Survey: Preliminary Findings* [online]. Available at: https://pure.strath.ac.uk/ws/portalfiles/portal/119024009/Taylor_etal_2021_Covid_19_and_Working_from_Home_Survey.pdf.

Trougakos, J.P., Hideg, I., Hayden Cheng, B. & Beal, D.J. (2014). Lunch breaks unpacked: The role of autonomy as a moderator of recovery during lunch. *Academy of Management Journal*, 57(2): 405–21.

de Vaujany, F., Leclercq-Vandelannoitte, A., Munro, I., Nama, Y. & Holt, R. (2021). Control and surveillance in work practice: Cultivating paradox in 'new' modes of organizing. *Organisation Studies*, 42(5): 675–95.

Weber, M. (1976). *The Protestant Ethic and the Spirit of Capitalism*. London: Allen and Unwin.

Wheatley, D. (2012). Work-life balance, travel-to-work, and the dual career household. *Personnel Review*, 41(6): 813–31.

Wheatley, D. (2017a). Autonomy in paid work and employee subjective well-being. *Work and Occupations*, 44(3): 296–328.

Wheatley, D. (2017b). Employee satisfaction and use of flexible working arrangements. *Work, Employment and Society*, 31(4): 567–85.

Wheatley, D. (2017c). *Time Well Spent: Subjective Well-being and the Organisation of Time*. London: Rowman and Littlefield International. ISBN: 9781783484256.

Wheatley, D. (2020). Changing places of work. In Holland, P. & Brewster, C. (eds), *Contemporary Work and the Future of Employment in Developed Societies*. London: Routledge.

Wheatley, D. (2021). Workplace location and the quality of work: The case of urban-based workers in the UK. *Urban Studies*, 58(11): 2233–57.

Wheatley, D. (2022a). Work time, place and space in the 'new normal'. In Holland, P., Bartram, T., Grant, K. and Garavan, T. (eds), *The Emerald Handbook of Work, Workplaces and Disruptive Issues in HRM*. Bingley, UK: Emerald Publishing, 459–78.

Wheatley, D. (2022b). *Well-being and the Quality of Working Lives*. Cheltenham, UK and Northampton, MA, USA: Edward Elgar.

Wheatley, D., Broome, M., Dobbins, T., Hopkins, B. & Powell, O. (2023). Navigating choppy water: Flexibility ripple effects in the Covid-19 pandemic and the future of remote and hybrid working. *Work, Employment and Society*. https://doi.org/10.1177/09500170231195230.

Zheng, C., Molineux, J., Mirshekary, S. & Scarparo, S. (2015). Developing individual and organisational work-life balance strategies to improve employee health and wellbeing. *Employee Relations*, 37(3): 354–79.

Zhu, P. (2013). Telecommuting, household commute and location choice. *Urban Studies*, 50(12): 2441–59.

5. Working from where? The dynamics of workplaces

Ilona Bučiūnienė, Rūta Kazlauskaitė, Tugce Yerlitas and Marius Kušlys

INTRODUCTION

Since the start of this century, the phenomenon of telework has attracted increasing public and research interest due to its espoused multiple merits to the economy, society and environment (Gohoungodji et al., 2022). With the advancement of information and communication technologies (ICT) and growing numbers of tasks in the knowledge-based economy that could be performed at any time and place through the use of ICT, coupled with the growing demand for work flexibility, telework was seen as a promising work arrangement and a tool for tackling multiple problems. These optimistic forecasts, however, failed to live up to the expectations until the surge of the Covid-19 pandemic, with only modest numbers of organisations opting to provide this possibility to their employees across the developed countries. Despite the espoused benefits, the adoption of telework faced multiple different level barriers, as it constituted a fundamental change in work arrangements and running a business (Allen et al., 2015). Thus, it was not until the outbreak of the Covid-19 pandemic that telework became a prevailing work arrangement; it is also likely to endure in the post-pandemic era, which has seen an unprecedented fast and widespread shift in work arrangements in modern history (Aksoy et al., 2022). The unexpected obligatory epidemic-induced telework has opened new insights and opportunities for telework for both employers and employees. Yet the pandemic being over, there still seems to be no general consensus on the benefits and drawbacks of this work arrangement, which calls for further research on this phenomenon.

The purpose of this chapter is to provide an overview of the developments of telework adoption by assessing the macro-, mezzo- and micro-level factors related to the dynamics of telework before the Covid-19 pandemic, as well as to review the trends of its development in the post-Covid period and the challenges associated with them. We start with a discussion of telework origins and conceptualisations and its developments until the Covid-19 pandemic. Next, we review macro, organisational and individual-level barriers to its adoption. Finally, we look at the trends of telework developments in the post-pandemic era, the process of returning to the 'new normal', that is, conventional telework, as well as legal and ethical challenges related to these new work arrangements.

DEFINITION OF TELEWORK AND RELATED WORK ARRANGEMENTS

The origin of telework dates back to the 1970s, when Nilles (1975) coined the term 'telecommuting networks' for the work performed outside the employer's premises through the use of computers and telecommunication tools, which later he replaced with the more general term of 'telework' (Nilles, 1988). Since then, a wide range of labels have been pinned to this phenomenon of work, such as telecommuting, remote work, remote e-work, home-based work, mobile work, distributed work, virtual teams, flexible work arrangements, flexplace, distance work etc. (Allen et al., 2015; Gohoungodji et al., 2022; Vartiainen, 2021). These diverse terms tend to overlap to a certain extent; however, they may also carry different meanings. To ease this conceptual ambiguity, a number of typologies have been proposed, which distinguish between different types of telework based on such characteristics as work location (home, remote or mobile), use of ICT and flexitime, and the extent of knowledge intensity and intra- and extra-organisational contact (Daniels et al., 2001; Vartiainen, 2021). Despite these efforts, a common, clear-cut definition of telework is still lacking, and its conceptualisation remains much debated in research (Gohoungodji et al., 2022).

Major international reports and regulatory frameworks also lack consistency in regards to the conceptualisation and operationalisation of telework, which also explains, at least to some extent, divergence in their reported findings (Aguilera et al., 2016). 'Telework' and 'remote work' are the two most prevalent terms in them, with the former being more widely used in Europe and Australia and the latter in the USA (Allen et al., 2015). For instance, in Europe, telework is defined as a work arrangement under which work is performed outside the employer's premises through the use of ICT (Eurofound[1]), while the US Department of the Interior[2] makes a distinction between remote work and telework based on the employee's station of duty, that is, a remote work location in case of remote workers, or the agency worksite in case of telework-

---

[1]   https://www.eurofound.europa.eu/topic/teleworking. Retrieved 26 February 2023.

[2]   https://www.doi.gov/telework. Retrieved 5 March 2023.

ers. ILO (2020: 5) views remote work as a broader concept under which 'work is fully or partly carried out on an alternative worksite other than the default place of work', while telework is viewed as a sub-category of remote work that specifically includes the use of personal electronic devices. In this chapter, we use the term telework and build on Allen et al.'s (2015: 44) definition of telework, which has been increasingly used in recent research: 'a work practice that involves members of an organization substituting a portion of their typical work hours (ranging from a few hours per week to nearly full-time) to work away from a central workplace – typically principally from home – using technology to interact with others as needed to conduct work tasks'.

TELEWORK DEVELOPMENTS IN THE PRE-COVID-19 ERA

Since its invention back in the 1970s, telework has undergone substantial developments, and three generations of telework may be distinguished in the pre-Covid-19 era (Messenger & Gschwind, 2016). In the first generation (the 1970s–1980s), referred to as 'home office', telework denoted work from one designated location outside work, usually an employee's home or a place in its vicinity, through electronic communication with the employer (Kurland & Bailey, 1999). In the early stages, it was mainly used by clerical staff, primarily in the ICT industries on the West Coast of the USA, from where it slowly spread to other industries and regions. Originally, telework was seen as a means to resolve traffic problems and reduce energy consumption, while later on, organisations started using it to address workforce shortages, improve employee work and life balance, and adhere to air pollution and equal opportunity requirements (Allen et al., 2015).

The second generation of telework refers to the emergence of the 'mobile office', which was prompted by rapid ICT developments, such as laptops, mobile phones etc., which enabled employees to work from almost anywhere, that is, telework was no longer attached to a single fixed location (Messenger, 2019; Vartiainen, 2021). At the time, however, mobile offices were mainly available for and used by managers and professionals in finance and marketing (Kurland & Bailey, 1999), which largely explains modest research interests and efforts on telework in the first two generations (Messenger, 2019). In addition, this period witnessed substantial legislative developments, such as, for instance, the signing of the *European Framework Agreement on Telework*,[3] which established the principles of telework and employer responsibilities.

---

[3] https://www.etuc.org/en/framework-agreement-telework. Retrieved 5 March 2023.

Finally, the emergence and spread of the Internet marked the rise of the third generation of telework, that is, 'virtual office'. In this generation telework has undergone significant developments, as information needed for work no longer had to be carried around all the time like in the second generation of the mobile office (Messenger, 2019). With improved security of information flows between the office and other workplaces and the emergence of cloud storage, information has become easily accessible from anywhere at any time, enabling work to move to the virtual office. Unlike work from the mobile office, work from the virtual office has enabled working from multiple locations, and ,in addition, has opened possibilities for work from global locales (Illegems & Verbeke, 2004; Messenger & Gschwind, 2016). Thus, it was not until the turn of the 21st century that telework started gaining global popularity (Gohoungodji et al., 2022).

MACRO-LEVEL ASPECTS RELATED TO WORKING FROM HOME

The early forecasts of the spread of telework were highly optimistic, suggesting that telework will become a new pattern of employment (Baruch, 2001; Toffler, 1980); however, telework did not live up to those anticipated levels in the pre-pandemic era despite the growing availability and affordability of personal computers, the spread of the Internet and developments in data storage and security. As of 2019, in the USA, those primarily teleworking comprised 5.7 per cent of the population (US Census Bureau, 2022), while in the European Union (EU), those usually teleworking constituted 5.4 per cent and those teleworking at least some time – 9 per cent of the working-age population (Eurostat, 2023a). The prevalence of telework, however, varied considerably across Europe. Before the pandemic, telework was most widely spread in Sweden and the Netherlands (over 30 per cent of the working-age population teleworking for at least some time), while in Bulgaria and Romania, the respective proportion was below 1 per cent (Eurostat, 2023a).

At the macro level, to some extent, these cross-national variations may be accounted for by differences in the industrial and occupational structure of employment (Milasi et al., 2021). Countries scoring higher in the use of telework also reported bigger proportions of employees in knowledge and ICT-intensive services, larger organisations (50 plus employees) and higher shares of those in high-skilled occupations, where most of the work is done on computers and employees are given higher degrees of autonomy. Statistics, however, also show sizeable differences in telework prevalence within the same sectors and occupations, which hints at the contribution of some other factors, such as, for instance, national policies on work conditions (Milasi et al., 2021; Sostero et al., 2020). National culture was also reported to have an influence on the use of telework so that it is higher in nations with stronger national values (Peters et al., 2016) and those scoring higher on future orientation, gender egalitarianism, humane orientation, assertiveness and performance orientation, while power distance and uncertainty avoidance are negatively related to the use of telework (Peretz et al., 2018).

Given that the adoption of telework necessitates certain ICT tools and skills, national differences in the technological environment may play an important role in the diffusion of telework. To evaluate these effects, we used a number of indicators from previous research. To measure the proportion of the workforce on remote work/teleworking, we used organisational-level data from the Cranet HRM survey 2010, 2015 and 2019 rounds (for more information on the Cranet survey, see Brewster et al., 2004) available for 16 countries in Europe and assessed the approximate proportion of teleworking employees in an organisation (answer scale $0 =$ not used; $1 = \leq 5\%$ of workforce on teleworking; $2 = 6–20\%$; $3 = 21–50\%$; $4 = \geq 50\%$). To evaluate the effects of the technological environment, we took the percentage of individuals aged between 16 and 74 having digital skills in information, communication, problem-solving and software skills (Eurostat, 2023b, 2023c) and the percentage of households that have access to the Internet (dial-up, leased lines, and broadband regardless of the type of device) used in each respective country (Euromonitor, 2023), as measures of the technological environment. Results of pooled OLS regression analysis revealed that only the households' access to the Internet had a positive effect on the mean of the proportion of teleworkers, while the relationship with digital skills was insignificant. Further, we examined the dynamics of the relationship between household access to the Internet in a country and the proportion of teleworkers in 2010, 2015 and 2019. The scatter plots in Figures 5.1–5.3 show the evolution of the relationship in three clusters of European countries. Countries in Western Europe (Figure 5.1) followed the same trend so that the use of telework increased along with the growth in Internet access.

Among the Nordic countries (Figure 5.2), some variation in the use of telework may be observed. In Finland, Norway and Sweden, an upward trend in the growth of both the proportion of teleworking and access to the Internet can be noted, while in Denmark and Iceland, the trend was the opposite, that is, despite increasing access to the Internet the proportion of telework use decreased.

Finally, the trends in Central and Eastern European countries (Figure 5.3) are the same as in Western Europe; however, the proportion of telework usage is lower in this region.

In line with our findings, such features of the technological environment as the adoption of enterprise information systems (e.g., ERP and CRM) and e-learning tools were also reported to be positively related to the use of telework (Neirotti et al., 2013). In addition to technological characteristics,

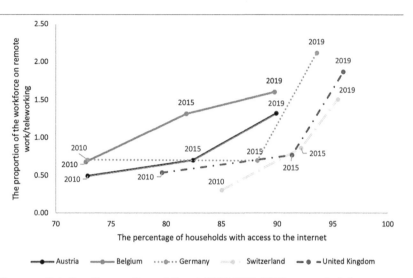

Source: Data from Euromonitor and Cranet (2010, 2015, 2019); own calculations.

Figure 5.1   *Use of telework and access to the internet in Western Europe*

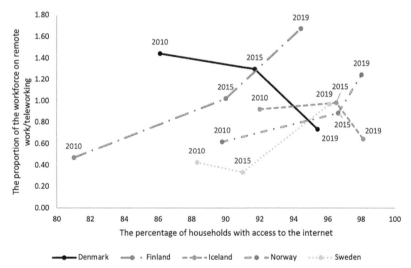

Source: Data from Euromonitor and Cranet (2010, 2015, 2019); own calculations.

Figure 5.2   *Use of telework and access to the internet in Nordic Europe*

telework was also reported to be more widely used in global vs local organi-

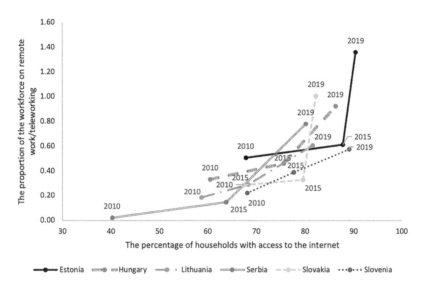

Source: Data from Euromonitor and Cranet (2010, 2015, 2019); own calculations.

Figure 5.3   *Use of telework and access to the internet in Central and Eastern Europe*

sations, larger organisations, service vs manufacturing organisations, private vs public organisations, high-tech organisations, and organisations with high proportions of younger, female and unionised employees (Peretz et al., 2018).

ORGANISATIONAL-LEVEL FACTORS RELATED TO THE ADOPTION OF TELEWORK

It is noteworthy, however, that in the pre-pandemic era, the growth of telework was not only lower than anticipated back in the 1980s; its usage even experienced some periods of decline. In 2013–17, some large corporations such as IBM, Yahoo, Bank of America, Best Buy, Aetna etc. reversed their teleworking policy and called their employees back to the office (Spector, 2017). A similar decline in telework use may be observed in some European countries too. Though in 2019, a higher EU average of employed teleworking persons (both among those teleworking sometimes and usually) was reported in comparison to 2015, in some countries, mostly in Central and Northern Europe, the trend was the opposite and with variance in its magnitude across countries (Eurostat, 2023a). In their official statements, organisations mostly justified their ban on telework by a growing need for creativity and collaboration, which they believed to be hindered by telework (Abrams, 2019). Empirical evidence, however, points to multiple organisational benefits of telework, including an increase in productivity and creativity (Gajendran & Harrison, 2007; Harker Martin & MacDonnell, 2012; Vega et al., 2015), which suggests organisations may have had other reasons to use telework in reservation.

Empirical evidence shows that managerial attitudes to telework constituted one of the major barriers that precluded the spread of telework in the pre-pandemic era (Bailey & Kurland, 2002; Mahler, 2012; Meroño-Cerdán, 2017; Peters & Heusinkveld, 2010). The amount of telework allowed in the organisation was found to depend on managerial judgement of employee trustworthiness and conscientiousness (Kaplan et al., 2018), meaning that managers tended to allow only their best employees to telework. This deficiency of trust, along with the lack of telework legislation, most likely explains why, in the pre-pandemic era, telework was largely used as an informal work arrangement in some countries and regions like, for instance, Britany, France (Aguilera et al., 2016). Among the perceived challenges of telework, managers often referred to the lack of face-to-face communication, teamwork interdependency, and perceived difficulties in managing and monitoring teleworkers' performance (Greer & Payne, 2014). Other barriers relating to managerial resistance to telework adoption and implementation include unwillingness to change existing work procedures, concerns over technology and its maintenance costs, perceived uncertain advantages and ease/difficulty in teleworker management and control, and insufficient knowledge of telework in smaller organisations in particular (Aguilera et al., 2016; Pérez et al., 2002). The perceived negative impact of teleworkers on the non-teleworkers – jealousy and perceived injustice in regards to increased workload in need to compensate for the teleworkers' absence – constitutes another barrier to managerial reluctance to adopt telework (Golden, 2007; Greer & Payne, 2014). Managerial attitudes towards telework, in turn, were found to be affected by their perceptions of telework usefulness, compatibility and ease of use as well as managers' experience in its use (Silva-C et al., 2019).

INDIVIDUAL-LEVEL FACTORS RELATED TO SLOW SPREAD OF TELEWORK

In addition to the macro- and organisational-level barriers discussed above, a number of major individual-level – personal, job-related and spatial – barriers (Vilhelmson & Thulin, 2016) precluded the individual use of telework before the Covid-19 pandemic. In terms of personal barriers, a typical teleworker of the pre-pandemic era was highly educated, held a permanent full-time high-status job with high income, was male, middle-aged and had children (Haddon & Brynin, 2005; Sostero et al., 2020). The results on the influence of demographic characteristics, however, are mixed and may depend on culture (Vilhelmson & Thulin, 2016).

Job-related barriers include some technological and attitudinal factors. Among the former, a survey of non-users of telework identified job unsuitability for telework and technical unfeasibility as the major reasons for not teleworking (Lott & Abendroth, 2020). As to the attitudinal barriers, like managers, employees also had some fears and negative interpretations and perceptions in regard to telework. The cultural influence of negative employee attitudes to telework stems from the ideal-worker norm (Lott & Abendroth, 2020), under which employees are expected to prioritise work over private and family life and be present at work (Kossek et al., 2009). Respectively, in organisations where such presence and high-performance culture prevail, teleworkers may suffer from flexibility stigma (Williams et al., 2013) and be perceived as less committed. In fear of negative career consequences, employees in such organisations would, in turn, be reluctant to telework. This flexibility stigma hypothesis has been supported empirically in a study of non-teleworkers (Lott & Abendroth, 2020).

Another attitudinal barrier to reluctance to telework relates to employee fear of social and professional isolation, which was identified as one of the major perceived disadvantages of telework (Allen et al., 2015). Teleworkers were reported to miss developmental and socialising possibilities such as interpersonal networking, informal learning and mentoring (Cooper & Kurland, 2002). They also feared that isolation may result in diminished rewards, especially when teleworker performance was not linked to measurable outcomes (Kurland & Cooper, 2002) and felt deprived of the possibility for social comparison, that is, using co-workers as social barometers to determine how well they were doing at work and providing a sense of belonging (Mann et al., 2000).

Willingness to telework may also be influenced by one's social network. More specifically, the telework status of those in one's social network and their relationship strength, so that having friends, neighbours and colleagues who did not telework was negatively related to one's decision to telework, with this relationship being stronger in case of closer friends and co-workers (Scott et al., 2012).

Employee negative perceptions of telework may also be shaped by the macro environment. A study conducted in Spain at the time of the 2008 financial crisis revealed that employees, middle-aged, middle-level managers, in particular, interpreted telework as a threat to their careers and jobs (Cañibano & Avgoustaki, 2022). This interpretation may have been evoked by the signal sent by the organisation that presented telework as a privilege, while in the context of high instability and uncertainty, the employees interpreted it as a threat. Provided that perceptions of telework are socially constructed, they may vary across countries, industries and organisations.

Finally, spatial barriers may also have had an influence on the use of telework in the pre-pandemic era, so that higher indices of teleworkers were reported in urban regions (Helminen & Ristimäki, 2007; Vilhelmson & Thulin, 2016). Spatial barriers also refer to the availability of space for work (at home or elsewhere) and the ability to control it (Mustafa & Gold, 2013). Not all individuals may have the space needed for work – some may have only limited or shared space. In addition, individuals may encounter other constraints and pressures while working at home, such as, for instance, the presence of dependants etc.

COVID-19 PANDEMIC AND EPIDEMIC-INDUCED TELEWORK

At the beginning of the Covid-19 pandemic and the mandatory lockdown, organisations were forced to switch from conventional telework to epidemic-induced telework characterised by a 'sudden, mandatory, and unprepared nature' (Carillo et al., 2021: 71) of full-time work from home. The epidemic-induced telework radically changed the patterns of jobs, opening new possibilities and exhibiting challenges of telework. Not surprisingly, since the pandemic, telework has received extensive research attention, which has looked into the organisational and individual benefits of telework as well as their pitfalls (Buomprisco et al., 2021; Lunde et al., 2022; Soga et al., 2022, among others).

Increased productivity and work-life balance have been identified as the main advantages of telework for both employers and employees (Buomprisco et al., 2021); however, research has failed to provide a clear answer as to how telework affects performance, leaving teleworker performance an unresolved dilemma (Ficapal-Cusí et al., 2023) and one of the most ambiguous issues, as teleworkers work longer hours (Saragih et al., 2021), suffer from work overload, which in turn generates fatigue (Ficapal-Cusí et al., 2023) and emotional exhaustion and leads to decreased performance (Junça Silva et al., 2022).

The Covid-19 pandemic demonstrated that telework may threaten employees' mental and physical health. Working from home leads to increased levels of stress and distress, anxiety, sleep disorders (Buomprisco et al., 2021; McPherson et al., 2021), depressive symptoms and even suicidal thoughts (O'Connor et al., 2021). In addition, telework leads to psycho-social problems, such as loneliness (Groarke et al., 2020) and a feeling of social isolation (Ficapal-Cusí et al., 2023). Furthermore, an inappropriate working environment and a workplace failing to meet ergonomic requirements may provoke physical health disorders (Buomprisco et al., 2021). Given all these issues, teleworkers' performance and well-being have been viewed as a double-edged sword.

TELEWORK IN THE POST-PANDEMIC ERA: WORKING FROM ANYWHERE

Return (Non-Return) to the Office: From Remote to – Hybrid – Full-Time Office Work

Telework has opened new possibilities and challenges for organisations and employees in the post-pandemic period too, raising a dilemma of how and where to work after the removal of lockdown measures. Employers had a range of opportunities in regards to work arrangements – fully remote, back in the office or in a hybrid form. The majority of companies have decided to adopt a hybrid working mode, allowing employees to work 3–4 days from home. The attitudes of employees and employers towards continued working from home, however, have been conflicting.

The pandemic has shaped new employee habits, and telework has become the new normal, which has remained highly appreciated by employees after the pandemic too. For instance, findings of the European Central Bank survey show that two-thirds of the respondents expressed interest in continued working remotely for at least one day per week (Da Silva et al., 2023). Another survey showed that up to 50 per cent of workers expected flexibility as to where and when to work, and more than 60 per cent said they would quit if required to return to full-time work in the office (Gutz, 2023). The 2022 Gallup survey of hybrid workers demonstrated that this form of work allowed them to better balance work and life, use time more efficiently, be more productive and flexible and experience lower levels of fatigue and burnout (Wigert & White, 2022). On the other hand, reduced access to equipment, weakened connectedness with the organisation, and decreased teamwork and interaction with co-workers were indicated as the main challenges of hybrid work.

Conversely from the employees, employers have not been so favourable towards teleworking. Since autumn 2022, claims that employees will be allowed to work in the hybrid mode, with one to two days per week in the office, have become less frequent and assertive (Nieto, 2023) supporting the argument of reduced productivity (Fox News, 2022) and have been increasingly replaced with the employers' pressure to return to the office. Such corporations as Disney, Ernst & Young, KPMG, Twitter (Christian, 2023), Apple (McAdams, 2022), coffee retailer Starbucks (Penley, 2023), Wall Street banks (Ballentine & Wong, 2022) and others have taken the decision to work three to four days per week in the office. The main arguments provided by employers in support of returning to the office relate to the importance of in-person contact, supervisor-employee communication and coaching and the need to foster teamwork, creativity, organisational culture and productivity. Respectively, the divide between employer and employee preferences regarding telework arrangements has grown, with employers exerting increasing pressure to return to in-person office work and employees favouring the telework option. Although there is no clear answer as to the teleworkers' performance yet, some survey findings report that employees working from home are even more productive than those in the office (Robinson, 2022). In addition, those performing well in the office were reported to work productively at home too, while those performing poorly in the office were likewise unproductive when working from home.

A number of strategies for tackling this dilemma and reaping the advantages of both working from the office and home have been offered so far. To optimise hybrid work, task differentiation has been suggested, as working from home allows employees to better focus on independent work tasks, engage in individual learning and development activities and avoid office-related distractions, whereas such tasks as organising meetings with colleagues, managers and customers as well as use of technologies and equipment that are not accessible from elsewhere are more appropriate for work in the office (Wigert & White, 2022). The Covid-19 pandemic has revealed the importance of employee self-control strategies in teleworking in relation to the establishment of the workplace and work environment, minimisation of distractions, dressing up as for work in the office, keeping regular contact with colleagues etc. (Troll et al., 2022). Individual cognitive resources covering realistic goal setting, planning of working and leisure time, and supporting autonomous motivation were identified as important individual factors leading to enhanced performance (Troll et al., 2022). Therefore, organisations seeking to find optimal solutions regarding the arrangement of in-office vs remote work have to reconsider which tasks may be performed more efficiently in the office and which remotely, what proportions of work time they should constitute, and adequately design hybrid work regimes.

In Search of Innovative Ways to When and Where to Work From

Despite employer preferences to return to the 'old normal' and to bring employees back to the offices once the pandemic was over, they have faced difficulty in convincing employees that it has become necessary to return to full-time work in the office, as employees have realised the benefits of teleworking and whether, how and what kind of work may be performed remotely. According to Prodoscore (n.d.), 80 per cent of employees now expect workplace flexibility, and it has become difficult to attract and retain employees without giving them the possibility to work in a hybrid mode at least (Prodoscore, n.d.).

The Covid-19 pandemic has accelerated the emergence of new forms of work arrangements, such as 'workcation', which originated in Japan and meant working while on vacation (Yoshida, 2021). During the pandemic, workcation gained a new meaning, encompassing travelling workers and allowing them to combine work and travel (Bassyiouny & Wilkesmann, 2023), which implies the possibility of working from anywhere. The possibility to telework is especially important for employees working in sectors with tight competition in the job market (such as IT, technology, engineering etc.). To attract and retain talent, such organisations need to search for innovative solutions for designing and scheduling jobs. For example, the Lithuanian business digitalisation company Baltic Amadeus has developed a hybrid work model called '11:1', under which employees can work 11 weeks from wherever they want, and all employees of one department or project have to return to the office and work together for one week (once a quarter) (Verslo Žinios, 2022). This hybrid work model and the weeks in the office restore social ties, help integrate new employees, strengthen teamwork and increase efficiency.

Some organisations use hybrid work as an attractive benefit in negotiations with jobseekers and as an argument when employees ask for a salary increase that the organisation may not afford (Vareikaitė-Mills, 2022). On the other hand, not every employee desires such flexibility, and working from home can even demotivate some, especially those who do not have a suitable working environment, have kids or dependent relatives at home they need to take care of. Therefore, companies need to look at telework as a new opportunity and reconsider the amount of time to be spent working in the office by taking into consideration the complexity of such factors as the rapidly changing macro environment, the specifics of organisational activities, team size, employee interests, customer needs and legal requirements.

The Covid-19 pandemic and changes in work arrangements have raised the need for adjusting the legislation of telework, and in 2021–22 the majority of European countries (such as Belgium, Denmark, Greece, Italy, Lithuania, Luxemburg, Norway, Poland, Portugal, Slovakia, Spain and Sweden) issued national regulations or guidelines on telework to ensure the safety and well-being of teleworking employees, including the provision of the necessary equipment and the assurance of the same rights and protection as the on-site employees. Some countries have established special requirements regarding telework. For example, the Lithuanian Labour Code obliges employers to allow teleworking to employees who are expecting babies, have recently given birth or are breastfeeding, have children, have health problems or are caring for a family member. The legal frameworks of Luxembourg, Italy and Greece, in addition to the general remote work regulations, emphasise the importance of disconnecting from work after working hours and provide guidelines for the use of digital equipment to protect employees' rest time, vacation and private as well as family lives (Lockton Global Compliance, 2023).

PERFORMANCE MANAGEMENT OF TELEWORKERS: ETHICAL AND LEGAL CONSIDERATIONS

Although some surveys show that remote work is as productive as in-office (Robinson, 2022), organisations have been concerned about the productivity of teleworkers and have increasingly implemented electronic monitoring technologies (such as software programme *bossware)* controlling teleworker activities (Browne, 2022). Even though employee performance monitoring is not a new phenomenon, the digital environment allows for gathering more comprehensive data, including real-time information regarding employee productivity, behaviour and physiological state (Ravid et al., 2020). These technologies capture and store different types of data, including data about employees' keyboard activities, real-time GPS information, log-in and log-out time, screenshots and browsing history. Furthermore, electronic monitoring software provides access to employee cameras and microphones (also detailed in Chapter 9). Despite the fact that electronic employee monitoring software is being promoted as a tool allowing employees to observe their productivity, better organise their work and increase performance, research findings suggest that electronic monitoring is not related to employee performance and has a negative effect on job satisfaction and well-being (Becker et al., 2022; Siegel et al., 2022). Moreover, electronic monitoring negatively affects employees' personal life through the crossover effects on family members (e.g. email monitoring leads to anxiety and affects relationships with other family members) (Becker et al., 2021), reduces the sense of agency among the monitored employees (accountability for their moral choses) (Thiel et al., 2021), and is even positively related to counterproductive work behaviour (Siegel et al., 2022).

Electronic monitoring of teleworkers also raises important ethical concerns related to the sensitivity of collected personal information and its usage by employers and others. Firstly, electronic monitoring relates to the violation of employee privacy, that is, 'the right to respect for his private and family life, his home and his correspondence' (Council of Europe, 2022: 11), as digital monitoring may provide access to sensitive personal information (Finkin et al., 2015), which requires employees' permission, and obliges employers to protect it from third parties (GDPR, 2016). For example, collecting keyboard activity records and screenshots allows one to view employees' passwords and access sensitive information like health records, bank account information etc. Moreover, with access to microphones and cameras, employers may activate these devices at any time, and monitor not only how employees work or where they do it from, but also their private life. Therefore, using these technologies without the consent of employees can be considered a violation of human rights.

Secondly, electronic monitoring is related to personal data security. When employers collect electronic monitoring information, they are required to ensure data storage security in the digital environment to avoid the risk of cyber-attacks. The leakage or theft of personal information can lead to ethical and legal problems. Even though organisations may choose to store personal data on their internal networks and thus protect it from external cyber-hackers, the risk of information leakage remains since other employees in the organisation may access the data. Therefore, given the sensitivity of the collected personal data, employees may face the risk of their colleagues using their personal data and putting human dignity at threat, which is another fundamental human right covering human privacy, honour and reputation (United Nations, 1948).

Thirdly, while accessing personal data may be an ethical issue by itself, the way the data are analysed and used can also lead to ethical issues. Some organisations track employees' emailing with customers and internal chats among employees to prevent information leakage, disclosure of work content and usage of discriminative language. Although this initiative seems legitimate, the dark side of digital applications relates to the possibility of using them as a tool to control employee voice (also see Chapter 8). Amazon chat application for employees' internal communication and getting feedback from managers is an example to understand the perils of such technologies (Thibodeau, 2022). The Amazon app monitors internal communication via artificial intelligence (AI) by detecting banned keywords, and based on these data, managers limit or ban employee conversation if they find it to be generating negative sentiments against the company (Anguiano, 2022) and, in this way, attempt to prevent employees from joining unions and to stifle their ability to criticise unfair interventions of the organisation (Klippenstein, 2022).

CONCLUSIONS

In this chapter, we looked at the evolution and dynamics of telework adoption across countries in the pre-pandemic era, seeking to understand the limited spread of this work arrangement until the outbreak of Covid-19, and disclose individual-, organisational- and macro-level barriers to its wider adoption. We also reviewed studies on telework induced by the Covid-19 pandemic and developments of telework in the post-pandemic period.

In the pre-pandemic era, at the macro level, the use of telework was shown to be dependent on a number of sectoral, technological, cultural and legal factors, which help to understand divergence in the use of telework across different national contexts. The major barriers, however, relate to organisational-level factors, and more specifically to negative attitudes and perceptions of employers to this work arrangement and their reluctance to adopt this mode of work, despite contradicting research findings on the positive organisational and individual outcomes. Those negative managerial attitudes, in turn, were passed onto their employees and inflicted some fears of telework. Individual willingness to telework was also shaped by personal features and one's social network. In addition, at the individual level, they were restricted by some personal features as well as technical and special factors related to their jobs and work environment.

The Covid-19-pandemic-induced telework has changed organisational and individual perceptions of telework, so it is no longer considered as a 'free or semi-free day' (Vareikaitė-Mills, 2022). Nevertheless, the question as to whether teleworkers work as productively as those in the office seems to remain open. The pandemic has exposed a number of challenges for organisations and employees, with some studies showing that telework leads to increased productivity and work-life balance (Buomprisco et al., 2021), while on the other hand, it comes at such costs as employee physical and mental health and well-being, as teleworkers tend to work more overtime, which increases fatigue and emotional exhaustion and leads to burnout and decreasing performance. Although there is no clear research answer on how teleworking affects employee productivity and well-being, the pandemic has changed people's habits irreversibly and developed their expectations for flexible work opportunities and at least partial telework. In trying to respond to employee preferences, organisations are looking for innovative solutions and evaluating what jobs and/or tasks may be best performed at what place (in the office or elsewhere), as well as how much time needs to be allocated to increase performance and guarantee employee well-being. When redesigning jobs and making decisions on telework arrangements, especially employee performance monitoring, the relevance of ethical considerations related to remote work increases. The Covid-19 pandemic has made telework the new reality, and national governments have taken up legislation to ensure the safety and well-being of teleworkers, seeking to guarantee them the same rights and protection as employees working on-site. Telework and related work arrangements are still in the process of development and remain a rich area for further investigations.

FUNDING

This research has been partially funded by the European Social Fund (project No. 09.3.3-LMT-K-712–01–0156) under grant agreement with the Research Council of Lithuania and ISM University of Management and Economics, Lithuania.

REFERENCES

Abrams, Z. (2019). The future of remote work. *APA, Monitor on Psychology, 10*. Retrieved 8 March 2023 from: https://www.apa.org/MONITOR/2019/10/COVER -REMOTE-WORK.

Aguilera, A., Lethiais, V., Rallet, A., & Proulhac, L. (2016). Home-based telework in France: Characteristics, barriers and perspectives. *Transportation Research Part A: Policy and Practice, 92*: 1–11. doi:https://doi.org/10.1016/j.tra.2016.06.021.

Aksoy, C.G., Barrero, J.M., Bloom, N., Davis, S.J., Dolls, M., & Zarate, P. (2022). *Working from home around the world*. National Bureau of Economic Research.

Allen, T.D., Golden, T.D., & Shockley, K.M. (2015). How effective is telecommuting? Assessing the status of our scientific findings. *Psychological Science in the Public Interest, 16*(2): 40–68.

Anguiano, D. (2022). Amazon to ban 'union' and other words from staff chat app – report. Retrieved 9 March 2023 from: https://www.theguardian.com/technology/2022/ apr/05/amazon-banned-words-list-union-internal-app.

Bailey, D.E., & Kurland, N.B. (2002). A review of telework research: Findings, new directions, and lessons for the study of modern work. *Journal of Organizational Behavior, 23*(4): 383–400. doi:10.1002/job.144.

Ballentine, C., & Wong, N. (2022). Wall Street Banks lead return-to-office with labor day push. Retrieved 15 March 2023 from: https://www.bloomberg.com/news/articles/ 2022–09–06/ wall -street -banks -lead -renewed -return -to -office -push -after -laborday ?leadSource=uverify%20all#xj4y7vzkg.

Baruch, Y. (2001). The status of research on teleworking and an agenda for future research. *International Journal of Management Reviews, 3*(2): 113–29.

Bassyiouny, M., & Wilkesmann, M. (2023). Going on workation – is tourism research ready to take off? Exploring an emerging phenomenon of hybrid tourism. *Tourism Management Perspectives, 46*: 101096. doi:https:// doi .org/ 10 .1016/ j .tmp .2023 .101096.

Becker, W.J., Belkin, L.Y., Conroy, S.A., & Tuskey, S. (2021). Killing me softly: Organizational e-mail monitoring expectations' impact on employee and significant other well-being. *Journal of Management, 47*(4): 1024–52. doi:10.1177/0149206319890655.

Becker, W.J., Belkin, L.Y., Tuskey, S.E., & Conroy, S.A. (2022). Surviving remotely: How job control and loneliness during a forced shift to remote work impacted employee work behaviors and well-being. *Human Resource Management, 61*(4): 449–64. doi: https://doi.org/10.1002/hrm.22102.

Brewster, C., Mayrhofer, W., & Morley, M. (2004). *Human resource management in Europe: Evidence of convergence?* Routledge.

Browne, R. (2022). HR's future of work glossary: Learn the words of work. Retrieved 9 March 2023 from: https://www.hrmonline.com.au/future-of-work/hr-future-of-work -glossary/.

Buomprisco, G., Ricci, S., Perri, R., & De Sio, S. (2021). Health and telework: New challenges after COVID-19 pandemic. *European Journal of Environment and Public Health, 5*(2): em0073.

Cañibano, A., & Avgoustaki, A. (2022). To telework or not to telework: Does the macro context matter? A signalling theory analysis of employee interpretations of telework in times of turbulence. *Human Resource Management Journal*, 1–17. doi:https://doi.org/10.1111/1748-8583.12457.

Carillo, K., Cachat-Rosset, G., Marsan, J., Saba, T., & Klarsfeld, A. (2021). Adjusting to epidemic-induced telework: Empirical insights from teleworkers in France. *European Journal of Information Systems, 30*(1): 69–88.

Christian, A. (2023). The companies backtracking on flexible work. Retrieved 12 March 2023 from: https://www.bbc.com/worklife/article/20230206-the-companies-backtracking-on-flexible-work.

Cooper, C.D., & Kurland, N.B. (2002). Telecommuting, professional isolation, and employee development in public and private organizations. *Journal of Organizational Behavior, 23*(4), 511–32. doi:10.1002/job.145.

Council of Europe. (2022). Guide on Article 8 of the European Convention on Human Rights.

Da Silva, A.D., Georgarakos, D., & Weißler, M. (2023). *How people want to work – preferences for remote work after the pandemic*. Retrieved 9 March 2023 from European Central Bank: https://www.ecb.europa.eu/pub/economicbulletin/focus/2023/html/ecb.ebbox202301_04~1b73ef4872.en.html.

Daniels, K., Lamond, D., & Standen, P. (2001). Teleworking: Frameworks for Organizational Research. *Journal of Management Studies, 38*(8), 1151–85. doi:10.1111/1467-6486.00276.

Euromonitor. (2023). Passport-economies and consumers annual data | historical/forecast. Retrieved 17 February 2023 from: https://www.portal.euromonitor.com/statisticsevolution/index.

Eurostat. (2023a). *Employed persons working from home*. Retrieved 18 February 2023 from: https://ec.europa.eu/eurostat/databrowser/product/page/lfsa_ehomp.

Eurostat. (2023b). Individuals' level of digital skills (from 2021 onwards). Retrieved 18 February 2023 from: https://ec.europa.eu/eurostat/databrowser/view/ISOC_SK_DSKL_I21__custom_5011729/default/table.

Eurostat. (2023c). Individuals' level of digital skills (until 2019). Retrieved 18 February 2023 from: https://ec.europa.eu/eurostat/databrowser/view/ISOC_SK_DSKL_I__custom_5011560/default/table.

Ficapal-Cusí, P., Torrent-Sellens, J., Palos-Sanchez, P., & González-González, I. (2023). The telework performance dilemma: Exploring the role of trust, social isolation and fatigue. *International Journal of Manpower*. doi:10.1108/IJM-08–2022–0363.

Finkin, M.W., Krause, R., & Takeuchi-Okuno, H. (2015). Employee autonomy, privacy, and dignity under technological oversight. In *Comparative labor law* (pp. 153–94). Edward Elgar Publishing.

Fox News. (2022). Economic analyst: Employees' remote work push has 'gone way overboard', impacts 'productivity'. Retrieved 12 March 2023 from: https://www.foxnews.com/media/economic-analyst-employees-remote-work-push-gone-way-overboard-impacts-productivity.

Gajendran, R.S., & Harrison, D.A. (2007). The good, the bad, and the unknown about telecommuting: Meta-analysis of psychological mediators and individual consequences. *Journal of Applied Psychology, 92*(6): 152g4–1541. doi:10.1037/0021–9010.92.6.1524.

GDPR. (2016). Regulation (EU) 2016/679 of The European Parliament and of The Council of 27 April 2016 on the protection of natural persons with regard to the processing of personal data and on the free movement of such data, and repealing Directive 95/46/EC (General Data Protection Regulation).

Gohoungodji, P., N'Dri, A.B., & Matos, A.L.B. (2022). What makes telework work? Evidence of success factors across two decades of empirical research: A systematic and critical review. *The International Journal of Human Resource Management*: 1–45. doi:10.1080/09585192.2022.2112259.

Golden, T. (2007). Co-workers who telework and the impact on those in the office: Understanding the implications of virtual work for co-worker satisfaction and turnover intentions. *Human Relations, 60*(11): 1641–67.

Greer, T.W., & Payne, S.C. (2014). Overcoming telework challenges: Outcomes of successful telework strategies. *The Psychologist-Manager Journal, 17*(2): 87.

Groarke, J.M., Berry, E., Graham-Wisener, L., McKenna-Plumley, P.E., McGlinchey, E., & Armour, C. (2020). Loneliness in the UK during the COVID-19 pandemic: Cross-sectional results from the COVID-19 Psychological Wellbeing Study. *PLoS One, 15*(9): e0239698.

Gutz, S. (2023). 2023 Monster work watch report: Research and trends on the world of work and what it means for the future. Retrieved 15 March 2023 from: https://learnmore.monster.com/monster-work-watch-report.

Haddon, L., & Brynin, M. (2005). The character of telework and the characteristics of teleworkers. *New Technology, Work and Employment, 20*(1): 34–46.

Harker Martin, B., & MacDonnell, R. (2012). Is telework effective for organizations? A meta-analysis of empirical research on perceptions of telework and organizational outcomes. *Management Research Review, 35*(7): 602–16. doi:https:// doi .org/ 10 .1108/01409171211238820.

Helminen, V., & Ristimäki, M. (2007). Relationships between commuting distance, frequency and telework in Finland. *Journal of Transport Geography, 15*(5): 331–42. doi:https://doi.org/10.1016/j.jtrangeo.2006.12.004.

Illegems, V., & Verbeke, A. (2004). Telework: What does it mean for management? *Long Range Planning, 37*(4): 319–34. doi:https://doi.org/10.1016/j.lrp.2004.03.004.

ILO. (2020). *Defining and measuring remote work, telework, work at home and home-based work.* Retrieved 14 March 2023 from: https:// www .ilo .org/ global/ statistics-and-databases/publications/WCMS_747075/lang--en/index.htm.

Junça Silva, A., Almeida, A., & Rebelo, C. (2022). The effect of telework on emotional exhaustion and task performance via work overload: The moderating role of self-leadership. *International Journal of Manpower.* doi:10.1108/IJM-08–2022–0352.

Kaplan, S., Engelsted, L., Lei, X., & Lockwood, K. (2018). Unpackaging manager mistrust in allowing telework: Comparing and integrating theoretical perspectives. *Journal of Business and Psychology, 33*(3): 365–82. doi:10.1007/s10869–017-9498–5.

Klippenstein, K. (2022). Leaked: New Amazon worker chat app would ban words like 'union', 'restrooms', 'pay raise', and 'plantation'. *The Intercept.* Retrieved 14 March 2023 from: https://theintercept.com/2022/04/04/amazon-union-living-wage-restrooms-chat-app/.

Kossek, E., Lewis, S., & Hammer, L.B. (2009). Work–life initiatives and organizational change: Overcoming mixed messages to move from the margin to the mainstream. *Human Relations, 63*(1): 3–19. doi:10.1177/0018726709352385.

Kurland, N.B., & Bailey, D.E. (1999). The advantages and challenges of working here, there anywhere, and anytime. *Organizational Dynamics, 28*(2): 53–68. doi:https://doi.org/10.1016/S0090–2616(00)80016–9.

Kurland, N.B., & Cooper, C.D. (2002). Manager control and employee isolation in telecommuting environments. *The Journal of High Technology Management Research, 13*(1): 107–26. doi: https://doi.org/10.1016/S1047–8310(01)00051–7.

Lockton Global Compliance. (2023). New remote working legislation around the world. Retrieved 10 March 2023 from: https://globalnews.lockton.com/new-remote-working-legislation-around-the-world/.

Lott, Y., & Abendroth, A.-K. (2020). The non-use of telework in an ideal worker culture: Why women perceive more cultural barriers. *Community, Work & Family:* 1–19.

Lunde, L.-K., Fløvik, L., Christensen, J.O., Johannessen, H.A., Finne, L.B., Jørgensen, I.L., … Vleeshouwers, J. (2022). The relationship between telework from home and employee health: A systematic review. *BMC Public Health, 22*(1): 47. doi:10.1186/s12889-021-12481-2.

Mahler, J. (2012). The telework divide: Managerial and personnel challenges of telework. *Review of Public Personnel Administration, 32*(4): 407–18. doi:10.1177/0734371X12458127.

Mann, S., Varey, R., & Button, W. (2000). An exploration of the emotional impact of tele-working via computer-mediated communication. *Journal of Managerial Psychology, 15*(7), 668–90. doi:10.1108/02683940010378054.

McAdams, P. (2022). Tech companies forcing a return to the office are ignoring the data. Retrieved 11 March 2023 from: https://www.forbes.com/sites/forbesbusine sscouncil/2022/11/03/tech-companies-forcing-a-return-to-the-office-are-ignoring -the-data/?sh=1f225a5c59ee.

McPherson, K.E., McAloney-Kocaman, K., McGlinchey, E., Faeth, P., & Armour, C. (2021). Longitudinal analysis of the UK COVID-19 Psychological Wellbeing Study: Trajectories of anxiety, depression and COVID-19-related stress symptomology. *Psychiatry Research, 304*: 114138. doi: https://doi.org/10.1016/j.psychres.2021 .114138.

Meroño-Cerdán, A.L. (2017). Perceived benefits of and barriers to the adoption of teleworking: peculiarities of Spanish family firms. *Behaviour & Information Technology, 36*(1): 63–74. doi:10.1080/0144929X.2016.1192684.

Messenger, J.C. (2019). *Telework in the 21st century*. Edward Elgar Publishing.

Messenger, J.C., & Gschwind, L. (2016). Three generations of telework: New ICTs and the (r)evolution from home office to virtual office. *New Technology, Work and Employment, 31*(3): 195–208. doi: https://doi.org/10.1111/ntwe.12073.

Milasi, S., González-Vázquez, I., & Fernández-Macías, E. (2021). Telework before the COVID-19 pandemic. *OECD Productivity Working Papers, 21*. doi:https://doi.org/10.1787/d5e42dd1-en.

Mustafa, M., & Gold, M. (2013). 'Chained to my work'? Strategies to manage temporal and physical boundaries among self-employed teleworkers. *Human Resource Management Journal, 23*(4): 413–29.

Neirotti, P., Paolucci, E., & Raguseo, E. (2013). Mapping the antecedents of telework diffusion: Firm-level evidence from Italy. *New Technology, Work and Employment, 28*(1): 16–36. doi: https://doi.org/10.1111/ntwe.12001.

Nieto, P. (2023). Starbucks CEO mandates corporate employees return to the office at least three days a week. Retrieved 9 March 2023 from: https://www.foxbusiness .com/economy/starbucks-ceo-mandates-corporate-employees-return-office-least -three-days-week.

Nilles, J.M. (1975). Telecommunications and organizational decentralization. *IEEE Transactions on Communications, 23*(10): 1142–7. doi:10.1109/TCOM.1975.1092687.

Nilles, J.M. (1988). Traffic reduction by telecommuting: A status review and selected bibliography. *Transportation Research Part A: General, 22*(4): 301–17. doi:https://doi.org/10.1016/0191-2607(88)90008-8.

O'Connor, R.C., Wetherall, K., Cleare, S., McClelland, H., Melson, A.J., Niedzwiedz, C.L., … Robb, K.A. (2021). Mental health and well-being during the COVID-19 pandemic: Longitudinal analyses of adults in the UK COVID-19 Mental Health &

Wellbeing study. *The British Journal of Psychiatry, 218*(6): 326–33. doi:10.1192/bjp.2020.212.

Penley, T. (2023). Wall Street CEO backs post-pandemic push to get employees back in the office in 2023. Retrieved 9 March 2023 from: https://www.foxbusiness.com/lifestyle/wall-street-ceo-backs-post-pandemic-push-employees-back-office-2023.

Peretz, H., Fried, Y., & Levi, A. (2018). Flexible work arrangements, national culture, organisational characteristics, and organisational outcomes: A study across 21 countries. *Human Resource Management Journal, 28*(1), 182–200. doi: https://doi.org/10.1111/1748–8583.12172.

Pérez, M.P., Sánchez, A.M., & de Luis Carnicer, M.P. (2002). Benefits and barriers of telework: Perception differences of human resources managers according to company's operations strategy. *Technovation, 22*(12), 775–83. doi:https://doi.org/10.1016/S0166–4972(01)00069–4.

Peters, P., & Heusinkveld, S. (2010). Institutional explanations for managers' attitudes towards telehomeworking. *Human Relations, 63*(1): 107–35.

Peters, P., Ligthart, P.E.M., Bardoel, A., & Poutsma, E. (2016). 'Fit' for telework'? Cross-cultural variance and task-control explanations in organizations' formal telework practices. *The International Journal of Human Resource Management, 27*(21): 2582–603. doi:10.1080/09585192.2016.1232294.

Prodoscore. (n.d.). What employees want and what employers need seem to be at odds. But, they're not. Retrieved 14 March 2023 from: https://www.prodoscore.com/results/.

Ravid, D.M., Tomczak, D.L., White, J.C., & Behrend, T.S. (2020). EPM 20/20: A review, framework, and research agenda for electronic performance monitoring. *Journal of Management, 46*(1): 100–26.

Robinson, B. (2022). 3 new studies end debate over effectiveness of hybrid and remote work. Retrieved 10 March 2023 from: https://www.forbes.com/sites/bryanrobinson/2022/02/04/3-new-studies-end-debate-over-effectiveness-of-hybrid-and-remote-ork/?sh=27d7eba559b2.

Saragih, S., Setiawan, S., Markus, T., & Rhian, P. (2021). Benefits and challenges of telework during the covid-19 pandemic. *International Research Journal of Business Studies, 14*(2): 129–35.

Scott, D.M., Dam, I., Páez, A., & Wilton, R.D. (2012). Investigating the effects of social influence on the choice to telework. *Environment and Planning A, 44*(5): 1016–31.

Siegel, R., König, C.J., & Lazar, V. (2022). The impact of electronic monitoring on employees' job satisfaction, stress, performance, and counterproductive work behavior: A meta-analysis. *Computers in Human Behavior Reports, 8*: 100227.

Silva-C, A., Montoya, R.I.A., & Valencia A.J.A. (2019). The attitude of managers toward telework, why is it so difficult to adopt it in organizations? *Technology in Society, 59*: 101133. doi: https://doi.org/10.1016/j.techsoc.2019.04.009.

Soga, L.R., Bolade-Ogunfodun, Y., Mariani, M., Nasr, R., & Laker, B. (2022). Unmasking the other face of flexible working practices: A systematic literature review. *Journal of Business Research, 142*: 648–62.

Sostero, M., Milasi, S., Hurley, J., Fernández-Macías, E., & Bisello, M. (2020). Teleworkability and the COVID-19 crisis: A new digital divide? *JRC Working Papers Series on Labour, Education and Technology 2020/05, JRC121193.*

Spector, N. (2017). Why are big companies calling their remote workers back to the office? *NBC News.* Retrieved 12 March 2023 from: https://www.nbcnews.com/business/business-news/why-are-big-companies-calling-their-remote-workers-back-office-n787101/.

Thibodeau, P. (2022). Amazon unexpectedly renews employee monitoring debate. Retrieved 10 March 2023 from: https://www.techtarget.com/searchhrsoftware/news/252515811/Amazon-unexpectedly-renews-employee-monitoring-debate.

Thiel, C.E., Bonner, J., Bush, J.T., Welsh, D.T., & Garud, N. (2021). Stripped of agency: The paradoxical effect of employee monitoring on deviance. *Journal of Management:* 01492063211053224.

Toffler, A. (1980). *The third wave.* William Collins Sons & Co.

Troll, E.S., Venz, L., Weitzenegger, F., & Loschelder, D.D. (2022). Working from home during the COVID-19 crisis: How self-control strategies elucidate employees' job performance. *Applied Psychology, 71*(3): 853–80.

United Nations. (1948). Universal Declaration of Human Rights.

Vareikaitė-Mills, A. (2022). Hibridinis darbas – metas susitaikyti, kad jo 'neiškraustysite'. Retrieved 11 March 2023 from: https://www.vz.lt/verslo-valdymas/2022/09/08/hibridinis-darbas--metas-susitaikyti-kad-jo-neiskraustysite&69edfdbca65ea.

US Census Bureau. (2022). The number of people primarily working from home tripled between 2019 and 2021. Press release. Retrieved from: https://www.census.gov/newsroom/press-releases/2022/people-working-from-home.html.

Vartiainen, M. (2021). Telework and remote work. In *Oxford research encyclopedia of psychology* (p. 30). Oxford University Press. Retrieved 11 March 2023 from https://doi.org/10.1093/acrefore/9780190236557.013.850.

Vega, R.P., Anderson, A.J., & Kaplan, S.A. (2015). A within-person examination of the effects of telework. *Journal of Business and Psychology, 30*(2): 313–23. doi:10.1007/s10869-014-9359-4.

Verslo Žinios. (2022). Lietuvio darbo vieta – visas pasaulis: kelionės plečia akiratį ir neleidžia atsipalaiduoti. Retrieved 11 March 2023 from: https://www.vz.lt/balticamadeus/2022/10/20/lietuvio-darbo-vieta--visas-pasaulis-keliones-plecia-akirati-ir-neleidzia-atsipalaiduoti.

Vilhelmson, B., & Thulin, E. (2016). Who and where are the flexible workers? Exploring the current diffusion of telework in Sweden. *New Technology, Work and Employment, 31*(1): 77–96.

Wigert, B., & White, J. (2022). The advantages and challenges of hybrid work. Retrieved from: https://www.gallup.com/workplace/398135/advantages-challenges-hybrid-work.aspx.

Williams, J.C., Blair-Loy, M., & Berdahl, J.L. (2013). Cultural schemas, social class, and the flexibility stigma. *Journal of Social Issues, 69*: 209–34.

Yoshida, T. (2021). How has workcation evolved in Japan? *Annals of Business Administrative Science, 20*(1): 19–32. doi:10.7880/abas.0210112a.

6. Work in the platform economy: a broad perspective and its policy implications

Angela Garcia Calvo

INTRODUCTION

Early analyses optimistically portrayed online platforms as new organisational forms that could create a more inclusive economy and increase opportunities for flexible work. This formulation has given way to a realisation that platforms are for-profit organisations and raised concerns about their ability to generate significant numbers of even mediocre quality jobs, their contribution to existing inequalities and the quality of work experiences of platform workers. In this chapter, we suggest that most studies of platform work have adopted a narrow perspective that focuses only on a small set of visible platforms that provide in-person and remote platform work. Such a narrow perspective provides only a partial view of the impact of platforms on work practices that may lead to biased assessments. We adopt instead a broader perspective that includes two other categories of platform-mediated work: platform vendors and virtual content provision. We use this perspective to highlight tensions between existing institutional arrangements and platforms in three key areas of work: management power and work processes, social protection and labour rights, and skills and career prospects. Some of these areas have yet to receive attention from scholars and policymakers. We use our insights to make recommendations for policymakers tasked with recasting policies in response to the rise and maturity of the platform economy.

ONLINE PLATFORMS AND WORK

Online platforms are virtual N-sided markets that mediate transactions and other exchanges of goods, services, and data/information (Cusumano et al., 2019; Plantin et al., 2018). They are a new institutional structure that differs from classic markets and hierarchies (Williamson, 1975) and networks (Powell,

1990) yet contain elements of all three (Frenken et al., 2020; Kretschmer et al., 2022). The expansion of online platforms across an ever-growing range of value creation activities has sparked the interest of academics and policy-makers in understanding how they impact work, what types of policies are available, and what their potential implications may be. However, there are two problems with existing assessments. First, most analyses on platform work are based on a small number of very salient platforms, such as Amazon Mechanical Turk (AMT), Deliveroo, Lyft, Uber, and Upwork, that operate in only a few areas of economic activity. For instance, the European Union's (EU) COLLEEM survey examines 52 platforms, 40 of which correspond to three categories of services rendered in person: personal transportation services, delivery services, and domestic work (de Groen et al., 2021). Yet, as platforms have expanded into an ever-growing range of economic activities, these analyses exclude a vast range of economic activities that are mediated, affected, or created by platform firms (Bearson et al., 2021; Garcia Calvo et al., 2023). For instance, the ETUI Internet and Platform Work Survey (Piasna et al., 2022) rules out large categories of platform income generation – influencers (YouTube, Instagram, Tiktok), app creators (Apple App Store and Google Play), online rentals (Airbnb), and product sales online (Amazon Marketplace, Etsy, etc.) that generate significant income. Even when these categories are included, existing taxonomies still exclude workers whose activities have been directly or indirectly transformed by platforms. To illustrate, activities that have been directly affected by platforms include finance, real estate, car sales, and healthcare, while activities that have been indirectly affected are those of professionals such as lawyers, scriptwriters, marketing specialists, and multimedia artists that assist platform content creators as well as legacy industries such as advertising or journalism that have been completely reorganised as a result of platforms. The effect of excluding all these activities is that the common understanding of the impact of platforms on work is vastly understated and possibly biased. Perhaps more importantly, such a limited view of platforms does not see the platform economy as a transformational force affecting most types of economic activities.

A second related problem is that although the number of initiatives is growing, few countries have adopted legislative responses that are specific to platform work (see also Chapter 7). Therefore, we have limited empirical knowledge about the way these processes shape perceptions about platform work, the impact and trade-offs of different policy choices, or the interaction effects between existing institutions, platform power, and policymaking. Recent developments in California, ground zero of the platform economy, epitomise these points. In the USA, where a broad range of social benefits and rights, including healthcare, pensions, and the right to unionise, depend on employee status, initial discussions on platform work regulation revolved around the legal status of employees. Thus, 2019's California Assembly Act 5 (AB5) established a test to determine a worker's employment status that would have resulted in many types of platform work being classified as employment. In response, a group of US platform firms, which had much to lose from a re-categorisation of platform workers as employees, sought to redefine the terms of the discussion from labour rights to worker flexibility, in line with their preferences. To do so, they dedicated over $200 million to support a ballot initiative known as Proposition 22. The initiative, which was endorsed by a California Court of Appeals in March 2023, exempts platform workers from the employee categorisation established in AB5 and creates instead a new hybrid category between employees and independent contractors. Under the new category, platform workers have access to some benefits, such as a healthcare subsidy, a guarantee of minimum earnings, or occupational accident insurance. However, Proposition 22 does not enable platform workers to organise or bargain collectively, and the status of platform workers under the new category is significantly inferior to that of employees in terms of salaries and benefits, including the cost of healthcare (McCullough et al., 2022).

This chapter addresses these issues through a three-step process. In contrast to the narrow perspective described above, it adopts a broad perspective that captures a greater range of platform-mediated activities. It then uses the broad perspective to provide an overview of the tensions between existing labour arrangements in advanced industrialised countries and platform-specific policy issues in three key areas: management power and work processes, social protection and labour rights, and skills and career prospects. The chapter then uses our analysis to provide recommendations for policymakers tasked with addressing the impact of platforms on value generation and value-capturing activities.

Our insights provide a broad yet nuanced view of the effects of online platforms on labour. The analysis should be of help to policymakers and scholars interested in the regulation of platform work. The chapter should also be of value to scholars interested in the impact of online platforms on the transformation of capitalism.

WHAT IS PLATFORM WORK? FROM THE NARROW TO THE BROAD PERSPECTIVE

Online platforms emerged in the late 1990s and expanded rapidly into an ever-greater range of activities since the introduction of the smartphone in 2008 (Bearson et al., 2021). A recent EU study identified over 500 active platforms in the EU alone (de Groen et al., 2021). In the USA, online platforms exist in 70 per cent of service sectors, representing 5.2 million establishments affected directly or indirectly (Kenney et al., 2021). As platforms have expanded, so has their capacity to reorganise and reconfigure work (Kenney & Zysman, 2016), but in doing so, platforms defy existing definitions of work, who is a worker, and how we measure and count workers. Most advanced countries understand work as a relatively permanent contractual relationship between an employer and a worker in which the employer assigns tasks and oversees the worker in exchange for monetary compensation and some form of labour and bargaining rights (Stone, 2006). By contrast, platform firms define themselves as technology firms that facilitate transactions between independent workers and their clients (Berg, 2016; Kuhn & Maleki, 2017).[1] Yet, there is no formal contract between the worker and the platform, no assumption of permanence or guaranteed compensation, no statutory labour or collective bargaining rights, and no formal managerial control. It follows that, in the eyes of most legal systems, platform firms do not provide jobs, they provide a marketplace in which sellers of goods and services can contract with their clients. As a result, conventional terms such as employment, labour or jobs are not appropriate labels to characterise work mediated by the platform. Instead, we use the term 'platform work' to capture the nature of these platform-mediated relationships and distinguish them from work in traditional settings. We also refer to the individuals who perform platform work as 'platform workers'.

The status of platform workers has been a major focus of scholarly and policy discussions regarding the impact of the platform economy. However, most studies of platform work and most policy initiatives adopted in response to platforms are based on what Garcia Calvo et al. (2023) characterise as the 'narrow' perspective. As discussed in the introduction, this view only considers a small subgroup of large, salient platforms which offer online or in-person services in a few industries, primarily transportation, delivery services, and domestic work (de Groen et al., 2021). The problem with such a narrow approach is that it excludes a vast amount of work that is mediated by the platform, created by the platform, or affected by the platform (Garcia Calvo et al., 2023). The exclusion of additional categories of platform work has important implications; namely, by adopting a narrow perspective, scholars and policymakers are skewing their analyses and failing to appreciate the transformative power of platforms across all types of value creation and value capture. The risk is that policies based only on such a narrow perspective will miss the mark, be insufficient to address key emerging issues such as the legal status of platform workers, power disparities between platform firms and workers or career development, cause more harm than good, or have large inadvertent

---

[1]   There is some disagreement here as some practitioners consider firms such as Uber, Airbnb, etc. as 'technology-enabled' firms, as they are not developing new technologies but rather applying existing ones in novel ways.

negative effects not only on the platform workers they aim to support but also on the business models of the platforms.

To appreciate the transformative impact of platforms, we adopt instead what Garcia Calvo et al. (2023) call the 'broad' perspective. When it comes to platform work, these authors characterise three perspectives on how platforms reorganise work: narrow, broad and systemic. The narrow perspective includes the two categories of platform-mediated work discussed above: in-person and remote services. In addition to these two types of work, the broad perspective adds two additional categories of work mediated by the platform: online content creators (YouTubers, TikTokers, app creators on Apple App Store and Google Play) and platform vendors (Amazon Marketplace, Etsy, etc.). Unfortunately, to date, there are no appropriate efforts to measure the value creation impact of different types of platforms, but these authors estimate that the two additional categories included in the broad perspective account for a much larger share of value than the few salient firms that have captured so much attention. The systemic perspective adds a vast and much more diverse set of work grouped into four additional categories: employment created directly by the platform firm (direct employees, contractors, and fulfilment workers); work in legacy industries such as advertising, journalism, real estate, hospitality, and, potentially, manufacturing that is being reorganised by the platform; indirect platform work – work provided by individuals that provide support for content creators and vendors such as legal services, audio-visual artists, web creators and scriptwriters; and prosumers, or individuals who *pro*duce the raw data that platform firms monetise as they con*sume* services and information through their interactions with the platforms (Lang et al., 2020; Ritzer & Jurgenson, 2010).

The systemic perspective raises a much broader range of policy issues than those derived from the narrow and the broad perspectives, but some of these are not exclusive to platforms. For instance, regular employees and contractors of platform firms raise issues of diversity, inclusion, sexual harassment, and ethics that are pervasive across white-collar professional and managerial occupations, where Asians tend to be overrepresented while women, Latinos, and Black people are underrepresented and concentrated in the lower-paid job categories (Bearson et al., 2021). Similarly, platform contractors and fulfilment workers have been linked to issues of compensation, labour conditions, precarious employment, and firms' resistance to unionisation. These issues also transcend platforms and are a manifestation of broader concerns about the impact of declining union membership, automation, globalisation, offshoring, and outsourcing on middle-skilled and middle-income jobs and permanent employment (Autor et al., 2015; Goos et al., 2014; Huws, 2009, 2014; Hyman, 2018; Weil, 2014). Finally, issues associated with prosumers affect vast swathes of the population and have been examined from the point of view of data governance and fundamental rights such as privacy or behavioural manipulation rather than labour (Bourreau et al., 2020; Caffarra & Valletti, 2020; Forbrukerrådet, 2018; Gawer, 2021; Lanier, 2018; Marsden & Podszun, 2019; Morton et al., 2019; Zuboff, 2015, 2019).

To concentrate on those issues that are linked to distinct platform features, we adopt the broad perspective. This enables us to reveal a wider range of policy issues derived from platform work besides workers' legal status while concentrating on four relatively well-defined categories of work mediated by the platform: online services, in-person services, content creators, and platform vendors. In the following section, we use the broad perspective to discuss the tensions between existing arrangements and platform work in three areas that are central to work arrangements in advanced economies.

TENSIONS BETWEEN CONVENTIONAL ARRANGEMENTS AND PLATFORM WORK

Management Power and Work Processes

A key purpose of labour law is to balance the inherent asymmetry of power between employers and workers to provide a measure of protection for workers. However, by defining themselves as technology firms that mediate between independent workers and their clients, platform firms create the illusion that there is no asymmetry of power and exempt themselves from labour laws. Despite this illusion, the reality is that platforms have a significant amount of power over workers (Cutolo & Kenney, 2021). Platform power derives from the platform firm's control over the technical architecture of the platform, its ability to attract and retain both workers and clients, its influence over participant behaviour, and its capacity to leverage network and long-tail effects (Berg & Johnston, 2019; Curchod et al., 2020; Cusumano et al., 2019; Cutolo & Kenney 2021; Mendonça & Kougiannou, 2023; Parker et al., 2016). Platform firms exercise their power through a variety of mechanisms. For example, Uber uses surge pricing, requiring acceptance of every passenger, account deactivation for cancelling unprofitable fares, a non-transparent rating and payment systems, GPS tracking, institutionalised nudging and decentralised, automated support systems to assign tasks and discipline drivers (Rosenblat & Stark, 2016). Deliveroo and UberEATS withhold information from workers to constrain their choices (Kougiannou & Mendonça, 2021; Veen et al., 2020). Some platforms also charge commission fees (Fabo et al., 2017) or use notifications, competition for desirable work shifts, and monetary incentives to exercise power (Ivanova et al., 2018).

The main instrument through which platforms exercise their power is through the use of algorithms or mathematical formulas (algorithmic management) (Lee et al., 2015). Algorithms transform most aspects of human resource management. They accelerate and facilitate recruitment: individuals who want to work for the platform only need to create an account and be approved. In more selective platforms, online assessments can help the platform identify and pre-select appropriate candidates (Ajunwa & Greene, 2019; Carpentier & Van Hoye, 2020; Carpentier et al., 2019; Salehi et al., 2017; Schaarschmidt et al., 2021; Valentine et al., 2017). Furthermore, platforms that provide remote services can easily and efficiently recruit from a large, global pool of candidates (Kellogg et al., 2020; Wood et al., 2019).

Algorithms also transform performance evaluation mechanisms. The constant stream of granular data about worker behaviour that platforms receive enables platform firms to evaluate worker performance in real time using internal and external resources. Platforms that provide in-person service, such as Uber, use geolocation positioning to match drivers and customers, collect data on cancelled trips and evaluate drivers (Rosenblat & Stark, 2016). Platforms that provide virtual services, such as AMT and Upwork, use keystroke loggers and random worker screenshots to ensure that the platform worker is doing the task and other technical means to assess speed and productivity and to monitor the work process (Wood et al., 2019). In addition to internal data, nearly all platforms utilise online reviews and rating systems to assess workers' performance. Yet online reviews are typically anonymous, and assessments can be volatile and contradictory. Furthermore, the opacity of algorithms means that workers have few means to understand the assessment procedure or challenge the rating and the algorithmic decisions based on it (Cameron & Rahman, 2022; Maffe, 2022; Orlikowski & Scott, 2014; Wexler, 2018). Moreover, because the ratings are provided by third parties, the platform is not legally responsible for their accuracy, leaving workers with little recourse.

Overall, algorithmic comprehensiveness, instantaneity, interactivity, and opacity afford platforms multiple mechanisms to control workers that are qualitatively different and often more intrusive than conventional forms of management control (Kellogg et al., 2020). Nonetheless, the absence of human supervision and the flexibility in deciding when, where, and how to work simultaneously grants workers more autonomy over their work (Mazmanian et al., 2013). Such a combination of intrusive control and flexibility has both positive and negative consequences for workers. Negative effects include isolation, precarity, anxiety, insecurity, irregular schedules, high levels of work intensity or even discrimination, which can affect workers' motivation and performance, leading to high levels of attrition (Bergvall-Kåreborn & Howcroft, 2014; Howcroft & Bergvall-Kåreborn, 2019; Lee et al., 2015; Rosenblat & Stark, 2016; Shapiro, 2018; Tomprou & Lee, 2022). Positive effects come in the form of higher levels of autonomy, flexibility, task variety, complexity, and, for some, long enjoyable conversations with others (Berg,

2016; D'Cruz & Noronha, 2016; Jabagi et al., 2019; Lee et al., 2015; Shapiro, 2018; Wood et al., 2019). Early on, flexibility was considered one of the great benefits of platform work. However, as discussed in Chapters 3 and 7, there is a growing degree of scepticism about flexibility in platform work since the pressure of earning enough and the high degree of uncertainty regarding future opportunities force workers to spend long hours working on the platform.

Few countries have adopted policy measures to address the opacity of algorithms or the negative impact of algorithmic management on workers. Platform firms oppose such measures on the basis that algorithms are key to their competitive advantage and should, therefore, remain private, creating a potential conflict between the logics of labour and competition policy. One country that has established such measures is Spain, where the 2021 Rider's Law mandates that platforms disclose information about their algorithms to ensure equal treatment between platforms and non-platform firms (see Chapter 7 for more detail). As expected, the requirement has been strongly opposed by the affected platform firms. Some, such as the UK's Deliveroo, left Spain soon after the enactment of the Rider's Law. Others, such as Glovo, a domestic delivery platform, have chosen to ignore the law and appear to perceive the subsequent economic sanctions as the cost of doing business (Garcia Calvo and Valdez, unpublished manuscript).

Social Protection and Labour Rights

Perhaps the most salient issue in both scholarly and policy debates regarding platform work has been the status of platform workers and the rights that should be attached to them. Platform workers contract with the purchaser of their services – not with the platform. For example, content creators' contract with the platform provides creators with the right to upload videos that may be monetised through advertising or sponsorships; on the other hand, e-viewers' implicit contract with the platform offers them the right to watch in exchange for their data. Therefore, the platform creates a market where the exchange takes place, but it neither employs the worker nor buys their product. The result is that since platform workers are not employees of the platform, the platform firm does not incur the responsibilities for social protection, taxes, and administrative costs associated with a conventional employment relationship, leaving workers without access to basic healthcare and social insurance protection. This situation is commonly referred to as the 'social protection gap' (Cappelli & Keller, 2013; de Groen et al., 2021). Because social protection is linked to either income taxes or employment contributions that are related to the legal status of platform workers, this issue has attracted significant attention from scholars and policymakers, becoming a central topic. However, there is no straightforward policy solution. One problem is that platform firms operate across national borders, and some types of platform work can take place remotely, whereas governments are constrained by national borders. An additional obstacle is that labour law and social protection systems vary significantly across countries, and, therefore, policy solutions need to build directly on existing systems, which makes it difficult to make broad recommendations. Finally, one needs to consider the willingness of platform firms to shape policy outcomes according to their benefit, yet platform firms appear to be more willing to flex their muscles to influence policy outcomes in their home countries rather than abroad, where, in some cases, they have simply opted to leave the market after national governments have introduced policies detrimental to their interests.

Despite these limitations, scholars have set forth proposals to define the status of platform workers and the social protection gap that derives from it. Such proposals fall into three main categories. The first sees platform work as a manifestation of broader trends towards the casualisation of work and the privatisation of risks. Accordingly, they argue that the social protection gap should be dealt with as part of broader policy packages aimed to manage insecure work (De Stefano, 2016; Joyce et al., 2019). A second line of thought recommends targeted policy approaches based on four possible options: redefining the concept of an employer to encompass the functions that platforms perform, redefining the concept of an employee based on their level of economic dependency, creating an intermediary category between those of employee and self-employed, or equating platform work to existing regulations (Prassl & Risak, 2017). A third view proposes reclassifying platform workers directly as employees and integrating platform work into existing industrial relations systems (Sieker, 2021).

Each of these proposals has strengths and weaknesses. The first rightly situates platform work within broader trends towards the increasing precarity of work but does not offer any concrete suggestions about how to address the problem and does not take into account the peculiarities of platform work. In fact, the particularities of some types of platform work may make this approach difficult to implement. Take the case of remote platform work, where the workers may be located in a different jurisdiction or that of content creators and influencers, for whom the line between professional and content is very difficult to draw.

The second highlights a variety of options, but at least one of them, creating an intermediary category for platform workers, is problematic since it could create ambiguities that are exploited by the platforms and leave workers unprotected. The third option may be suitable for systems where industrial relationships rely on high levels of cooperation across a broad range of subjects, but it is less likely to deliver fruitful outcomes in countries where industrial relations are adversarial or focus primarily (and almost solely) on salary negotiations.

Some jurisdictions have recently debated or adopted measures to define the status of platform workers. A brief assessment of two of these cases showcases the broad variety of responses from across jurisdictions and the positions of both governments and platform firms. As mentioned earlier, in 2021, Spain, the country with the highest rate of platform workers in the EU (Pesole et al., 2018), adopted the Riders' Law. The law applies only to platform delivery workers and presumes that the workers have the status of an employee, with the same rights and responsibilities as regular workers under the Workers' Statute. The Riders' Law also establishes a right to algorithmic transparency, obliging platforms to disclose to work councils those algorithmic features 'that may affect working conditions and access to and maintenance of employment, including profiling' (Government of Spain Royal Decree Law 9/2021, of May 11, 2021). Delivery platform firms' reactions to the Riders' Law have varied from platform to platform: Deliveroo left the country, Glovo/Delivery Hero found a loophole that enabled it to circumvent the norm, and JustEats/Takeway.com adapted its business model to conform to the norm.

At the opposite end of the spectrum, recent US initiatives have upheld the independent worker status of delivery and ridesharing workers. California's 2019 AB5 established a test that classified most delivery and ridesharing workers as employees. In a show of force in 2020, large platforms responded by supporting Proposition 22, a ballot initiative that exempts delivery and ridesharing platform workers in California from employee classification. An initial ruling deemed Proposition 22 unconstitutional, but a 2023 decision upheld Proposition 22 in appeal, in what amounts to a victory for platform firms (Chen & Padin, 2021; Gedye, 2023).

Skills and Career Prospects

Finally, platform work raises significant issues regarding existing educational and vocational training systems. This is an area that to date has received minimal attention from policymakers and scholars. Yet, as platform work continues to grow, it will require dedicated attention from policymakers.

The skills required for platform work vary broadly depending on the types of platforms and types of tasks considered. Uber drivers require little more than a driver's licence, but workers on other platforms, such as Upwork, require complex cognitive skills in subjects such as legal advice or software that take years to acquire. Meanwhile, Youtubers, Tiktokers, and other influencers rely on non-cognitive skills such as persuasion, agility, creativity, and curiosity that are not usually taught through formal education programmes. Such diversity makes it difficult to think of platform work skills as a single package or to develop broad programmes that address skills demand for platform firms.

Despite these obstacles, there are some overarching areas in which platform work challenges existing arrangements. Unlike conventional employers, platform firms do not assume any responsibility for the development of platform workers' skills (Margaryan, 2019). This requires workers to develop self-management, self-reflection, and strategic planning skills to identify gaps and develop appropriate plans to fill them, a major gap in most educational and skills systems. Workers' responsibility is underscored by platforms' use of algorithmic management, which forces workers to develop their own career goals (Zimmerman & Kitsantas, 2005). Compounding the problem is the fact that in the absence of human performance reviews, opaque algorithmic rating weights and potentially volatile and contradictory customer reviews do not necessarily provide workers with the information they need to develop their own skill development plans. Unlike conventional settings, skills demand in platform environments evolve rapidly, as platforms change their algorithms. This requires workers to also adapt rapidly. These three factors: lack of platform responsibility for skill development, algorithmic management, and skill transiency explain why, while platform workers in advanced economies tend to have some form of tertiary education, they tend to prioritise the development of just-in-time skills through informal channels such as online communities, feedback from clients, or YouTube videos rather than rely on formal educational or vocational training programmes (CEDEFOP, 2020).

Yet, the prevalence of non-standardised skills development schemes has downsides. The most important is that it makes workers more dependent on the platform because their skills, reputations, and experience are often validated through client reviews and platform certificates and badges that are attached to the platform. This makes skill portability a key issue, especially as workers seek to develop their careers, operate through other platforms, or seek work outside the platform. Nonetheless, there are no easy solutions. Platforms have few incentives to facilitate skill portability since it would diminish the power of the platform firm over the worker. There are also technical and regulatory challenges associated with the sharing of personal data. Regulatory challenges vary by country, based on the characteristics of their data protection regulation. In addition, even when the worker can take their data, it can be difficult to gauge the quality of non-standardised skills (CEDEFOP, 2020, 2021).

In addition to these issues, career formation can vary significantly depending on the type of work performed. There is little in the way of career development in ridesharing or micro-tasking, but even in those platforms that provide opportunities for more complex work, platforms provide little additional incentives in the form of seniority or compensation. For content creators, influencers, and platform vendors, career development is constrained by their dependence on the platform, although there may be opportunities to develop complementary careers beyond the platform.

CONCLUSIONS

The expansion of the platform economy has created new types of work and reorganised existing work across a vast range of value creation and value capture activities. In doing so, platforms challenge existing legal definitions of employment, work, and labour. These definitions matter because each category involves a different set of rights and benefits for workers and different levels of costs and responsibilities for platform firms. Accordingly, scholars and policymakers face the challenge of reformulating policies and concepts to respond to this new reality. Such reformulation is essential if governments are to devise effective responses to platform work. Otherwise, we may end up devising 20th-century solutions to a 21st-century challenge.

Much of the literature has adopted what we call a narrow perspective, which focuses on in-person and remote services. A derivation of that approach is that emerging policy discussions have tended to focus on a small set of issues that are more salient for such types of workers, especially the legal status of delivery and ridesharing workers. While this issue is certainly important, it is only one of multiple areas in which platform work challenges existing institutional arrangements. Using the broad perspective, we show that platform work raises a much broader set of policy issues, including power disparities, changes in work processes derived from algorithmic management, mismatches between existing skills systems and skills demand, and issues regarding career development prospects. Addressing these issues efficiently will require governments to adopt a comprehensive rather than a piecemeal approach to the platform economy. Such an approach could centre on labour regulation and policy but should also encompass adjacent areas such as education and training, policies regarding the transfer of personal data, the definition of entrepreneurs and competition policy. Our brief description of recent policies in Spain and the USA shows that policy strategies so far have focused on a very narrow set of policy areas, yet, even in those areas, national strategies can differ significantly as a function of existing institutions, domestic coalitions, and political and economic goals. Platform firms are also likely to flex their muscles in support of policy solutions that back their interests since certain types of solutions have a direct impact on the viability of their business models. Therefore, when addressing the impact of the platform economy, policymakers should do well to abandon siloed approaches and consider both the needs of workers and the priorities and needs of firms simultaneously. As the platform economy continues to mature, we expect to see an increasing number of initiatives that will impact workers, platforms, and large swaths of economic activity. The result will likely have a transformative effect not only on labour but on the dynamics of different forms of capitalism as a whole.

REFERENCES

Ajunwa, I. & Greene, D. (2019). Platforms at work: automated hiring platforms and other new intermediaries in the organization of work. In S.P. Vallas and A. Kovalainen (eds), *Work and Labour in the Digital Age*. Bingley: Emerald Publishing, pp. 61–91.

Autor, D.H., Dorn, D. & Hanson, G.H. (2015). Untangling trade and technology: evidence from local labour markets. *Economic Journal*, 125(584): 621–46.

Bearson, D., Kenney, M. & Zysman, J. (2021). Measuring the impacts of labour in the platform economy: new work created, old work reorganized, and value creation reconfigured. *Industrial and Corporate Change*, 30(3): 536–63.

Berg, J. (2016). Income security in the on-demand economy: findings and policy lessons from a survey of crowdworkers. *Comparative Labour Law & Policy Journal*, 37(3): 543–76.

Berg, J. & Johnston, H. (2019), Too good to be true? A comment on Hall and Krueger's analysis of the labour market for Uber's driver-partners. *Industrial & Labour Relations Review*, 72(1): 39–68.

Bergvall-Kåreborn, B. & Howcroft, D. (2014). Amazon Mechanical Turk and the commodification of labour. *New Technology Work and Employment*, 29(3): 213–23.

Bourreau, M., Caffarra, C., Chen, Z., Choe, C., Crawford, G., Duso, T., Genakos, C. Heudues, P., Peitz, M., Rønde, T., Schnitzer, M., Schutz, N., Sovinsky, M., Spagnolo, G., Toivanen, O., Valletti T. & Vergé, T. (2020). Google/Fitbit will monetise health data and harm consumers. CEPR Policy Insights No. 107. https:// euagenda .eu/ upload/publications/policyinsight107.pdf. Accessed 15 December 2022.

Caffarra, C. & Valletti, T. (2020). Google/Fitbit review: privacy IS a competition issue. Vox EU/CEPR. 4 March. https:// cepr .org/ voxeu/ blogs -and -reviews/ googleftbit -review-privacy-competition-issue. Accessed 14 January 2023.

Cameron, L.D. & Rahman, H. (2022). Expanding the locus of resistance: understanding the co-constitution of control and resistance in the gig economy. *Organization Science*, 33(1): 38–58.

Cappelli, P. & Keller, J.R. (2013). Classifying work in the new economy. *Academy of Management Review*, 38(4): 575–96.

Carpentier, M. & Van Hoye, G. (2020). Managing organizational attractiveness after a negative employer review: company response strategies and review consensus. *European Journal of Work and Organizational Psychology*, 30(2): 274–91.

Carpentier, M., Van Hoye G. & Weijters, B. (2019). Attracting applicants through the organization's social media page: signaling employer brand personality. *Journal of Vocational Behavior*, 115: 1–14.

CEDEFOP. (2020). Developing and matching skills in the online platform economy: findings on new forms of digital work and learning from CEDEFOP's Crowd Learn study. CEDEFOP reference series 116. Luxembourg: Publications Office of the European Union.

CEDEFOP. (2021). Skill development in the platform economy. Comparing microwork and online freelancing. CEDEFOP research paper No. 81. Luxembourg: Publications Offce of the European Union.

Chen, B. & Padin, L. (2021). Prop 22 was a failure for California's app-based workers. Now it's also inconstitutional. National Employmen Law Project. Blog post 16 September. https://www.nelp.org/blog/prop-22-unconstitutional/. Accessed 18 May 2023.

Curchod, C., Patriotta, C., Cohen, L. & Neysen, N. (2020). Working for an algorithm: power asymmetries and agency in online work settings, *Administrative Science Quarterly*, 65(3): 644–76.

Cusumano, M.A., Gawer, A. & Yoffe, D.B. (2019). *The Business of Platforms*. New York: Harper Business.

Cutolo, D. &. Kenney, M. (2021). Platform-dependent entrepreneurs: power asymmetries, risks, and strategies in the platform economy. *Academy of Management Perspectives*, 35(4): 584–605.

D'Cruz, P. & Noronha, E. (2016). Positives outweighing negatives: the experiences of Indian crowdsourced workers. *Work Organisation, Labour & Globalisation*, 10(1): 44–63.

De Groen, W.P., Kilhoffer, Z., Westhoff, L., Postica, D. & Shamsfakhr, F. (2021). Digital labour platforms in the EU. Mapping and business models. Prepared by CEPS for the European Commission, Directorate-General for Employment, Social Affairs and Inclusion (DG EMPL). Brussels: European Commission.

De Stefano, V. (2016). The rise of the just-in-time workforce: on-demand work, crowdwork, and labour protection in the 'gig-economy'. *Comparative Labour Law and Policy Journal*, 37(3): 471–504.

Fabo, B., Beblavy, M., Kilhoffer, Z. & Lenaerst, K. (2017). Overview of European platforms: scope and business models. Luxembourg: Publications Office of the European Union.

Forbrukerrådet. (2018). Deceived by design. How tech companies use dark patterns to discourage us from exercising our rights to privacy. Oslo. https://fl.forbrukerradet .no/ wp -content/ uploads/ 2018/ 06/ 2018–06–27 -deceived -by -design -fnal .pdf. Accessed 15 December 2022.

Frenken, K., Vaskelainen, T., Fünfschilling, L. & Piscicelli, L. (2020). An institutional logics perspective on the gig economy. In *Theorizing the Sharing Economy: Variety and Trajectories of New Forms of Organizing*. Bingley: Emerald Publishing. pp. 83–105.

Garcia Calvo, A. & Valdez, J. (unpublished manuscript). To be or not to be an employee: how do governments respond to platform work? American Association of Political Science 2023 Proceedings.

Garcia Calvo, A., Kenney, M. & Zysman, J. (2023). Understanding work in the online platform economy: the narrow, the broad, and the systemic perspectives. *Industrial and Corporate Change*:1–20. https://doi.org/10.1093/icc/dtad005.

Gawer, A. (2021). Digital platforms' boundaries: the interplay of firm scope, platform sides, and digital interfaces. *Long Range Planning*, 54(5): 1–16.

Gedye, G. (2023). Court upholds California Prop. 22 in big win for gig firms like Lyft and Uber. Cal Matters. 13 May 2023. https://calmatters.org/economy/2023/03/prop -22-appeal/. Accessed 18 May 2023.

Goos, M., Manning, A. & Salomons, A. (2014). Explaining job polarization: routine-biased technological change and offshoring. *American Economic Review*, 104(8): 2509–26.

Government of Spain. (2021). Ryders' Law Royal Decree Law 9/2021, of May 11, 2021. Boletin Oficial del Estado N233. Sec. I, 119341-119344. 29 September.

Howcroft, D. & Bergvall-Kåreborn, n. B. (2019). A typology of crowdwork platforms. *Work, Employment and Society*, 33(1): 21–38.

Huws, U. (2009). The making of a cybertariat? Virtual work in a real world. *Socialist Register*, 37: 1–23.

Huws, U. (2014). *Labour in the Global Digital Economy: The Cybertariat Comes of Age*. New York: NYU Press.

Hyman, L. (2018). *Temp: How American Work, American Business, and the American Dream Became Temporary*. New York: Penguin Random House.

Ivanova, M., Bronowicka, J., Kocher, E. & Degner, A. (2018). The app as a boss? Control and autonomy in application-based management. Arbeit | Grenze | Fluss – Work in Progress interdisziplinarer Arbeitsforschung No. 2, Viadrina: Frankfurt, Oder.

Jabagi, N., Croteau, A.-M., Audebrand, L.K. & Marsan, J. (2019), Gig-workers' motivation: thinking beyond carrots and sticks. *Journal of Managerial Psychology*, 34(4): 192–213.

Joyce, S., Stuart, M., Forde, C. & Valizade, D. (2019). Work and social protection in the platform economy in Europe. *Advances in Industrial and Labour Relations*, 25: 153–84.

Kellogg, K.C., Valentine, M. & Christin, A. (2020). Algorithms at work: the new contested terrain of control. *Academy of Management Annals*, 14(1): 366–410.

Kenney, M. & Zysman, J. (2016). The rise of the platform economy. *Issues in Science and Technology*, 32(3): 61–9.

Kenney, M., Bearson, D. & Zysman, J. (2021). The platform economy matures: measuring pervasiveness and exploring power. *Socio-Economic Review*: 1–33.

Kougiannou, N.K. & Mendonça, P. (2021). Breaking the managerial silencing of worker voice in platform capitalism: the rise of a food courier network. *British Journal of Management*, 32(3): 744–59.

Kretschmer, T., Leiponen, A., Schilling, M. & Vasudeva, G. (2022). Platform ecosystems as meta-organizations: implications for platform strategies. *Strategic Management Journal*, 43(3): 405–24.

Kuhn, K.M. & Maleki, A. (2017). Micro-entrepreneurs, dependent contractors, and instaserfs: understanding online labour platform workforces. *Academy of Management Perspectives*, 31(3): 183–200.

Lang, B., Dolan, R., Kemper, J. & Northey, G. (2020). Prosumers in times of crisis: definition, archetypes and implications. *Journal of Service Management*, 32(2): 179–89.

Lanier, J. (2018). *Ten Arguments for Deleting Your Social Media Accounts Right Now*. London: Bodley Head.

Lee, M.K., Kusbit, D., Metsky, E. & Dabbish, L. (2015). Working with machines: the impact of algorithmic and data-driven management on human workers. Paper presented at the Proceedings of the 33rd Annual ACM Conference on Human Factors in Computing Systems, April, pp. 1603–12.

Maffe, M.D. (2022). The perils of laundering control through customers: a study of control and resistance in the ride-hail industry. *Industrial & Labour Relations Review*, 75(2): 348–72.

Margaryan, A. (2019). Comparing crowdworkers' and conventional knowledge workers self-regulated learning strategies in the workplace. *Human Computation*, 6(1): 83–97.

Marsden, P. & Podszun, R. (2019). Restoring balance to digital competition – sensible rules, effective enforcement. Konrad Adenauer Stiftung. https:// www .kas .de/en/ single-title/ -/ content/ restoring -balance -todigital -competition -sensible -rules -effective-enforcement. Accessed 15 December 2022.

Mazmanian, M., Orlikowski, W.J. & Yates, J. (2013). The autonomy paradox: the implications of mobile email devices for knowledge professionals. *Organization Science*, 24(5): 1337–57.

McCullough, E., Dolber, B., Scoggins, J., Muña, E.M. & Treuhaft, S. (2022). Prop 22 depresses wages and deepens inequities for California workers. 21 September. https://nationalequityatlas.org/prop22-paystudy. Accessed 10 August 2023.

Mendonça, P. & Kougiannou, N.K. (2023). Disconnecting labour: the impact of intraplatform algorithmic changes on the labour process and workers' capacity to organise collectively. *New Technology, Work and Employment*, 38(1): 1–20.

Morton, S. Bouvier, Ezrachi, A., Jullien, B., Katz, R., Kimmelman, G., Melamed, D. & Morgenstern, J. (2019). *The Stigler Report*. Committee for the Study of Digital Platforms, Market Structure and Antitrust.

Orlikowski, W.J. & Scott, S.V. (2014). Exploring apparatuses of valuation in the travel sector. *Organization Science*, 25(3): 868–91.

Parker, G.G., Van Alstyne, M.W. & Choudary, S.P. (2016). *Platform Revolution: How Networked Markets Are Transforming the Economy and How to Make Them Work for You*. New York: W.W. Norton & Company.

Pesole, A., Urzi Brancati, M.C., Fernandez-Macias, E., Biagi, F. & Gonzalez Vazquez, I. (2018). *Platform Workers in Europe*. Brussels: JRC Science for Policy Report, European Commission.

Piasna, A., Zwysen, W. & Drahokoupil, J. (2022). The platform economy in Europe: results from the second ETUI Internet and Platform Work Survey. European Trade Union Institute Working Paper 2022–5.

Plantin, J.C., Lagoze, C., Edwards, P.N. & Sandvig, C. (2018). Infrastructure studies meet platform studies in the age of Google and Facebook. *New Media & Society*, 20(1): 293–310.

Powell, W.W. (1990). Neither market nor hierarchy: network forms of organization. *Research in Organizational Behavior*, 12: 295–336.

Prassl, J. & Risak, M. (2017). The legal protection of crowdworkers: four avenues for worker's rights in the virtual realm. In P. Meil & V. Kirov (eds), *Policy Implications of Virtual Work. Dynamics of Virtual Work*. E-book. Cham: Palgrave Macmillan, pp. 273–95.

Ritzer, G. & Jurgenson, N. (2010). Production, consumption, prosumption: the nature of capitalism in the age of the digital 'prosumer'. *Journal of Consumer Culture*, 10(1): 13–36.

Rosenblat, A. & Stark, L. (2016). Algorithmic labour and information asymmetries: a case study of Uber's drivers. *International Journal of Communication*, 10: 3758–84.

Salehi, N., McCabe, A., Valentine, M. & Bernstein, M. (2017). Huddler: convening stable and familiar crowd teams despite unpredictable availability. Paper presented at the Proceedings of the 2017 ACM Conference on Computer Supported Cooperative Work and Social Computing. Association of Computing Machinery, New York, pp. 1700–13.

Schaarschmidt, M., Walsh, G. & Ivens, S. (2021). Digital war for talent: how profile reputations on company rating platforms drive job seekers' application intentions. *Journal of Vocational Behavior*, 131: 1–20.

Shapiro, A. (2018), Between autonomy and control: strategies of arbitrage in the 'on-demand' economy. *New Media & Society*, 20(8): 2954–71.

Sieker, F. (2021). Platform work and access to social protection across major European countries. Hertie School of Governance.

Stone, K.V. (2006). Legal protections for atypical employees: employment law for workers without workplaces and employees without employers. *Berkeley Journal of Employment and Labour Law*, 27: 251–86.

Tomprou, M. & Lee, M.K. (2022). Employment relationships in algorithmic management: a psychological contract perspective. *Computers in Human Behavior*, 126: 106997.

Valentine, M.A., Retelny, D., To, A., Rahmati, N., Doshi, T. & Bernstein, M.S. (2017). Flash organizations: crowdsourcing complex work by structuring crowds as organizations. Paper presented at the Proceedings of the 2017 CHI Conference on Human Factors in Computing Systems, Denver, Colorado, 6–11 May. Association of Computing Machinery, New York, pp. 3523–37.

Veen, A., Barratt, T. & Goods, C.C. (2020). Platform-capital's 'app-etite' for control: a labour process analysis of food-delivery work in Australia. *Work, Employment and Society*, 34(3): 388–406.

Weil, D. (2014). *The Fissured Workplace*. Cambridge, MA: Harvard University Press.

Wexler, R. (2018). The odds of justice: code of silence: how private companies hide flaws in the software that governments use to decide who goes to prison and who gets out. *Chance*, 31(3): 67–72.

Williamson, O.E. 1975. *Markets and Hierarchies*. New York: Free Press.

Wood, A.J., Graham, M., Lehdonvirta, V. & Hjorth, I. (2019). Good gig, bad gig: autonomy and algorithmic control in the global gig economy. *Work, Employment and Society*, 33(1): 56–75.

Zimmerman, B.J. & Kitsantas, A. (2005). The hidden dimension of personal competence: self-regulated learning and practice. In A.J. Elliot and C.S. Dweck (eds), *Handbook of Competence and Motivation*. New York: Guilford Publications, pp. 509–26.

Zuboff, S. (2015). Big other: surveillance capitalism and the prospects of an information civilization. *Journal of Information Technology*, 30(1): 75–89.

Zuboff, S. (2019). *The Age of Surveillance Capitalism: The Fight for a Human Future at the New Frontier of Power*. London: Profile Books.

7. Employment from the pandemic onwards: European trends on platform work and teleworking and the case of Spain

Amaya Erro-Garcés, Angel Belzunegui-Eraso and Antonio Fernández García

INTRODUCTION

'New ways of organising' (Kelliher & Richardson, 2012), 'New ways to work' (Peters et al., 2014), 'New ways of working' (Gerards et al., 2018) or, more recently, 'The future of work' (Beane & Leonardi, 2022) are terms with which the academic literature refers to new forms of employment (NFE) in the labour market. In line with the conclusions of Eurofound (2020), NFE have consolidated themselves in recent decades, with many of them featuring Information and Communication Technology (ICT) and affecting variables such as the workplace (ICT-based mobile work, platform work), the ability of companies to control (platform work), the time worked (platform work, job sharing), the duration of the contractual relationship (casual work, interim management), remuneration (voucher-based work), etc. Perhaps the most notable features of these NFE are platform work and teleworking (ICT-based mobile work modality), particularly during and after the Covid-19 pandemic.

The characteristics of these forms of employment do not lie so much in their novelty but in their spread. While remote platforms or teleworking from home had been developing to a different extent and intensity in Europe and Spain, it was only after the experience of lockdown during the pandemic that these forms began to acquire a previously unknown dimension.[1]

---

[1] In Spain, from March to June 2020 with a total shutdown of activities considered non-essential, and from June 2020 until the summer of 2021, with major restrictions on mobility and gatherings of people.

As Belzunegui-Eraso and Erro-Garcés (2020) point out, in the early days of the pandemic, teleworking kept employment going during months when a good part of physical activity in the economy had stopped completely. In those circumstances of great uncertainty, teleworking (in its different forms and updates) highlighted the fact that a large number of jobs could be performed remotely online, taking advantage of the opportunities offered by this option; mainly saving time and the impact of lower mobility on a better environment in towns and cities. The application of remote working as a consequence of the pandemic drove two levels of action that are still being explored: on the one hand, anything to do with new developments that facilitate working remotely, from new tools (hardware and software) to new working procedures (rethinking in terms of work by objectives, new ways of managing, collaborative work, etc.), and on the other, the regulatory changes that emerged from this wide-ranging experience of working remotely. These changes have affected – and continue to do so – both European and Spanish labour legislation.

The new forms of employment, and particularly those created as a result of the experience of the pandemic, challenge European labour legislation in some aspects, for example, Directive 2003/88/CE of the European Parliament and the Council of 4 November 2003 concerning certain aspects of the organisation of working time and Directive (UE) 2019/1152 of the European Parliament and the Council of 20 June 2019 on transparent and predictable working conditions in the European Union (EU). The EU has also been obliged to regulate new phenomena related to ICTs such as artificial intelligence, used in platform work and increasingly extended to any business activity. Work has been done since 2021 on a proposed regulation to establish harmonised rules in the field of artificial intelligence (Law on Artificial Intelligence). In the same direction, we can refer to the Proposal for a Directive of 9 December 2021 concerning the improvement of working conditions in platform work.

As regards platform work, Eurofound distinguishes up to ten modalities of remunerated work, in which the matching of supply to demand is a key factor through an online platform where the on-location platform-determined routine work stands out. In other words, the provision of services that do not require particular skills, such as the transport of passengers or the delivery of food and goods (Eurofound, 2018: 23). This last-mentioned activity (riders) affected 24 per cent of the 28.2 million platform workers in the EU, and it is also the modality that has grown fastest due to the Covid-19 pandemic (European Commission, 2021: 97). It is estimated that 5 million workers are erroneously classified as self-employed when they should be salaried employees. In Spain, workers in this category are called 'false self-employed'. This occurs precisely in on-location platform-determined routine workers, a practice challenged in a series of legal systems (Guerrero & Fernández, 2022). The restrictions on social mobility produced by the pandemic favoured the emergence of *in itinere* jobs such as those related to the home delivery of goods and services. This kind of work has renewed the debate on the recognition of the activity provided, similar to how teleworking was questioned in the last decade of the 20th century, being considered – in part and for certain activities – as a kind of outsourcing of a service provision.

As regards teleworking, each Member State has developed (or is developing) its own legislation, in many aspects, based on the European Framework Agreement on Teleworking of 2003, the result of community social dialogue, although its application is not binding. The Covid-19 pandemic has been a key factor in the increase of this kind of service provision: according to Eurostat, 5.5 per cent of workers were teleworking in 2019, while the figure rose to 13.6 per cent in 2021. The main exponents were Ireland (33 per cent, with only 7 per cent in 2019), Luxembourg (28.4 per cent, 11 per cent in 2019) and Sweden (27.7 per cent, 6.1 per cent in 2019). For its part, 4.8 per cent of workers in Spain were teleworking in 2019, with the figure rising to 11 per cent in 2020 and 9.6 per cent in 2021. In general, around 40 per cent of workers in the EU started to telework at the beginning of the pandemic, according to data from Eurofound (2020); 34 per cent did so exclusively from home. In the months of confinement, Belgium stood out as the country where most employees teleworked from home (around 50 per cent), followed by France, Spain, Italy and Ireland, where people working from home represented around 40 per cent of the total. Obviously, these figures are distributed in a very unequal way based on productive sectors. Moreover, according to Eurofound, teleworking was much more prevalent in the EU in the knowledge-based, financial and insurance sectors, without forgetting its impact on the education and publishing sectors.

This chapter focuses on the Spanish case in an attempt to learn how labour legislation has performed in the face of the pandemic and the new ways of working. Specifically, given the spread of teleworking and delivery work through digital platforms. We shall also address the issue of temporary work; according to Eurostat, Spain was already seeing a rate of temporary work around 20–22 per cent, being the biggest Member State with these figures, only surpassed in 2019 by Montenegro (26.1 per cent) and followed by the Netherlands (20.8 per cent) and Serbia (19.4 per cent). This rate has been maintained between 11.8 per cent and 12.9 per cent in the EU since 2009.

These two dimensions that we address in this chapter (teleworking and work done through digital platforms) and temporary work are strongly associated with the Spanish case. The latter has often been used in Spain as a way to match supply and demand in the labour market. Far from only affecting less skilled jobs, temporary work has spread as a form of labour relations that shows discontinuous career profiles among the workforce. In the final analysis, this has long-term effects on workers' contributory pensions, as well as short- and medium-term effects that put Spain among the EU countries with the highest number of working people at risk of falling into poverty.

THE LEGAL CONTEXT OF A CONTRACT THAT EMERGED FROM THE PANDEMIC

The Covid-19 pandemic represented the biggest drop-off in the economy since the oil crisis of the 1970s, leading to the urgent production of legislation aimed at offsetting the impact on jobs, among other things. This legislation is very varied but always sets out to maintain employment, avoiding redundancies by improvements to internal flexibility measures: the temporary lay-off mechanism (ERTE in Spanish). The processing of layoffs, the payment of extra unemployment benefits and other advantages to maintain jobs were all facilitated.

Two other labour regulations came into effect during the pandemic, aimed at regulating teleworking and the provision of services via digital delivery platforms.

Teleworking was regulated by Spanish Royal Decree-Act 28/2020 of 22 September 2020 on remote working. It became effective on 13 October 2020 and later became Act 10/2021 of 9 July 2021 on remote working, although without major changes. It emerged from a social dialogue between the government, trade unions and employers, enacted in the midst of the pandemic due to the urgent need to improve the legislation that was regulating teleworking at the time. We should clarify that teleworking is not a type of employment contract but a clause that can take effect in different contract modalities. It is limited to training contracts and those signed by minors. Nevertheless, it is an important employment modality, and it is interesting to observe its evolution, particularly because its regulation imposes a series of economic obligations on the employer (provision of equipment, compensation for expenses, etc.) that should also be negotiated with the workers' legal representatives (works council, etc.), which could complicate its general application.

Regarding the provision of services through digital delivery platforms, Act 12/2021 of 28 September 2021 (known as the 'Riders Act'), which modifies the revised text of the Law on the Statute of Rights for Workers – approved by Legislative Royal Decree 2/2015 of 23 October 2015 – to guarantee the labour rights of delivery workers through digital platforms. The result of social dialogue between the government, the trade unions CCOO and UGT and the employers' organisations CEOE and CEPYME, this law states that:

> The activity of persons who provide remunerated services consisting of the delivery or distribution of any commodity or goods by employers who exercise business faculties of organisation, management and control in a direct, indirect or implicit

manner through the algorithmic management of the service or the working conditions applicable, through a digital platform that is considered an employment relationship as employed by others.

Therefore, digital platforms are obliged to contract people as employees, although not in all areas of the platform economy, just in the fields of delivery or distribution. For example, this law would not be applied to Uber or Cabify, companies that transport passengers.

The 'Riders Act' is based on the criteria followed by the jurisprudence of the Spanish Supreme Court (STS 805/2020 of 25 September 2020) in the case of the company Glovo. While some platforms have accepted the new rules and even agreed the regulation of employment terms with the main trade unions (e.g., Just Eat), others are still not applying the law and maintaining a commercial relationship with their delivery men/women (false self-employed), which has meant the inclusion of a new offence in criminal law that is applicable to these cases, given the impotence of the administrative system of sanctions vis-à-vis companies that prefer to pay fines while they continue with their illicit practices.

Once the hardest phase of the Covid-19 pandemic had been overcome, Royal Decree-Act 32/2021 of 8 December 2021 was enacted. It consisted of urgent labour market reform measures, a guarantee of stability in employment and the transformation of the labour market in order to comply with the requirements laid down by the EU to activate the funding instruments for receiving Next Generation Funds. It is a major labour reform with the backing of social dialogue, agreed between the government, trade unions and employers (CCOO, UGT, CEOE and CEPYME) that sets out to put an end to unemployment and temporary and precarious work to take on economic crises without losing jobs in the process. It includes measures such as the reformulation of the recruitment of workers to reduce the level of temporary work (also encouraging the hiring of women and young people), new internal flexibility measures based on the urgent measures applied during the pandemic (the temporary lay-off system) and changes in subcontracting and collective bargaining to correct the provisions of the labour reform of 2012.

In relation to contracting, it boosts the permanent seasonal contract (CFD in Spanish) with the aim of replacing temporary contracts for specified work and services. These are repealed, although they could exist until 30 September 2022. It is a permanent contract modality that involves certain periods of inactivity, during which the worker may receive unemployment benefits. From 30 March 2022, the permanent seasonal contract is applicable to: (i) work of a seasonal nature or related to productive seasonal activities; (ii) work that does not have this seasonal nature but, being provided intermittently, has particular, determinate or indeterminate periods of performance; (iii) the provision of services within the framework of the performance of mercantile or administrative contracts. These being foreseeable, they are part of the ordinary activity of a company (the periods of inactivity are a maximum of three months unless the collective agreement for the sector stipulates another time limit); (iv) between a temporary agency and a person contracted to be transferred to the user company.

The labour reform also modifies one of the most commonly used contracts: the contract to cover demand for production (CCP in Spanish), which can only be applied in two scenarios from 30 March 2022 onwards:

- *Scenario 1*: the occasional and unforeseeable increase of an activity and oscillations (including holidays), even though it is a case of the company's normal activity, that creates a temporary imbalance between the stable employment available and what is required, provided that these do not respond to cases that would come under a permanent seasonal contract. The maximum duration is six months, although this could be extended to one year under a sectoral collective agreement.
- *Scenario 2*: to cover occasional, foreseeable situations of short duration (and marked out in time), duly identified in the contract. The maximum duration is 90 days in the calendar year, which cannot be applied in a continuous manner.

The aim is that this type of contract should also be replaced by a permanent seasonal contract. In general, the aim is to reduce the extent of temporary work, as indicated above. However, until 30 June 2023, CCP contracts may abide by legislation prior to its modification, which would allow for more scenarios than those described.

The application of this new legislation, created during the pandemic, highlights three circumstances that have had – and continue to do so – a direct impact on the configuration of the labour market in Spain. In summary:

1. Temporary contracting has been reduced in favour of the permanent seasonal contract, which in turn favours the contracting of women and young people.
2. The 'Riders Act' has led to an increase in the number of workers employed in the category 'Home delivery personnel on foot or in a non-motorised form of transport' (94331026 of CNO-11), reducing the number of self-employed workers in that occupation.
3. After the hardest phase of the pandemic the number of people teleworking has been reduced due to deficiencies in the Act, which imposes undesired conditions on companies, despite the fact that the regulation was approved with the support of employer stakeholders.

CHARACTERISTICS OF THE EMPLOYMENT CONTRACT: TEMPORARY AND PERMANENT CONTRACTS

One of the most pressing problems in the European labour market, and particularly in Spain, is the so-called 'duality'; in other words, the existence of two groups of workers with different conditions in their employment contract (Simoni & Vlandas, 2021).

The duality of the labour market generates rigidity in the balance between supply and demand in the market and increases inequality. Indeed, a large part of legislative reforms of the labour market seek to liberalise the supply of jobs and solve the duality of the market. As described by Simoni and Vlandas (2021), the reforms developed by the public sector with these aims often come up against the opposition of the trade unions, who tend to defend contracted workers as opposed to unemployed people. This situation is exacerbated even more when the economic context is favourable.

Various authors (Busemeyer & Kemmerling, 2020; Vlandas, 2020) claim that the protective measures that have been implemented in the labour market have varied and have affected diverse groups in different ways.

The starting hypothesis – reducing temporary contracting after the Covid-19 pandemic – comes precisely within a context of economic crisis. As pointed out previously, this context can lead to the implementation of economic policies of a liberal nature in the labour market, and thereby reduce the level of temporary work.

In the specific case of Spain, and despite the fact that the characteristics of the Spanish labour market are similar to those in other European countries, Spain usually shows greater oscillations than its European counterparts. The Spanish labour market is characterised by a higher unemployment rate than the European average and a higher proportion of temporary employment. Specifically, the Spanish labour market shows a higher temporary employment rate, in particular in the case of women, and a lesser presence of part-time contracts (Delgado et al., 2020).

As described above, the starting hypothesis examined in this chapter envisages the reduction of temporary employment to the benefit of permanent seasonal contracts. We also consider that these contracts are of greater benefit to women and young people, the groups most affected by temporality. To validate this hypothesis, we resort to data from Eurostat on temporality in Europe.

First, we would highlight the situation of the labour market in Spain in comparison with the European average of temporary employment. Table 7.1 shows that the temporary employment rate in Spain is one of the highest in

Table 7.1　　　*Rate of temporality in Europe (totals)*

TIME	2010	2011	2012	2013	2014	2015	2016	2017	2018	2019	2020	2021
EU: 27 countries (from 2020)	12.1	12.3	12.1	12.0	12.4	12.7	12.8	12.9	12.7	12.2	11.1	11.2
Euro area: 20 countries (from 2023)	12.3	12.5	12.2	12.0	12.3	12.7	12.9	13.2	13.3	12.9	11.7	12.2
Euro area: 19 countries (2015–22)	12.3	12.6	12.2	12.0	12.3	12.7	12.8	13.2	13.3	12.9	11.7	12.2
Belgium	6.5	7.1	6.6	6.6	7.0	7.4	7.5	8.5	8.5	8.5	8.0	8.0
Bulgaria	3.9	3.6	4.0	5.0	4.7	3.9	3.6	3.9	3.6	3.9	3.2	3.0
Czechia	6.6	6.4	6.6	7.4	7.8	8.1	7.9	7.8	6.9	6.3	5.7	5.3
Denmark	6.8	7.0	7.0	7.2	6.8	6.9	10.9	9.5	8.2	8.3	8.7	8.8
Germany	11.7	11.9	11.3	10.9	10.7	10.8	10.9	10.7	10.5	9.9	9.1	9.2
Estonia	3.2	3.9	2.9	3.0	2.6	2.8	3.1	2.7	2.7	2.5	2.2	1.3
Ireland	7.5	8.1	8.0	7.9	7.5	7.0	6.5	6.7	7.4	7.1	6.6	6.9
Greece	8.3	7.7	6.6	6.5	7.6	7.9	7.5	7.7	7.7	8.8	7.1	7.0
Spain	20.3	20.8	19.2	18.9	19.6	20.7	21.5	22.1	22.3	21.9	20.1	20.9
France	10.9	11.2	11.2	11.2	11.8	12.5	12.5	12.9	12.6	12.1	11.2	11.9
Croatia	9.8	10.5	10.7	11.9	14.0	16.9	18.6	17.5	17.1	15.5	13.0	11.4
Italy	9.4	9.9	10.3	9.9	10.3	10.6	10.7	11.8	13.1	13.1	11.7	12.9
Cyprus	11.6	11.9	12.8	14.5	15.7	15.8	14.3	13.5	12.0	11.9	11.6	11.6
Latvia	5.5	5.2	3.7	3.3	2.5	2.8	2.8	2.2	2.1	2.3	2.1	2.3
Lithuania	2.1	2.4	2.2	2.3	2.3	1.8	1.6	1.4	1.2	1.1	1.0	1.6
Luxembourg	5.9	6.0	6.4	5.9	6.7	8.5	7.4	7.6	8.5	7.9	6.5	7.9
Hungary	8.1	7.6	8.1	9.3	9.2	9.7	8.3	7.5	6.2	5.6	5.0	5.1
Malta	3.9	5.0	5.3	5.9	6.1	6.1	6.0	4.9	6.4	7.2	6.4	6.3
Netherlands	20.6	20.6	21.4	22.1	22.8	21.7	21.9	22.5	21.9	20.8	19.2	19.4
Austria	5.6	5.8	5.8	5.9	6.0	6.1	6.2	6.7	6.7	6.3	5.7	5.8
Poland	21.6	21.4	21.4	21.5	22.7	22.5	22.1	21.0	19.5	17.4	14.7	11.7
Portugal	18.3	18.3	17.2	17.8	18.0	18.6	18.9	18.7	18.8	17.6	15.1	14.3
Romania	0.8	1.1	1.2	1.1	1.2	1.1	1.1	1.0	0.9	1.2	1.0	2.0
Slovenia	15.6	16.6	15.9	15.1	15.1	16.5	16.0	16.5	14.5	12.3	10.4	9.6
Slovakia	3.1	3.7	3.8	3.8	5.0	6.0	5.7	5.3	4.5	4.4	3.7	3.4
Finland	14.1	14.2	14.1	13.9	13.9	13.7	14.2	14.5	14.8	14.1	13.5	12.9
Sweden	12.3	13.0	12.6	12.9	13.4	13.3	13.0	12.8	12.6	12.3	11.9	11.6
Iceland	9.4	9.0	10.1	11.0	10.7	9.9	9.2	8.5	7.1	6.3	6.5	9.8

TIME	2010	2011	2012	2013	2014	2015	2016	2017	2018	2019	2020	2021
Norway	7.8	7.6	8.3	8.3	7.6	7.9	8.4	8.3	8.3	7.7	7.6	7.7
Switzerland	7.1	6.9	7.0	7.3	7.5	8.2	7.9	7.9	7.8	7.6	7.9	8.0
Montenegro	:	14.4	17.6	21.6	21.8	23.7	26.1	23.3	25.3	26.1	23.9	:
North Macedonia	11.9	10.7	10.6	10.9	11.3	9.4	10.2	10.6	11.5	13.2	14.6	:
Serbia	:	12.5	13.2	13.7	15.1	17.8	19.2	18.7	19.5	19.4	17.7	17.6
Türkiye	6.5	7.1	7.0	7.0	7.8	7.9	8.0	8.0	7.6	7.0	6.8	:

Note: (:) No data.
Source: Eurostat (2023a).

Europe (20.9 per cent in Spain, in contrast to the European average of 11.2 per cent in 2021).

The figures also confirm that this situation affects women more. They show a temporary employment rate of 24.1 per cent in comparison with the European average of 12.4 per cent in 2021, while the temporary employment rate in Spain is 18.2 per cent in men and 10.1 per cent in Europe (Table 7.2). This mainly affects young people, with a temporary employment rate of 51.2 per cent (working people under 29 years of age) as opposed to a European average of 32.8 per cent in 2021 (Figure 7.1).

In other words, the situation of the labour market in Spain explains the need to act on the temporary employment rate and justifies the Spanish government's action to restrict temporary contracts from 30 March 2022.

To validate the effectiveness of this policy, the number of temporary contracts in different periods has been analysed. Specifically, prior to 30 March 2022 and before the entry into force of the new labour contracting system, from 30 March (with the new policies on temporary contracts), and from 30 September 2022, when all temporary contracts for specified work and services ended, and from 30 June 2023, the date when there were still contracts to cover production regulated according to the previous regulation, which would allow more scenarios (Table 7.3).

The most notable fall in temporary contracting in Spain occurred in April 2022 (Table 7.3), from 1,158,164 contracts in March 2022 to 751,447 in April 2022. This seems to be the result of the new policies on temporary contracting applicable from 30 March 2022.

It will be interesting to observe the evolution from June 2023, when the last contracts to cover production regulated by the previous legislation ceased to exist (this legislation allowed more scenarios to justify contracting). In any event, a reduction in temporary contracting is observed in the first months of 2023. This is highly relevant if a comparison is made with the same months in 2022 (a 50.62 per cent reduction in January and 47.52 per cent in February).

Table 7.2   Temporary employment rate in Europe (by sex)

TIME	2015		2016		2017		2018		2019		2020		2021	
GENDER	M	F	M	F	M	F	M	F	M	F	M	F	M	F
European Union: 27 countries (from 2020)	11.8	13.7	11.8	13.8	11.9	14.0	11.7	14.0	11.3	13.3	10.1	12.2	10.1	12.4
Euro area: 20 countries (from 2023)	11.8	13.8	11.9	13.9	12.2	14.4	12.3	14.5	12.0	13.9	10.8	12.8	11.0	13.5
Euro area: 19 countries (2015–22)	11.7	13.7	11.9	13.9	12.2	14.3	12.3	14.4	12.0	13.9	10.8	12.8	11.1	13.5
Belgium	6.9	7.8	7.0	8.1	8.1	9.0	8.0	9.1	8.2	8.9	7.7	8.4	7.0	9.0
Bulgaria	4.0	3.9	3.8	3.4	4.1	3.7	3.7	3.6	4.0	3.8	3.4	3.0	3.4	2.6
Czechia	6.5	10.2	6.3	9.9	6.0	10.0	5.0	9.2	4.8	8.2	4.6	7.1	4.1	6.7
Denmark	5.8	8.2	9.0	13.0	8.1	11.0	6.7	9.8	7.0	9.8	6.8	10.7	7.1	10.8
Germany	10.2	11.5	10.3	11.5	10.2	11.2	10.2	10.8	9.7	10.2	8.9	9.3	9.0	9.4
Estonia	3.1	2.5	3.4	2.7	2.9	2.5	2.8	2.7	2.4	2.6	2.1	2.4	1.3	1.3
Ireland	6.4	7.7	5.7	7.4	6.0	7.5	6.5	8.4	6.2	8.2	5.7	7.6	6.3	7.6
Greece	7.0	9.3	6.4	9.1	6.2	9.9	6.0	10.2	7.0	11.2	5.7	9.0	5.3	9.3
Spain	19.7	21.9	20.3	22.9	20.5	24.0	20.7	24.2	20.2	23.8	18.0	22.5	18.2	24.1
France	11.4	13.7	11.6	13.5	11.8	14.0	11.5	13.8	11.2	13.0	10.1	12.4	10.7	13.2
Croatia	16.5	17.3	17.6	19.7	17.0	18.1	16.2	18.1	14.0	17.3	11.7	14.5	9.4	13.6
Italy	9.7	11.9	9.7	11.9	10.8	13.1	11.9	14.6	12.1	14.4	10.9	12.9	11.7	14.6
Cyprus	10.9	20.8	9.7	19.1	10.3	16.8	9.0	15.3	8.0	16.2	7.5	16.3	8.0	15.5
Latvia	3.2	2.3	3.2	2.4	2.6	1.9	2.2	2.0	2.7	2.0	2.2	2.1	2.7	1.9
Lithuania	2.0	1.6	1.7	1.5	1.6	1.1	1.3	1.1	1.1	1.0	1.0	0.9	1.6	1.6
Luxembourg	8.4	8.6	7.2	7.7	7.2	8.1	7.7	9.4	7.8	8.0	6.0	7.2	7.1	8.8
Hungary	9.9	9.5	8.0	8.6	7.1	8.0	5.7	6.7	5.2	6.1	4.5	5.5	4.7	5.5
Malta	5.0	7.8	5.0	7.7	4.0	6.3	5.7	7.4	6.0	9.1	4.7	8.8	5.0	8.2
Netherlands	19.3	24.4	19.5	24.6	20.0	25.2	19.4	24.8	18.6	23.4	17.0	21.5	17.3	21.8
Austria	6.0	6.2	5.9	6.6	6.6	6.9	6.4	7.0	6.0	6.7	5.5	6.0	5.4	6.2
Poland	21.6	23.6	21.0	23.4	19.7	22.6	18.0	21.3	15.7	19.5	13.2	16.5	10.7	12.9
Portugal	18.2	19.0	18.4	19.5	18.2	19.2	18.0	19.6	16.7	18.5	14.2	16.0	13.6	15.1
Romania	1.3	0.9	1.3	0.8	1.1	0.8	1.0	0.8	1.4	0.9	1.2	0.7	2.7	1.0
Slovenia	14.9	18.4	14.1	18.3	14.5	18.7	12.5	16.8	10.3	14.8	8.7	12.4	8.1	11.4
Slovakia	5.7	6.4	5.6	5.8	5.2	5.5	4.2	4.9	4.0	4.9	3.2	4.1	3.0	3.8
Finland	10.7	16.9	11.3	17.4	11.3	18.0	11.5	18.3	11.1	17.4	10.8	16.4	10.2	15.8

TIME	2015		2016		2017		2018		2019		2020		2021	
Sweden	11.7	15.1	11.4	14.7	11.2	14.6	10.9	14.4	10.7	14.1	10.2	13.7	9.8	13.6
Iceland	8.3	11.7	7.7	10.9	7.1	10.1	5.4	9.0	4.9	7.8	5.0	8.2	8.0	12.0
Norway	6.0	9.9	6.5	10.4	6.7	10.0	7.0	9.7	6.0	9.5	6.0	9.4	6.0	9.5
Switzerland	7.9	8.5	7.4	8.3	7.4	8.4	7.5	8.3	7.2	8.1	7.5	8.4	7.4	8.7
Montenegro	21.4	26.5	25.6	26.8	22.5	24.2	24.7	26.1	26.1	26.0	24.6	23.0	:	:
North Macedonia	9.8	8.8	10.8	9.4	11.1	9.9	12.2	10.5	13.7	12.3	15.7	13.0	:	:
Serbia	18.2	17.4	20.1	18.0	18.9	18.3	20.1	18.7	19.3	19.5	17.1	18.5	16.8	18.6
Türkiye	8.8	5.9	8.8	6.3	8.7	6.5	8.1	6.4	7.4	6.1	7.6	5.3	:	:

Note: (:) No data.
Source: Eurostat (2023a).

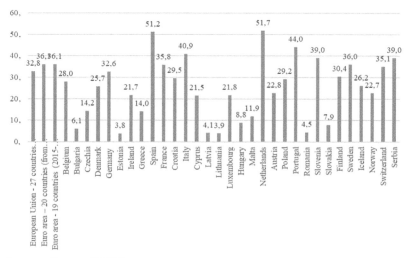

Source: Eurostat (2023a).

Figure 7.1   Temporary employment rate in Europe in young people (15–29 years of age)

The summer months also show an increase in temporary contracting, mainly arising from the type of work typical of summer months (closely related to tourism – hotel and catering, etc.) that fits into the nature of the permanent seasonal contract.

In summary, the reduction of temporary employment is one of the challenges facing the European labour market. This is even more the case in Spain,

Table 7.3 Number of temporary contracts in Spain 2022–23

| | 2022 | | 2023 | | ANNUAL VARIATION | | | |
| | | | | | MONTHLY DATA | | YEARLY DATA | |
	MONTHLY	ACCUMULATED	MONTHLY	ACCUMULATED	ABSOLUTE	RELATIVE	ABSOLUTE	RELATIVE
JANUARY	1,357,660	1,357,660	670,443	670,443	-687,217	-50.62	-687,217	-50.62
FEBRUARY	1,127,216	2,484,876	591,602	1,262,045	-535,614	-47.52	-1,222,831	-49.21
MARCH	1,158,164	3,643,040						
APRIL	751,447	4,394,487						
MAY	910,168	5,304,655						
JUNE	985,393	6,290,048						
JULY	969,523	7,259,571						
AUGUST	777,060	8,036,631						
SEPTEMBER	884,936	8,921,567						
OCTOBER	826,804	9,748,371						
NOVEMBER	809,047	10,557,418						
DECEMBER	725,765	11,283,183						

Source: Servicio Público de Empleo Estatal (SEPE, Public Service of State Employment (2023).

given its high temporary employment rate, in particular in young people and women, and especially in the former. The legislation approved in Spain in recent years aims at reducing this temporary employment, and in the light of results in the last months of 2022 and the first months of 2023 it seems to have been effective. Therefore, we examine the hypothesis that labour market reforms have led to an increase in permanent contracts to the detriment of temporary ones, as shown in Figure 7.2.

PLATFORM WORK

In the first year since the application of the 'Riders Act', the total number of workers in the delivery sector under an employment contract doubled, from 5,464 in May 2021 to 10,980 in August 2022. The new regulation has had a positive impact in terms of the introduction of employment contracts for riders. The improvement has also been clear in qualitative terms, as most new

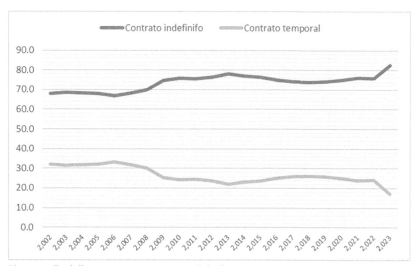

Note: Dark line: permanent contracts; light line: temporary contracts.
Source: In-house based on Active Population Survey issued by the National Statistics Institute.

Figure 7.2   *Evolution of permanent and temporary contracts in Spain (2002–23)*

workers are under permanent contracts. During the period in which the legislation has been in force permanent contracting has increased by 167 per cent, according to the Ministry of Employment. However, since the application of the regulation, only a few companies have contracted delivery staff as workers with permanent contracts, that is, subject to the rights that those workers have as a result of that contract modality. Other companies have got around the law by maintaining their riders as self-employed after modifying their conditions and implementing models to avoid the presumption of an employment relationship.

This problem has not been exclusive to Spain; the European Commission presented a draft directive in 2021 that aimed to end the false provision of services by self-employed people to large platforms. The draft includes five criteria, and if two of these are met, it is necessary to recognise an employment relationship. The five criteria included in the Directive are: (1) effectively determining or setting upper limits for the level of remuneration; (2) requiring the person performing platform work to respect specific binding rules with regard to appearance, conduct towards the recipient of the service or performance of the work; (3) supervising the performance of work or verifying the quality of the results of the work including by electronic means, including by electronic means; (4) effectively restricting the freedom, including through sanctions, to organise one's work, in particular the discretion to choose one's working hours or periods of absence, to accept or to refuse tasks or to use subcontractors or substitutes; and (5) effectively restricting the possibility to build a client base or to perform work for any third party. Companies may refute the presumption of an employment contract, but they – not the employee – will have to demonstrate that such an employment relationship does not exist.

Both European and Spanish legislation improves the working conditions of workers in these platforms, as once their situation has been regularised, they will have the basic rights involved in a contractual relationship, such as a minimum wage, the right to representation by trade unions and collective bargaining, the regulation of working hours and healthcare, paid holidays, protection if they suffer an accident at work, unemployment or sickness benefits and a contribution towards a contributory pension for retirement.

While it is true that a causal relationship cannot be established between the socioeconomic crisis produced by the pandemic and the regulation of this sector, the two phenomena are not disassociated from each other. Workers on these platforms were considered essential in the first (and strictest) phase of confinement, which was when their working conditions became more visible in general. As a result of complaints about what was clearly an employment contract, paradoxically outside labour regulation, the institutions were urged to increase the protection of this group through legal reforms.

WORKING MODALITIES: TELEWORKING

As for teleworking, our starting hypothesis is based on the fact that the number of people teleworking in Spain fell after the period of confinement. This was the result, on the one hand, of a regulatory framework that did not clearly define the conditions for teleworking, and on the other, due to historical misgivings of middle managers and supervisors about this way of working, based on a deep-rooted approach in Spain to seeing an employment relationship as a conflictive one. This idea is not so much the case in private companies, but it is deeply rooted in the Administration. This is why teleworking has been reduced considerably in all the areas of the Administration.

We should point out once more that the pandemic gave rise to a boom in teleworking (Belzunegui-Eraso & Erro-Garcés, 2020). Specifically, the percentage of workers in Europe rose from 5.5 per cent in 2019 to 12.2 per cent in 2020 at the harshest time of the pandemic, and to 13.6 per cent in 2021. Teleworking, according to these authors, facilitated the continuity of business activity during confinement, as well as the provision of services by the Administration (e.g., education, healthcare, etc.). These reasons explain the increase in the percentage of teleworkers based on the pandemic.

It is also important to note that teleworking during the confinement period shows certain characteristics, as it was implemented without specific legislation, although several European countries (including Spain) approved measures to regulate the situation. In the specific case of Spain, legislation was enacted that specified conditions for teleworking during the pandemic and other conditions after this period (Royal Decree-Act 28/2020 of 22 September, on remote working, which later became Act 10/2021 of 9 July on remote working). In this respect, employment contracts were not modified during the pandemic despite the implementation of teleworking. Later, a large part of the negotiation of working conditions for teleworking was left to collective bargaining, following the guidelines set out in the European Framework Agreement on teleworking, which, as mentioned above, was not binding on the parties but did establish some minimum recommendations for consensus-based functioning.

Table 7.4 shows the evolution of teleworking from before the pandemic to 2021. The figures confirm the boom of teleworking in 2020 as a result of confinement and later restrictions on mobility, which were maintained for about a year. As stated previously, these figures reflect a very particular experience of teleworking, given the need to combine work at home with looking after children because schools were closed. Moreover, the implementation of teleworking at the time took place without previous planning, and the workers provided the necessary technical means themselves. In any case, the implementation of teleworking in the pandemic showed that many jobs could be done – at least partially – remotely. It also showed that the technology was sufficiently developed to spread this working modality.

After the hardest phase of the pandemic, teleworking fell away in some countries (e.g., Spain), although it increased generally in relation to the situation prior to the pandemic (Table 7.4).

As regards our hypothesis, focusing on the rejection of teleworking by middle managers and supervisors, various authors cite reasons outside the legislation to explain the reduction in the percentage of teleworkers in some countries, among them the case of Spain. Specifically, the need to adapt organisational culture to these changes, misgivings among middle managers about the loss of power through the reduced physical presence of workers, or the need to adapt the hierarchical structure and the way of managing were some of the obstacles in the way of the development of teleworking (e.g., López Peláez et al., 2021). In other words, not only did the deficiencies in the legislation prevent a wider extension of teleworking, but organisational factors explain, to a certain extent, why this working modality was held back. This agrees with studies made on resistance to teleworking: most of them observe mistrust as the reason for rejection, and this is more prevalent in countries where a conflictive vision of labour relations has prevailed over a more consensus-based one. This is the case of Mediterranean countries in which labour relations come within this more conflictive vision and in which tripartite negotiation is relatively recent when it comes to accommodating different interests in productive sectors. There seems to be a relationship between greater participation of workers in business decisions (as in the case of Germany, a clear example of a consensus-based approach and a higher level of teleworking maintained in comparison with countries in which labour relations are based on the idea of a struggle between powers and not on cooperation (e.g. Spain or Italy)).

There is also evidence that most workers were satisfied with this way of working, which facilitates a work-life balance and improves flexibility. According to data from Eurofound (2020), most teleworkers prefer to continue working remotely, combining it with presence-based work (hybrid mode). This poses major challenges that have to do with other areas of people's lives, for example, work-life balance and, basically, satisfaction at work as a driver of productivity.

In conclusion, we can partially accept the hypothesis of a greater presence of teleworking and, at the same time, a reduction if we take the most intense moments of the pandemic as a reference. It has increased if we compare it with levels prior to Covid-19, although since the pandemic abated, its presence has not been so strong. Furthermore, this is not only due to restrictions in the legislative framework; there have also been reasons of an organisational nature, despite the positive perception by workers of the experience of working remotely.

Table 7.4   Teleworking in Europe

TIME	2010	2011	2012	2013	2014	2015	2016	2017	2018	2019	2020	2021
European Union - 27 countries (from 2020)	5.1	5.5	5.6	4.9	4.9	4.9	4.8	5.2	5.3	5.5	12.2	13.6
Belgium	9.8	10.0	9.3	8.9	8.7	8.2	7.2	6.9	6.6	7.0	17.3	26.4
Bulgaria	0.4	0.6	0.5	0.5	0.4	0.3	0.2	0.3	0.3	0.5	1.2	2.8
Czechia	3.2	3.2	3.4	3.3	3.4	3.5	3.9	3.9	4.0	4.6	7.3	7.2
Denmark	11.5	12.6	12.3	11.5	10.3	9.4	8.7	9.2	8.2	8.1	17.7	18.9
Germany	3.3	3.7	3.6	3.4	3.3	3.3	3.3	4.9	5.1	5.3	13.8	17.3
Estonia	4.8	4.9	5.7	6.2	5.5	5.5	5.8	5.8	7.4	6.7	12.3	15.1
Ireland	7.1	7.0	4.9	4.1	3.6	3.8	3.4	5.0	6.6	7.1	21.9	33.0
Greece	1.9	2.1	2.2	2.2	2.7	2.6	2.6	2.3	2.1	1.9	7.0	6.7
Spain	3.8	4.0	4.4	4.3	4.3	3.6	3.5	4.3	4.3	4.8	11.0	9.6
France	11.1	11.4	11.7	7.4	6.9	7.1	7.0	6.8	6.7	7.1	16.0	17.3
Croatia	0.9	1.0	0.9	1.0	1.4	1.3	1.4	1.5	1.4	1.9	3.1	4.7
Italy	3.1	3.0	3.3	3.1	3.2	3.4	3.3	3.5	3.6	3.6	12.3	8.3
Cyprus	1.0	0.9	1.1	1.6	1.7	1.5	1.6	1.2	1.2	1.3	4.5	6.7
Latvia	2.8	2.1	2.0	2.1	2.4	2.1	2.6	2.2	2.9	3.0	4.5	11.0
Lithuania	3.5	3.4	4.0	3.9	4.1	3.0	2.8	2.6	2.5	2.4	5.4	9.2
Luxembourg	12.4	12.1	11.5	12.5	14.2	13.1	12.0	12.7	11.1	11.5	23.2	28.4
Hungary	2.3	2.8	3.1	3.9	3.4	3.4	3.0	2.5	2.3	1.2	3.6	4.6
Malta	1.7	1.7	1.8	2.3	2.7	2.7	3.7	4.5	5.9	6.2	15.0	15.1
Netherlands	11.5	11.8	12.1	13.2	13.8	14.3	14.2	14.6	14.9	15.0	18.9	24.0
Austria	10.7	11.1	10.7	10.7	11.0	10.5	10.2	9.7	10.2	10.2	18.5	16.2
Poland	4.5	4.7	4.6	4.0	4.6	5.6	5.4	4.5	4.6	4.6	8.9	6.9
Portugal	0.9	5.6	6.3	6.8	6.6	6.2	6.3	5.9	6.1	6.6	14.0	14.5
Romania	0.2	0.5	0.4	0.3	0.4	0.5	0.5	0.4	0.4	0.8	2.6	2.4
Slovenia	6.8	6.7	6.6	7.1	7.6	8.0	7.5	7.2	7.0	6.9	7.5	10.6
Slovakia	3.1	3.6	3.5	3.5	3.6	3.2	3.3	3.5	3.6	3.7	5.7	6.6
Finland	9.4	10.0	10.0	10.9	10.8	12.3	12.2	12.6	13.7	14.5	25.9	25.5
Sweden	4.3	4.4	4.6	4.9	5.0	5.2	5.1	5.1	5.4	6.1	:	27.7
Iceland	9.2	8.9	7.6	7.8	7.5	8.2	8.0	7.6	6.8	5.9	9.1	:
Norway	4.7	4.4	4.8	5.4	4.6	4.3	5.0	5.2	5.7	5.1	4.8	17.1
Switzerland	4.2	4.2	4.1	4.1	4.2	4.4	4.5	4.2	4.3	4.1	5.1	16.6
United Kingdom	3.0	3.6	3.6	3.5	3.8	3.9	4.2	4.1	4.5	4.8	:	:

TIME	2010	2011	2012	2013	2014	2015	2016	2017	2018	2019	2020	2021
Montenegro	:	4.7	5.9	4.4	5.9	8.3	7.5	8.1	6.4	5.8	7.5	:
Serbia	5.2	6.4	6.8	6.5	5.6	4.2	3.8	3.1	3.3	4.9	7.2	5.0
Türkiye	2.4	2.0	1.3	1.6	1.9	1.9	1.9	2.2	2.3	2.2	3.1	:

Note: (:) No data.
Source: Eurostat (2023b).

CONCLUSION: CHANGES IN THE WORKPLACE AND SOCIAL DIALOGUE

The response to the Covid-19 crisis has highlighted the need for collaboration as a basis for solving the problems our societies are facing. In the field of labour relations in Spain, the Covid-19 crisis has been seen as an opportunity to relaunch social dialogue on several aspects, among them the maintenance of jobs and secure income for workers. The Spanish case is a good example of an attempt to overcome a conflict-based conception of labour relations to adopt a more consensus-based approach. However, this has not occurred without problems that continue to affect day-to-day negotiations. No model has been replaced, although it can be said that Spain is currently in a hybrid model phase between conflict-based and consensus-based approaches. There are political and economic factors that will mark the agenda in the coming years and will tip the Spanish model in one direction or the other. We will have to see how events play out first, however.

The tripartite model in Spain has benefited from new leadership and the drive of the government after years in which disagreements between workers' representatives and employer stakeholders have been the norm. The social agreements reached have shown the ability of social dialogue to solve problematic situations that affect citizens in general. This does not mean that there have been no disagreements and differences of opinions and postures among the three main players in the Spanish corporatist model, although it has been possible to reach consensus with the well-being of the population in mind through concertation. The corporatist model, based on agreement and consensus, does not exclude social conflict or take social issues out of the debate, although the scenario of the pandemic introduced another element which, from our point of view, strengthens the attempts made to reach consensus. This new element is the role that the EU needs to play at times (and in situations) of systemic crisis. The social stakeholders have probably been the first to understand the need to provide a joint and supportive response to the socioeconomic crisis that threatened to carry everything before it. Unilateral solutions would have been disastrous for the economy in which companies and workers participate. This is where we can consider that the pandemic may have functioned as a stimulus for European social cohesion. The relevant question now is whether the social construction of Europe (the social agenda referred to by Belzunegui-Eraso & Moreno-Fernández, 2020) can only be carried out in stressful situations for the Member States (e.g., the crisis we lived through) or if it is worthwhile going for a model that combines both social and other aspects in which clear successes have been seen (e.g., caring for the environment). Labour relations should be part of that social agenda that will harmonise social policies to ensure good living standards for European citizens in the face of contingencies and catastrophes (which seem to be recurrent, at least at the level of climate).

If the recent economic crisis (2008–15) was a setback for progress in common policies in the EU, a period in which the lack of solidarity of certain countries towards others was evident, the recent socioeconomic crisis has had a different impact in terms of joint response by the EU, and also a greater awareness of the vulnerability of the European system in international geopolitics. In this greater awareness, we believe that the social stakeholders have shown themselves to be above the interests of political stakeholders. As a result, social dialogue has emerged stronger at the European level.

Social dialogue during the pandemic highlighted the need for the social stakeholders to have sufficient muscle in terms of representing the people whose interests they promote. Policies that propitiate the weakening of social stakeholders in favour of economic regulation based on the invisible hand of the market have undesirable consequences when a commitment is required of the people represented. In contrast, giving a voice to social stakeholders and strengthening them as sources of legitimate representation helps pool efforts that can be essential in cohesive societies.

Furthermore, this idea of pooling a response to a crisis has also been taken on board by the EU when it comes to addressing the consequences of a crisis. Without this response, we would surely be speaking of a more chaotic situation, one in which 'every man for himself' would have prevailed at the national level.

The mechanisms adopted in social dialogue in Spain, and also by the government, have been effective in dealing with the economic crisis created by the pandemic. The guarantees offered to safeguard jobs and the income of workers have been the objectives on which this social dialogue has been based. This has also benefited thousands of small, medium and large companies because it has enabled them to get through the downtime suffered as a result of lack of production.

The health crisis and its impact on the labour market has also served to make certain rules more flexible, among them guarantees to certain groups who had found themselves in a situation of great vulnerability in labour and social terms. An example is the situation of young people of foreign origin between 18 and 21 years of age. They were quickly granted residence and work permits for two years, renewable for another two, that are valid for the whole of Spanish territory, with no restrictions on occupations or sectors of activity.

In other words, an analysis of the situation of diverse groups in the labour market following the Covid-19 crisis has served to improve certain aspects of their living conditions. This is the basic tool of social dialogue, or expressed another way, the fundamental usefulness of social dialogue. Without fear of contradiction, we can affirm that during this period in Spain's recent history the social stakeholders have given us an example of how agreement and consensus can be reached despite their differences, and how these agreements benefit society in general.

REFERENCES

Beane, M.I., & Leonardi, P.M. (2022). Pace layering as a metaphor for organizing in the age of intelligent technologies: Considering the future of work by theorizing the future of organizing. *Journal of Management Studies*. https://doi.org/10.1111/joms.12867.

Belzunegui-Eraso, A., & Erro-Garcés, A. (2020). Teleworking in the context of the Covid-19 crisis. *Sustainability*, 12(9): 3662.

Belzunegui-Eraso, A., & Moreno-Fernández, L. (2020). *La Agenda Social Europea. Cohesión social y lucha contra las desigualdades en Europa*. Pamplona: Thomson Reuters Aranzadi.

Busemeyer, M., & Kemmerling, A. (2020). Dualization, stratification, liberalization, or what? An attempt to clarify the conceptual underpinnings of the dualization debate. *Political Science Research and Methods*, 8(2): 375–9.

Delgado, J.L.G., Sánchez, R.M., Sueiras, J.C., Torres, A.G., Jiménez, J.C., Alonso, J.A., & Morales, J.M.L. (2020). *Lecciones de economía española*. Pamplona: Thomson Reuters Aranzadi.

European Commission. (2021). *Study to support the impact assessment of an EU initiative to improve the working conditions in platform work. Final Report*. Luxembourg: Publications Office of the European Union.

Eurofound. (2018). *Employment and working conditions of selected types of platform work*. Luxembourg: Publications Office of the European Union.

Eurofound. (2020). *New forms of employment: 2020 update*. Luxembourg: Publications Office of the European Union.

Eurostat (2023a). Temporary employees as percentage of the total number of employees. https://ec.europa.eu/eurostat/databrowser/view/tesem110/default/table?lang=en (accessed 6 March 2023).

Eurostat (2023b). Employed persons working from home as a percentage of the total employment, by sex, age and professional status. https://ec.europa.eu/eurostat/databrowser/view/LFSA_EHOMP__custom_4659348/default/table?lang=en (accessed 6 March 2023).

Gerards, R., De Grip, A., & Baudewijns, C. (2018). Do new ways of working increase work engagement? *Personnel Review*, 47(2): 517–34.

Guerrero, E., & Fernández, A. (2022). The impact of new forms of self-employment on employment law. *E-Journal of International and Comparative Labour Studies*, Joint Issue (Vol. 10 No. 03/2021 and Vol. 11 No. 01/2022): 1–23.

Kelliher, C., & Richardson, J. (2012). Recent development in new ways of organizing work. In C. Kelliher & J. Richardson (Eds.), *New ways of organizing work: Developments, perspectives and experiences* (pp. 1–15). London: Routledge.

López Peláez, A., Erro-Garcés, A., Pinilla García, F.J., & Kiriakou, D. (2021). Working in the 21st century. The coronavirus crisis: A driver of digitalisation, teleworking, and innovation, with unintended social consequences. *Information*, 12(9): 377.

Peters, P., Poutsma, E., Van Der Heijden, B.I.J.M., Bakker, A.B., & Bruijn, T.D. (2014). Enjoying new ways to work: An HRM-process approach to study flow. *Human Resource Management*, 53(2): 271–90.

Servicio Público de Empleo Estatal, SEPE. (2023). Número de empleos temporales en España. https:// sepe .es/ HomeSepe/ que -es -el -sepe/ estadisticas/ datos -avance/ contratos.html (accessed 6 March 2023).

Simoni, M., & Vlandas, T. (2021). Labour market liberalization and the rise of dualism in Europe as the interplay between governments, trade unions and the economy. *Social Policy & Administration*, 55(4): 637–58.

Vlandas, T. (2020). The political consequences of labor market dualization: Labor market status, occupational unemployment and policy preferences. *Political Science Research and Methods*, 82: 362–8.

PART III

Working and communication in the virtual workplace

8. Workplace communication in the age of virtual flexibility

Nadia K. Kougiannou and Peter Holland

INTRODUCTION

With the pandemic arguably accelerating the development of hybrid and remote work, this has revitalised the debate around flexible work patterns. With the widespread adoption of smart technology, employees are no longer confined (nor indeed want to be) to a physical workspace and it is now possible (for those whose work allows it) to be able to work from any location with an internet connection. The continuing redefinition of the workplace in terms of place and space (Grant et al., 2023; Wheatley et al., 2021) has enabled employees at least potentially to have more control over their schedules and work-life balance, which may positively impact their working lives. However, the shift to remote work may also have unintended consequences on communication structures within organisations. With the decentralisation of the workforce, it may be more difficult for employees to interact effectively with each other and management, leading to fragmentation and potentially a breakdown in systems such as the voice mechanisms. In addition, the lack of face-to-face interaction may make it more challenging for employees to build relationships and trust with their colleagues and superiors, which are crucial elements of an effective voice and working relationships (Holland & Kougiannou, 2021; Kougiannou & Holland, 2022). These points illustrate the significant and critical role that employee voice plays in the workplace. As noted by Pyman et al. (2010), employee voice serves as a means for workers to voice their concerns, influence decision-making processes and express their opinions. For employers, it provides a platform for two-way communication with the workforce, enabling management to gather valuable information and gauge employees' reactions on various issues. Thus, voice is critical in facilitating (quality) information transfer and building trust within the workplace (Tzafrir, 2005). In other words it builds the fabric of the workplace.

As such, the intersection and consequences of these new patterns of flexible work on employee voice is an emerging issue that needs to be addressed

(Wheatley et al., 2021). Indeed, voice may be the bulwark to the worst excesses of work intensification under these new work patterns that have emerged in research post-pandemic (Grant et al., 2023). This chapter explores the relationship between flexible work patterns on employee voice to examine potential outcomes for both employees and organisations in this 'new normal' workplace of the post-pandemic era. The chapter delves into several emerging issues and the consequences of unchecked or unchallenged flexible work on employee voice.

VOICE IN THE NEW NORMAL

The COVID-19 pandemic has accelerated the adoption of digital and social media platforms for work and communication (Sanders et al., 2020). However, limited literature exists on the specific voice mechanisms employees adopt during uncertain events, with the exception of a few studies (Martin et al., 2015; Zeitoun & Pamini, 2021). For example, while the study by Zeitoun and Pamini (2021) highlights the importance of unions in supporting employee voice during a recession, Martin and colleagues (2015) found reduced use of social media for constructive voice during an external financial crisis. Some research suggests that employees may choose to remain silent during external crises due to a feeling of helplessness (Prouska & Psychogios, 2018, 2019), while others explore measures to promote a prosocial or constructive voice (Kim & Lim, 2020).

These new flexible ways of working can also be viewed as fragmenting an increasingly virtual and isolated workforce, thereby distorting the entire system. Our concerns also revolve around the possibility of a more unitarist voice system emerging in this virtual environment to fill the void. A typical example of this we have found is the CEO/senior management-led virtual forums that provide opportunities to post questions, allowing management to set and lead the agenda while also operating and filtering the questions they respond to in these virtual forums. A second issue is the emergence of virtual or online management culture surveys, which again enable management to filter information before disseminating it, further distorting information flows between management and the workforce. In other words a constructed silence of the workforce.

We argue that the pandemic, while ushering in a new paradigm of work, could usher in a new approach to voice. However, despite the favourable workplace ecology of moving work and the workplace online, little has been done or spoken about in developing employee voice at a similar rate or style, which appears to be a significant paradox in developing the virtual workplace. We argue that such an approach to work needs to be reflected in the voice systems. Such systems can be enhanced by using the speed and quality of the virtual workplace to increase efficient and effective two-way decision-making and, we suggest, facilitate the development of a more democratic workplace by giving everyone an immediate voice in workplace issues.

We find this situation paradoxical because in this volatile, uncertain, complex and ambiguous (VUCA) environment, the ability is now at employee and employer fingertips to respond in real-time to issues to enhance workplace information flows and decision-making processes and from this employee engagement, which has never been so important (Boxall & Purcell, 2016; Mowbray et al., 2022). The key here might be to draw attention to what Martin and his colleagues (2015) point to as authentic management support requiring a real-time response, which can mean management dealing with issues that they may not want to in real-time (Miles & Mangold, 2014). However, we argue that this goes to the heart of effective management.

THE DARKER SIDE OF THE NEW WORKPLACE

Although working from home may have been mandated because of the pandemic, as we have intimated, its legacy could be the disruption of key workplace mechanisms such as voice. With the significant shift to remote and hybrid working arrangements traditional employee voice structures, such as in-person meetings, 'town hall' sessions, and face-to-face conversations, but more so collective voice arrangements can decline. In remote working, typical messaging channels are individualised to email, instant messaging and video conferencing. While these channels allow employees to express their opinions, they may not always be as effective as in-person or physical group interactions. Conveniently for some management, this disruption could negate information and issues they may not want to deal with (Miles & Mangold, 2014). We refer to this as 'structural silence', where management can appear to hide behind legitimate variations in work patterns and practices to either allow a deaf-ear approach to voice (Pinder & Harlos, 2001) or fill the vacuum with management-led voice through senior management initiatives such as virtual forums.

The shift to remote and hybrid working also presents several challenges for maintaining equitable employee voice structures. One of the primary challenges is ensuring that all employees have equal opportunities to express their opinions. Remote working may lead to inequalities, such as employees who are not as technologically proficient, those who may not have access to the necessary equipment to participate fully, or simply being uncomfortable about voicing their opinion directly to management. Employers must ensure all employees have equal opportunities to participate in information and communication technology (ICT)-based employee voice structures, and have confidence in doing so in these forums. Another challenge is ensuring that remote and hybrid working does not result in a lack of transparency or accountability. Employers must ensure that all employees are aware of the decisions that are being made and how their feedback is being incorporated. In hybrid working, it is important to ensure that employees who work remotely are not left out of meaningful conversations and decision-making processes. Maintaining a sense of community and connection among employees is also critical for effective employee voice structures. Employers must find ways to foster a sense of belonging and engagement, even in a remote or hybrid working environment. This can include virtual team-building activities, social events and regular check-ins with employees or simply in-person meeting on major issues with virtual options. For management this means a significant and ongoing (resource) investment in these virtual and hybrid systems.

SOCIAL MEDIA AND VOICE

As the pandemic has shown, the utilisation of technology and digital media has emerged as a critical aspect of work (Foss, 2021; Soto-Acosta, 2020). With its ease of use and ability to offer instant access to information and geographically dispersed individuals, social media (SM) has attracted more than four billion users, making it a valuable component of an organisation's communication system (Chen & Wei, 2020). The surge in remote work due to the pandemic has been a catalyst for further adoption of SM and other ICT applications as organisations accelerate the adoption of the digital workplace (Foss, 2021; Kamal, 2020).

We argue that SM also holds the potential for enriching employee voice, which is increasingly recognised as essential for enhancing individual and organisational outcomes (Bashshur & Oc, 2015; Burris et al., 2013). Despite this, the extent to which SM facilitates employee voice is still understudied (Holland et al., 2019a). Furthermore, most research has approached the subject from an information systems (IS) perspective and has focused on top-down communication or voice only in the form of reporting problems. As such it is worthwhile investigating how SM can serve as a more flexible voice in a more flexible work environment rather than simply a vehicle for top-down communication, even if it was not intentionally designed or implemented for that purpose. This inquiry is particularly significant post-pandemic, where the work landscape is changing for voice and can be limited or denied (Khan et al., 2023).

So, what is the benchmark for developing voice in light of emerging work patterns? We argue, firstly, that voice is more critical than ever as a two-way communication mechanism between management and employees in the emerging dynamic environment. Therefore, virtual networks can provide the infrastructure to facilitate the development of a contemporary hybrid voice system compatible with the new dynamic workplace. Prior to the pandemic, organisations such as HP and IBM had developed internal virtual voice systems, where voice became a real-time communication arrangement. Such systems allow for immediate feedback from the workforce, enabling management to deal with issues as they arise and gauge the workforce's views while also allowing for issues to be refined and (bubble) sorted from the most to least pressing.

The literature on employee voice highlights the significance of perceived psychological safety when expressing voice (Gruman & Saks, 2020). An organisational climate that encourages and supports voice and voice/communication mechanisms that offer privacy and anonymity can provide psychological safety (Khan et al., 2023) in contrast to the argument that digital media reduces employees' perceived safety to express challenging voice (Knoll et al., 2022). Anonymity can promote voice on sensitive topics (e.g., personal concerns or dissenting ideas/opinions) that employees might otherwise hesitate to express. Although employees may not always prefer anonymity, research demonstrates that anonymity can increase whistleblowing (Holland, 2018). For example, the likelihood of reporting fraudulent behaviour (Johansson & Carey, 2016) is increased in a voice culture, particularly concerning challenging voice.

In social media, discussions held in virtual town halls and meetings on platforms like MS Teams are stored and retrievable (if recorded), enabling employees to view issues discussed and how the recipients of voice responded (Khan et al., 2023). The voice literature suggests that employee voice is influenced by others' voice outcomes and how targets respond to voice (Carnevale et al., 2020; Liu et al., 2023). The archived discussions, created, may allow employees to evaluate their safety to give voice based on previous voice outcomes related to collective and individual interests (e.g., salaries and working conditions), criticism or challenging voice (Khan et al., 2023). In addition, organisations can archive posts where employees have engaged in debates or brainstorming sessions in the form of frequently asked questions (FAQs), communities or repositories of information (Treem et al., 2020). These archived discussions can refine future suggestions and concerns and encourage others to contribute ideas or solutions to issues raised, facilitating constructive voice. Additionally, the persistence of information can create a sense of accountability for voice targets because the recordings of meetings and discussions on SM platforms are accessible to others (Khan et al., 2023). When concerns or grievances are voiced on these platforms, voice targets can be held accountable for their responses, enabling employees to evaluate the effectiveness of SM voice-based platforms (Miles & Mangold, 2014).

In contemporary work environments, virtual voice and SM have provided employees with alternative ways of organising and expressing their concerns and opinions, particularly in the absence of traditional unions. This development necessitates a reconsideration of the concept of organised and collective voice in the context of digital technology. By leveraging SM platforms, employees can expand their audience and potentially garner greater collective support to capture management's attention. Bhuiyan (2019) and Palmer (2020) argue that using SM can allow geographically dispersed employees to mobilise a collective voice, associate with peers who share similar issues, and develop support for their concerns. Several recent studies attest to this use.

Walker's (2021) study on Australian Uber drivers reveals that participation in forum discussions on ICT/SM enabled gig workers to build solidarity and develop a shared understanding of concerns and possible actions. Facebook Groups and WhatsApp have become important platforms for lateral voice because they are beyond the purview of management and easy to use. In their study on Indian platform-based ride-share drivers, Parth et al. (2023) demonstrate how these drivers leveraged Facebook Groups and WhatsApp to organise collective action, including sharing technical loopholes and workarounds and staging protests to defend their rights. Kougiannou and Mendonça (2021) investigate the managerial silencing of workers' voice in platform capitalism. However, workers have developed alternative modes of communication, such as Facebook Groups and WhatsApp, and have organised to contest this silencing. By utilising qualitative data from interviews with food couriers and online communication analysis, the authors analyse the emergence of a worker-led network that challenges dominant managerial discourse and promotes collective action. Li's (2022) recent study demonstrated how online platforms provided temporary migrant workers with the means to access information and each other to protect themselves from exploitation. These online interactions served as a form of resistance, whereby workers warned each other (and potential future workers) of exploitative employers and practices. These examples illustrate how SM can enable employees to reach out to others and express dissent, which can then be expressed vertically to exert influence.

Of course, some management teams may read this with significant concerns, likely reflecting a focus on controlling and minimising employee input to the work systems. In addition, continued resource allocation is necessary not only to set up such systems but also ensure that people are educated on how it works, and most of all, there must be trust in managing it. Nothing will negate such a system as much as a perception of democracy being undermined by management focused on controlling and manipulating 'the message' in terms of the issues they deem fit for the agenda they are trying to set. For example, managers may force employees to change or delete dissenting content posted on organisational sites, fearing that such voice on online platforms challenges their authority (Stumpf & Süß, 2022).

The utilisation of SM platforms by employees presents an opportunity for their voices to be made more visible and accessible to others, thereby increasing their ability to express their views. However, although these features allow employees to express themselves, they can also result in important matters being ignored or silenced. This is particularly evident in cases with high visibility of messages and low anonymity, such as MS Teams and Yammer. In such situations, the fear of social sanctions when expressing opinions that counter those held by the majority (or management) can discourage minority voices, leading to their suppression (Khan et al., 2023).

Furthermore, research shows that employees often present overly cautious or edited opinions/ideas on SM platforms rather than engaging in substantive discussions of issues (Gode et al., 2019). Although having the ability to edit content may seem beneficial for enhancing your image or refining your message, it may also restrict the expression of ideas or issues that are important to employees. As a result, while the ability to edit or be visible may assist with diverse communication needs, their inherent nature and lack of additional supportive features (such as anonymity) can create obstacles to expression, especially when it conflicts with the prevailing viewpoint.

STRUCTURING VOICE OR STRUCTURED SILENCE

The consequence of creating or allowing a vacuum in voice to emerge due to the changing nature of work to the virtual or working from home hybrid environment is that while the traditional systems may be maintained, they have the potential to whither as structural voice systems become structured silence. This adds to our argument that the void needs to be filled by a SM-style voice. However, in the initial period post-pandemic, we increasingly see a management-led voice – with associated chat boards in which management appears to engage with the workforce but, by managing the chat board we argue, they are, in fact, manipulating the system. This leads to another form of structured silence. Managerial-driven or structured employee silence refers to situations where employees do not speak up or share their opinions, suggestions or concerns due to a lack of psychological safety or fear of negative repercussions or simply a feeling they are not being listened to. In hybrid and remote working arrangements, employees may feel less connected to their colleagues and managers, leading to a lack of trust and a reluctance to speak up. One reason for this is the decreased frequency of face-to-face interactions, which can create a lack of emotional connection between managers and employees. Additionally, remote and hybrid working can make it difficult for employees to gauge the emotional responses of their colleagues and managers, making it challenging to interpret the intent behind their actions.

Furthermore, hybrid and remote working may also lead to increased managerial-driven employee silence due to the use of monitoring tools. Organisations are increasingly using these tools to monitor employee activity (see the Chapter 9 in this volume), both in the office and when working remotely. These tools can track everything from keystrokes and mouse movements to website and application usage and of course conversation between employees online. While these tools are used for detecting productivity issues and identifying areas for improvement, they can also create a sense of surveillance among employees. The use of monitoring tools can make employees feel like they are constantly being watched, undermining trust and making them hesitant to share their opinions or express dissenting views. Employees may feel that their actions are being scrutinised and that any deviation from the norm could lead to negative consequences. As a result, employees may be less likely to speak up in meetings or share their thoughts with their colleagues, which can harm team dynamics and ironically overall productivity, thus undermining the very purpose for which much monitoring and surveillance is developed.

Additionally, monitoring tools can reinforce a power hierarchy between managers and subordinates, granting managers greater authority over shared information and expressed viewpoints. Consequently, a milieu may be created in which employees are pressured to conform to their managers' beliefs rather than voicing their individualist perspectives. This circumstance can stifle ingenuity and innovation since employees may avoid proposing fresh ideas or approaches for fear of contradicting their superiors' expectations. Additionally, this conformity-oriented culture can lead to an absence of diversity in concepts and approaches. When employees sense that their opinions and views are not highly valued, they may be less inclined to express themselves (employee silence), resulting in a limited scope of ideas being considered. Ultimately, this can curtail the organisation's potential for growth and development, as well as impede the organisation's capacity to react to changes in circumstances or capitalise on emerging opportunities.

IMPLICATIONS FOR EMPLOYEES, TRADE UNIONS AND MANAGEMENT

Through an examination of the literature, it becomes clear that the relationship between employees, trade unions, management and ICTs is socially mediated and dialectical (Geelan, 2021). Individuals within society develop and produce technologies, and their use can potentially enable, constrain or influence human activities in unpredictable ways (Geelan, 2021). Thus, the impact of technology on society, and consequently work and voice, cannot be definitively determined but is marked by multiple conflicting effects (Kougiannou

& Mendonça, 2021). While the internet, SM and artificial intelligence have the potential to be used for exploitation, control and surveillance, they can also be used as tools for empowerment and resistance (Fuchs, 2020; Mendonça & Kougiannou, 2023). The shift to virtual and hybrid workplaces and digital communication tools is changing the way employees interact with their colleagues and managers. While this has increased the potential for employee voice, it has also created new challenges for ensuring that all employees have an equal opportunity to be heard and that their views are considered. This is a challenge for management.

Effective communication and trust-building between employees and management in a virtual or hybrid workplace present further difficulties. The nature of these workplaces may provide fewer opportunities for informal communication and less face-to-face interaction, resulting in a limited ability to build relationships based on trust. This makes it harder for employees to raise concerns and for management to address them effectively. Trust is a vital element in any workplace, especially in virtual and hybrid workplaces where communication is largely mediated by technology. In such workplaces, employees may feel a sense of detachment from the organisation, leading to a lack of commitment and motivation and consider leaving in an environment with significant skill scarcity post-pandemic. Without effective communication channels, employees may be unable to discuss their concerns with management, and management may not be able to provide the necessary support to employees (Kougiannou et al., 2015). The lack of trust can result in increased conflict and tension in the workplace (Kougiannou et al., 2022), leading to decreased productivity and job satisfaction.

To address this challenge, it is crucial to establish employee voice channels that facilitate regular interactions between management and employees. These channels should enable open dialogue, active listening and feedback mechanisms that allow employees to express their opinions and concerns. Management should ensure that employees are aware of these channels and encouraged to use them. Additionally, virtual team-building activities and regular video meetings can help create a sense of community and belonging, fostering trust and effective communication between employees and management.

The use of digital tools for voice and communication in virtual and hybrid workplaces can also pose a significant challenge. For instance, discussion boards or chat rooms may seem to be a means for employees to voice their opinions, but management may be able to manage and manipulate these platforms. This can create a perception of a lack of authenticity and credibility, undermining trust between employees and management. Moreover, using digital tools may require additional training and support for employees to use them effectively. This can be a resource issue for organisations, especially those with limited resources. As a result, employees may be unable to utilise these tools effectively, leading to ineffective communication and misunderstandings. Furthermore, the use of digital tools can also create issues related to information security and data privacy. As more organisations shift to virtual and hybrid workplaces, there is an increased risk of cyber-attacks and data breaches. This can result in the loss of sensitive information and undermine employee trust in the organisation's ability to protect their personal data.

The virtual and hybrid workplace presents both challenges and opportunities for unions (Barnes et al., 2019). In adapting to new ICTs, unions may encounter difficulties in maintaining their presence in the workplace and engaging with employees in a meaningful way. However, the virtual workplace also provides new opportunities for unions to connect with their members and reach a wider audience (Holland et al., 2019b) and is the focus of Chapter 10. The question of how the trade union movement is adapting to new ICTs to retain and increase their power is a significant issue in the contemporary debate on union revitalisation (Carneiro & Costa, 2022; Pasquier et al., 2020). Union mobilisation has traditionally relied on interpersonal and mass communication methods, such as union journals, leaflets, pamphlets, newspapers, radio, film and television, to organise workers and influence public opinion. Unions have also been involved in struggles over the means of communication, including which political, economic and social issues are discussed in the media, as well as how ICTs are integrated into the labour process. Research has shown that unions can use digital platforms for virtual collective bargaining and advocacy for their members' rights (Geelan, 2021).

The use of ICTs and SM presents both challenges and opportunities for trade unions, which can impact their influence depending on their ability to effectively use these tools for revitalisation (Frege & Kelly, 2004). However, using ICTs and SM effectively requires significant resources in terms of expertise, funding and personnel to manage online communication (Rego et al., 2016). It is important to recognise the socially mediated impact of technology and the importance of choices, as technology is shaped by various actors seeking to further their own interests, including corporations, trade unions and civil society (Hodder & Houghton, 2020).

Currently, corporations dominate the digital age and shape technology use in societies to meet their needs (Holtgrewe, 2014; McChesney, 2013). This can be seen in organisations such as Uber and Deliveroo, which exploit ICTs to undercut workers' capacity to organise collectively (Kougiannou & Mendonça, 2021). In the gig economy context, unilateral intraplatform algorithmic changes disconnect workers from the platform, the labour process and each other, leading to increased surveillance, fragmentation and disempowerment (Kougiannou & Mendonça, 2021). In addition, tech organisations have developed largely invisible collaborative arrangements with state security apparatuses that use the internet to monitor and suppress political organisation and dissent (McChesney, 2013). Anti-union employers are also increasingly using surveillance of online protest activities to counter-mobilise against trade union campaigns, activists and dissenting employees (Thompson et al., 2020). Moreover, a significant threat of cyber-attacks targeting the trade union movement poses a serious challenge (Geelan & Hodder, 2017). However, ICTs also present trade unions with opportunities. For example, trade unions can amplify the impact of 'offline' collective action, strengthen a sense of collective identity among dispersed workforces and enhance the legitimacy of union campaigns by using ICTs (Pasquier & Wood, 2018).

Lastly, the shift to virtual and hybrid workplaces presents a significant challenge for management, who must adapt to new ways of communicating with employees and ensuring their voices are heard. Effective communication in virtual and hybrid workplaces is crucial, as remote workers can often feel isolated and disconnected from the organisation, reducing productivity and job satisfaction. Therefore, management must establish new channels of communication that are compatible with the virtual workplace, such as real-time messaging and video conferencing, to keep employees informed and engaged, and of course resource this.

However, while it is important for management to encourage employee voice, it is also important to avoid manipulating or controlling it. If employees feel that their voice is being manipulated or suppressed, it can lead to a perception of structured silence (Holland & Kougiannou, 2021) and a lack of trust in the organisation (Kougiannou et al., 2021). This can have a significant impact on employee morale and engagement, as well as on the overall effectiveness of the organisation.

Moreover, potential power dynamics are at play in virtual and hybrid workplaces, where management can easily control and monitor communication. To ensure that employee voice is not suppressed or manipulated, management should provide opportunities for anonymous feedback and ensure that communication channels are transparent and accessible to all employees. This can help build trust and ensure employee voice is valued and respected, leading to a more engaged and productive workforce.

The virtual and hybrid workplace also presents opportunities. Digital communication tools can provide a platform for real-time feedback and engagement, enhancing the efficiency and effectiveness of decision-making. This can facilitate the development of a more democratic workplace by giving everyone an immediate voice on workplace issues. Moreover, virtual networks can provide the infrastructure that can be the bridge to facilitate the development of a contemporary voice system compatible with the new workplace.

It is clear the virtual and hybrid workplace has significant implications for employee voice, and all stakeholders must adapt to the changing nature of work to ensure that employee voice remains effective and meaningful. This requires developing new communication channels, using technology to facilitate employee voice and a commitment to transparency and trust-building from management. By embracing these changes, organisations can ensure that employee voice remains a critical mechanism for employee engagement, decision-making and organisational success.

CONCLUSION

Employee voice and flexibility have not been studied together. The pandemic has brought remote work to the forefront of redefining the workplace and impacting employee voice structure and quality. The flexibility of remote work can positively impact employee voice, but it may also have unintended consequences. Decentralisation of the workforce could lead to breakdowns in communication and voice mechanisms, and the lack of face-to-face interaction may hinder the building of relationships and trust necessary for effective voice.

Voice scholars have called for further investigation into the current state of employee voice on SM and other ICTs, as recent reviews have only touched on this emerging trend. The impact of flexible work patterns on employee voice is an emerging issue that needs to be addressed as organisations adapt to the post-pandemic workplace. Investigating the potential impact of flexible work patterns on employee voice is crucial to promote positive outcomes for both employees and organisations.

In the current context of hybrid work, there is a lack of proactive management approaches to employee voice, which could lead to a unitarist voice system emerging in virtual environments. Virtual forums and management culture surveys can be seen as examples of this. However, it is concerning that there has been a lack of new voice systems emerging, despite the potential benefits of internal SM-style systems to enhance voice.

REFERENCES

Barnes, A., Balnave, N., Thornthwaite, L. & Manning, B. (2019). Social media: union communication and member voice. In P. Holland, J. Teicher & J. Donaghey (eds), *Employee Voice at Work*. Singapore: Springer, pp. 91–112.

Bashshur, M.R. & Oc, B. (2015). When voice matters: a multilevel review of the impact of voice in organisations. *Journal of Management*, 41(5), 1530–54.

Bhuiyan, J. (2019). How the Google walkout transformed tech workers into activists. Retrieved 12 March 2024 from: https:// www .latimes .com/ business/ technology/ story/2019–11–06/google-employeewalkout-tech-industry-activism.

Boxall, P.F. & Purcell, J. (2016). *Strategy and Human Resource Management*, 4th edn. London: Palgrave.

Burris, E.R., Detert, J.R. & Romney, A.C. (2013). Speaking up vs. being heard: the disagreement around and outcomes of employee voice. *Organization Science*, 24(1), 22–38.

Carneiro, B. & Costa, H. (2022). Digital unionism as a renewal strategy? Social media use by trade union confederations. *Journal of Industrial Relations*, 64(1), 26–51.

Carnevale, J.B., Huang, L., Uhl-Bien, M. & Harris, S. (2020). Feeling obligated yet hesitant to speak up: investigating the curvilinear relationship between LMX and employee promotive voice. *Journal of Occupational and Organizational Psychology*, 93, 1–25.

Chen, X. & Wei, S. (2020). The impact of social media use for communication and social exchange relationship on employee performance. *Journal of Knowledge Management*, 24(6), 1289–314.

Foss, N.J. (2021). The impact of the Covid-19 pandemic on firms' organizational designs. *Journal of Management Studies*, 58(1), 268–72.

Frege, C. & Kelly, J. (2004) *Varieties of Unionism: Strategies for Union Revitalisation in a Globalizing Economy*. Oxford: Oxford University Press.

Fuchs, C. (2020) *Communication and Capitalism: A Critical Theory*. London: University of Westminster Press.

Geelan, T. (2021). Introduction to the Special Issue – the internet, social media and trade union revitalisation: still behind the digital curve or catching up? *New Technology, Work and Employment*, 36(2), 123–39.

Geelan, T. & Hodder, A. (2017). Enhancing transnational labour solidarity: the unfulfilled promise of the internet and social media. *Industrial Relations Journal*, 48(4), 345–64.

Gode, H.E., Johansen, W. & Thomsen, C. (2019). Employee engagement in generating ideas on internal social media: a matter of meaningfulness, safety and availability. *Corporate Communications: An International Journal*, 25(2), 263–80.

Grant, K., McQueen, F., Osborn, S. & Holland, P. (2023). Re-configuring the jigsaw puzzle: balancing time, pace, place and space of work in the Covid-19 era. *Economic and Industrial Democracy*. https://doi.org/10.1177/0143831X231195686.

Gruman, J.A. & Saks, A.M. (2020). Employee and collective voice engagement: being psychologically present when speaking up at work. In A. Wilkinson, J. Donaghey, T. Dundon & R.B. Freeman (eds), *Handbook of Research on Employee Voice*, 2nd edn. Cheltenham, UK and Northampton, MA, USA: Edward Elgar, pp. 397–417.

Hodder, A. & Houghton, D. (2020) Unions, social media and young workers – evidencefrom the UK. *New Technology, Work and Employment*, 35(1), 40–59.

Holland, P. (2018) Workplace bullying and the role of voice and ethical leadership. In P. Holland, J. Teicher & J. Donaghey (eds), *Employee Voice at Work*. Singapore: Springer, pp. 129–48.

Holland, P. & Kougiannou, N. (2021). Employee voice. In N. Dodd, C. Brewster & P. Holland (eds), *Contemporary Issues in Human Resources Management*, 5th edn. Cape Town, South Africa: Oxford University Press, pp. 295–314.

Holland, P., Cooper, B. & Hecker, R. (2019a). Social media at work: a new form of employee voice? In P. Holland, J. Teicher & J. Donaghey (eds), *Employee Voice at Work*. Singapore: Springer, pp. 73–89.

Holland, P., Teicher. J. & Donaghey, J. (eds) (2019b). *Employee Voice at Work*. Singapore: Springer.

Holtgrewe, U. (2014) New new technologies: the future and the present of work in information and communication technology. *New Technology, Work and Employment*, 29(1), 9–24.

Johansson, E. & Carey, P. (2016). Detecting fraud: the role of the anonymous reporting channel. *Journal of Business Ethics*, 139(2), 391–409.

Kamal, M.M. (2020). The triple-edged sword of COVID-19: understanding the use of digital technologies and the impact of productive, disruptive, and destructive nature of the pandemic. *Information Systems Management*, 37(4), 310–17

Khan, M., Mowbray, P.K., & Wilkinson, A. (2023). Employee voice on social media – an affordance lens. *International Journal of Management Reviews*, 1–20.

Kim, Y. & Lim, H. (2020). Activating constructive employee behavioural responses in a crisis: examining the effects of pre-crisis reputation and crisis communication strategies on employee voice behaviours. *Journal of Contingencies and Crisis Management*, 28(2), 141–57.

Knoll, M., Feldt, M. & Zacher, H. (2022). Effects of technology enabled flexible work arrangements on employee voice: toward a nuanced understanding. *Management Revue*, 33(3), 303–34.

Kougiannou, N. & Holland, P. (2022). Employee voice and silence in the digital era. In P. Holland, T. Bartram, T. Garavan & K. Grant (eds), *The Emerald Handbook of Work, Workplaces and Disruptive Issues in HRM*. Bingley: Emerald Group Publishing, pp. 513–31.

Kougiannou, N.K. & Mendonça, P. (2021). Breaking the managerial silencing of worker voice in platform capitalism: the rise of a food courier network. *British Journal of Management*, 32(3), 744–59.

Kougiannou, K., Redman, T. & Dietz, G. (2015). The outcomes of works councils: the role of trust, justice and industrial relations climate. *Human Resource Management Journal*, 25(4), 458–77.

Kougiannou, N.K., Dundon, T. & Wilkinson, A. (2021). Forming effective employee information and consultation: a five-stage trust and justice process. *British Journal of Management*, 32(1), 200–18.

Kougiannou, N.K., Wilkinson, A. & Dundon, T. (2022). Inside the meetings: the role of managerial attitudes in approaches to information and consultation for employees. *British Journal of Industrial Relations*, 60(3), 585–605.

Li, Y.-T. (2022). Digital togetherness as everyday resistance: the use of new media in addressing work exploitation in rural areas. *New Media & Society*. doi.org/10.1177/14614448221080717.

Liu, X., Mao, J.Y., Chiang, J.T.J., Guo, L. & Zhang, S. (2023). When and why does voice sustain or stop? The roles of leader behaviours, power differential perception and psychological safety. *Applied Psychology*, 72(3): 1209–47.

Martin, G., Parry, E. & Flowers, P. (2015). Do social media enhance constructive employee voice all of the time or just some of the time? Social media and employee voice. *Human Resource Management Journal*, 25(4): 541–62.

McChesney, R. (2013) *Digital Disconnect: How Capitalism Is Turning the Internet against Democracy*. New York: New Press.

Mendonça, P. & Kougiannou, N.K. (2023). Disconnecting labour: the impact of intraplatform algorithmic changes on the labour process and workers' capacity to organise collectively. *New Technology, Work and Employment*, 38, 1–20.

Miles, S.J. & Mangold, W.G. (2014). Employee voice: untapped resource or social media time bomb? *Business Horizons*, 57(3), 401–11.

Mowbray, P.K., Wilkinson, A. & Tse, H.H. (2022). Strategic or silencing? Line managers' repurposing of employee voice mechanisms for high performance. *British Journal of Management*, 33(2), 1054–70.

Palmer, A. (2020). Hundreds of Amazon employees risk firing to protest the company's climate policies. Retrieved 12 March 2024 from: https://www.cnbc.com/2020/01/27/amazon-employees-protestexternal-communications-policy.html.

Parth, S., Bathini, D.R. & Kandathil, G. (2023). Actions in physical space: work solidarity and collective action among app-based cab drivers in India. *New Technology, Work and Employment*, 38(2): 206–29.

Pasquier, V. & Wood, A.J. (2018). *The Power of Social Media as a Labour Campaigning Tool: Lessons from OUR Walmart and the Fight for 15*. Brussels: European Trade Union Institute.

Pasquier, V., Daudigeos, T. & Barros, M. (2020) Towards a new flashmob unionism: the case of the Fight for 15 movement. *British Journal of Industrial Relations*, 58(2), 336–63.

Pinder, C. & Harlos, K. (2001). Employee silence: quiescence and acquiescence as responses to perceived injustice. In G.R. Ferris (ed.), *Research in Personnel and Human Resource Management*, vol. 20. Greenwich, CT: JAI Press, pp. 331–69.

Prouska, R. & Psychogios, A. (2018). Do not say a word! Conceptualising employee silence in a long-term crisis context. *The International Journal of Human Resource Management*, 29(5), 885–914.

Prouska, R. & Psychogios, A. (2019). Should I say something? A framework for understanding silence from a line manager's perspective during an economic crisis. *Economic and Industrial Democracy*, 40(3), 611–35.

Pyman, A., Holland, P., Teicher, J. & Cooper, B. (2010). Industrial relations climate, employee voice and managerial attitudes to unions. An Australian study. *British Journal of Industrial Relations*, 48(2), 460–80.

Rego, R., Sprenger, W., Kirov, V., Thomson, G. & Di Nunzio, D. (2016). The use of new ICTs in trade union protests – five European cases. *Transfer: European Review of Labour and Research*, 22(3), 315–29.

Sanders, K., Nguyen, P.T., Bouckenooghe, D., Rafferty, A. & Schwarz, G. (2020). Unraveling the what and how of organizational communication to employees during COVID-19 pandemic: adopting an attributional lens. *The Journal of Applied Behavioral Science*, 56(3), 289–93.

Soto-Acosta, P. (2020). COVID-19 pandemic: shifting digital transformation to a high-speed gear. *Information Systems Management*, 37(4), 260–6.

Stumpf, R. & Süß, S. (2022). The valuation of social media voice: an experimental investigation. *Management Revue*, 33(3), 240–68.

Thompson, P., McDonald, P. & O'Connor, P. (2020) Employee dissent on social media and organisational discipline. *Human Relations*, 73(5), 631–52.

Treem, J.W., Leonardi, P.M. & van den Hooff, B. (2020). Computer-mediated communication in the age of communication visibility. *Journal of Computer-Mediated Communication*, 25(1), 44–59.

Tzafrir, S. (2005), The relationship between trust, HRM practices and firm performance. *International Journal of Human Resource Management*, 16(9), 1600–22.

Walker, M. (2021). Peer-to-peer online voice as emergent collective action. *Journal of Industrial Relations*, 63(5): 777–97.

Wheatley, D., Buglass, S. & Hardill, I. (eds) (2021). *Remote Work and Worker Well-being in the Post-COVID-19 Era: Impacts, Challenges, and Opportunities*. Hershey, PA: IGI Global.

Zeitoun, H. & Pamini, P. (2021). A promise made is a promise kept: union voice, HRM practices, implicit contracts and workplace performance in times of crisis. *Human Resource Management Journal*, 31(1), 277–92.

9. The dark side of 21st century flexible work

Tse Leng Tham, Peter Holland and Debora Jeske

INTRODUCTION

On 11 March 2020, the World Health Organization (WHO) declared COVID-19 a global pandemic. This was only the beginning of the ripple which brought on a tidal wave of stay-at-home orders, emptying offices overnight, turning kitchen counters and living rooms into offices as millions around the world were forced into embracing remote work. Whilst the practice of telecommuting and remote work has been in existence for many years, (and explored in more depth elsewhere in this book), employees working remotely and flexibly remained few and far between, often limited to advanced market economies (Lund et al., 2021). However, the context of the COVID-19 pandemic inadvertently accelerated the remote working trend potentially by decades, as organisations globally were forced to rapidly develop and deploy their remote working capabilities such as videoconferencing, document-sharing tools, and new ways of managing, all out of necessity (Bick et al., 2020). As a result, in response to one of the biggest forced social experiments, we have overcome cultural and technological barriers which once prevented remote work in the past, triggering a lasting structural and behavioural reshaping of where, when, and how work takes place.

Many recognise the opportunities and benefits of remote working – for workers, this represented increased flexibility and autonomy, particularly in helping reconcile demands from work and home, resulting in greater productivity and satisfaction (Grant et al., 2023); for organisations, remote working allowed significant and long-term potential of real estate cost savings, more effective deployment of their workforce, and a means of attracting (virtual) international talent. Herein, as we emerge from the pandemic, many organisations are opting to either shift to a hybrid or completely remote working models. For instance, a study by Gartner reports that 74 per cent of CFOs surveyed intend to have at least a proportion of their workforce continue working remotely on a long-term basis (Lavelle, 2020). Elsewhere, a study by IBM indicates that 54 per cent of American respondents wished to continue remote working arrangements (Bick et al., 2020). However, it is important to note that such autonomous remote and flexible work is ironically linked with a dark side of work, where organisations have adopted tracking, monitoring, and surveillance tools in order to exert control over as well as support remote workers' flexibility (Aloisi & De Stefano, 2022; Wang et al., 2021). This gives rise to the term, the flexibility paradox, wherein higher levels of flexibility beget greater and wider forms of control.

Given the erosion of the once-clear demarcation between work and home in remote and flexible working arrangements, and the increasing proliferation of artificial intelligence (AI) being applied to data collected via electronic monitoring and surveillance in key HR activities, the rise of flexible and remote work does not come without challenges and consequences related to privacy, discrimination, ethics, and trust in the employment relationship. As recent forecasts and modelling indicate, advancements in technology have created the capacity for nearly four to five times as many people to potentially work from home in some form compared to before the pandemic (Lund et al., 2021). However, the rapid permeability and adoption of such developments into the private household have far-outpaced the development of clear legal guidelines pertaining to the electronic tracking, monitoring, and surveillance of work and of course privacy. As such, HR and management are increasingly at the forefront of managing these new ways of working. This includes having to carefully balance the benefits and costs of how to manage and support flexible and remote work. These issues and their far-reaching consequences need to be more fully understood by HR professionals to ensure that the implementation of new patterns of work do not cause more harm than problems they propose to resolve, particularly now that rather than being the exception, remote and flexible work is fast becoming our new normal.

THE RISE OF REMOTE WORK AND THE PANDEMIC PARADIGM

Recent advancements in technology and events such as the COVID-19 pandemic have fast-tracked the emergence of new ways of working, characterised by 'a wide range of practices placed on a continuum of work flexibilisation and diversification, from remote work to collaborative entrepreneurship and digital nomadism' (Aroles et al., 2019, p. 286). Whilst technology has sometimes been introduced as a means of connecting geographically dispersed remote workers and of enabling their performance, it has also been leveraged as a means of monitoring and surveillance, particularly for managers who remain embedded in a 20th century management model that workers can't be trusted to be productive in absence of management (Mazmanian et al., 2013). Indeed, this was particularly a major concern during the pandemic and was quickly dubbed, the 'productivity paranoia' (Christian, 2022). In a survey of 20,000 people across 11 countries, Microsoft reported that 85 per cent of leaders struggled to trust their remote/hybrid working employees were being productive. As a result, many organisations worldwide raced to find electronic means of 'keeping an eye' on employees given it was no longer possible to do so physically. This fuelled demand for worker surveillance tools (Kurkowski, 2021). By 2022, it was estimated that the number of large firms tracking, monitoring, and surveilling their workers had increased two-fold since the start of the pandemic (Migliano, 2022; Morgan & Nolan, 2023).

Tracking is often a feature of many monitoring systems which may be utilised to capture certain employee and production statistics. Electronic monitoring is often therefore more directed to certain activities or operations. More specifically, it involves the use of electronic instruments and/or devices such as audio, video, computer systems or software to collect, store, analyse, and report on individual or group actions and performance (Nebeker & Tatum, 1993; Siegel et al., 2022). Electronic surveillance, on the other hand, is often more encompassing, continuous, discerning, discrete, intrusive, and comprehensive than electronic monitoring. It may also be more indiscriminate and rolled out more widely, beyond key performance indicators or production indices. It is important to note that whilst tracking can support both monitoring and surveillance, monitoring and surveillance are not by default one or the same. The critical point here is how much information is collected, why information is collected, and with whom this information is shared.

Monitoring is often legitimate and legally required to safeguard the well-being of workers, track progress on business goals, and working hours. Organisations may monitor data access and transferrals to protect their customers' privacy, data, and IP (e.g., code). Surveillance is more akin to a risk management approach. The use of more cloud and networked resources to allow employees to work from various locations make organisations increasingly vulnerable to outside attacks and intellectual property (IP) theft. Powered by advancements in AI and machine learning, organisations are also making use of electronic data from employees to predict risks associated with employee behaviours such as burnout, quitting, and espionage (Kurkowski, 2021). Additionally, organisations may also be motivated to engage in electronic monitoring and surveillance (EMS) on employees as it can serve as a basis of evidence-based management (EBM), evidence-based HRM (EBHRM), and HR analytics (Greasley & Thomas, 2020). The adoption of such methods is also increasingly widespread given it permits a means of using seemingly more 'scientific' knowledge in analysing human capital and in improving business performance (Fitzenz, 2010; Greasley & Thomas, 2020). This, in turn, has the potential to strengthen the position in which the HR function occupies in organisations, moving into a more strategic, performance, and analytically oriented role (Lawler et al., 2004; Levenson, 2005; Mondore et al., 2011).

Whilst we have witnessed a significant increase in the frequency and scope of EMS as a function of the widespread adoption of remote and flexible work, it is important to note that the practice of tracking, monitoring, and surveillance is not new. Arguably these practices are inextricably bound with modern management and bureaucracies. The foundations of modern workplace surveillance can be traced back to the Ford Motor Company, which on top of high surveillance workplace management, developed a Sociology Department, where officers physically patrolled, monitored, and spied on factory workers and their families, outside of their rostered shifts, to ensure there was compliance with a 'moral' and 'healthy' lifestyle (e.g., no excessive alcohol consumption and gambling). These were taken as 'productivity metrics' (beyond clocking in, counting output) as they were conditions which were perceived to have a significant impact on their productivity levels on the factory floor. Poor scores on such 'metrics' had significant implications for individual's compensation and benefits, and employment (Sarpong & Rees, 2014; Vitak & Zimmer, 2021). An illustrative metaphor in understanding the impact of such monitoring and surveillance practices at the workplace is Foucault's use of Benthem's panopticon prison design. Central to this metaphor is the concept of self-supervision as the central tower where the guard observes from is strategically placed where it permits the observation of prisoners in all prison cells at any point in time. Whilst the guard may not be visible to the prisoners, prisoners monitor and adjust their own behaviours as they must operate under the assumption of being permanently visible (Bauman & Lyon, 2013; Foucault, 1979). Whilst you may consider this anachronistic management practices of a by-gone age, the fact that work and your organisation are now in your private space at home may make you reconsider this.

In the midst of the emerging 4th Industrial Revolution, advancements in digital technologies and AI have made significant progress in efforts to support the rapid switch to widespread remote and flexible work. Such progress has made EMS cheaper and more efficient, thereby allowing it to be more readily available for adoption and implementation in more workplaces. Increasingly, we see this paradox of flexibility emerge, where remote working can be introduced as a way for workers to have greater levels of flexibility and autonomy (Fried et al., 2013), yet, 'productivity paranoia' associated with hybrid, remote, and flexible forms of work means managers remain sceptical on work productivity in their physical absence (Mazmanian et al., 2013). In response, organisations enlist EMS as means of maintaining supervisory control over productivity in increasingly office-free environments, resulting in a higher number of electronically monitored employees. Some scholars have argued that such trends are not too surprising, as the use of such technology at the workplace is, in fact, a natural evolution and extension of the Fordist Sociology Department. Instead of employing officers to spy on factory workers, this is being replaced by the omnipresent, invisible, and unblinking digital eye(s) of technology (Holland & Tham, 2020; Sarpong & Rees, 2014).

What is distinctive about EMS through the pandemic paradigm is its pervasiveness, ubiquitousness, and intrusiveness. This is partly enabled by the advancements in digital devices, software, and systems, creating a portable panopticon (De Saulles & Horner, 2011; Holland & Brewster, 2021) that is capable of watching and recording every word, keystroke, and click as we work in our homes. Indeed, with the increasing adoption of remote and flexible working models, melting boundaries between where and when work begins and ends only exacerbates the potential intrusiveness of EMS. For instance, designed as a means of fostering interconnectedness among remote workers, Sneek is a videoconferencing call software that is perpetually on, taking webcam pictures of employees and uploading them on 'a virtual wall' so managers can observe the whole team whilst they work remotely (Holmes, 2018). Software allowing managers to have remote access to employees' systems attempts to replicate the openness and informality of managers walking around and lending team members a helping hand has also emerged. Other software has been designed to track and collect electronic data on employees. Time Doctor, Teramind, ActivTrack, and Insightful are among some of the most popular EMS software which allow discrete and intermittent recordings of employees' screens whilst they work and track a range of activities such as login times, keystrokes, active time spend on applications (e.g., MS Word), search histories, and bandwidth utilisation as a means of productivity. Managers are sent notifications when tracked data indicate the employee is distracted (e.g., on social media), perceived to be taking excessive breaks, or engaging in potentially suspicious activities (Migliano, 2022). In combination with advancements in biometric data collection, EMS software and equipment today also boasts capabilities in collecting such data in office-free working environments. For instance, employees may be required to scan fingerprints or faces to clock-in and out, or their eye movements can be scanned via webcams to track employee attention (Morgan & Nolan, 2023).

The contemporary EMS landscape is a combination of AI and machine learning, with the potential to power exponential growth in volume, scope, and depth of data organisations and collection on workers. This enables new ways of 'assessing performance' and policing behaviours, ultimately performing the role of a 'virtual Sociology Department'. In applying algorithms, software like Produscore calculates a daily 'productivity score' from weighing and aggregating data collected via tracking individuals' emails, messaging apps, browsers, and databases. Even seemingly innocuous applications many of us use daily such as Microsoft 365 has capabilities to produce productivity scores and charts based on individual activity across various applications such as email (MS Outlook), calendars, and calls (MS Teams) (Cyphers & Gullo, 2020). AI recognition technology scans facial expression, tone of voice, together with the mining of emails and chat communications; software such as Read, an extension application to Zoom (virtual meeting platform) can produce insights on individual engagement and sentiment. Other AI monitoring technology coupled with predictive analysis can also be used to flag whether a worker is likely to engage in certain undesirable behaviours, for example, quit, espionage, theft. For instance, Veriato scans the text of individuals' emails and chats, and calculates a daily 'risk score' for each worker, representing the probability that they may be disgruntled and may engage in behaviours which may harm the organisation. As such, the expansive practice and capabilities of EMS today require much careful consideration, especially as these are often carried out in uncharted and unregulated (legal) terrains. The following sections explore the issues associated with EMS in our increasingly distributed and flexible workforces.

THE VALUE OF ELECTRONIC MONITORING AND SURVEILLANCE IN REMOTE WORK

There are several key and practical factors that encourage organisations to engage in EMS to 'watch' their employees, particularly in instances where workers are engaging in work remotely. The first and foremost being the ability to monitor, manage, and improve performance of individuals, and thereby, the organisation (Gagné & Bhave, 2011). In fact, the simple presence of electronic monitoring has been reported to encourage higher levels of accountability, integrity, and concentration (Ball, 2010; Iedema & Rhodes, 2010; Ravid et al., 2022; Wang et al., 2021), therefore encouraging higher quality of performance. Research has suggested that individuals are more likely to engage in helpful behaviours beyond the requirements of their jobs if they perceive such behaviours are being monitored (Bhave, 2014). Although research by Holland et al. (2015), (discussed below) disputes this. Additionally, EMS also enables the accurate, timely, and consistent collection of information on workers' workflow processes and 'performance', which could be helpful in providing insights on *how* managers can support the development of individual and team productivity, whilst effectively managing wastage, inefficiencies, and inappropriate behaviours (e.g., social or cyber loafing, theft) (Sarpong & Rees, 2014). Productivity scores, dashboards, charts generated by software such as Produscore or Microsoft 365's MyAnalytics provide the opportunity for managers to pinpoint chock points in the work system such as team members being bogged down by too many virtual meetings or requiring developmental help with tasks. Indeed, research has found that electronic monitoring, when used in a developmental and supporting manner, can improve performance, job satisfaction, and well-being (Ravid et al., 2022; Wells et al., 2007). The question here though that needs to be asked: Is this really a quality approach to productivity or default form of EMS?

A second point relates to the issue of safety and security. This can include the protection of individuals' safety and well-being, including employees and other critical stakeholders such as the community or the public, and the safeguarding of corporate interests and trade secrets (Ball, 2010; West & Bowman, 2016). Fundamentally, employers have a basic duty of care to ensure the safety and well-being of their workers. Software tracking productivity (e.g., Teramind tracking keystrokes, time spent on applications) and levels of engagement (e.g., Read application on Zoom uses AI facial scanning) could alert a manager that an individual may be at the early stages of burnout if he or she is normally very active, participative, and engaged in meetings, chats, and emails but begins to clock metrics of much lower activity and engagement levels. This enables a manager to take proactive measures in minimising stress and other psychosocial risks for workers, despite having limited visibility in physically observing them (Aloisi & De Stefano, 2022). However, the authors have yet to come across support for this proactive management strategy. Another threat to individual well-being in remote and flexible working environments relates to social isolation. Managers may use electronic monitoring tools to help in recreating the sense of cohesion that one would experience when working in a shared physical space. For instance, Pesto reads and synchronises individuals' calendars and music playlists while Sneek captures webcam photos of workers intermittently and circulates among team members to replicate the sense of 'proximity' and togetherness that one would experience working in the same office. Although Grant et al. (2023), found no evidence on this in their study of remote working, during and post-pandemic. In certain workplaces, EMS tools may also be used to protect workers against potential lawsuits or formal complaints. In the context of call centre workers, Sewell et al. (2012) noted that individuals felt at ease, knowing recordings of customer interactions existed to protect them in instances of complaints. For customers, organisations are compelled to ensure that their data, especially of a sensitive nature such as health and credit card information, are handled with utmost care. EMS software such as RemoteDesk leverages real-time facial recognition via webcams and object detection technology to alert workers when they are in instances of potential security breach. This might be when a recording device (e.g., phone) comes into view, ensuring their workers are always operating in secure environments, no matter where and when that might be. For employers, electronic means of monitoring including emails, Internet usage and footprint could serve to protect against the risks of sabotage, data theft, hacking and espionage activities (Vitak & Zimmer, 2021). As noted, software such as Veriato and KeenCorp uses data collected via EMS and predictive analysis to flag potential risks of misconduct behaviours and disengaged employees based on a score generated from existing data available in the daily workflow such as word patterns in emails (Bales & Stone, 2020; KeenCorp, 2018).

A third point is when effectively designed and implemented, electronic monitoring and collection of accurate data could offer data-based insights to support faster and more effective decision-making practices aimed at improving processes and performance (West & Bowman, 2016). Employees working under conditions of having their performance electronically monitored have also reported to perceive that their treatment by management is more procedurally fair (McNall & Roch, 2007) as they believe their performance is more accurately captured thereby, positively impacting task satisfaction (Stanton & Julian, 2002). However, this research is reasonably old now and the level of sophistication and intrusion of EMS has increased significantly since this research was undertaken. More generally, Bekkers et al. (2013) also note that electronic monitoring has the potential to facilitate higher levels of transparency, clarity, and accountability in decision-making. These, in turn, not only help reinforce HR's strategic function in organisations (Greasley & Thomas, 2020; Lawler et al., 2004), but can potentially aid in improving workers' levels of trust in their organisation (Bekkers et al., 2013).

Whilst there may be several relevant reasons and benefits for the use of EMS to track, monitor, and surveil workers, there are also various cautionary considerations organisations and managers need to be aware of, particularly in an era where such technology is readily available and easily implementable. This firstly, includes the overreliance on such wholesale datafication in making key HR decisions such as hiring, performance evaluations, promotions, and disciplinary actions. Central to this concern stems from the limited checks and balances in ensuring reliability and validity in the data collected via EMS, and the potential ethical issues which may arise when applied to making key decisions in the employment relationship. Secondly, organisations and managers should be wary of how EMS can quickly go down the slippery 'functional creep' slope, where monitoring initially used for one purpose is extended (often without the knowledge of those being monitored) to other purposes (Vitak & Zimmer, 2021). For instance, webcam-based EMS technology such as RemoteDesk could be initially introduced as a means of ensuring workers handling sensitive data in their work are in a secure working environment to avoid potential security breaches. However, the same EMS technology may also be leveraged to track how often workers may be distracted on their mobile phones as this is also considered a device with recording capabilities and would be flagged by the EMS system as a potential security breach. The pervasiveness and unboundedness of EMS' functional creep capabilities is exacerbated not just by the advancements in technology, but by the rapid growth of flexible working arrangements and together with it, the blurring boundaries between work and non-work environments (Grant et al, 2023; Hansen & Weiskopf, 2021; Tham & Holland, 2022). Together, this has the potential to rewrite the informational and power asymmetry in the employment relationship, allowing the organisation to have heightened visibility over their workers' every move, thought, and intention (Adler-Bell & Miller, 2018). Whilst we may have, overtly, increasing flexibilisation of work arrangements, it may be accompanied by a dark side of being subjected to greater levels of 'invisible' and total control that EMS can enable organisations and managers to have or what has been termed the flexibility paradox (Adler-Bell & Miller, 2018; Ball, 2021; Hansen & Weiskopf, 2021). To a certain extent, these issues are driven by the fast and widespread adoption in workplaces in response to the forced move to remote working as mandated by COVID-19 stay-at-home orders (Vitak & Zimmer, 2023). These developments have far outpaced the legal or HR boundaries in many countries which govern workers' rights to the protection and privacy of their data, particularly in increasingly office-free working environments (Ball, 2010; Tham & Holland, 2022; Vitak & Zimmer, 2023). Together, these factors have the impact of challenging the boundaries of privacy and ethics and, therefore, the quality and integrity of the employment relationship. The following section explores these potential complex ethical, legal, and social negative implications of EMS in the context of increasing flexibilisation of work.

THE DARK SIDE OF ELECTRONIC MONITORING AND SURVEILLANCE IN REMOTE WORK

One of the primary arguments for engaging in EMS is its capacity to track, monitor, and develop employee performance by being able to conduct accurate and timely performance appraisals and provide constructive and specific feedback (Holman, 2002; McNall & Roch, 2009). However, research indicates that EMS specifically for performance purposes could elicit significant negative impact on performance, employee attitudes, and behaviours, and the employment relationship that outweighs the perceived positive effects (Aloisi & Gramano, 2019).

In some circumstances, EMS may even induce unintended consequences, some of which may be the exact counterproductive or undesirable behaviours EMS is meant to discourage in the focus on greater productivity (Tham & Holland, 2022). When EMS is being used to watch certain behaviours in determining one's level of productivity, it sends clear signals as to which behaviours are expected and valued in an organisation (Holland et al., 2015).

Indeed, research substantiates this notion as evidence suggests that tasks which are monitored are perceived by individuals to be more critical and worthy of attention as opposed to non-monitored tasks (Ball, 2010). Since the pandemic simple proxies such as keystrokes, number of emails sent, and time spent on applications are being used as productivity metrics and may appear to support 'evidence-based' HR decisions in the absence of physical managerial observation, contrarily it can inadvertently encourage new forms of what Zuboff (1988) described as anticipatory conformity. This is essentially where individuals engage in self-monitoring behaviours, which are often safe, passive, and docile to ensure they conform to the behaviours the organisation is monitoring and using as a measure of performance. This can promote an overly narrow focus on the quantified proxy measures (e.g., keystrokes, number of messages sent) and may come at the expense of quality activities critical to individual, team, and organisational performance such as ideation, brainstorming, planning, and collaborative teamwork (e.g., 'if it isn't counted, it doesn't count'), activities which may be critical in generating tangible results (Hanley & Hubbard, 2020). For instance, in a sample of remote workers, Bakewell et al. (2018) found that engineers avoided assisting a colleague as that time spent would have been considered unaccounted for in their newly introduced, continuously monitoring EMS system and performance metrics, thereby discouraging what would have been a naturally occurring organisational citizenship behaviour (OCB). Indeed, research has also found that high levels of intrusive EMS encourage individuals to minimise the frequency of OCBs and positive social exchanges with colleagues (Grant & Mayer, 2009; Korsgaard et al., 2010). These in turn, can compound feelings of workplace isolation (Mulki et al., 2008), a common challenge for those working remotely or virtually and a threat to overall productivity, worker well-being, and turnover.

Using EMS for performance could also unintentionally encourage undesirable and ultimately unproductive behaviours as workers may identify ways to 'game' the system. It was not long before the Internet and social media had numerous posts on such tips and tricks for example, hoisting the laptop lid open with a wine cork pressing down on a key on the keyboard, so it appears as though a worker is constantly typing furiously on a blank MS Word document. Other examples include putting the mouse on a rover vacuum cleaner to give the appearance of constant movement. Research also found that workers may rather engage in time-consuming behaviours to hide problems encountered at work as opposed to formally requesting assistance and risk leaving a digital trace of it (Bakewell et al., 2018). For example, productivity dashboards that make individual productivity metrices visible to all team members are meant to foster transparency, collaborative troubleshooting, and a felt sense of cohesion in geographically dispersed teams. However, these can also have the unintended effect of engendering 'lateral surveillance', where individuals are watched by not just their managers, but their peers as well. This, in turn, may also encourage individuals to engage in ultimately unproductive behaviours such as masking problems encountered in work tasks rather than engage in collaborative problem-solving, all for the sake of appearing 'productive'. Research evidence supporting the use of EMS for enabling higher levels of performance is few and far between, with evidence generally supporting a negative impact of performance (e.g., Becker & Marique, 2014). In fact, a recent meta-analysis by Siegel et al. (2022) finds that overall, there is no significant relationship between monitoring and performance.

Another instrumental reason organisations and managers engage in EMS is to capture and assess worker performance more accurately and fairly as its reach far exceeds manager's physical observation. This has traces of the logic of scientific management which attempted to take conflict out of the process by using 'science' as the arbiter. Whilst this can be particularly valuable given workers are increasingly geographically dispersed through remote and flexible working arrangements, there are concerns related to the accuracy, reliability, and validity and therefore interpretation of using EMS-collected data in determining performance (Mateescu & Nguyen, 2019). EMS systems which have experienced a significant boom since the COVID-19 pandemic, include, Hubstaff, Teramind, and Insightful, which track and record productivity 'proxy' measures such as keystrokes and mouse movements to calculate a productivity score which can be shared with both individual workers and their managers. As we note, the concerning issue is that these 'proxy' metrics can be overly narrow, rigid, and at times, may ultimately be an inaccurate measure of individual productivity. For example, as a social experiment, together with his supervisor, a *New York Times* journalist trialled Hubstaff for several weeks and found that it consistently reported his productivity scores as less than 50 per cent despite working up to 14-hour days. The EMS tool only tracked his typing and mouse movements and did not capture time spent making phone calls and other essential non-computer work (Santariano, 2020).

The reliance on EMS data to determine performance may not always be free of bias. For instance, webcams combined with AI recognition technology scanning used to track workers' time spent at work, facial expression, tone of voice, etc. to determine individual levels of productivity and engagement levels may have ingrained inaccuracies and biases. This can be attributable to the fact that AI models are built based on previously available data which may be biased as minorities may already be underrepresented (Ball, 2021). Particularly, facial recognition technology has been shown to suffer from gender and racial bias. AI algorithms struggle to accurately identify people with darker skin tones, with reports of workers therefore consistently having trouble being recognised by facial recognition systems in ways their colleagues with lighter skin did not (e.g., being signed out of systems for prolonged inactivity despite being in front of their screens and having to spend time re-scanning) (Raposo, 2023). This creates obvious concerns around whether their 'performance' is being accurately captured by such EMS technology. Such concerns have been cautioned by scholars, where the widespread and unchecked use of EMS technology and AI in automising key HR decisions and processes could further perpetuate discriminatory biases (Aloisi & Gramano, 2019).

Contemporary use of EMS technology in remote and flexible working environments also raises some significant and unique concerns related to privacy and ethics (as noted above), especially with increasingly enmeshed temporal and spatial boundaries that are used to clearly demarcate 'work' and 'private' spheres. Advancements in EMS technology also allow for monitoring powers which far surpass that of our human gaze or traditional analogue surveillance systems. Increasingly, many of us working remotely and flexibly are being exposed to omnipresent, real-time, and individualised EMS that is not confined to the workplace or working time (Katsabian, 2019), giving managers and employers essentially an 'open window' to workers' homes and private lives – the 'pandemic panoption' (Aloisi & De Stefano, 2022).

Webcam-based EMS technology such as Sneek can be constantly on. This may mean that it could be actively watching and listening in to workers even outside of work, including time, conversations, and spaces that are private given the difficulties in clearly delineating when the former stops and the latter begins in remote working settings. With an example of a *New York Times* writer who repurposed his kitchen as his home office spot, the EMS software would capture his family members and their private background conversations (Santariano, 2020). In other cases, workers completing work on personal computers are still required to be subjected to their organisation's EMS, whether that is allowing intermittent screenshots of their screens to be taken or supervisors and/or colleagues being able to remotely access their computers. This means that employers potentially have access to personal private information such as banking, passwords, medical records, and correspondences with doctors and the potential for such information to be hacked via work. Accordingly, scholars and international watchdogs alike have highlighted growing concerns pertaining to the scope and intensity of privacy invasion in contemporary forms of EMS adopted in remote working settings (Ball, 2021; Hern, 2020; Vatcha, 2020). These concerns can be exacerbated as it can often be unclear when such data might be collected, how such data are being used and stored, and what measures are put in place to ensure the capturing of data related to non-work activities (or time) are discounted and not used in punitive ways against workers (Vitak & Zimmer, 2021).

The adverse impact of EMS systems on work intensification and workers' well-being are also well known (Chillakuri & Vanka, 2021; Wang et al., 2021). Particularly in instances where EMS is implemented in ways that are punitive, limits individual autonomy, or used as a means of pressurising high performance, it is likely to increase workers' stress levels (cf. Alge & Hansen, 2013; Backhaus, 2019; Holland et al., 2015; Mallo et al., 2007; Ravid et al., 2022). Being subjected to EMS over a working day, across a large proportion of our adult lives could have significant negative implications for an individual's health and well-being in the long run (Funder & Ozer, 2019).

Contemporary forms and uses of EMS in remote and flexible working environments have stretched the boundaries of the granularity, scale, and frequency of data collection (Vitak & Zimmer, 2021). Such 'digital exhaust' has the capacity to compound EMS' negative effects on individual wellbeing (Leonardi, 2021). Indeed, recent research evidence from studies conducted during the pandemic of remote working indicates that EMS can exacerbate presenteeism tendencies, a concerning trend particularly among remote workers (e.g., Bathini & Kandathil, 2020; Bulińska-Stangrecka & Bagieńska, 2021; Sinclair et al., 2020). Individuals working remotely report higher levels of work intensification (Mallett et al., 2020), ultimately, working longer hours than before (Bolisani et al., 2020; DeFilippis et al., 2020; Rees, 2020). Workers subjected to high levels of EMS tend to report higher levels of anxiety (Indiparambil, 2019), emotional exhaustion (Baer et al., 2015), stress (Mallo et al., 2007), and burnout (Mastracci & Adams, 2018).

An illustrative example of such impact of EMS in contemporary remote working settings is the case of Barclays. The British bank came under the Information Commissioner's Office's investigation in 2020, where it faced a potential fine of £865 million for breaching privacy laws when it used Sapience Analytics surveillance software to track its remote workers. Initially launched to monitor staff anonymously, without the knowledge of its workers, Barclays enabled a feature which allowed managers to track individual employees' productivity score – which included a calculated percentage of working time in 'the zone' (high concentration and productivity). Employees were sent automatic alerts of their scores and prompts throughout the day on how to improve their time in 'the zone' (e.g., putting mobile phones away). What raised concerns was the fact that the software would also log bathroom visits as 'unaccounted activity', which could negatively impact their productivity scores. The whistleblower described 'the stress this (use of Sapience Analytics) is causing is beyond belief', with employees' accounts detailing how they were too anxious to step away from their desks to fetch water or use the bathroom in case it had negative repercussions for their performance.

Related to the discussion above, research has also found the potential of highly intrusive EMS to have an adverse impact on employee attitudes and behaviours. From a stress perspective, scholars have purported that EMS' pressure on work intensification is likely to have a flow-on effect in hampering job satisfaction (Holman, 2002; Holland et al, 2015). From the work design lens (Parker, 2014), there may be a tendency to simplify job tasks (in complexity and variety) as this makes monitoring and tracking EMS easier, effectively reducing employee's autonomy and, thereby, job satisfaction. To this end, several studies (Alge & Hansen, 2013; Backhaus, 2019; Ravid et al., 2022) and meta-analysis (Siegel et al., 2022) have found a negative relationship between EMS and job satisfaction. The presence of EMS technology can also signal a lack of trust – undermining the foundations of the employer-employee relationship (Migliano, 2022). Indeed, if workers perceive EMS to be a signal of mistrust and a violation of the employment relationship, individuals will likely restore equity in the relationship by disengaging (Migliano, 2022), reducing levels of OCB (Jeske, 2011), and commitment to colleagues, supervisors, and the organisation (Ball, 2021). In some cases, employees may even retaliate by engaging in counterproductive work behaviours and ultimately turnover (Bakewell et al., 2018; Martin et al., 2016).

THE FUTURE

We conclude this chapter with a few final propositions for discussions for practitioners and managers. One of the key challenges, when we discuss the dark side of flexibility, is that our concepts and understanding of privacy at work are often insufficiently explicit, clear, and mutually agreed (Lockwood & Nath, 2021). A nebulous sense of privacy as well as implicit and largely vague psychological contracts formed by the workforce can increase the likelihood that employees and organisations experience a conflict over tracking, monitoring, and surveillance practices. Transparency in communication, mutual commitment, and accountability are all key to ensuring that both the workers and the organisation clearly outline their expectations around privacy and work in a way that supports the adoption of solutions and work practices (Vatcha, 2020). Communication and conversion are important before fully fledged employee surveillance is developed (Hagen et al., 2018; Indiparambil, 2019; McParland and Connolly, 2020; West and Bowman, 2016).

Another area for more discussion around 'flexible work' or 'remote work' (Bal & Izak, 2021) is the importance to reflect on our use of the term 'at work'. For the majority of managers and employees, the idea of 'at work' still implies a fixed location like an office and/or time. This location specificity around working and our assumptions about work require a rethink, similar to how we now store data in the cloud and distributed data centres, rather than specific office-based servers. Not all organisations are ready for a digital transformation of their business and business model that could support a fully remote workforce. Similarly, many organisations are still clinging on to older leadership models that emphasise control, rather than other leadership models such as inclusive (Antonacopoulou & Georgiadou, 2021), servant leadership

(Al-Asfour et al., 2022), or liberating leadership (although it is clear that these leadership models also have their limitations, see Picard & Islam, 2019). The COVID-19 pandemic has initiated new interest in leadership in changing times as non-coercive and supportive (Crevani et al., 2021). Situationally appropriate leadership competencies are, in addition to business transformation, HR operational and budget reviews, important cornerstones of future remote working ambitions.

This also connects to divergent workforce expectations. Since the pandemic, many organisations adopted new work practices to support the needs of the business and to meet workers' requests for more flexibility (Allstrin et al., 2022). Many organisations are not equipped to meet all requests for employee and work flexibility. In short, workforce flexibility may be operationally and organisationally dependent: as sometimes a possibility, and not in all instances and at all times. The cross-functional collaboration required to implement many monitoring and surveillance tools further complicates matters for many of these organisations (Jeske & Calvard, 2022). These circumstances require open discussion and efforts to reach agreement with workers in order to counteract potential conflicts in expectations regarding the forms of flexibility that will be open to remote workers in the future (Bal & Izak, 2021).

REFERENCES

Adler-Bell, S. & Miller, M., (2018). *The Datafication of Employment*, TCF: The Century Foundation. Retrieved from https://policycommons.net/artifacts/1329055/the-datafication-of-employment/1932345/.

Al-Asfour, A., Charkasova, A., Rajasekar, J. & Kentiba, E. (2022). Servant leadership behaviors and the level of readiness to covid-19 pandemic: Evidence from USA higher education institutions. *International Journal of Leadership in Education*. https://doi.org/10.1080/13603124.2022.2108505.

Alge, B.J. & Hansen, S.D. (2013). Workplace monitoring and surveillance research since '1984': A review and agenda. In M.D. Coovert & L.F. Thompson (Eds.), *The Psychology of Workplace Technology* (pp. 209–37). Routledge, New York.

Allstrin, S., Grafström, J., Stern, L. & Weidenstedt, L. (2022). Managing work from anywhere: Six points to consider for HR professionals. Ratio Seminar Series, 2 November 2022. Unpublished paper uploaded on ResearchGate.

Aloisi, A. & De Stefano, V. (2022). Essential jobs, remote work and digital surveillance: Addressing the COVID-19 pandemic panopticon. *International Labour Review*, *161*(2), 289–314.

Aloisi, A. & Gramano, E. (2019). Artificial intelligence is watching you at work: Digital surveillance, employee monitoring, and regulatory issues in the EU context. *Comparative Labour Law & Policy Journal*, *41*, 95.

Aroles, J., Mitev, N. & de Vaujany, F.-X. (2019). Mapping themes in the study of new work practices. *New Technology, Work and Employment*, *34*, 285–99.

Antonacopoulou, E.P. & Georgiadou, A. (2021). Leading through social distancing: The future of work, corporations and leadership from home. *Gender, Work &*

Organization, 28(2), 749–67. https://onlinelibrary.wiley.com/doi/full/10.1111/gwao .12533.

Backhaus, N. (2019). Context sensitive technologies and electronic employee monitoring: A meta-analytic review. In R. Chatila & E. Yoshida (Eds.), *2019 IEEE/ SICE International Symposium on System Integration (SII)* (pp. 548–53). Sorbonne Université, Paris. ISSN: 2474–2325.

Baer, M., Dhensa Kahlon, R., Colquitt, J., Rodell, J.B., Outlaw, R. & Long, D. (2015), Uneasy lies the head that bears the trust: The effects of feeling trusted on emotional exhaustion. *Academy of Management Journal, 58*(6), 1637–57.

Bakewell, L.L., Vasileiou, K., Long, K.S., Atkinson, M., Rice, H., Barreto, M., ... & Vines, J. (2018). Everything we do, everything we press: Data-driven remote performance management in a mobile workplace. In *Proceedings of the 2018 CHI Conference on Human Factors in Computing Systems* (pp. 1–14).

Bal, P.M. & Izak, M. (2021). Paradigms of flexibility: A systematic review of research on workplace flexibility. *European Management Review, 18*(1), 37–50.

Bales, R.A. & Stone, K.V. (2020). The invisible web at work: Artificial intelligence and electronic surveillance in the workplace. *Berkeley Journal of Employment & Labor Law, 41*, 1.

Ball, K. (2010). Workplace surveillance: An overview. *Information, Technology and People, 25*(4), 376–94.

Ball, K. (2021). *Electronic Monitoring and Surveillance in the Workplace. Literature Review and Policy Recommendations.* Luxembourg: Publications Office of the European Union. ISBN 978–92–76–43340–8, doi:10.2760/5137, JRC125716.

Bathini, D.R. & Kandathil, G.M. (2020). Bother me only if the client complains: Control and resistance in home-based telework in India. *Employee Relations: The International Journal, 42*(1), 90–106.

Bauman, Z. & Lyon, D. (2013). *Liquid Surveillance: A Conversation.* Polity Press, Cambridge.

Becker, T.E. & Marique, G. (2014). Observer effects without demand characteristics: An inductive investigation of video monitoring and performance. *Journal of Business and Psychology, 29*, 541–53.

Bekkers, V., Edwards, A. & de Kool, D. (2013). Social media monitoring: Responsive governance in the shadow of surveillance? *Government Information Quarterly, 30*(4), 335–42.

Bhave, D.P. (2014). The invisible eye? Electronic performance monitoring and employee job performance. *Personnel Psychology, 67*, 605–35.

Bick, R., Hazran, E., Khan, H., Lacroix, S. Sarrazin, H. & Welchman, T. (2020). The future of work; Reskilling and remote working in the 'next normal'. McKinsey Co., Retrieved from https://www.mckinsey.com/capabilities/mckinsey-digital/our -insights/the-future-of-work-reskilling-and-remote-working-to-recover-in-the-next -normal.

Bolisani, E., Scarso, E., Ipsen, C., Kirchner, K. & Hansen, J.P. (2020). Working from home during COVID-19 pandemic: Lessons learned and issues. *Management & Marketing. Challenges for the Knowledge Society, 15*(s1), 458–76.

Bulińska-Stangrecka, H, & Bagieńska, A. (2021). The role of employee relations in shaping job satisfaction as an element promoting positive mental health at work in the era of COVID-19. *International Journal of Environmental Research and Public Health, 18*(4), 1903.

Chillakuri, B. & Vanka, S. (2021). Examining the effects of workplace well-being and high-performance work systems on health harm: A sustainable HRM perspective. *Society and Business Review*, *16*(1), 71–93.

Christian, A. (2022). The 'productivity paranoia' managers can't shake, BBC Worklife. Retrieved from https://www.bbc.com/worklife/article/20221130-the-remote-helicopter-bosses-who-stunt-worker-resilience.

Crevani, L., Uhl-Bien, M., Clegg, S. & Todnem By, R. (2021). Changing leadership in changing times II. *Journal of Change Management*, *21*(2), 133–43. https://doi.org/10.1080/14697017.2021.1917489.

Cyphers, B. & Gullo, K. (2020). Inside the invasive, secretive 'bossware' tracking workers. Electronic Frontier Foundation.

De Saulles, M. & Horner, D.S. (2011). The portable panopticon: Morality and mobile technologies. *Journal of Information, Communication & Ethics in Society*, *9*(3), 206–16.

DeFilippis, E., Impink, S.M., Singell, M., Polzer, J.T. & Sadun, R. (2020). Collaborating during coronavirus: The impact of COVID-19 on the nature of work. Working Paper No. w27612. National Bureau of Economic Research.

Fitzenz, J. (2010). *The New HR Analytics: Predicting the Economic Value of Your Company's Human Capital Investments* (1st edn). American Management Association, New York.

Foucault, M. (1979). *Discipline and Punishment: The Birth of the Prison*. Penguin, Harmondsworth.

Fried, J., Hansson, D.H. & Lowman, R. (2013). *Remote: Office Not Required*. Vermillion, New York.

Funder, D.C. & Ozer, D.J. (2019). Evaluating effect size in psychological research: Sense and nonsense. *Advances in Methods and Practices in Psychological Science*, *2*(2), 156–68.

Gagné, M. & Bhave, D. 2011. Autonomy in the workplace: An essential ingredient to employee engagement and well-being in every culture. In V.I. Chirkov, R.M. Ryan & K.M. Sheldon (Eds.), *Human Autonomy in Crosscultural Context*, Vol. 1 (pp. 163–87). Springerm Dordrecht, Netherlands.

Grant, A.M. & Mayer, D.M. (2009). Good soldiers and good actors: Prosocial and impression management motives as interactive predictors of affiliative citizenship behaviors. *Journal of Applied Psychology*, *94*(4), 900.

Grant, K., McQueen, F., Osborn, S. & Holland, P. (2023). Reconfiguring the jigsaw puzzle: Balancing time, pace, place and space of work in the Covid-19 era. doi:10.1177/0143831X231195686.

Greasley, K. & Thomas, P. (2020). HR analytics: The onto-epistemology and politics of metricised HRM. *Human Resource Management Journal*, *30*(4): 494–507.

Hagen, C.S., Bighash, L., Hollingshead, A.B., Shaikh, S.J. & Alexander, K.S. (2018). Why are you watching? Video surveillance in organizations. *Corporate Communications: An International Journal*, *23*(2), 274–91.

Hanley, D. & Hubbard, S. (2020). Eyes everywhere: Amazon's surveillance infrastructure and revitalizing worker power. Open Markets Institute.

Hansen, Hans K. & Weiskopf, R. (2021). From universalizing transparency to the interplay of transparency matrices: Critical insights from the emerging social credit system in China. *Organization Studies*, *42*, 109–28.

Hern, A. (2020), Shirking from home? Staff feel the heat as bosses ramp up remote surveillance. *Guardian*. Retrieved from https://www.theguardian.com/world/2020/sep/27/shirking-from-home-staff-feel-the-heat-as-bosses-ramp-up-remote-surveillance.

Holland, P. & Brewster, C. (2021). Redesigning Work as a Response to the Global Pandemic: Possibilities and Pitfalls. In D. Wheatley, S. Buglass & I. Hardill (Eds.), *Remote Work and Worker Well-being in the Post-COVID-19 Era: Impacts, Challenges, and Opportunities* (pp. 104–21). IGI Global, Hershey, PA.

Holland, P. & Tham, T.L. (2020). Total surveillance: Electronic monitoring and surveillance in the 21st century. In P. Holland & C. Brewster (Eds.), *Contemporary Work and the Future of Employment in Developed Countries* (pp. 135–50). Routledge, London.

Holland, P., Cooper, B. & Hecker, R. (2015). Electronic monitoring and surveillance in the workplace: The effects on trust in management, and the moderating role of occupational type. *Personnel Review, 44*(1), 161–75.

Holman, D. (2002). Employee wellbeing in call centres. *Human Resource Management Journal, 12*(4), 35–50.

Holmes, K. (2018). *Mismatch: How Inclusion Shapes Design.* MIT Press, Cambridge.

Indiparambil, J.J. (2019), Privacy and beyond: socio-ethical concerns of 'on-the-job' surveillance. *Asian Journal of Business Ethics, 8*(1), 73–105.

Iedema, R. & Rhodes, C. (2010). The Undecided space of ethics in organizational surveillance. *Organization Studies, 31*(2), 199–217. https://doi.org/10.1177/0170840609347128.

Jeske, D. (2011). *Electronic performance monitoring: Employee perceptions and reactions.* Unpublished doctoral dissertation, Northern Illinois University, De Kalb.

Jeske, D. & Calvard, T.S. (2022). Cross-functionality in practice: Electronic performance monitoring. In P.C. Nunes Figueiredo, E.L. de Campos Soares Tomé & J.C.D. Rouco (Eds.), *Handbook of Research on Challenges for Human Resource Management in the COVID-19 Era* (pp. 403–25). IGI Global, Hershey, PA.

Katsabian, T. (2019). Employees' privacy in the internet age. *Berkeley Journal of Employment and Labor Law, 40*(2), 203–55.

KeenCorp (2018). Your people: Do you know how they are really doing? KeenCorp. Retrieved from http://www.keencorp.com/ or https://perma.cc/Q7QP-A7PE.

Korsgaard, M.A., Meglino, B.M., Lester, S.W. & Jeong, S.S. (2010). Paying you back or paying me forward: Understanding rewarded and unrewarded organizational citizenship behavior. *Journal of Applied Psychology, 95*(2), 277.

Kurkowski, H. (2021). Monitoring remote workers: The good, the bad and the ugly. *Forbes.* Retrieved from https://www.forbes.com/sites/forbesagencycouncil/2021/12/08/monitoring-remote-workers-the-good-the-bad-and-the-ugly/.

Lavelle, J. (2020). Gartner CFO survey reveals 74% intend to shift some employees to remote work permanently. Gartner press release. Retrieved from https://www .gartner .com/ en/ newsroom/ press -releases/ 2020–04–03 -gartner -cfo -surey -reveals -74 -percent -of -organizations -to -shift -some -employees -to -remote -work -permanently2#:~:text=A%20Gartner%2C%20Inc.,remote%20positions%20post%2DCOVID%2019.

Lawler, E.E., III, Levenson A. & Boudreau J.W. (2004). HR metrics and analytics: Use and impact. *Human Resource Planning, 27*, 27–35.

Leonardi, P.M. (2021). COVID-19 and the new technologies of organizing: Digital exhaust, digital footprints, and artificial intelligence in the wake of remote work. *Journal of Management Studies, 58*(1), 249.

Levenson A. (2005). Harnessing the power of HR analytics. *Strategic HR Review,* 4(3), 28–31.

Lockwood, G. & Nath, V. (2021). The monitoring of tele-homeworkers in the UK: Legal and managerial implications. *International Journal of Law and Management, 63*(4), 396–416.

Lund, S., Madgavkar, A., Manyika, J., Smit, S., Ellingrud, K., Meaney, M. & Robinson, O. (2021). The postpandemic economy: The future of work after COVID-19. McKinsey Global Institute. Retrieved from https://www.mckinsey.com/~/media/mckinsey/featured%20insights/future%20of%20organizations/the%20future%20of%20work%20after%20covid%2019/the-future-of-work-after-covid-19-report-vf.pdf.

Mallett, O., Marks, A. & Skountridaki, L. (2020). Where does work belong anymore? The implications of intensive homebased working. *Gender in Management: An International Journal, 35*(7/8), 657–65.

Mallo, J., Nordstrom, C.R., Bartels, L.K. & Traxler, A. (2007). The effect of age and task difficulty. *Performance Improvement Quarterly, 20*, 49–63.

Martin, A.J., Wellen, J.M. & Grimmer, M.R. (2016). An eye on your work: How empowerment affects the relationship between electronic surveillance and counterproductive work behaviours. *The International Journal of Human Resource Management, 27*(21), 2635–651.

Mastracci, S. & Adams, I. (2018). 'That's what the money's for': Alienation and emotional labor in public service. *Administrative Theory & Praxis, 40*(4), 304–19.

Mateescu, A. & Nguyen, A. (2019). Algorithmic management in the workplace. Data & Society Research Institute. Retrieved from https://datasociety.net/library/explainer-algorithmic-management-in-the-workplace/.

Mazmanian, M., Orlikowski, W.J. & Yates, J. (2013). The autonomy paradox: The implications of mobile email devices for knowledge professionals. *Organization Science, 24*, 1337–57.

McNall, L.A. & Roch, S.G. (2007). Effects of electronic monitoring types on perceptions of procedural justice, interpersonal justice, and privacy. *Journal of Applied Social Psychology, 37*, 658–82.

McNall, L.A. & Roch, S.G. (2009). A social exchange model of employee reactions to electronic performance monitoring. *Human Performance, 22*(3), 204–24.

McParland, C. & Connolly, R. (2020). Dataveillance in the workplace: Managing the impact of innovation. *Business Systems Research, 11*(1), 106–24.

Migliano, S. (2022). Employee surveillance software demand up 58% since pandemic started, blog. Retrieved from https://www.top10vpn.com/research/covid-employee-surveillance.

Mondore, S., Douthitt, S. & Carson, M. (2011). Maximizing the impact and effectiveness of HR analytics to drive business outcomes. *People & Strategy: Journal of the Human Resource Planning Society, 34*(2), 20–7.

Morgan, K. & Nolan, D. (2023). How worker surveillance is backfiring on employers. BBC Worklife. Retrieved from https://www.bbc.com/worklife/article/20230127-how-worker-surveillance-is-backfiring-on-employers.

Mulki, J.P., Jaramillo, J.F. & Locander, W.B. (2008). Effect of ethical climate on turnover intention: Linking attitudinal- and stress theory. *Journal of Business Ethics, 78*(4), 559–74.

Nebeker, D.M. & Tatum, B.C. 1993. The effects of computer monitoring, standards, and rewards on work performance, job satisfaction, and stress. *Journal of Applied Social Psychology, 23*, 508–36.

Parker, S.K. (2014). Beyond motivation: Job and work design for development, health, ambidexterity, and more. *Annual Review of Psychology, 65*(1), 661–91.

Picard, H. & Islam, G. (2019). Free to do what I want? Exploring the ambivalent effects of liberating leadership. *Organization Studies*, *41*(3), 393–414. https://doi.org/10.1177/0170840618814554.

Raposo, V.L. (2023). When facial recognition does not 'recognise': Erroneous identifications and resulting liabilities. *AI & Society*. https://doi.org/10.1007/s00146-023-01634-z.

Ravid, D.M., White, J.C., Tomczak, D.L., Miles, A.F. & Behrend, T.S. (2022). A meta-analysis of the effects of electronic performance monitoring on work outcomes. *Personnel Psychology*, ePub 14 April 2022. https://doi.org/10.1111/peps.12514.

Rees, G. (2020), Employee-monitoring technology: Productivity vs privacy. Retrieved from https://www.intheblack.com/articles/2020/09/01/employee-monitoring-technology-productivity-privacy.

Santariano, (2020). How my boss monitors me when I work from home. *New York Times*. Retrieved from https://www.nytimes.com/2020/05/06/technology/employee-monitoring-work-from-home-virus.html.

Sarpong, S. & Rees, D. (2014). Assessing the effects of 'big brother' in a workplace: The case of WAST. *European Management Journal*, *32*, 216–22.

Sewell, G., Barker, J.R. & Nyberg, D. (2012). Working under intensive surveillance: When does 'measuring everything that moves' become intolerable? *Human Relations*, *65*(2): 189–215.

Siegel, R., König, C.J. & Lazar, V. (2022). The impact of electronic monitoring on employees' job satisfaction, stress, performance, and counterproductive work behavior: A meta-analysis. *Computers in Human Behavior Reports*, *8*, 100227.

Sinclair, R.R., Allen, T., Barber, L., Bergman, M., Britt, T., Butler, A., ... & Yuan, Z. (2020). Occupational health science in the time of COVID-19: Now more than ever. *Occupational Health Science*, *4*, 1–22.

Stanton, J.M. & Julian, A.L. (2002). The impact of electronic monitoring on quality and quantity of performance. *Computers in Human Behavior*, *18*, 85–101.

Tham, T.L. & Holland, P. (2022). Electronic monitoring and surveillance: The balance between insights and intrusion. In P. Holland., T. Bartram., T. Garavan & K. Grant (Eds.), *The Emerald Handbook of Work, Workplaces and Disruptive Issues in HRM* (pp. 493–512). Emerald, Bingley, UK.

Vatcha, A. (2020). Workplace surveillance outside the workplace: An analysis of e-monitoring remote employees. *iSChannel*, *15*(1), 4–9.

Vitak, J. & Zimmer, M. (2021). Workers' attitudes toward increased surveillance during and after the Covid-19 pandemic. *Items: Insights from the Social Sciences*.

Wang, B., Liu, Y., Qian, J. & Parker, S.K. (2021). Achieving effective remote working during the covid-19 pandemic: A work design perspective. *Applied Psychology*, *70*(1), 16–59.

Wells, D.L., Moorman, R.H. & Werner, J.M. 2007. The impact of the perceived purpose of electronic performance monitoring on an array of attitudinal variables. *Human Resource Development Quarterly*, *18*, 121–38.

West, J.P. & Bowman, J.S. (2016). Electronic surveillance at work: An ethical analysis. *Administration & Society*, *48*(5), 628–51.

Zuboff, S. (1988). *In the Age of the Smart Machine*. Basic Books, New York.

10. Treading water or dead in the water? The future of unions revisited through power analysis

Anthony Forsyth

INTRODUCTION

The transformation of the world of work wrought by more than 30 years of globalisation, economic restructuring and technological innovation has not only undermined the standard employment model (as demonstrated in the other chapters in this volume). It has also presented major challenges to trade unions (Visser 2019), which have seen their power and influence decline in the face of rising hostility from employers and the state in many countries. Along with the proliferation of atypical and insecure forms of work, the deployment of new technologies and business models (Weil 2019; Aloisi and De Stefano 2022) has further loosened the attachments which traditionally linked workers and their collective representatives.

So, are trade unions globally treading water or dead in the water? The optimistic conclusion of my recent research on the future of unions was that, despite over 30 years of declining membership in many countries, there were bright signs of innovation and revitalisation that would help secure their survival. However, that outcome was only possible if unions committed to a project of reimagination, including through technology, to meet the expectations of young employees and to satisfy the demands of marginalised workers for a more confrontational form of unionism (Forsyth 2022, p. 12). My sanguine view was subsequently shattered by the release in my home country of the biennial Australian Bureau of Statistics data on trade union membership in December 2022 (ABS 2022). It showed that union density (the proportion of Australian employees who are union members) had fallen even further, from 14.3 per cent in August 2020 to 12.5 per cent in August 2022 (in 1992, union density in Australia was 41.1 per cent). Of even greater concern for unions, only 2 per cent of 15–19-year-olds were union members in 2022 (down from 5 per cent in 2020) and only 5 per cent of those aged 20–24 (down from 6 per cent). Union membership has also declined further in two of the other countries covered in my study. In the USA density fell from 10.8 per cent in 2020 to 10.1 per cent in 2022 (Bureau of Labor Statistics 2023), and in the UK from 23.7 per cent to 22.3 per cent over the same period (Department for Business and Trade 2023).[1]

The continuing and pervasive nature of falling union membership compels me to re-evaluate the main conclusions of my research. These included that unions could return to a position of influence (although not necessarily to the membership levels of the past), by supplementing traditional organising with digital tools to forge connections between workers who traditionally have not joined unions, and being open to less rigid forms of engagement (or who counts as a 'member') (Forsyth 2022, pp. 192–208; see also Visser 2019, pp. 10, 68–70). I also examined the role of labour law in accounting for union decline, and the importance of labour law reform in union revitalisation, concluding that unions need to view campaigning for changes to the law as one element in the project of union revival – rather than as an end in itself (Forsyth 2022, pp. 208–25). However, there was a significant gap in my analysis, and that is the 'power' dimension of union decline and how to reverse it. In this chapter, I use power analysis – most clearly articulated by Holgate (2021) – to reassess 'the future of unions'. I do this by examining a number of recent examples of trade union campaigning and activism: the seemingly successful organising drives at Amazon and Starbucks in the USA; and the conclusion to the experiment of Australia's first digital union, Hospo Voice. I shall now explain the conceptual framing of worker and union power which will inform my assessment of the above examples and my ultimate conclusions.

THE CONCEPT OF WORKER AND UNION POWER

Jane Holgate's book *Arise: Power, Strategy, and Union Resurgence* was published just before mine, but I did not have the benefit of reading it until my book had gone to press. Much of Holgate's inquiry is directed at explaining how strategies for union renewal in the UK over the last 30 years, in particular the adoption of the US organising model (and its Australian equivalent; see Heery 2015; ACTU 2023), have not produced 'the panacea that was hoped for' (Holgate 2021, p. 16). In her view, this is because organising has been too narrowly focused 'on recruitment, tactics and individual campaigns rather

---

[1]   The recent fall in membership density in the UK followed three successive years of increases between 2017 and 2020 (Forsyth 2022, p. 17). As for Italy, the other nation considered in my study, OECD data shows a marginal fall in union density from 32.6 per cent in 2018 to 32.5 per cent in 2019 (OECD undated).

than a strategic review of where power lies and how it can be (re-)created' (p. 4). Union leaders have been too 'concerned with a cost-benefit analysis of whether the investment in organising was paying off in terms of membership gains', whereas for Holgate, 'deep and transformative organising is about building capacity and self-reliance among workers so they are able to use their own agency to effect change through collective action – or at least the credible threat of it' (p. 15). This more transformational approach to union renewal requires 'a focus on power – the essential factor needed for workers to effect change to improve their terms and conditions of employment' (p. 16; see also Marinescu and Rosenfeld 2022, p. 1).

Holgate then explores and elucidates three inter-related dimensions of worker power (2021, pp. 30–4).[2] Firstly, *'associational power* is at the heart of what trade unions are about': union members and leaders 'acting in concert ... to challenge the power of employers'. She explains that union density is often mistaken for associational power, but this misses important factors at the sectoral or workplace level such as 'how strongly the members identify with their union'. Secondly, *'structural power* arises from the position of workers in the economic system': their bargaining capacity in the context of conditions in the labour market, and (for example) whether their jobs are susceptible to offshoring or whether production processes are exposed to the 'structural power of disruption'. Thirdly, *'institutional power* ... is the capacity to hold employers to account through laws and regulations at transnational, national and local levels'. However, Holgate (2021, pp. 32–33) warns that 'institutional power is effectively power "borrowed" from more traditional bases', such as associational power:

> Primarily, the power of trade unions within institutions rests on their ability to enforce change. If that power has been eroded, then their institutional power will, in general, also decline.

McAlevey and Lawlor echo Holgate's scepticism about an institutional pathway (on its own) to union recovery, arguing that labour law reforms like European-style sectoral bargaining would founder in the US context without the necessary workplace-based power structures. For McAlevey and Lawlor (2023, p. 212), while it would improve on the current US enterprise-focused bargaining system: 'sectoral bargaining is still a form of negotiations. Like any negotiations, workers' success at the table depends directly on strong worker organization.' This view stems from their conception of union collective

---

[2]   Note, in addition, the dimensions of 'ideational power' and 'coalitional power' discussed in Rudman and Ellem (2022).

bargaining campaigns and negotiations as processes premised on 'build[ing] maximum power' through 'intentional, mass participation', with the goals not only of obtaining a collective agreement but also 'strengthening the workers' organisation and the labour movement as a whole' (p. 6). For this approach to succeed, unions have to be prepared to 'transform' how they negotiate from a 'closed' process 'with little worker involvement into [one] that serves as a key lever for rebuilding worker participation and power' (p. 12). Australian union leader Godfrey Moase has likewise argued for a direct (rather than representational) form of unionism, in which workers are empowered to 'actively [grab] hold of their own destiny and struggle' and union membership 'is the vehicle which creates the power necessary to win the change [workers] want to see' (Moase 2012, pp. 287, 280, 284–6). Similarly, Holgate contends that the narrowly conceived project of organising-for-membership in the UK must develop into 'a way of supporting union members to build power to improve their pay and conditions through their own self-activity' (2021, p. 183). Further:

> To become an 'organising union' requires a strategic vision, articulated by leaders, as to what could be won by the collective action of members. It is the vision of change that then attracts activists and gives confidence and hope to members. People join in the belief that being part of the union is a step toward winning a positive change in the workplace. (p. 184)

BUILDING UNION POWER ON HOSTILE GROUND: RECENT SUCCESSES IN THE USA (AND THEIR LIMITS)

Amazon

I opened my book with the story of the global e-commerce giant Amazon's extensive efforts to prevent its workers from unionising, all over the world but especially in the USA. I recounted how Amazon utilised the union-busting tactics perfected by US employers over many decades, to defeat a ballot for recognition of the Retail, Wholesale and Department Store Union (RWDSU) at its warehouse in Bessemer, Alabama in early 2021 (Forsyth 2022, pp. 1–2).[3] I also noted that an advocate of the safety rights of Amazon staff in Staten Island, New York, during the COVID-19 pandemic, Chris Smalls, was using

---

[3]   1,798 voters opposed union recognition, with only 730 in favour, out of 5,876 eligible employees. In a rerun of the Bessemer vote in March 2022 (ordered due to Amazon's unlawful tactics in the original vote), the RWDSU was again unsuccessful (993 to 875 with 400 ballots challenged) (Clark 2022a).

'the profile generated by his dismissal to kick-start a [wider] protest move-ment demanding higher pay' and better conditions for the company's workers (pp. 2–3; see also Healy 2022, pp. 39–44). By April 2022, Smalls had led the independent, grassroots Amazon Labor Union (ALU) to a landmark victory over the tech behemoth, with workers at the Staten Island JFK8 warehouse voting 2,654 to 2,131 in favour of union recognition (Kim 2022a). Smalls and his ALU activist colleagues ran an effective on-the-ground organising drive at JFK8 (and the nearby LDJ5 Amazon sorting centre). They used the bus stop sitting between the two locations as a focal point for discussions with workers, seeking to win their support for a $30 per hour minimum wage and more regular rest breaks (Velasquez 2022). Amazon rolled out the usual anti-union tactics including confiscation of ALU flyers and holding 'captive audience' meetings with the workforce (meetings which employees are compelled to attend to hear management's position without union representatives present); the ALU countered with TikTok videos, mass phone calls to workers and media profiles of Smalls and other union leaders (Kim 2022a).

ALU's independence from mainstream unions is considered a key ingredi-ent of its success at JFK8. Smalls explained: 'We felt that going the independ-ent route, starting something brand new and worker-led would be the better way to organize Amazon because we know the company' (Velasquez 2022). In its victory at Bessemer, Amazon had been able to portray the RWDSU as an (unhelpful) outside agent, but as Milkman (2022) explains, this tactic did not gain the same traction in New York because the ALU's leaders and activists came from the JFK8 workforce and reflected its generational and racial mix. The differences in attitudes to unions in 'right to work' Alabama and more union-friendly New York may also explain the divergent outcomes (Weise and Scheiber 2022). Yet while the ALU victory at Staten Island was hailed as an 'historic breakthrough' for organised labour in the USA (Weise and Scheiber 2022), McAlevey (2022) rightly pointed out that 'winning the union election is only step one' and 'now the real fight begins'. She argued further that:

> … the ALU must consolidate and build on the power it has amassed. This starts with it going all out to win a second election at LDJ5 [the nearby sorting facility]. … After that second election is in the rearview, the focus shifts to how to force Amazon to the negotiating table.

If the workers can build to a supermajority strike by walking off the job, there is no Prime Delivery. There is no delivery, period. So workers have essential, strategic workplace leverage. To get to the negotiating table, the ALU must act like a certified union despite the employer's stalling tactics.

However, things have turned out rather differently. The ALU lost the LDJ5 vote in late April 2022, workers voting 618 to 380 against union recognition

(Clark 2022b). It then lost another vote at Amazon's ALB1 warehouse in upstate New York, and some months after the Staten Island success it still had not forced the company into contract negotiations (Press 2023). That remains the case at the time of writing, 18 months after the JFK8 vote in favour of union recognition for collective bargaining. Again reverting to 'union-busting 101', Amazon has refused to accept that outcome and launched legal challenges to the vote through the National Labor Relations Board (NLRB), enabling it to delay the commencement of any discussions over a collective agreement (Sainato 2023a). In the meantime, fractures have emerged within the ALU itself: an 80-member ALU Democratic Reform caucus has emerged, raising concerns about Smalls's huge public profile and questioning the wisdom of the leadership's attempts to win other recognition votes before securing a contract at Staten Island (Leon 2023; Sainato 2023a).

Starbucks

Another major new site for union organising in the USA has been the wave of successful recognition votes at Starbucks coffee stores across the country. Like the ALU at Amazon, Starbucks Workers United (SWU) is a grass-roots, rank-and-file organisation although it is affiliated with a mainstream labour organisation, the Service Employees International Union (SEIU) (Press 2022a). In mid-December 2021, workers at a store in Buffalo, New York, voted to become the first unionised Starbucks in the country, an improbable victory (Jaffe 2022a). This became the trigger for a nationwide surge in SWU organising to obtain recognition for collective bargaining, demanding on behalf of Starbucks baristas not only improved pay and conditions but also greater respect from management:

> Starbucks workers from California to Maine, from Florida to Washington, face a lot of the same issues such as short staffing and unpredictable schedules. Low wages and unaffordable healthcare. Sexual and racial harassment, broken equipment, unfair discipline, and workplace favoritism. For this reason, we are seeking a national framework of agreements with Starbucks that, when signed, will solve these issues we're all facing. (SWU, undated)

Starbucks is trenchantly anti-union, its founding CEO Howard Schultz positioning the company as a progressive enterprise that looks after its 350,000 US employees so well they should not need union representation (Kim 2022b; Press 2022a). Not surprisingly, therefore, Starbucks has sought to defeat the SWU organising drive with tactics such as temporarily closing stores with high levels of union activism, flooding stores with 'support managers' to counter union messaging among staff, and firing SWU activists (Jaffe 2022a; Logan 2022; Press 2022b).

Schultz has placed himself at the heart of the battle for workers' hearts and minds, returning from retirement to the CEO role in April 2022. He spoke directly to workers prior to the union vote at the Buffalo store and, several months later, testified at a Congressional hearing to defend the company's opposition to the union campaign, stating that: 'We do nothing that is nefarious. We put our people first … and we have the track record to prove it' (Jaffe 2022b). In a leaked video call, he portrayed the SWU as 'an outside force that is trying to disrupt the future of our company' and urged Starbucks store managers to vigorously contest the unionisation drive (Lichtenstein 2022). Yet despite all these efforts, the SWU campaign has become 'a national movement' (Sainato 2022), holding successful recognition votes at 359 stores and roasteries covering 9,023 employees as at October 2023 (Reuning undated; see also Kochan et al. 2022, pp. 18–19). Even so, as with the ALU at Amazon, the real challenge for the SWU is to convert these NLRB vote successes into contract negotiations and, ultimately, genuine improvements in workers' pay and conditions through collective agreements. But like Amazon, Starbucks refuses to negotiate, and as Kim (2022b) observes: 'How to force Starbucks to the table is potentially an existential question for [the SWU]. It's unclear what tactic, other than focussed large-scale strikes, could pressure the company into meaningful talks.' Although the workers have engaged in several walkoffs and strikes over the last 18 months (see further the Analysis section below), this has not altered the company's position as the stand-off has become mired in legal proceedings over alleged unfair labour practices by Starbucks (Sainato 2023b; see also Stack 2023).

UNIONISM REIMAGINED: THE FINALE TO AUSTRALIA'S 'HOSPO VOICE' DIGITAL UNION PROJECT

The United Workers Union's (UWU) digital union, Hospo Voice, was examined in my research as one of a number of 'new union models and digital prototypes' since 2016, which had demonstrated 'some of the most creative experimentation by several Australian unions using new forms of … activism and a redefinition of the very concept of a "union"' (Forsyth 2022, p. 95). Established in 2018, Hospo Voice was marketed to young café, bar and restaurant workers through a Netflix-style membership, offering them access to online tools to contest underpayment and sexual harassment for A$9.99 per month. For several years, Hospo Voice was very effective in exposing wage theft and other forms of exploitation by Australian hospitality businesses and obtaining justice for the workers affected (Forsyth 2022, pp. 96–7). However, there was always a question mark over the start-up union's longevity, whether its members would 'move in significant numbers' from paying a notional monthly membership fee 'to full UWU membership', and whether it could make the transition from campaigning 'to become a strong workers' organisation which negotiates wages and conditions' (Forsyth 2022, p. 200).

In July 2021, the leaders of Hospo Voice announced changes to its membership model in an apparent effort to deal with some of these questions about its future direction. Presented as 'Hospo Voice 2.0', the new tiered membership structure offered members a choice between 'Hospo Voice Basic' for A$10 per month (access to the Hospo Voice community, campaigns and union discounts on various goods and services), 'Hospo Voice Standard' for A$29 per month (Basic + access to the Mobilise app's digital information tools, workshops and masterclasses) and 'Hospo Voice Plus' for A$79 per month (Basic/Standard + unlimited access to the UWU member-rights team, one-on-one support and more) (Hospo Voice 2021). However, the attempted transformation met with a fierce backlash from many of Hospo Voice's grassroots members and activists, who organised a petition in protest at what they saw as an undemocratic decision (Espejo 2021). Typical of this sentiment was the online critique from one anonymous member, lambasting Hospo Voice as 'not fit for purpose' because 'its officials view members as a passive source of revenue, rather than potential activists who can and must, with patience and effort, get organised to resist in their workplaces'. Questioning the wisdom and benefit of the new tiered membership structure, the member's tirade also highlighted the challenges inherent in Hospo Voice's quest to evolve from its original incarnation into something more sustainable:

> Shouldn't the union be trying to fight to win back unpaid wages for all its members, building collective power along the way? Apparently that doesn't fit the commercialised understanding of unionism that prevails at Hospo Voice, where the 'union' is a service provider extracting revenue from a passive membership. And even if you pay for 'Plus', don't expect any real organising. 'Personalised support to win back your unpaid wages' is more likely to mean help with lodging a Fair Work [underpayment] claim, not workplace organising. (Hospo Voice Member 2021)

It seems that Hospo Voice's leaders did not communicate effectively with its members about the rationale for the transition. In a subsequent UWU evaluation of the Hospo Voice project, it was acknowledged that 'our new tiered membership model initially met with strong resistance from some activists who believed that access to services should not be determined by membership level' – although the tiered approach 'proved to be quite uncontroversial with new members' (Petterson 2022, p. 29). In July 2022, the UWU decided to wind up Hospo Voice, National Secretary Tim Kennedy observing that the union learned (from the attempt to introduce the three-tier membership structure) 'that transactional unionism doesn't work'. Hospo Voice members were encouraged to join together with UWU members 'across industries … as one big powerful union' to 'ramp up' the fights against unfairness and exploitation in hospitality, leveraging the union's existing strength in casinos and licensed clubs, hotels, restaurants and cafés (Workplace Express 2022).

Hospo Voice's leadership considered that 'it certainly achieved its goals' in that '[i]n a young and mostly casual sector that has long been considered un-organisable, we signed up 2500 members in over four years and developed 400 impressive young activists' (Petterson 2022, p. 6). However, it seemed to measure success in terms of media hits and social media traffic ('creating explosive media moments that could be amplified via digital campaigning'; Petterson 2022, p. 19). The limitations of this approach were revealed, for example, by Hospo Voice's series of blog posts on common problems faced by workers in the industry, which had 'over 100,000 page views … but did not result in a noticeable increase in joins. … We essentially struggled to connect our solution – union membership – to the problems we engaged cold workers around' (Petterson 2022, p. 23). Hospo Voice was also limited by its premise that the hospitality sector is 'ill-suited to a standard bargaining and field organising strategy' and its main focus on using 'digital demonstrations of union power' against issues like wage theft 'to create compelling "join moments"' (Petterson 2022, pp. 9, 13).

ANALYSIS AND CONCLUSIONS

The three examples of union organising and activism examined in this chapter illustrate, in different ways, how innovative approaches can be used to build new forms of associational power among workers – but also, the limits of that form of power without an accompanying capacity (or ambition) to utilise structural power as a means to obtain enduring positive outcomes for the workforce. Such constraints are in part due to the erosion of the institutional power of unions over the last 30 years, especially in the USA. The prevalence of the union-busting industry, enabled by a broken labour law system with virtually no effective (and certainly no timely) remedies against employer obstruction of union organising, places US unions constantly on the defensive. That is why the successes of the ALU at Amazon and the SWU at Starbucks are so remarkable. Winning union recognition in such hostile terrain is a vindication of the strategic vision of the leaders of these grassroots unions. They have built associational power among vulnerable, exploited workers from the ground up, and instilled in these workers the belief that by joining together, they can contest the arbitrary power wielded by management every day in Amazon warehouses and Starbucks stores. However, as noted earlier, in each case the achievement of recognition is only half of the battle won. What matters now is whether the ALU and SWU can move from recognition to obtaining first collective agreements for the workers they represent.

The barriers here are formidable: both Amazon and Starbucks continue to exploit US labour laws, contesting the legitimacy of the unions' hard-fought recognition and engaging in 'surface bargaining' to draw out negotiations (i.e., technically complying with legal good faith bargaining requirements but with no intention of ever concluding an agreement). The unions need a circuit-breaker and that is where structural power comes into play. As McAlevey argued in relation to Amazon, and Kim in respect of Starbucks, the only real way to force these corporate titans into negotiations would be through large-scale strikes – or as Holgate put it, by deploying 'the structural power of disruption'. I noted in my research that a 2017 'Black Friday' strike by members of the main Italian union confederations at an Amazon warehouse led to negotiation of the company's first-ever collective agreement globally (Forsyth 2022, pp. 142–3). Amazon workers at the Staten Island warehouse have, as McAlevey suggested, 'essential, strategic workplace leverage'. They could significantly disrupt Amazon's supply chain in New York City. However, as we saw earlier, the ALU has not been able to build on the success of its victory at the JFK8 warehouse. As well as losing recognition votes at other locations, there seems to be no momentum towards strike action to force Amazon to negotiate, as the associational power built by the ALU has fractured due to internal tensions among its leaders.

At Starbucks, in contrast, the growth of the worker movement unleashed by the SWU's first success in Buffalo in late 2021 shows no sign of slowing down. Every week, more stores become unionised. Is there any prospect, then, of a mass strike to get Starbucks management to the negotiating table? Around 3,500 workers at over 150 US Starbucks stores went on strike in June 2023, protesting against a perceived change in company policy about whether LGBTQI+ Pride decorations could be displayed in the stores (Guardian staff and agency 2023). This followed walkoffs by SWU members in mid-November 2022 aimed at shutting down more than 100 stores on 'Red Cup Day', when Starbucks marks the start of the holiday season by serving coffee in festive red cups (one of its busiest trading days of the year) (Durbin 2022). There is, then, a clear willingness on the part of the newly-mobilised Starbucks workers to wield structural power. The SWU leaders are also aware of the 'crunch points' in the production chain where such power can have maximum effect. But given the company has more than 15,000 US stores, the SWU will need to significantly scale up any future strikes, if it is to pressure the company into negotiations and convert recognition success (at almost 360 stores and counting) into collective agreements.

The Hospo Voice story illustrates the ability for new forms of unionism to develop through a combination of digital (online) and direct action (offline) strategies, harnessing the force of mainstream and social media to attract young workers to contest their exploitation. This was an important attempt to build associational power in the largely union-free environment of Australian cafés and restaurants, and it succeeded up to a point. Hospo Voice's collective strength – a vibrant network of members and activists, built over its first few years – splintered when the union tried to implement a self-sustaining membership model. This inevitably contributed to the UWU's decision to end Hospo Voice, but the seeds of its demise lie deeper than that. Implicit in its leaders' prioritisation of digital campaigning and media hits was a lowering of ambition as to what could be achieved for hospitality workers. It seemed to be enough to highlight a case of egregious underpayment by a café, restaurant or hotel chain, obtain some form of recompense for the affected workers, then move onto the next target. Structural power is nowhere to be found in this strategy, which was based on a view that for Hospo Voice to ultimately engage in collective bargaining with employers is too difficult in the hospitality sector. That view may be partly valid for reasons including limits on the institutional power of Australian unions, in particular labour laws that have (until recently) precluded collective bargaining across multiple employers.[4] However, the UWU has succeeded in organising and obtaining collective agreements for other 'unorganisable' workers, such as migrant farm labourers, in the last five years (Underhill et al. 2020; Forsyth 2022, pp. 111–15). In addition, the Starbucks campaign in the USA demonstrates that start-up unions *can* organise hospitality workplaces for more than simply correcting injustices, and credibly work towards the goal of securing collective agreements (although, as has been noted, greater structural power will need to be exercised to realise that objective).

What does all of this mean for the conclusions I reached in my research on 'the future of unions'? I remain of the view that unions must continue to evolve, including through technology, to appeal to young and marginalised workers. The Amazon, Starbucks and Hospo Voice examples all demonstrate that innovation in union forms and tactics will attract new members and activists, and enable associational power to take root in previously union-free sites. However, something more is clearly needed to empower workers, as Moase (2012) put it, to grab hold of their own destiny and utilise their union to win the change they want to see. That something is structural power, driven by the members but enabled by the kind of union leadership Holgate described as the vision of change that gives members confidence that they can win through collective action. It is the pursuit – and securing – of real improvements in pay and other conditions that will convince workers of the benefits of union mem-

---

[4]   Significant amendments to Australian federal labour legislation were passed by Parliament in late 2022, including new mechanisms for workers and unions to engage in multi-employer collective bargaining (although it is unclear as yet how effective these changes will be in practice) (see Stewart et al. 2023).

bership. The need to successfully deliver on this core union function through leadership that energises workers to take the risky path of industrial action was probably under-emphasised in my book's conclusions about how unions can recover (see the brief discussion of 'the bolder "strike-ready" union' in Forsyth 2022, pp. 206–7).

In the UK, there has been widespread industrial action by unions covering rail, bus and postal workers, civil servants, teachers and National Health Service staff since mid-2022 (Wall 2022; Office for National Statistics 2023). Combative union leaders like Mick Lynch of the National Union of Rail, Maritime and Transport Workers and Pat Cullen of the Royal College of Nursing have inspired their members to take part in many months of rolling strikes, pushing the boundaries of the public's tolerance of disruption to vital public services (Nevett 2022; Triggle 2023). Unions have ramped up their deployment of structural power to pressure the UK government to agree to new pay deals in the context of rapidly rising inflation, with some success (see, e.g., Standley 2023). Their campaign has also connected with a wider sense of community resentment after many years of austerity-driven cuts to public services, and increasing demands to address inequality and the cost of living crisis (Enough is Enough Ltd undated). We are yet to see whether this recent wave of industrial action leads to increased membership for UK unions. It is also worth noting that the sites for this recent wave of strikes are mostly in economic sectors which were traditional strongholds of union power, rather than in newer services-focused or technology-enabled industries like those considered in the three case studies in this chapter. The barriers to taking industrial action are more formidable for low-wage warehouse, hospitality and café workers, in workplaces built on temporary forms of employment and the constant threat of retribution for collective organising.

The organising successes at Amazon and Starbucks in the USA, and the UWU's attempt to reimagine unionism through the Hospo Voice experiment, represent significant examples of the efforts of trade unions globally[5] to meet the myriad challenges presented by the 'new world of work' which have been considered in this volume. The three examples considered here also illustrate the ongoing *need* for unions as a bulwark against employer power in the hyper-flexible modern workplace, where artificial intelligence and other technologies have become new instruments of surveillance, performance management and discipline of employees (Del Castillo 2018; Wood 2021; Aloisi 2022). Unions are therefore by no means dead in the water, but a significant reorientation in strategy may be needed to enable them to move from constantly treading water to confidently swimming atop the waves. My reassessment of

---

[5]   See further Ramos et al. (2023).

the future of unions through the lens of Holgate's power analysis leads me to the following conclusion: unions that build capacity in workers to transform their working lives through collective action (translating associational power into structural power) have far greater prospects of attracting new members than unions which pursue a narrow 'organising for recruitment' pathway or simply operate in the institutional space of pushing for labour law reforms.

REFERENCES

ABS. (2022). *Trade Union Membership*, Australian Bureau of Statistics, Canberra.

ACTU. (2023). *Organising Works Review*, Australian Council of Trade Unions, Melbourne, June.

Aloisi, A. (2022). '*Boss Ex Machina*: Employer Powers in workplaces governed by algorithms and artificial intelligence', in Lo Faro, A (ed.), *New Technology and Labour Law: Selected Topics*, Giappichelli, Torino.

Aloisi, A. & De Stefano, V. (2022). *Your Boss Is an Algorithm: Artificial Intelligence, Platform Work and Labour*, Hart Publishing, Oxford.

Bureau of Labor Statistics. (2023). Union members 2022, News release, US Department of Labor, Washington DC.

Clark, M. (2022a). 'Union files objections to Amazon's actions in Bessemer, AL election', *The Verge*, 9 April.

Clark, M. (2022b). 'Amazon Labor Union stumbles as workers vote down union at second NYC facility', *The Verge*, 3 May.

Del Castillo, A. (2018). 'Artificial intelligence: A game changer for the world of work', Foresight Brief #05, European Trade Union Institute, Brussels.

Department for Business and Trade. (2023). *Trade Union Membership, UK 1995–2022: Statistical Bulletin*, National Statistics.

Durbin, D. (2022). 'Starbucks workers strike at more than 100 stores in largest labor action since union campaign', *PBS NewsHour*, 17 November.

Enough is Enough Ltd. (undated), *Enough is Enough!* at: https://wesayenough.co.uk/. Accessed 18 October 2023.

Espejo, D. (2021). 'Hospitality workers petition against tiered union membership', *Honi Soit*, 7 July, at: http:// honisoit .com/ 2021/ 07/ hospitality -workers -petition -against-tiered-union-membership/. Accessed 18 October 2023.

Forsyth, A. (2022). *The Future of Unions and Worker Representation: The Digital Picket Line*, Hart Publishing, Oxford.

Guardian staff and agency. (2023). 'Workers at over 150 US Starbucks stores to strike over Pride decorations', *Guardian*, 23 June.

Healy, M. (2022). *Organising during the Coronavirus Crisis: The Contradictions of Our Digital Lives*, Palgrave Macmillan, Singapore.

Heery, E. (2015). 'Unions and the organising turn: Reflections after 20 years of organising works', *Economic and Labour Relations Review*, 26(4): 545.

Holgate, J. (2021). *Arise: Power, Strategy and Union Resurgence*, Pluto Press, London.

Hospo Voice. (2021). 'Introducing Hospo Voice 2.0: A membership for every kind of worker', email to Hospo Voice members, 2 July (on file with the author).

Hospo Voice Member. (2021). 'Hospo Voice is terrible and it's getting worse', *Red Flag*, 12 July, at: https://redflag.org.au/article/hospo-voice-terrible-and-its-getting -worse. Accessed 18 October 2023.

Jaffe, G. (2022a). 'A Rhodes scholar barista and the fight to unionize Starbucks', *Washington Post*, 12 February.

Jaffe, G. (2022b). 'Lexi Rizzo fought to unionize her Starbucks. Now she's out of a job. Her struggle is just beginning', *Washington Post*, 17 June.

Kim, E. (2022a). 'How to unionize at Amazon', *The New Yorker*, 7 April.

Kim, E. (2022b). 'The upstart union challenging Starbucks', *The New Yorker*, 2 August.

Kochan, T., Fine, J, Bronfenbrenner, K., Naidu, S., Barnes, J., Diaz-Linhart, Y., Kallas, J., Kim, J., Minster, A., Tong, D., Townsend, P. & Twiss, D. (2022). *U.S. Workers' Organizing Efforts and Collective Actions: A Review of the Current Landscape*, Worker Empowerment Research Network, June.

Leon, L. (2023). 'Reform caucus rises, sues for elections in Amazon Labor Union', *Labor Notes*, 10 July.

Lichtenstein, N. (2022). 'Starbucks workers are demanding management stop acting like petty dictators', *Jacobin*, April.

Logan, J. (2022). '10 reasons why the Starbucks campaign is bad news for anti-union corporations', *The Hill*, 20 March.

Marinescu, I. & Rosenfeld, J. (2022). 'Worker power and economic mobility: A landscape report', WorkRise Research Report, Urban Institute.

McAlevey, J. (2022). 'The Amazon Labor Union's historic victory was the first step', *The Nation*, May 2/9.

McAlevey, J. & Lawlor, A. (2023). *Rules to Win By: Power and Participation in Union Negotiations*, Oxford University Press, Oxford.

Milkman, R. (2022). 'The Amazon Labor Union's historic breakthrough', *Dissent*, 8 April.

Moase, G. (2012). 'A new species of shark: Towards direct unionism', *Interface: A Journal for and about Social Movements*, 4(2): 280.

Nevett, J. (2022). 'Mick Lynch: Union leader who's in the national spotlight', *BBC News*, 13 December.

OECD. (undated). *OECD Data on Trade Union Density*, at: https://stats.oecd.org/Index.aspx?DataSetCode=TUD. Accessed 18 October 2023.

Office for National Statistics. (2023). *The Impact of Strikes in the UK: June 2022 to February 2023*.

Petterson, T. (2022). *Australia's First Digital Union: Final Report*, UWU, November.

Press, A. (2022a). 'The Starbucks union drive is spreading with impressive speed', *Jacobin*, February.

Press, A. (2022b). 'Starbucks is desperate to stop unionization, so it's firing worker leaders', *Jacobin*, April.

Press, A. (2023). 'Right now is the most exciting time to join the labor movement in decades', *Jacobin*, May.

Ramos, J., Priday, G., Browne, R. & Chimal, A. (2023). 'Trade Unions navigating and shaping change', ILO/ACTRAV Working Paper, International Labour Organization.

Reuning, K. (undated). *Union Election Data – Current Starbucks Statistics*, at: https://unionelections.org/data/starbucks/. Accessed 18 October 2023.

Rudman, A. & Ellem, B. (2022). 'Union purpose and power: Regulating the fissured workplace', *Economic and Industrial Democracy*. doi: https://journals.sagepub.com/doi/10.1177/0143831X221139333.

Sainato, M. (2022). '"This is a national movement": Union drives surge at US Starbucks stores', *Guardian*, 11 February.

Sainato, M. (2023a). '"War of attrition": Why union victories for US workers at Amazon have stalled', *Guardian*, 8 April.

Sainato, M. (2023b). '"The law is finally catching up": The union contract fight at Starbucks', *Guardian*, 12 May.

Stack, M. (2023). 'Inside Starbucks' dirty war against organized labor', *New York Times*, 21 July.

Standley, T. (2023). 'Teacher strikes in England end as all four unions accept pay deal', *BBC News*, 31 July.

Stewart, A., McCrystal, S. & Forsyth, A. (2023). 'Will pay be better and jobs more secure? Analysing the Albanese government's first round of fair work reforms', *Australian Journal of Labour Law*, 36(2), 104.

SWU. (undated). *Our Proposals*, at: https:// sbworkersunited .org/ proposal -update. Accessed 18 October 2023.

Triggle, N. (2023). 'Nurses strike because patients are dying – RCN union boss Pat Cullen', *BBC News*, 16 May.

Underhill, E., Groutsis, D., van den Broek, D. & Rimmer, M. (2020). 'Organising across borders: Mobilising temporary migrant labour in Australian food production', *Journal of Industrial Relations*, 62(2): 278.

Velasquez, J. (2022). 'Meet Christian Smalls and Derek Palmer, the DIY duo behind the Amazon Labor Union's guerrilla bid to make history', *The City*, 24 March.

Visser, J. (2019). 'Trade unions in the balance', ILO/ACTRAV Working Paper, International Labour Organization.

Wall, T. (2022). 'Industrial disputes in UK at the highest in five years as inflation hits pay', *Guardian*, 3 April.

Weil, D. (2019). 'Understanding the present and future of work in the fissured workplace context', *RSF: The Russell Sage Foundation Journal of the Social Sciences*, 5(5): 147.

Weise, K. & Scheiber, N. (2022). 'Amazon workers on Staten Island vote to unionize in landmark win for labor', *New York Times*, 1 April.

Wood, A. (2021). 'Algorithmic management: consequences for work organisation and working conditions', JRC Working Paper Series on Labour, Education and Technology, No. 2021/07, European Commission, Joint Research Centre, Seville.

Workplace Express. (2022). 'UWU shutters pioneering digital union', *Workplace Express*, 22 July.

PART IV

Contemporary aspects of flexible work

11. Learning, development and employability

Valerie Anderson

INTRODUCTION

This chapter discusses the skill and employability implications arising from the changes to work and employment relationships, discussed in detail in the previous chapters of this book, that have been linked to increased digitisation, automation and other technological developments. Labour market changes since the 1980s have been characterised by a proliferation of different forms of non-standard, virtual, remote and precarious work arrangements. To different extents, in different regions of the world, work that is becoming most precarious or at risk of automation is expected to have the greatest negative effect on members of already disadvantaged groups. However, accurate predictions about 'the shape of things to come' are elusive (Battisti et al., 2023). Alongside this, at a global level, patterns of global labour migration, as well as changes in the geography of production, distribution and value chains, raise questions about whether traditional approaches to vocational training and employability remain appropriate (Keep, 2021; WEF, 2018).

This chapter focuses on learning, training, development, vocational education and employability. These are important topics as vocational education, and skill development and deployment have long been understood to be a driver of a nation's wealth with direct and indirect impact on individual's careers, employability and life chances and on organisational productivity and performance (Becker, 1964; Garavan et al., 2018; Paprock, 2006; Schultz, 1961). Therefore, the questions addressed in this chapter are:

1. What are the main features of learning, training and employability systems at the macro (global environment), meso (national and sector) and micro (organisational and individual) levels, and how do these systemic features interact with each other?

2. What effects will global developments such as technological change, environmental and social sustainability challenges, and patterns of global migration have on skill demands and employability?
3. What learning, training, education and employability policy and practice responses will be necessary to address the consequences?

NATIONAL SYSTEMS OF LEARNING, TRAINING AND VOCATIONAL EDUCATION

To address the opening question, a systems perspective is taken as a basis from which to examine the role, purpose, beneficiaries and key stakeholders involved in national-level systems of learning, training and vocational education. Learning, education, training and employability issues feature in analysis and debates in a multitude of different policy, practice and research specialisms, for example, economics, education, labour market studies, career studies, and so on. Human Resource Development (HRD), which is concerned with three principal constructs; people, learning and organisations, is used in this chapter as a framing from which these different perspectives can be synthesised to examine the systemic features of vocational education and training, workplace training and development, organisation development and social and individual skill and personal development. Specifically, the field of National Human Resource Development (NHRD) provides a useful basis from which learning, training and employability systems, policies and practices at institutional, regional, organisational and individual levels can be both described and explained (Garavan et al., 2018). Pertinent to the questions raised in this chapter, NHRD focuses on describing and explaining how and why investment in education and training systems at different levels and by different 'actors' affect economic development, business performance, social and civic development, and individual level well-being and employability (Garavan et al., 2018).

The principal assumption of NHRD is that vocational education, training, learning and development have important effects on both economic and non-economic outcomes and life chances (McLean, 2004). Although NHRD as a field is grounded in systems theory (Checkland, 1994; Wang & Swanson, 2008), economic concepts derived from human capital theory (Becker, 1964; Schultz, 1961) are dominant in most considerations of the relationship between learning, training and vocational education and individual, organisational and societal-level outcomes. The assumption is that investment in NHRD will generate 'high skills' required to meet labour demand and so contribute to economic growth and poverty alleviation (Brown et al., 2021). Assumptions from social theory, especially the work of Bourdieu (1986), also underpin NHRD's explanation of the role of education, highlighting the opportunities it provides for individuals and groups to accumulate and deploy social capital resources from which to obtain social and economic advantage through, for example, increased social status, professional standing, employability and income generation. Social capital is, therefore, understood as the means of access to social and employment networks providing opportunities for socialisation into the implicit and explicit norms and values that help people to fully exploit employment opportunities and achieve career advancement (Bourdieu, 1986; Coleman, 1988).

At a national level, most NHRD policies are firmly grounded in human capital theory. They assume that the demand side of the labour market, driven by competitive market forces, creates skill demands. The role of education and training is, therefore, to supply the skills needed to meet demand. Some national-level policies may operate a mostly voluntarist approach to skill supply, leaving the process of skill development to 'independent' bodies such as educational institutions and employers or trade bodies. Others may take a more interventionist approach to encourage or mandate specific skill supply activities (Anderson et al., 2020; Stuart & Cooney, 2008). These assumptions pervade macro-level, 'supra-national' institutional advocacy by the Organisation for Economic Co-operation and Development (OECD) and World Economic Forum (WEF) as well as those of other global institutions such as the World Bank, the International Labour Organization (ILO) and the United Nations Educational, Scientific and Cultural Organization (UNESCO). These institutions publish international benchmarks and national performance measures grounded in the supply of education and training to encourage policy improvements to national skill supply systems in order to meet labour market demands (Keep, 2021).

However, the rapid economic growth achieved in the 1980s by countries such as Hong Kong, Taiwan, Singapore and South Korea (the so-called Asian Tiger economies) raises questions about whether the assumption that skill supply can only respond to skill demand generated through competitive market forces. At this time, the state encouraged investment in physical, informational and technological infrastructure alongside changes to education and vocational training, resulting in substantially accelerated economic, social and educational development (Blumenfeld & Malik, 2017; Riain, 2000). This 'Developmental State' approach, adopted latterly by other Asian economies with different degrees of success, therefore, highlights the limitations of reliance on assumptions that NHRD is a derivative and reactive activity dependent on liberal or free market economic theory. It further illustrates how learning, training and employability policy and practice are better understood as a part of interactional cultural, political, economic, technological and ecological systems.

Recognition of the interactivity between education, learning, development and employability systems with wider societal, political and economic policies focuses attention on the ways in which national-level systems of education and training constrain or enhance outcomes for individuals, employers and civil society. As a result, societal assumptions about participation or exclusion from education have economic as well as cultural consequences. In addition, occupationally directed 'upskilling' initiatives at national and regional levels are dynamically interrelated with wider cultural and social systems. This interrelatedness means that industry and sector-wide lobby groups, employers and training and vocational education providers are important actors, as well as beneficiaries, of NHRD processes and outcomes. Employers form an important 'pivot point' in the interactivity of NHRD systems. Their business development provides the basis of skill demand in national and local labour markets, but their investment in skill development through workplace education and training and career development at the workplace level further affects skill supply within the labour market system (Garavan et al., 2023). Processes of skill supply and demand are further nested within, and interact with, other patterns of national-level demographics, such as the age and health of the workforce. Figure 11.1 illustrates the complex, multi-level and interrelated features of NHRD in different country settings that are themselves sensitive to global business and economic fluctuations. NHRD occurs as a result of, and influences, macro-level political and economic power dynamics and 'trade-offs' that are further influenced by other factors such as global and local patterns of labour migration, changing forms of international regulation, and unanticipated global events such as pandemics or regional conflicts (Keep, 2021).

THE FUTURE OF WORK AND THE FUTURE OF SKILLS

Learning, development, training and vocational education and employability configurations vary according to national contexts and are further affected by other systemic features and developments, such as technological change and other changes to work and employment systems. This section assesses these developments and their potential impact on employability and employment-related learning, training, development and education.

A challenge for this discussion is that the extent to which technological advances in digital interconnectivity and 'smart' automation will affect work and employment, and therefore learning, training and vocational education, is contested (Philbeck & Davis, 2018). However, there is little doubt that in many high-income economies, technological change since the 1970s has been linked with a substantial decline in demand for traditional industrial skills and an increase in demand for skills relevant to which is often referred to

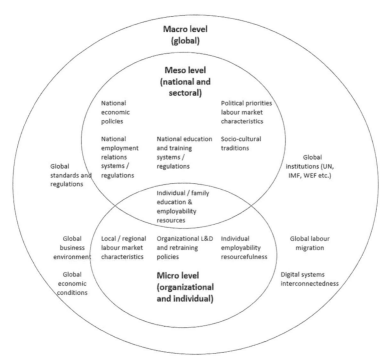

Source: Adapted from Garavan et al. (2018: 294).

Figure 11.1   Influences on learning, development and employability

as a 'knowledge economy' (Hadad, 2017). However, although technology, and especially computerisation, has increasingly prompted the exchange and commodification of knowledge in many Western economies, industrial manufacturing and production value chains have not disappeared but have shifted to other parts of the world (Mangan & Lalwani, 2016). Increasingly rapid technological developments in social, commercial and manufacturing practice, generated through machine learning, increased automation, artificial intelligence (AI), mobile robotics and 'smart systems' have led to further suggestions that a further shift to labour market structures is likely, referred to increasingly as the Fourth Industrial Revolution (4IR) (Philbeck & Davis, 2018). This proposal is grounded in an assessment of the effect of increases in automation and the opportunities provided by self-monitoring technological systems to replace human expertise in work systems. These opportunities, it is argued, mean that operational-level problem diagnosis, analysis and solution can occur more reliably and efficiently through technology replacing the demand for substantial numbers of human workers to carry out such work. This scenario suggests that labour markets will be substantially destabilised and restructured (Bag & Wood, 2022).

Two competing theoretical approaches have emerged to explain the potential effect of substantial technological change on labour markets and, therefore, on learning, training and employability. One theoretical lens, referred to as labour scarcity theory, suggests that technological transformation will result in a scarcity of appropriately skilled labour with new skill requirements arising at pace (Brown, 2021). Labour scarcity theory predicts that employment in sectors where non-routine, semi-skilled and semi-professional skills which comprise much of the curriculum of advanced-level training and education will quickly be dispensed with as robotics, machine learning technology, algorithmic management and big data manipulation will provide more reliable and efficient means for these tasks to be carried out (Frey & Osborne, 2017). However, labour scarcity theorists also predict high levels of demand for work involving high-level cognitive tasks requiring depth and breadth of human perception, for example, tasks involving negotiation, persuasion, care and human creativity (WEF, 2018). The challenge, according to this view, is that existing provision of vocational training and education, which has traditionally been slow to respond to changes, will fuel an over-supply of inappropriate or out-of-date skills and an insufficient supply of high-level cognitive and creative skills.

Taken as a whole, labour scarcity theory predicts a substantial restructuring of labour markets, and especially an extensive 'hollowing-out' of middle-income work. However, it also suggests that increased demand for high-level cognitive skills, in addition to the retention of some low-income (care-related) manual occupations within the labour market, will occur. Advocates for this interpretation, such as the World Economic Forum (WEF, 2018), argue for urgent investment in early childhood education as the basis for foundational cognitive and socio-behavioural skills needed in the 4IR context. Advocates further argue for increased provision of further education and vocational training, with a focus on analytical thinking and innovation, technology design and programming, as well as increased emotional intelligence and leadership capabilities. Such investment, it is assumed, will facilitate employability through adaptation to technological transformation with resultant societal and individual-level benefits from new opportunities and technological imperatives.

The second theoretical lens, job scarcity theory, takes a more critical approach. This approach focuses on patterns of advantage and disadvantage in work and employment across societies and sectors taken as a whole. Job scarcity theory suggests that the deployment of technology and other resources rarely acts in a neutral way; there are always 'winners' and 'losers'. Job scarcity theory, therefore, suggests that the consequences of technological advances will not be benign. In considering the likely impact of future-orientated scenarios concerning the 4IR, some groups will benefit from greater productivity made possible with automation and the new business opportunities that will arise. However, other groups of workers will lose their livelihoods as jobs and employment prospects disappear from the labour market. Therefore, a job scarcity theory approach suggests a transformation of labour markets and employability as a result of technological change that will eradicate the demand for much manual and semi-skilled work as well as remove the need for much of the 'knowledge work' currently carried out by those in mid-level professional, higher technical and managerial roles. This, according to job scarcity theory, will occur as AI and machine learning technologies increasingly erode and automate the 'knowledge processing' features of much work currently labelled as professional (Brown et al., 2010; Susskind & Susskind, 2015).

Job scarcity theory, therefore, critiques assumptions inherent in human capital theory that investment in high-level skills will always lead to increased employability. Instead, job scarcity theory predicts that, in the context of technological transformation, there will be an over-supply of skills and abilities generated from existing approaches to further and higher education and advanced training systems (Srnicek, 2017; Susskind & Susskind, 2015). Emerging challenges to graduate employability in developed Western economies, where the supply of qualified and skilled graduates already exceeds demand by employing organisations (Anderson & Tomlinson, 2021) might be understood in this context. From the job scarcity theory perspective, therefore, technological transformation will lead to a surplus of well-qualified individuals who find themselves without the opportunity to build a meaningful career and who will be forced into precarious forms of employment for which they are over-qualified and over-skilled (Murgia & Poggio, 2014).

Taken to its extreme, the assumptions underpinning job scarcity theory invite speculation that the technological transformation scenario will challenge taken-for-granted assumptions about the working life span and the extent to which employability can remain a valid feature of an individual's personal identity. Aroles et al. (2020), for example, suggest that automation and technological transformation processes require a systemic 're-think' about whether 'full-time work' in a standard employment relationship over a 40-year work-life period will remain feasible. In summary, job scarcity theory challenges current assumptions that human capital investment in education or skills will deliver positive employability outcomes. In contrast to labour scarcity theory, it suggests that education, training and learning focused explicitly on employability-related skills will make things worse by leading to labour market congestion with an over-supply of qualified candidates for a labour market characterised by fewer employment opportunities.

Job demand and job scarcity theories reach different conclusions about the implications for learning, development and employability of technological transformation. However, both approaches are grounded in the same starting assumption. Both assume an inevitability in the increased use and spread of technology. Both also assume that technology will have a generally applicable and universal effect on skill demands and employability. However, this technological determinist stance has been critiqued as being over-reliant on the experiences and assumptions of Western developed economies that may not apply in different regions of the world (Trauth-Goik, 2021). For example, although industrial and manufacturing employment in Western developed economies has declined since the late 20th century, it has remained stable in the rest of the world and continues to rise in East Asia (World Bank, 2019). In addition, in developing economies where access to technology is more limited, low-skill work and employment are less at risk. Further, although concerns about increased work precarity and non-standard work arrangements have increased in Western economies since the turn of the 21st century, informality in employment relationships has been the norm and has remained stable in other parts of the world (Anderson, 2022). Historical analyses also question the 4IR scenario predictions of unprecedented effects on work and employment. Instead, historical trends indicate that 'ruptures' to employment and skills, leading to patterns of 'lagged' over-supply of outdated skills, have consistently occurred as changes to technology (whether engineering, electronic or digital) have been developed (Frey & Osborne, 2017). Commentators have also suggested that, in addition to variations in the rate of job loss over time, societal and macro-level cultures and policies will lead to variations affecting issues such as employability and different forms of employment relationships (Peters, 2020).

To summarise, most estimates of the proportion of skills at risk as a result of technological change are 'worst case' projections. In addition, employer decision-making and local contexts are likely to either exacerbate or suppress the effects on employability. Arntz et al. (2016), for example, suggest that country-specific economic, legal, social and ethical regulations and barriers may limit the effects of automation on employability as well as on learning, training and development in workplace settings. Different interpretations of the implications of any future transformative deployment of technology also lead to very different conclusions about the effect on labour markets, work and employment.

THE FUTURE FOR TRAINING, SKILLS AND EMPLOYABILITY

The argument of this chapter is that learning, training and development at micro, meso and macro levels have traditionally been viewed as an important means by which skill demands in the labour market are met and through which economic and social prosperity can be achieved. The chapter has further evaluated and compared different approaches to interpreting the extent of, and potential effect of, technological change on the learning, training and employability 'ecosystem'. Although predictions are contested and uncertain, it is important to consider the potential implications of these developments, disputed though they are for training, vocational education, workplace development and employability.

As Figure 11.1 illustrates, learning, training, employability and vocational education form part of a dynamic and interrelated set of systems. This means that, in addition to technological developments that may affect them, other global demographic changes may also add additional effects on labour market structures and skill demand and supply issues. For example, the size of the population available for work (the global population) is increasing year on year, fuelled by sustained improvements in healthcare programmes and life expectancy in many parts of the world. Global life expectancy at birth has increased over a 20-year period from 66.8 years in 2000 to 73.4 years in 2019 (WHO, 2023). This means that the supply of people seeking employment and expecting to be active in labour markets is increasing without the necessity of equivalent increases in labour demand as automation and production efficiency continue to rise. Further factors such as geopolitical conflicts, wide-scale natural disasters resulting from climate change, and increasing inequality between citizens in different regions of the world are also predicted to trigger unprecedented and difficult to quantify levels of labour migration. For example, data from 2019 estimated the number of international labour migrants as 164 million people (United Nations, n.d), with 31 per cent of the international migrants located in Asia, 30 per cent in Europe, 26 per cent in the Americas, 10 per cent in Africa and three per cent in Oceania (Migration Data Portal, n.d.). Such shifting labour supply volumes in different regions of the world will increasingly affect national-level labour markets, generating shortages in some regions and surpluses in others, resulting in an imbalance and mismatch between skill supply and labour demand in different continents (Keep, 2021).

Therefore, predictions about future trends for learning, development and employability are difficult. However, the analysis of this chapter suggests four areas where substantial rethinking is necessary: education and training provision (skill supply), workplace learning, reconceptualising employability and lifelong learning.

Rethinking Education and Training Provision

The assessment of this chapter is that labour markets, like other features of the business world, are likely to become increasingly volatile, uncertain, complex and ambiguous (Canzittu, 2022; Sobotka, 2021). This means that employers' skill demands will change frequently. Traditional approaches by education and training providers that assume stability of skill demand are insufficiently adaptive for such a scenario. This suggests a substantial rethink in three features of training and education provision by vocational training providers at both further and higher education levels. First, the deployment of data analytics and more responsive assessments of skill demand trends to better predict changing labour market demand will be needed. Second, traditional approaches to developing and delivering vocational training curricula will need to be replaced with systems that are more responsive to minimise 'lag' in the supply of skills to the labour market and the opportunities for learners to gain employment. Indeed, both curriculum and lead times for education and training delivery will require substantial reduction to meet emergent skill needs and implement timely vocational training responses. This will require a continuation of the 'digital pedagogy pivot' prompted (but rarely welcomed) in many parts of the world by the Covid-19 pandemic (Anderson, 2020). Traditional approaches to vocational education and training and assessment are increasingly likely to be replaced by 'smart' delivery of vocational education and training programmes.

Third, assumptions about the learner population for vocational training and education will change radically as vocational education and (re)training will be necessary for adult learner cohorts in addition to younger, first-time labour market entrants. Demand for vocational education for older learners whose career progression has radically altered will increase substantially and, in instances where inward labour migration occurs, further adult-level socialisation into different socio-cultural work norms and expectations will be necessary.

Rethinking Workplace Learning

Figure 11.1 indicates the important role of learning, development and retraining policies and practices in workplace settings as a feature of the learning, development and employability landscape. Workplace environments have always been an important feature of sustainable skill supply and deployment and organisational performance. Workplace learning is consequential for both individual-level employability and career development but also for organisation development and performance (Lundgren & Poell, 2020). Employers invest substantial funds in providing formal training processes (Statista, 2023; Winterbotham et al., 2020). However, the workplace is frequently overlooked as a site for developing adults' skills and knowledge (Bound et al., 2018). In addition, most attention by those responsible for learning and training in the workplace focuses on classroom-based or off-the-job forms of training and development. Much less recognition has been given to the importance of the workplace itself as a learning environment in which situated learning and skill enhancement or adaptation occurs (Poell & Van Der Krogt, 2016). However, as skill demands fluctuate in unpredictable and dynamic ways, workplace learning can provide a means for organisations to identify, assimilate and transform their skill availability to respond to changes in the volume, quality and nature of their skill demands caused by technological advances and opportunities (Economist, 2023; Loon, 2020).

Therefore, working in collaboration with vocational learning and development providers, an important implication for those with responsibility for training and organisation development in work settings, whether in larger or small organisations, is to rethink their approach to workplace learning. First, proactive development of informational systems and data analytics capability is necessary as a basis from which technological adoption effects can indicate skill development priorities. Second, making use of technological advances such as AI and machine learning, more personalised learning and reskilling experiences for workers can be developed. This will be possible through automated data processing of learner's preferences to match training opportunities with individual needs and availability. Third, a radical review of assumptions about workplace learning by individuals is necessary to encourage workers towards proactivity in self-development as technology increasingly makes it possible for personalisation of objective setting, learning pace and learning methods and timing.

Fourth, opportunities for workplace learning will be necessary for the increasing proportion of workers employed on non-standard employment contracts, including contract and 'gig'-work (Pingali et al., 2017; World Bank, 2019). This means that a rethink of the scope of workplace learning is necessary so that training and skill development are encouraged and available for all those who work on behalf of the organisation and not just those with permanent employment contracts. Failure to recognise the skill and capability development needs and to encourage career development by those in non-standard forms of employment will negatively affect organisational adaptability and productivity.

Reliance on increasing availability of formal and informal training and learning in the workplace will, however, only address short-term skill demands issues (Keep, 2021). Therefore, a fifth 'rethink' area for those responsible

for workplace learning is to review the longer-term impacts of technological advances on the nature of work and on career development pathways.
Longer-term skill development processes to foster human creativity, innovation and development of important 'soft skills' will also form the basis for
organisational and individual-level resilience as work contexts are increasingly
infused by computerisation and digital automation. For example, in addition
to technical skills, other workplace learning priorities may be the development
of interpersonal intelligence, creative thinking, cross-cultural competency,
data-based reasoning, multi-disciplinary reasoning, information management
and collaborative working (Institute for the Future, 2011).

Finally, in a context of potential job scarcity in some parts of the labour
market, and as employment relationships become increasingly non-standard,
it is likely that workplace learning processes may progressively intersect with
out-of-work or external activities carried out by those who work on behalf of
the organisation. Although the focus of workplace learning tends to focus on
immediate skill demands, as employment relationships become increasingly
non-standard, workplace learning is likely to increasingly intersect with
out-of-work or external activities carried out by workers, leading to a different
relational balance between individual employability, skill deployment, and
organisational flexibility and adaptiveness in the context of fast-changing skill
needs (Torraco & Lundgren, 2020).

To summarise, technological advances provide the opportunity to rethink
and substantially enlarge the role of workplace learning. Traditional approaches
and timescales for training needs analysis and delivery, focused on present
rather than future skills will no longer be sufficient. A more proactive approach
to training 'transfer' that emphasises knowledge sharing in different workplace
settings and a more inclusive understanding of those who are considered 'in
scope' for workplace learning opportunities will be necessary.

Rethinking Employability

Technological change also has profound implications for the way that
employability is understood. Employability currently dominates the agenda
of employers, policymakers, individuals, economists and politicians (Smith
et al., 2018). The concept conflates the notions of individual 'ability' with
'work-readiness' (Suleman, 2018). Systems of education and training are
expected to provide occupational skills and qualifications for those seeking
employment but also to equip individuals with more general qualities to assist
their work readiness. Once in employment, however, the onus of responsibility
for employability is assumed to shift to the individual. In a changing labour
demand context, workers are expected to continually upgrade their technical
digital competencies and to constantly refresh their work-related interper-

sonal skills and qualities whilst also advancing higher-level capabilities such as thinking skills and creativity (Akkermans et al., 2023; Rakowska & de Juana-Espinosa, 2021).

Grounded in human capital theory, employability difficulties are explained as the result of an individual's failure to engage with education and prepare for or adapt to changing skill and employment demands. However, in the context of rapid technological change in workplace and employment settings, individual-level employability will become increasingly important as work opportunities and the skills required change or are displaced. This is likely to challenge an individual's 'employability self-concept' and will confront traditionally understood occupational and social identities. 'Mobility capital' or 'employability capital' is likely to be necessary as the basis from which individuals can transition from one job or occupational field to another. This will require a substantial rethinking of skill-related and career mobility resources provision and acquisition, requiring new knowledge, skills, and attitudes to deploy social capital resources to be able to move from one occupation or employer to another (Forrier et al., 2009; Peeters et al., 2019).

However, worker flexibility and willingness to upskill or retrain to meet emerging skill supply issues will be ineffective if current employers' policies to 'hire in' new skills rather than to develop them 'in-house' remain as they are currently operated. For example, evidence from employer organisations and professional bodies suggests that skills deficits and business growth plans are most usually addressed by employers through the recruitment of new employees in preference to the encouragement of upskilling or retraining of their existing workers (WEF, 2018). Recruitment and job search are prioritised, including employment of temporary workers, alongside changes to pay and conditions to make job roles more attractive to new workers (Green et al., 2020). This approach means fewer opportunities for existing workers to develop new skills and engage in other forms of workplace education and training as a means to maintain their employability.

An employability rethink is necessary, therefore, not just at the level of employers but also at national policy levels. In place of short-term and pragmatic approaches to skill development, employers can engage more proactively with workers' employability development as some forms of work, including professional and other knowledge work, are challenged by the adoption of AI, robotics and other forms of computerised automation (Susskind & Susskind, 2015). Employability in this different context requires explicit encouragement by employers of individual development, growth in skills and adaptation, and individual versatility to better equip people to navigate their working life in more flexible, agile ways (Jackson & Tomlinson, 2020). At the national level, it requires opportunities for vocational retraining and development to be available for individuals at all stages of their work-life trajectory.

Rethinking Lifelong Learning

The fourth conclusion of this examination of the future of learning, development and employability in the context of restructured labour markets is that fundamental changes to lifelong learning policies and practices are necessary. The concept of lifelong learning was originally developed in the 1970s alongside economic development and expansion processes that occurred in Europe and North America in this decade. The concept of lifelong learning was initially grounded in a humanistic and developmental purpose and described opportunities for individuals to participate in education and training throughout their life span. Lifelong learning, therefore, is conceptually aligned with ideas about self-development and the achievement of self-realisation by both individuals and communities as a basis for well-being and civic advancement (Bynner, 2017; Preece, 2009). It was described as involving 'learning to know' (knowledge and understanding), 'learning to do' (skills and capabilities), 'learning to live together' (social cohesion) and 'learning to be' (self-realisation and fulfilment) (Delors, 1998).

This broad and humanistic aspiration can still be seen in macro-level policy rhetoric. For example, the European Union Lifelong Learning Index (ELLI) (CEDEFOP, 2023) and the Composite Learning Index (CLI) of Canada (UNESCO, 2023) draw on this idea within their comparative metrics relating to learning, training and education. However, the dominance of human capital theory assumptions and the development of neoliberal economic policies in many parts of the world has led to a redefinition in the practice of lifelong learning as something that is a tool to be deployed for short-term economic growth and increased national competitiveness (Kim, 2016). Rather than being regarded as something beneficial for all citizens, therefore, policies focus on lifelong learning as a social mechanism to address poverty, low wages and underemployment (Müller et al., 2015). Lifelong learning, in current policy discourse, is a means through which 'pathways' of access to vocationally orientated higher or further education programmes can be 'opened up' to disadvantaged adults aged over 25 years (UNESCO Institute for Lifelong Learning, n.d.).

However, the analysis of this chapter suggests that, in contexts where job scarcity is likely, a rethink of lifelong learning will be necessary as an increasing proportion of the population in many countries may experience frequent dislocations to full-time employment opportunities (Bynner, 2017). This means that national and local-level provisions for lifelong learning will be necessary and available for learners at different points of their life spans. Failure to address this need is likely to have negative consequences for an individual's well-being, as well as for employment readiness required by employers as well as problems for civic engagement and social cohesion. This has substantial implications for trade unions, employer organisations, universities and civil society organisations, in addition to sectoral or occupational training and development organisations. It also represents an important opportunity to be grasped by those whose role involves leadership of learning, development and employability to show the social cohesion and positive economic outcomes that can result from a rethinking of lifelong learning. However, this will require leaders in the learning, development and education fields to engage in consistent advocacy and consensus-building across different systemic levels (Keep, 2021).

CONCLUSION

Predictions about technological change and its impact on work and learning are difficult. Skill demands and skill supply processes vary substantially across different regions of the world and in different industries and sectors. Nonetheless, developments in technological capability combined with other changes in the macro-level environment are likely to destabilise existing labour markets. The argument of this chapter is that this should prompt a re-evaluation of the assumptions underpinning learning, development and employability.

Four conclusions can be drawn from the arguments that have been examined in this chapter. First, at the macro level, education and training policies require review so that people of all ages can develop the necessary levels of skill and capability. In addition to cognitive, linguistic and numerical abilities, non-cognitive interpersonal and personal development skills will be important as a basis from which individuals can respond appropriately to increasingly uncertain labour market circumstances. Second, vocational education and training providers throughout the system will need to identify and respond to emerging skills demands more quickly and in ways that meet the needs of learning of all ages and backgrounds. Third, a paradigm change in assumptions about the purpose of workplace learning is necessary as a basis from which inclusive forms of skill development and organisational agility and responsiveness can be achieved. Fourth, for workers, personal responsibility for continual development, lifelong learning and recognition of the value of mobility and employability capital will be necessary. However, it is also likely that individuals will experience periods of employment transition requiring interventions and reskilling for which they can only prepare with a proactive approach towards lifelong learning. This is likely to require both individual commitment and national-level funding.

In many, but not all, parts of the world, support and commitment towards matters of diversity, equity, inclusion and social justice are increasing. Advocates for technological change suggest that it has the potential to further accelerate opportunities for wider participation in social and economic pro-gress. Others are more sceptical and suggest that existing patterns of disadvantage may be further exaggerated as a result of the impact of technology on work and work identity. The argument of this chapter is that, although predictions are difficult, a new understanding of the purpose of learning and development at macro, meso and micro systemic levels is necessary as a basis for productive and fulfilling work, employment and citizenship in the 21st century.

REFERENCES

Akkermans, J., Tomlinson, M., & Anderson, V. (2023). Initial employability development: Introducing a conceptual model integrating signalling and social exchange mechanisms. *European Journal of Work and Organizational Psychology*: 1–13.

Anderson, D., Brown, M., & Rushbrook, P. (2020). Vocational education and training. In *Dimensions of adult learning* (pp. 234–50). New York: Routledge.

Anderson, V. (2020). A digital pedagogy pivot: Re-thinking higher education practice from an HRD perspective. *Human Resource Development International*, 23(4): 452–67.

Anderson, V. (2022). Human Resource Development, professions and precarious workers. In *The Emerald Handbook of Work, Workplaces and Disruptive Issues in HRM* (pp. 277–301). Bingley, UK: Emerald Publishing.

Anderson, V., & Tomlinson, M. (2021). Signaling standout graduate employability: The employer perspective. *Human Resource Management Journal*, 31(3): 675–93.

Arntz, M., Gregory, T., & Zierahn, U. (2016). The risk of automation for jobs in OECD countries: A comparative analysis. OECD Social, Employment, and Migration Working Papers 189. OECD, Paris.

Aroles, J., Granter, E., & de Vaujany, F.X. (2020). 'Becoming mainstream': The professionalisation and corporatisation of digital nomadism. *New Technology, Work and Employment*, 35(1): 114–29.

Bag, S., & Wood, L.C. (2022). Guest editorial: Human resource development in the digital age: Recent issues and future research directions. *International Journal of Manpower*, 43(2): 253–62.

Battisti, M., Dustmann, C., & Schönberg, U. (2023). Technological and organizational change and the careers of workers. *Journal of the European Economic Association*, 21(4): 1551–94.

Becker, G.S. (1964). *Human Capital: A Theoretical and Empirical Analysis with Special Reference to Education*. New York: National Bureau of Economic Research.

Blumenfeld, S., & Malik, A. (2017). Human capital formation under neo-liberalism: The legacy of vocational education training in Australasia and implications for the Asia-Pacific region. *Asia Pacific Business Review*, 23(2): 290–8.

Bound, H., Evans, K., Sadik, S., & Karmel, A. (2018). *How Non-Permanent Workers Learn and Develop: Challenges and Opportunities*. Oxon: Routledge.

Bourdieu, P. (1986). Forms of social capital. In J.C. Richards (ed.), *Handbook of Theory and Research for Sociology of Education* (pp. 241–58). New York: Greenwood.

Brown, P. (2021). Education, technology and the future of work in the Fourth Industrial Revolution. Digital Futures of Work Research Programme, Working Paper 2.

Brown, P., Lauder, H., & Ashton, D. (2010). *The Global Auction: The Broken Promises of Education, Jobs, and Incomes*. New York: Oxford University Press.

Brown, P., Sadik, S., & Souto-Otero, M.(2021). Digital futures of work: Reimagining jobs, skills and education for the digital age. Digital Futures of Work Research Programme, Working Paper 1.

Bynner, J. (2017). Whatever happened to lifelong learning? And does it matter. *Journal of the British Academy*, 5: 61–89.

Canzittu, D. (2022). A framework to think of school and career guidance in a VUCA world. *British Journal of Guidance & Counselling*, 50(2): 248–59.

CEDEFOP. (2023). ELLI – European lifelong learning indicators: Making lifelong learning tangible. https://www.cedefop.europa.eu/en/news/elli-european-lifelong-learning-indicators-making-lifelong-learning-tangible.

Checkland, P. (1994). Systems theory and management thinking. *American Behavioral Scientist*, 38(1): 75–91.

Coleman, J.S. (1988). Social capital in the creation of human capital. *American Journal of Sociology*, 94: 95–120.

Delors, J. (1998). *Learning: The Treasure within*. Unesco.

Economist. (2023). Bridging the Skills gap. fuelling careers and the economy in Asia Pacific. https://impact.economist.com/perspectives/sites/default/files/bridging_the_skills_gap_fuelling_careers_and_the_economy_in_asia_pacific.pdf.

Forrier, A., Sels, L., & Stynen, D. (2009). Career mobility at the intersection between agent and structure: A conceptual model. *Journal of Occupational and Organizational Psychology*, 82(4): 739–59.

Frey, C.B., & Osborne, M.A. (2017). The future of employment: How susceptible are jobs to computerisation? *Technological Forecasting and Social Change*, 114: 254–80.

Garavan, T., Wang, J., Matthews-Smith, G., Nagarathnam, B., & Lai, Y. (2018). Advancing national human resource development research: Suggestions for multi-level investigations. *Human Resource Development International*, 21(4): 288–318.

Garavan, T., Wang, J., Nolan, C., Lai, Y., O'Brien, F., Darcy, C., ... & McLean, G. (2023). Putting the individual and context back into national human resource development research: A systematic review and research agenda. *International Journal of Management Reviews*, 25(1): 152–75.

Green, A., Owen, D., Atfield, G., Baldauf, B, Bramley, G., & Kispeter, E. (2020). *Employer decision-making around skill shortages, employee shortages and migration: Literature Review*. Report Commissioned by the Migration Advisory Committee. https:// assets .publishing .service .gov .uk/ government/ uploads/ system/ uploads/ attachment_data/file/936388/131120_FINAL_literature_review_for_publication.pdf.

Hadad, S. (2017). Knowledge economy: Characteristics and dimensions. *Management Dynamics in the Knowledge economy*, 5(2): 203–25.

Institute for the Future (2011). *Future Work Skills 2020*. https:// www .iftf .org/ futureworkskills/.

Jackson, D., & Tomlinson, M. (2020). Investigating the relationship between career planning, proactivity and employability perceptions among higher education students in uncertain labour market conditions. *Higher Education*, 80(3): 435–455.7

Keep, E. (2021). Initial thoughts on policy issues for the future of work. Digital Futures of Work, Research Programme, Working Paper 3.

Kim, J. (2016). Development of a global lifelong learning index for future education. *Asia Pacific Education Review*, 17(3): 439–63.

Loon, M. (2020). Self-directed learning and absorptive capacity: The mediating role of trust and human capital. In M. Loon, J. Stewart, & S. Nachmias (eds),

The Future of HRD, Vol. II. Cham: Palgrave Macmillan. https://doi.org/10.1007/978–3–030–52459–3_4.

Lundgren, H., & Poell, R.F. (2020). Human resource development and workplace learning. In *The 2020 Handbook of Adult and Continuing Education* (pp. 275–86). San Franscico, CA: Jossey-Bass.

Mangan, J., & Lalwani, C. (2016). *Global Logistics and Supply Chain Management*. Chichester: John Wiley & Sons.

McLean, G.N. (2004). National human resource development: What in the world is it? *Advances in Developing Human Resources*, 6(3): 269–75.

Migration Data Portal. (n.d.). The bigger picture. https://www.migrationdataportal.org/?i=stock_abs_&t=2017&m=1.

Müller, R., Remdisch, S., Köhler, K., Marr, L., Repo, S., & Yndigegn, C. (2015). Easing access for lifelong learners: A comparison of European models for university lifelong learning. *International Journal of Lifelong Education*, 34(5): 530–50.

Murgia, A., & Poggio, B. (2014). At risk of deskilling and trapped by passion: A picture of precarious highly educated young workers in Italy, Spain and the United Kingdom. In *Young People and Social Policy in Europe: Dealing with Risk, Inequality and Precarity in Times of Crisis* (pp. 62–86). Basingstoke: Palgrave Macmillan.

Paprock, K.E. (2006). National human resource development in transitioning societies in the developing world: Introductory overview. *Advances in Developing Human Resources*, 8(1): 12–27.

Peeters, E., Nelissen, J., De Cuyper, N., Forrier, A., Verbruggen, M., & De Witte, H. (2019). Employability capital: A conceptual framework tested through expert analysis. *Journal of Career Development*, 46(2): 79–93.

Peters, M.A. (2020). Beyond technological unemployment: The future of work. *Educational Philosophy and Theory*, 52(5): 485–91.

Philbeck, T., & Davis, N. (2018). The Fourth Industrial Revolution. *Journal of International Affairs*, 72(1): 17–22. ISSN 0022–197X.

Pingali, S.R., Rovenpor, J., & Shah, G. (2017). From outsourcing to best-sourcing? The global search for talent and innovation. In *Human Capital and Innovation* (pp. 161–91). London: Palgrave Macmillan.

Poell, R.F., & Van Der Krogt, F.J. (2016). Employee strategies in organising professional development. In S. Billett, D. Dymock, & S. Choy (eds), *Supporting Learning across Working Life. Professional and Practice-Based Learning*, Vol. 16. (pp. 29–46). Cham: Springer.

Preece, J. (2009). Lifelong learning and development: A perspective from the 'South'. *Compare*, 39(5): 585–99.

Rakowska, A., & de Juana-Espinosa, S. (2021). Ready for the future? Employability skills and competencies in the twenty-first century: The view of international experts. *Human Systems Management*, 40(5): 669–84.

Riain, S.Ó. (2000). The flexible developmental state: globalization, Information technology, and the 'Celtic tiger'. *Politics & Society*, 28(2): 157–93.

Schultz, T.W. (1961). Investment in human capital. *The American Economic Review*, 51(1): 3.

Smith, M., Bell, K., Bennett, D., & McAlpine, A. (2018). *Employability in a Global Context: Evolving Policy and Practice in Employability, Work Integrated Learning, and Career Development Learning*. Wollongong, Australia: Graduate Careers Australia.

Sobotka, B. (2021). Labour market changes and challenges for education in the VUCA era. *Journal of Modern Science*, 46(1): 191–208.

Srnicek, N. (2017). *Platform Capitalism*. New York: John Wiley & Sons.

Statista (2023). Average spending on workplace learning per employee worldwide, 2008–2021. https://www.statista.com/statistics/738519/workplace-training-spending-per-employee/.

Stuart, M., & Cooney, R. (2008). Training and the limits of supply-side skill development. *Industrial Relations Journal*, 39(5): 346–53.

Suleman, F. (2018). The employability skills of higher education graduates: Insights into conceptual frameworks and methodological options. *Higher Education*, 76: 263–78.

Susskind, R.E., & Susskind, D. (2015). *The Future of the Professions: How Technology Will Transform the Work of Human Experts*. New York: Oxford University Press.

Torraco, R.J., & Lundgren, H. (2020). What HRD is doing – what HRD should be doing: The case for transforming HRD. *Human Resource Development Review*, 19(1): 39–65.

Trauth-Goik, A. (2021). Repudiating the Fourth Industrial Revolution discourse: A new episteme of technological progress. *World Futures*, 77(1): 55–78.

United Nations. (n.d.). Migration. https://www.un.org/en/global-issues/migration#:~:text=According%20to%20the%20IOM%20World,the%20global%20population%20in%202019.

United Nations Educational, Scientific and Cultural Organization (UNESCO). (2023). The Composite Learning Index and European Lifelong Learning Indicators. https://www.ibe.unesco.org/en/geqaf/annexes/technical-notes/composite-learning-index-and-european-lifelong-learning-indicators.

UNESCO Institute for Lifelong Learning. (n.d.). Collection of lifelong learning policies and strategies. https://uil.unesco.org/lifelong-learning/lifelong-learning-policies.

Wang, G.G., & Swanson, R.A. (2008). The idea of national HRD: An analysis based on economics and theory development methodology. *Human Resource Development Review*, 7(1): 79–106.

Winterbotham, M., Kik, G., Selner, S., Menys, R., Stroud, S., & Whittaker, S. (2020). *Employer Skills Survey 2019: Training and Workforce Development Research Report*. https://assets.publishing.service.gov.uk/government/uploads/system/uploads/attachment_data/file/936487/ESS_2019_Training_and_Workforce_Development_Report_Nov20.pdf.

World Bank. (2019). *World Development Report: The Changing Nature of Work*. http://documents1.worldbank.org/curated/en/816281518818814423/pdf/2019-WDR-Report.pdf.

World Economic Forum (WEF). (2018). *The Future of Jobs Report: 2018*. http://www3.weforum.org/docs/WEF_Future_of_Jobs_2018.pdf.

World Health Organization (WHO). (2023). The Global Health Observatory. https://www.who.int/data/gho/publications/world-health-statistics.

12. Flexibility and the disadvantaged, disabled and precarious worker

Hannah Meacham and Alyssa Chhim

INTRODUCTION

Traditional, or standard work patterns are conceptualised as full-time, permanent work contracts with one employer that provides statutory benefits such as sick leave (Shuey & Jovic, 2013). Non-standard work patterns became more prevalent in the 1970s when employers started looking for a more flexible workforce to keep up with consumer demand and societal changes (Laß & Wooden, 2020). Non-standard employment may consist of temporary work, part-time or short-term contracted workers (Smith & Halpin, 2019). Research and social commentators (Oddo et al., 2021) have incorporated non-standard work into the concept of precarious employment which focuses on the negative features of non-standard work, for example, having a lack of defined benefits such as sick leave. Although job quality variation exists amongst non-standard work, typically, non-standard work has been portrayed as 'flexible work patterns' to workers in promoting the benefits (Kreshpaj et al., 2020). However, it does not take into consideration the variations on precarity it can produce for workers (Shuey & Jovic, 2013). As the term 'flexible work patterns' is now commonly used through research and practice, it will be used throughout this chapter as an umbrella term for all non-standard work practices.

Over the decades flexible work patterns have become attractive to workers and employers alike, in response to the changing needs of the workforce (Rubery et al., 2016). Flexible work patterns are working without boundaries around places, schedules and contracts (Groen et al., 2018) , that is, where, when and how an employee works. It has been reported in the academic literature (Choi, 2020; Ipsen et al., 2021) that flexible work patterns can be advantageous to disadvantaged workers (Rubery et al., 2016). Early flexible work patterns included 'part-time', 'flexi-work' and 'telework', with newer terms emphasising the virtual and mobile nature of the contemporary technologically based work environment including 'co-workspaces', 'on-call work' and 'virtual work' (Soga et al., 2022).

A key feature of flexible work patterns is the expected ability to accommodate workforce diversity by offering a range of work opportunities. While flexible work patterns may appear to open up opportunities for disadvantaged workers, they may in fact open them up to greater prejudice in the workplace (Chung & Van der Horst, 2020). The negative impact of flexible work patterns can be seen in work relationships, home-work conflicts and the health and wellbeing of workers (Soga et al., 2022), issues which came to prominence during the COVID-19 pandemic for all workers. For example, remote work or working from home can cause greater social isolation, work-family conflict and exclusion from promotion and training opportunities (Royle, 2023).

These are important issue as the workforce becomes more diverse through care responsibilities, younger workers are combining work and study, older workers are staying in the workforce longer and more workers with disabilities are attempting to enter the mainstream workforce being supported in many advanced market economies by proactive legislation (Chung, 2020). This perceived flexibility comes, however, at a cost of potentially much lower pay and promotion opportunities as employers still stereotype those requiring flexible work patterns as lacking commitment (Fernandez-Lozano et al., 2020). While recruitment advertisements offering flexible work may in theory open up jobs for disadvantaged workers to apply, they still have to compete with 'typical' workers who potentially have more experience in the workplace (Rubery, 2015). Groups such as women, ethnic minorities, older workers and workers with disabilities may be perceived to lack either competence, commitment or may simply not fit in with the typical work group (Madsen, 2004). For example, younger workers are often seen as lacking experience, while older workers are more vulnerable to redundancy due to a perception of falling productivity or inability to learn new ways of working (Yeung et al., 2021). Therefore, it is imperative that management understand how flexible work patterns may benefit their organisation, along with disadvantaged workers, and how deep-rooted discriminations may continue regardless of the flexibility given (Rubery et al., 2016).

The chapter will discuss low-income earners and welfare recipients and their reliance on flexible work. This is followed by a focus on the 'gig' economy and its perception as flexible work. The issue of flexibility as a stigma for women in the workplace and voluntary and involuntary flexibility within the white-collar workforce are examined in detail. The chapter concludes with a discussion on mental health concerns and the needs of people with disabilities.

FLEXIBILITY AND LOW-INCOME EARNERS AND WELFARE RECIPIENTS

Workers on low incomes and those receiving welfare are often also disadvantaged in other ways (Cai et al., 2022) . In Australia, the federal government reports that most low-income earners were either female or a person with a disability, as these groups are over-represented in low-income sectors such as healthcare and hospitality (ABS, 2019–20). In the UK, low-income earners were represented by ethnic minorities and households where one person has a disability (Francis-Devine, 2023). In Europe, women are more likely to be low-income earners than men (Eurostat, 2021), while in America, the Black and Hispanic communities are more likely to report low-income wages (Creamer et al., 2022). It is therefore important to discuss the intersectionality of low-income earners and welfare recipients. While flexible work patterns may be of benefit to these low-income workers, many may find themselves trapped in poor paying jobs, with low or unstable hours (Anwar & Graham, 2021). Industries such as contract cleaning and the broadening gig economy are two examples of where this can occur (Rho et al., 2020). Flexible work patterns may involve disadvantaged workers being available for work, or on call, over a longer period than their actual paid working hours (Chen et al., 2020). The Trade Union Congress (TUC) in the UK has stated 'Gig economy platforms are using new technologies to carry out the age-old practice of worker exploitation. Too often gig workers are denied their rights and are treated like disposable labour' (Jones, 2021: 1). Financial planning and stability can also become more difficult due to the irregularities in income (Marica, 2020). This means achieving an acceptable living wage may be difficult (Dube, 2019), particularly if it involves working for multiple employers who may each require flexible availability over the week. Unions across the Western world are campaigning against gig work platforms due to the substandard working conditions available to them. 'Those classified as self-employed also have less rights than workers. It is vital that pay and conditions for gig workers are improved to protect those who rely on this work as a source of income' (Jones, 2021: 1).

The perceived benefits of on-demand work (gig work/on-call/zero hours work) often attract disadvantaged workers to such work due to the promised flexible work patterns and possible supplementation of income (Soga et al., 2022). A Forbes study found that 63 per cent of survey participants indicated that flexibility is the main reason for them choosing gig work (Wilson, 2023). However, for low-income earners who rely on on-demand work, it can be unpredictable without any commitment from organisations to provide hours creating an unstable income for the most disadvantaged individuals in society, yet these workers are often dependent on such organisations (with little legislative support) due to their limited work experience (Jacobs & Padavic, 2015). These unpredictable schedules create additional stress in negotiating family logistics and finance due to the unpredictability of weekly hours (Henly & Lambert, 2014). For example, Deliveroo has been accused of a 'hollow' PR move when signing a deal with the GMB union in the UK. Under the deal, riders will be paid minimum wage during the time they are on delivery. However, while they are waiting for a pick-up they remain unpaid. Considering the additional time, the IWBG union noted that this takes delivery riders under the minimum wage. However, the GMB union has stated that this deal gives riders collective bargaining, consultation and representation rights (Butler, 2021). As noted, regulatory gaps surrounding on-demand work has further distanced disadvantaged workers from a stable income due to a lack of sufficient employment laws in many countries (Kaine & Josserand, 2019). Attempts have been made to regulate the gig economy to negate such issues. The Victorian State government in Australia has implemented legislation in 2023 that requires platforms to inform workers potential earnings, any incurred costs such as equipment (bike/car costs) and work conditions so they can make informed decisions as to take on the work (Gordon, 2022; Redrup, 2022). The UK government has clarified the employment status of gig workers which includes employment protections such as pay, leave entitlements and working conditions (Department for Business Energy and Industrial Strategy, 2022). In November 2022, Deliveroo announced it was exiting the Australian market citing 'achieving a sustainable position of leadership in the market is not possible without a disproportionate level of investment'. However, this came at a time when they had also lost a Fair work commission case for firing a rider for being too slow during deliveries (Taylor, 2022).

THE FLEXIBLE PERCEPTION OF THE 'GIG ECONOMY'

The rise of the 'gig economy' has seen a major shift in power towards employers using workers' desire for 'flexible work' (Anwar & Graham, 2021). Employment contracts are now as temporary as employers would like them to be with 'gig work' undermining the safety of traditional employment systems (Mehta, 2020; Wu et al., 2019), despite, as noted above, attempts to legislate protection for these vulnerable workers. For example, the transcription service Rev cut its base rate it pays transcription workers with no notice or consultation (Weinberg, 2019). These types of employment contracts are only likely to grow (MacDonald & Giazitzoglu, 2019). 'Gig' workers are usually young individuals between the ages of 16 and 30 (Doshi & Tikyani, 2020). From a flexibility and employment perspective, it is perceived such work patterns and practices provide opportunities for young and disadvantaged workers to enter the job market and gain valuable work experience and allows more freedom and control than other forms of employment if, for example, they have study or care responsibilities (Wood et al., 2019).

However, this perceived increase in control can often be short-lived, where workers find themselves being exploited (Mehta, 2020). Research in the retail sector found that the use of flexible scheduling can impact future work, with managers often punishing workers who turned down shifts (MacDonald & Giazitzoglu, 2019). As such, 'gig workers' are likely to have schedules altered or cut if they turn down shifts, causing stress for workers (Anwar & Graham, 2021; Mehta, 2020). In the UK for example, the use of zero hours contracts is increasing, where employers do not need to offer a set amount of hours and can alter the number of hours offered down to zero without notice (Greeves, 2023). As detailed above, with gig workers being more likely to be low-income earners (Doshi & Tikyani, 2020), this means that those in the most need of work are either punished for not being flexible enough or have to sacrifice the wellbeing of themselves or family to be able to earn (Tan et al., 2021). The perceived 'flexible' gig work can often isolate workers from each other where they do not have regular ongoing contact with other workers (Webster, 2016) and can put workers in direct competition with each other creating a 'race to the bottom' in terms and conditions (Riezzo, 2021). This can be clearly seen in the case of rideshare work such as Uber or delivery services such as Uber Eats where workers work on their own and must be available for work at any time of the day to earn money (Hasegawa et al., 2022). This isolation forces individuals to live from job to job with no financial security, stability or social connection, having a negative impact on workers' wellbeing (Wu et al., 2019). This employer exploitation leads to personal exploitation, as workers are made to maximise their earning potential by being always available, negating any real flexibility or control (Wood et al., 2019). This personal exploitation can start a negative spiral where workers are seemingly forced into continual availability to earn a perceived decent wage, however, when they do not they sacrifice their work-life balance and wellbeing just to earn a living wage (Wu et al., 2019). Therefore, to be able to earn a decent wage, workers must have a constant blurred line between work and home life, being always on call to secure work in a competitive market (MacDonald & Giazitzoglu, 2019; Riezzo, 2021). Therefore this 'flexible work' becomes inflexible as workers are forced into working during times when they might not want to. For example, busy periods for Uber may be evenings, late nights and weekends when workers may traditionally be able to spend time with family.

WORKING WOMEN AND FLEXIBILITY STIGMA

Flexible work patterns are increasingly becoming a popular method to allow working mothers opportunities to re-enter the workforce after a period of leave, and a way to tackle the gender inequalities in the labour market (Chung & Van der Horst, 2018). As such, research has shown that flexible work patterns can help reduce the gender pay gap as these help women maintain their previous job positions after returning from maternity leave, for example (Chung, 2022). However, the stigma associated with requesting and working flexible work patterns remains and can burden women and working mothers (Chung, 2020; Piasna & Plagnol, 2018). Flexibility stigma is the biased notion that workers who use flexible work patterns to care for family members are less productive and less committed to the workplace (Chung, 2022). Thus, workers may not feel comfortable requesting or taking up flexible working arrangements when flexibility stigma is prevalent in their workplaces. Flexibility stigma can be seen as not working long hours or working non-traditional work hours (outside of the 9–5 routine) to meet care demands. Flexibility stigma is mainly felt by women and often amplified during parenthood (Jacobs & Padavic, 2015). In most Advanced Market Economies, this is due to an unequal gender division of labour where most mothers carry out the majority of childcare (Kurowska, 2020) while men can prioritise work over home life (Chung, 2020; Lott, 2020). This can lead to management discrimination, co-worker resentment and negative career outcomes (Van Der Lippe & Lippényi, 2020).

When comparing men and women, men are more likely to be seen in a positive light when asking for flexible work patterns, with women more likely to judge other women for working flexibly (Chung, 2020). Women are also more likely to believe that they will receive more negative career outcomes if asking for flexible work patterns compared to men (Rubery, 2015). Male and female perceptions of flexibility stigma can also differ, as women are usually the ones requiring flexible work patterns to care for children (Chung & Van der Horst, 2018; Kim et al., 2020). As men are more likely to have to adhere to a 'typical' worker culture of high performance and increased hours, they are therefore less likely to request flexible work patterns for fear of not performing in their roles and are more aware of negative career consequences (Chung, 2020). On an organisational level, employers may assume that women, when asking for flexible work patterns, will restrict their working roles to fit in with their family demands, further restricting job performance. On the other hand, men, when working flexibly, still prioritise work (Kim et al., 2020). Therefore, when men use flexible work patterns, they increase their overtime and gain promotions/pay increases, yet women work much longer hours to prove their performance while receiving no additional remuneration or promotion opportunities (Lott, 2020).

VOLUNTARY VS INVOLUNTARY FLEXIBLE WORK

Flexible work, while seemingly voluntary, or chosen by workers, may in fact be dictated by employers (Kaduk et al., 2019).The notion of involuntary flexible work practices may present itself as employer-driven flexibility to meet business needs. For example, white-collar workers in global teams where they may be required to work after hours to attend meetings with colleagues in other time zones (Mockaitis et al., 2018). Such staffing policies have their origins in hospitality 'just in time' style rostering where workers are called in or sent home based on customer demand (Lai & Baum, 2005). Just in time style rostering gives workers little to no notice, especially in industries where workers may depend on a certain number of hours to earn a living wage (Perdomo-Verdecia et al., 2022).

This reimagined flexible work is convenient for the employer yet challenging for the employee (Kaduk et al., 2019) especially regarding these 'always available' policies where it is expected workers work at home in the evenings and on weekends to keep up with the demands of the job, as well as completing the traditional 9–5 workday. Technology advances also mean that workers are in easy contact with managers and clients (Ter Hoeven et al., 2016). Global demands, plus these technology advances, mean that workers are required to be contactable from not only a local but a global workforce (Mockaitis et al., 2018). This has been especially prevalent since the COVID-19 pandemic (Vyas, 2022).

These white-collar professional workers may be pushed into involuntary flexible work due to their high work demands, work overload and availability expectations (late nights/weekends) to suit global teams (Blagoev & Schreyögg, 2019). This was highlighted by media stories outlining the -hour expected days by EY (Tadros, 2023) where workers reported that 12-hour days and weekend working were seen as 'normal'. As such, these involuntary flexible work practices are seen as a demand, instead of an incentive for workers (Allen et al., 2021). Remote work may be a strategy for workers to cope with high work demands (Kaduk et al., 2019) rather than splitting regular work hours between the office and home. However, remote workers are more likely to work additional hours, suggesting that remote work comes on top of regular work hours (Noonan & Glass, 2012). Professional workforces, such as consultancy companies or banks, may even be unwilling to acknowledge these practices as they are often seen as 'part of the job' (Delfino & Van Der Kolk, 2021). This was detailed by staff at KPMG who noted that 'burnout was very common and others reported long nights [as] a normal expectation' (Wootton, 2021). This perceived, or real, obligation to an overloaded and variable schedule impacts negatively on employee mental health (Blagoev & Schreyögg, 2019), family interactions (Bouwmeester et al., 2021) and emotional exhaustion (Boswell et al., 2014). We saw the impact of this during (and since) the COVID-19 pandemic with the transition to many workforces working from home, and even now the working from home phenomenon remains. While debates continue as to the productivity of workers while at home (Seva et al., 2021), research has shown that those who continued working during the COVID-19 pandemic worked longer hours and suffered increased work-related stress (André & van der Zwan, 2023; Kantamneni, 2020).

Voluntary flexible work practices, such as remote work or variable work hours that are chosen by workers, can increase job satisfaction, turnover intentions and lower stress (Choi, 2020). However, involuntary flexible work practices, such as remote work after hours, where workers do not feel in control of their work hours, can impact work-life balance and mental health (Allen et al., 2021; Delfino & Van Der Kolk, 2021). Therefore, it is important to distinguish between these forms of flexibility and define who has control in the specific work practice, and whether that practice is voluntary or involuntary (Kaduk et al., 2019). It is important to note here the increasing use of 'right to disconnect' policies. Countries such as Belgium, Spain, Portugal and Italy are introducing legislation that states employers cannot contact employees outside of work hours (Von Bergen & Bressler, 2019), with the UK and Australia looking to do the same (Tran, 2023). This may go some way to counteract extended work hours, however, mindset and culture changes still need to come into effect for employees to stop 'logging on' after work (Chung, 2022). For example, in Australia, the 'right to disconnect' amendment to the Fair Work Act (2009) (Cth) proposed in 2023 states that employers must not contact employees outside of work hours, including leave periods, unless it is an emergency, a welfare check or the employee is in receipt of an 'availability allowance' (an allowance to remain available during a set period). However, the Act does not state what 'hours of work' are (e.g., 9 am–5 pm) or how many 'availability allowances' one employee can receive, suggesting this could be up for interpretation and exploitation.

MENTAL HEALTH CONCERNS

The mental health of workers, and society has become an increasing concern, especially since the COVID-19 pandemic (Bufquin et al., 2021). Previous research has highlighted a negative relationship between precarious employment conditions and poor mental health (Vancea & Utzet, 2017), while workers with standard work patterns (permanent full-time employment) showed better mental health (Waenerlund et al., 2014). Workers with flexible work patterns that are termed precarious have a clear psychological vulnerability (Escudero-Castillo et al., 2023), which may manifest into a variety of negative outcomes including suicidal thoughts (Min et al., 2015). Poor mental health for these workers may be exacerbated by concerns over the requirement to maintain standards of living, job insecurity, and the lack of control over work hours (Escudero-Castillo et al., 2023). In an empirical study regarding the use of prescription mental health drugs, Moscone et al. (2016) found that workers on temporary or part-time contracts were more likely to be on prescription medication for mental health concerns compared to workers on permanent full-time contracts. The authors also found that shifting from a permanent contract to a temporary or part-time contract decreased employee mental well-being, while the opposite was true for workers transitioning from a temporary contract to a permanent one (Moscone et al., 2016). Workers experiencing involuntary flexible work hours can also encounter poor sleep patterns, mental health concerns and poor general wellbeing (Schneider & Harknett, 2019)). A clear example can be found during and post the COVID-19 pandemic where gig economy workers were struggling to keep up with work demands while also trying to obtain a living wage (Cameron et al., 2021). Additionally, those workers working from home experienced increased job demands and workload along with longer working hours (Kantamneni, 2020) all while dealing with the circumstantial stresses of a pandemic situation.

PEOPLE WITH DISABILITIES

According to the World Health Organization, disability can be defined as any impairment or condition that impacts daily activities and limits socio-environmental participation in activities, such as employment. People with disabilities are more likely to work in precarious work where they are exposed to poor work conditions, including the ability to obtain and maintain suitable work (Bartram et al., 2021). For example, being engaged in part-time work, short-term contracts and earning a lower income (Meacham et al., 2017). Low-quality employment for people with disabilities can contribute to societal exclusion and poor health outcomes (Beatty et al., 2019).

The digitalisation of the workforce, especially since COVID-19 has left some workers with disabilities even more isolated than they were before (Soga et al., 2022). They often rely on going into the office for social interaction and stimulation, however, they are no longer able to do so (Schur et al., 2020) or when they do they find other workers are still working from home so there is little benefit to inclusion from either working from home or the office (Soga et al., 2022). This isolation may lead to increased stress and anxiety. Digital platforms such as Zoom or Microsoft Teams, used for both formal work and informal chats, may constrain workers with disabilities and negatively impact

Table 12.1   *Summary of issues faced by workers surrounding flexibility and solutions*

Issue	Workers	Solution
Job contracts	Gig	Gig workers need additional protections within their job contracts to bring them level with permanent workers. Greater legislation is needed around the world to offer gig workers protections such as sick and holiday pay. Governments and unions need to take the lead in partitioning the gig economy to offer fair and equitable job contracts.
Exploitation	Low income	Linked to the job contracts issue above is the exploitation of low-income earners who may use flexible work to supplement their income. Again, governments and unions need to be legislating contracts such as zero hours contracts and the right of workers to have clear regular hours, so they can support family requirements. Training and development programmes, either through government-assisted places or employer programmes, should be utilised to increase the skills and experiences of these workers to lift them out of the low-income cycle.
Flexibility stigma	Working parents	While standards in parental leave have increased in recent years, with fathers gaining additional leave benefits to support families, it is mothers who still bare the burden of the default parent. Leave options and flexible practices need to be made available to all parents with those on flexible (part-time) contracts given the ability to develop and progress their careers through targeted career development programmes.

Issue	Workers	Solution
Inclusion	People with a disability	For works with disabilities, it is important to consult workers to understand their individual needs and required supports. This may be in the form of flexible work; however, it is important to note that some workers benefit from office social interaction. Give the worker the option to both work from home and the office by setting up a safe, inclusive office environment. For example, a quiet desk away from distractions.
Involuntary flexibility	White collar	'Right to disconnect' policies go some way to solving this issue, however, organisations need to change their workplace cultures to foster better work-time habits of workers. Job design and workload allocation can assist by reducing the need for workers to work into their evenings/weekends and leaders leading by example by allocating fair workload and minimising the expectation to work long hours.

Source: Authors' own.

their communication and learning (Soga et al., 2022), as well as limit their ability to reach out for help. Schur et al. (2020) found that people with disabilities felt more isolated when having to telework. This digitalisation during and post-COVID-19 can also put the onus on the employee to perform work autonomously. For workers without disabilities this may have been a welcome addition (Van Der Lippe & Lippényi, 2020), yet, for those with disabilities who require more supervision and direction, this may lead to stress and anxiety over completing job tasks (Beatty et al., 2019). Email and 'digital housekeeping' workload can also create challenges for workers with disabilities who do not have the skills or time to fix tech issues (McDowall & Kinman, 2017). Such digital platforms often require a steep learning curve requiring workers to adapt quickly, with little on-demand support if workers with disabilities are working remotely. This can result in additional workplace stress for workers with disabilities who struggle to learn in conventional ways (Bonaccio et al., 2020).

While remote work for people with disabilities was recommended by the World Health Organization during the COVID-19 pandemic due to health concerns (Ned et al., 2020), it has been reported that remote work can place severe restrictions on the types of work and the increased social capital available for people with disabilities (Schur et al., 2020), especially as people with disabilities are often socially isolated from society (McNaughton et al., 2014). For example, Ameri et al. (2022) found that people with disabilities reported further health issues, such as poorer mental health outcomes once they were isolated through telework. While remote work can certainly assist people with disabilities gain employment (Bosua & Gloet, 2021), the types of jobs currently held by most people with disabilities often do not suit remote or telework (Schur et al., 2020). Workers with disabilities are more likely to be in service or manufacturing jobs that require workers to be on site (Sullivan, 2021), meaning they are unlikely to be able to take advantage of remote, tele-work or flexible work patterns. Even when remote work is available to people with disabilities they are often paid less and have fewer opportunities afforded to them (Schur et al., 2020).

People with disabilities utilising flexible work practices (such as temporary work) other than remote work (or working from home) may also be at a dis-advantage in not having their accommodation needs met (Jetha et al., 2020). Disability workplace accommodations tend to parallel the distribution of other employment protections, such as sick leave, particularly for workers with disa-bilities in temporary work arrangements. Research concluded that people with disabilities on temporary contracts were less likely to have any further accom-modations, such as physical amendments to workplaces, due to the temporary arrangement of their employment (Shuey & Jovic, 2013). This could be due to temporary workers not feeling comfortable to disclose their disability if they are only on a fixed-term temporary contract (Lindsay et al., 2019).

FLEXIBILITY ISSUES POST-COVID-19 PANDEMIC AND POTENTIAL SOLUTIONS

This chapter has outlined the potential dangers of flexible work policies and practices for different types of workers. Table 12.1 offers a summary of the issues faced by workers surrounding flexibility, and the possible solutions.

CONCLUSION

Flexibility can offer workers an avenue to enter, return to or maintain work-force participation. Working mothers, people with disabilities and students, for example, can fit work around their studies, health concerns and home life. However, as this chapter has shown, there is a dark side to flexible work that can create more potential issues than it purports to solve. Flexible work, to the disadvantaged or those on low incomes may be inadvertently manipulated by employers into working long hours for below minimum wage standards. It is not just disadvantaged workers, white-collar consultants employed at 'the big

4' often report a 12-hour day as 'normal'. While flexible work may offer clear advantages for some, it is often wise to proceed with caution that flexible work practices are not in fact more inflexible than other work options.

REFERENCES

Australian Bureau of Statistics (ABS). (2019–20). Household Income and Wealth, Australia. https://www.abs.gov.au/statistics/economy/finance/household-income-and-wealth-australia/latest-release. Accessed 13 September 2023.

Allen, T.D., Merlo, K., Lawrence, R.C., Slutsky, J., & Gray, C.E. (2021). Boundary management and work-nonwork balance while working from home. *Applied Psychology, 70*(1): 60–84.

Ameri, M., Kruse, D., Park, S.R., Rodgers, Y., & Schur, L. (2022). Telework during the pandemic: Patterns, challenges, and opportunities for people with disabilities. *Disability and Health Journal*: 101406.

André, S., & van der Zwan, R. (2023). The influence of the COVID-19 pandemic on changes in perceived work pressure for Dutch mothers and fathers. *Gender, Work & Organization, 30*(3): 1015–34.

Anwar, M.A., & Graham, M. (2021). Between a rock and a hard place: Freedom, flexibility, precarity and vulnerability in the gig economy in Africa. *Competition & Change, 25*(2): 237–58.

Bartram, T., Cavanagh, J., Meacham, H., & Pariona-Cabrera, P. (2021). Re-calibrating HRM to improve the work experiences for workers with intellectual disability. *Asia Pacific Journal of Human Resources, 59*(1): 63–83. doi: https://doi.org/10.1111/1744-7941.12230.

Beatty, J.E., Baldridge, D.C., Boehm, S.A., Kulkarni, M., & Colella, A.J. (2019). On the treatment of persons with disabilities in organizations: A review and research agenda. *Human Resource Management, 58*(2): 119–37. doi: https://doi.org/10.1002/hrm.21940.

Blagoev, B., & Schreyögg, G. (2019). Why do extreme work hours persist? Temporal uncoupling as a new way of seeing. *Academy of Management Journal, 62*(6): 1818–47.

Bonaccio, S., Connelly, C.E., Gellatly, I.R., Jetha, A., & Martin Ginis, K.A. (2020). The participation of people with disabilities in the workplace across the employment cycle: Employer concerns and research evidence. *Journal of Business and Psychology, 35*(2): 135–58. doi: https://doi.org/10.1007/s10869-018-9602-5.

Bosua, R., & Gloet, M. (2021). Telework and People with disabilities: Perspectives of managers and employees from Australia. In *Research Anthology on Digital Transformation, Organizational Change, and the Impact of Remote Work* (pp. 1119–37). IGI Global.

Boswell, W.R., Olson-Buchanan, J.B., & Harris, T.B. (2014). I cannot afford to have a life: Employee adaptation to feelings of job insecurity. *Personnel Psychology, 67*(4): 887–915.

Bouwmeester, O., Atkinson, R., Noury, L., & Ruotsalainen, R. (2021). Work-life balance policies in high performance organisations: A comparative interview study with millennials in Dutch consultancies. *German Journal of Human Resource Management, 35*(1): 6–32.

Bufquin, D., Park, J.-Y., Back, R.M., de Souza Meira, J.V., & Hight, S.K. (2021). Employee work status, mental health, substance use, and career turnover intentions:

An examination of restaurant employees during COVID-19. *International Journal of Hospitality Management, 93*: 102764.

Butler, S. (2021). Deliveroo accused of 'cynical PR move' with union deal for couriers. *Guardian.* https:// www .theguardian .com/ business/ 2022/ may/ 12/ deliveroo -union -deal-couriers-minimum-wage-gmb-iwgb. Accessed 10 September 2023.

Cai, R.Y., Gallagher, E., Haas, K., Love, A., & Gibbs, V. (2022). Exploring the income, savings and debt levels of autistic adults living in Australia. *Advances in Autism.* https://doi.org/10.1108/AIA-01-2022-0004.

Cameron, L.D., Thomason, B., & Conzon, V.M. (2021). Risky business: Gig workers and the navigation of ideal worker expectations during the COVID-19 pandemic. *Journal of Applied Psychology, 106*(12): 1821.

Chen, B., Liu, T., & Wang, Y. (2020). Volatile fragility: New employment forms and disrupted employment protection in the new economy. *International Journal of Environmental Research and Public Health, 17*(5): 1531.

Choi, S. (2020). Flexible work arrangements and employee retention: A longitudinal analysis of the federal workforces. *Public Personnel Management, 49*(3): 470–95.

Chung, H. (2020). Gender, flexibility stigma and the perceived negative consequences of flexible working in the UK. *Social Indicators Research, 151*(2): 521–45.

Chung, H. (2022). *The Flexibility Paradox: Why Flexible Working Leads to (Self-) Exploitation*: Policy Press.

Chung, H., & Van der Horst, M. (2018). Women's employment patterns after childbirth and the perceived access to and use of flexitime and teleworking. *Human Relations, 71*(1): 47–72.

Chung, H., & Van der Horst, M. (2020). Flexible working and unpaid overtime in the UK: The role of gender, parental and occupational status. *Social Indicators Research, 151*(2): 495–520.

Creamer, J., Shrider, E., Burns, K., & Chen, F. (2022). *Poverty in the United States* (pp. 60–277). United States Census Bureau. https://www.census.gov/library/publications/2022/demo/p60–277.html. Accessed 19 September 2023.

Delfino, G.F., & Van Der Kolk, B. (2021). Remote working, management control changes and employee responses during the COVID-19 crisis. *Accounting, Auditing & Accountability Journal, 34*(6): 1376–87.

Department for Business Energy and Industrial Strategy. (2022). New guidance brings clarity on employment status for workers and businesses, Press release. https://www .gov.uk/ government/ news/ new -guidance -brings-clarity -on-employment-status-for -workers-and-businesses. Accessed 19 September 2023/

Doshi, B.M., & Tikyani, H. (2020). A theoretical integration of GIG economy: Advancing opportunity, challenges and growth. *International Journal of Management (IJM), 11*(12): 3013–19. dhttps://doi.org/ 10.34218/IJM.11.12.2020.282.

Dube, A. (2019). *Impacts of Minimum Wages: Review of the International Evidence* (pp. 268–304). *Independent Report.* UK Government Publication.

Escudero-Castillo, I., Mato Diaz, F.J., & Rodriguez-Alvarez, A. (2023). Effects of precarious work on mental health: Evidence from Spain. *Applied Economics, 55*(14): 1603–20.

Eurostat. (2021). Living conditions in Europe – poverty and social exclusion. https:// ec .europa .eu/ eurostat/ statistics -explained/ index .php ?title = Living _conditions _in_Europe_-_poverty_and_social_exclusion&oldid=584082. Accessed 9 September 2023.

Fernandez-Lozano, I., González, M.J., Jurado-Guerrero, T., & Martínez-Pastor, J.-I. (2020). The hidden cost of flexibility: A factorial survey experiment on job promotion. *European Sociological Review, 36*(2): 265–83.

Francis-Devine, B. (2023). *Poverty in the UK: Statistics* (7096). UK Parliament. https:// commonslibrary.parliament.uk/research-briefings/sn07096/. Accessed 10 August 2023.

Gordon, J. (Producer). (2022). Gig economy companies placed on notice ahead of new laws. https://www.theage.com.au/national/victoria/gig-economy-companies-placed -on-notice-ahead-of-new-laws-20221020-p5brbq.html.

Greeves, M. (2023). What are my rights on a zero-hours contract? *Good Housekeeping.* https:// www.goodhousekeeping.com/uk/consumer-advice/consumer-rights/ a38103417/zero-hour-contract/. Accessed 19 September 2023.

Groen, B.A., Van Triest, S.P., Coers, M., & Wtenweerde, N. (2018). Managing flexible work arrangements: Teleworking and output controls. *European Management Journal, 36*(6): 727–35.

Hasegawa, Y., Ido, K., Kawai, S., & Kuroda, S. (2022). Who took gig jobs during the COVID-19 recession? Evidence from Uber Eats in Japan. *Transportation Research Interdisciplinary Perspectives, 13*: 100543.

Henly, J.R., & Lambert, S.J. (2014). Unpredictable work timing in retail jobs: Implications for employee work–life conflict. *Ilr Review, 67*(3): 986–1016.

Ipsen, C., van Veldhoven, M., Kirchner, K., & Hansen, J.P. (2021). Six key advantages and disadvantages of working from home in Europe during COVID-19. *International Journal of Environmental Research and Public Health, 18*(4): 1826.

Jacobs, A.W., & Padavic, I. (2015). Hours, scheduling and flexibility for women in the US low-wage labour force. *Gender, Work & Organization, 22*(1): 67–86.

Jetha, A., Martin Ginis, K.A., Ibrahim, S., & Gignac, M.A. (2020). The working disadvantaged: The role of age, job tenure and disability in precarious work. *BMC Public Health, 20*: 1–12.

Jones, A. (2021). Big increase in number of workers in gig economy. *The Leader.* https://www.leaderlive.co.uk/news/19696654.big-increase-number-workers-gig -economy/. Accessed 23 August 2023.

Kaduk, A., Genadek, K., Kelly, E.L., & Moen, P. (2019). Involuntary vs. voluntary flexible work: Insights for scholars and stakeholders. *Community, Work & Family, 22*(4): 412–42. doi:10.1080/13668803.2019.1616532.

Kaine, S., & Josserand, E. (2019). The organisation and experience of work in the gig economy. *Journal of Industrial Relations, 61*(4): 479–501.

Kantamneni, N. (2020). The impact of the COVID-19 pandemic on marginalized populations in the United States: A research agenda. *Journal of Vocational Behavior, 119*: 103439.

Kim, J., Henly, J., Golden, L., & Lambert, S. (2020). Workplace flexibility and worker well-being by gender. *Journal of Marriage and Family, 82*(3): 892–910.

Kreshpaj, B., Orellana, C., Burström, B., Davis, L., Hemmingsson, T., Johansson, G., … Bodin, T. (2020). What is precarious employment? A systematic review of definitions and operationalizations from quantitative and qualitative studies. *Scandinavian Journal of Work, Environment & Health, 46*(3): 235–47.

Kurowska, A. (2020). Gendered effects of home-based work on parents' capability to balance work with non-work: Two countries with different models of division of labour compared. *Social Indicators Research, 151*(2): 405–25.

Laß, I., & Wooden, M. (2020). Trends in the prevalence of non-standard employment in Australia. *Journal of Industrial Relations, 62*(1): 3–32.

Lai, P.C., & Baum, T. (2005). Just-in-time labour supply in the hotel sector: The role of agencies. *Employee Relations, 27*(1), 86–102.

Lindsay, S., Cagliostro, E., Leck, J., Shen, W., & Stinson, J. (2019). Disability disclosure and workplace accommodations among youth with disabilities. *Disability and Rehabilitation, 41*(16): 1914–24.

Lott, Y. (2020). Does flexibility help employees switch off from work? Flexible working-time arrangements and cognitive work-to-home spillover for women and men in Germany. *Social Indicators Research, 151*(2): 471–94.

MacDonald, R., & Giazitzoglu, A. (2019). Youth, enterprise and precarity: Or, what is, and what is wrong with, the 'gig economy'? *Journal of Sociology, 55*(4): 724–40.

Madsen, P.K. (2004). The Danish model of 'flexicurity': Experiences and lessons. *Transfer: European Review of Labour and Research, 10*(2): 187–207.

Marica, M.-E. (2020). Employee sharing: A new type of employment, opportune in a globalized context. Paper presented at the Proceedings of the International Conference on Business Excellence.

McDowall, A. and Kinman, G. (2017), The new nowhere land? A research and practice agenda for the 'always on' culture. *Journal of Organizational Effectiveness: People and Performance, 4*(3), 256–66. https://doi.org/10.1108/JOEPP-05-2017-0045.

McNaughton, D., Rackensperger, T., Dorn, D., & Wilson, N. (2014). 'Home is at work and work is at home': Telework and individuals who use augmentative and alternative communication. *Work, 48*(1): 117–26.

Meacham, H., Cavanagh, J., Shaw, A., & Bartram, T. (2017). HRM practices that support the employment and social inclusion of workers with an intellectual disability. *Personnel Review.* https://doi.org/10.1108/PR-05–2016–0105.

Mehta, B.S. (2020). Changing nature of work and the gig economy: Theory and debate. *FIIB Business Review*: 2319714520968294.

Min, K.-B., Park, S.-G., Hwang, S.H., & Min, J.-Y. (2015). Precarious employment and the risk of suicidal ideation and suicide attempts. *Preventive Medicine, 71*: 72–6.

Mockaitis, A.I., Zander, L., & De Cieri, H. (2018). The benefits of global teams for international organizations: HR implications. *The International Journal of Human Resource Management, 29*(14), 2137–58. doi:10.1080/09585192.2018.1428722.

Moscone, F., Tosetti, E., & Vittadini, G. (2016). The impact of precarious employment on mental health: The case of Italy. *Social Science & Medicine, 158*: 86–95.

Ned, L., McKinney, E.L.M., McKinney, V., & Swartz, L. (2020). COVID-19 pandemic and disability: Essential considerations. *Social and Health Sciences, 18*(2): 136–48.

Noonan, M.C., & Glass, J.L. (2012). The hard truth about telecommuting. *Monthly Labor Review., 135*: 38.

Oddo, V.M., Zhuang, C.C., Andrea, S.B., Eisenberg-Guyot, J., Peckham, T., Jacoby, D., & Hajat, A. (2021). Changes in precarious employment in the United States: A longitudinal analysis. *Scandinavian Journal of Work, Environment & Health, 47*(3): 171.

Perdomo-Verdecia, V., Sacristán-Díaz, M., & Garrido-Vega, P. (2022). Lean management in hotels: Where we are and where we might go. *International Journal of Hospitality Management, 104*: 103250.

Piasna, A., & Plagnol, A. (2018). Women's job quality across family life stages: An analysis of female employees across 27 European countries. *Social Indicators Research, 139*(3): 1065–84.

Redrup, Y. (Producer). (2022). Gig economy laws coming in first half of 2023. https:// www .afr .com/ technology/ gig -economy -laws -coming -in -first -half -of -2023–20220904-p5bf9k. Accessed 10 August 2023.

Rho, H.J., Brown, H., & Fremstad, S. (2020). A basic demographic profile of workers in frontline industries. *Center for Economic and Policy Research, 7*(10).

Riezzo, C. (2021). An exploration of employee motivation and job satisfaction in the gig economy. *The Elphinstone Review*: 61.

Royle, O. (2023). Are remote workers lonely? Probably – and experts warn it has damaging side effects on productivity, engagement, and progression. *Fortune.* https://fortune.com/2023/03/14/is-remote-work-lonely-side-effects-on-productivity-engagement-and-progression/. Accessed 10 August 2023.

Rubery, J. (2015), Change at work: Feminisation, flexibilisation, fragmentation and financialisation. *Employee Relations, 37*(6), 633–44. https://doi.org/10.1108/ER-04-2015-0067.

Rubery, J., Keizer, A., & Grimshaw, D. (2016). Flexibility bites back: The multiple and hidden costs of flexible employment policies. *Human Resource Management Journal, 26*(3): 235–51.

Schneider, D., & Harknett, K. (2019). Consequences of routine work-schedule instability for worker health and well-being. *American Sociological Review, 84*(1): 82–114.

Schur, L.A., Ameri, M., & Kruse, D. (2020). Telework after COVID: A 'silver lining' for workers with disabilities? *Journal of Occupational Rehabilitation, 30*(4): 521–36.

Seva, R.R., Tejero, L.M.S., & Fadrilan-Camacho, V.F.F. (2021). Barriers and facilitators of productivity while working from home during pandemic. *Journal of Occupational Health, 63*(1): e12242.

Shuey, K.M., & Jovic, E. (2013). Disability accommodation in nonstandard and precarious employment arrangements. *Work and Occupations, 40*(2): 174–205.

Smith, V., & Halpin, B. (2019). Non-standard work and non-standard workers. In *Handbook of the Politics of Labour, Work and Employment* (pp. 281–97). Edward Elgar Publishing.

Soga, L.R., Bolade-Ogunfodun, Y., Mariani, M., Nasr, R., & Laker, B. (2022). Unmasking the other face of flexible working practices: A systematic literature review. *Journal of Business Research, 142*: 648–62.

Sullivan, T.A. (2021). Who are the marginal workers? In *Marginal Workers, Marginal Jobs* (pp. 13–24). University of Texas Press.

Tadros, E. (2023). In their own words: What staff say about EY. *Financial Review.* https://www.afr.com/companies/professional-services/in-their-own-words-what-staff-say-about-ey-20230726-p5drjd. Accesed 29 July 2023.

Tan, Z.M., Aggarwal, N., Cowls, J., Morley, J., Taddeo, M., & Floridi, L. (2021). The ethical debate about the gig economy: A review and critical analysis. *Technology in Society, 65*: 101594.

Taylor, J. (2022). Deliveroo quits Australia citing 'challenging economic conditions'. *Guardian.* https://www.theguardian.com/business/2022/nov/16/deliveroo-quits-australia-citing-challenging-economic-conditions. Accessed 10 September 2023.

Ter Hoeven, C.L., van Zoonen, W., & Fonner, K.L. (2016). The practical paradox of technology: The influence of communication technology use on employee burnout and engagement. *Communication Monographs, 83*(2): 239–63.

Tran, C. (2023). Ban on Australian bosses contacting workers out of hours: Careers expert Sue Ellson predicts pay impact over bombshell proposal. *7 News.* https://7news.com.au/lifestyle/ban-on-australian-bosses-contacting-workers-out-of-hours-careers-expert-sue-ellson-predicts-pay-impact-over-bombshell-proposal--c-11664791. Accessed 20 July 2023.

Van Der Lippe, T., & Lippényi, Z. (2020). Co-workers working from home and individual and team performance. *New Technology, Work and Employment, 35*(1): 60–79.

Vancea, M., & Utzet, M. (2017). How unemployment and precarious employment affect the health of young people: A scoping study on social determinants. *Scandinavian Journal of Public Health, 45*(1): 73–84.

Von Bergen, C.W., & Bressler, M.S. (2019). Work, non-work boundaries and the right to disconnect. *The Journal of Applied Business and Economics, 21*(2): 51–69.

Vyas, L. (2022). 'New normal' at work in a post-COVID world: Work–life balance and labor markets. *Policy and Society, 41*(1): 155–67.

Waenerlund, A.-K., Gustafsson, P.E., Hammarström, A., & Virtanen, P. (2014). History of labour market attachment as a determinant of health status: A 12-year follow-up of the Northern Swedish Cohort. *BMJ Open, 4*(2): e004053.

Webster, J. (2016). Microworkers of the gig economy: Separate and precarious. Paper presented at the New Labor forum.

Weinberg, A. (2019). *Mother Jones*. https://www.motherjones.com/media/2019/11/a-transcriptionist-reveals-the-perils-of-the-gig-economy/. Accessed 10 September 2023.

Wilson, N. (2023). Flexibility and earning potential, two lures of the gig economy. *Forbes*. https://www.forbes.com/sites/nigelwilson/2023/02/15/flexibility-and-earning-potential-two-lures-of-the-gig-economy/?sh=78c0a97e4db0. Accessed 25 May 2023.

Wood, A.J., Graham, M., Lehdonvirta, V., & Hjorth, I. (2019). Good gig, bad gig: Autonomy and algorithmic control in the global gig economy. *Work, Employment and Society, 33*(1): 56–75.

Wootton, H. (2021). 'Borderline slavery': Staff lambast 'brutal' hours at big four consultancies. *Financial Review*. https://www.afr.com/companies/professional-services/borderline-slavery-staff-lambast-brutal-hours-at-big-four-consultancies-20210114-p56tz9. Accessed 26 April 2023.

Wu, Q., Zhang, H., Li, Z., & Liu, K. (2019). Labor control in the gig economy: Evidence from Uber in China. *Journal of Industrial Relations, 61*(4): 574–96.

Yeung, D.Y., Zhou, X., & Chong, S. (2021). Perceived age discrimination in the workplace: The mediating roles of job resources and demands. *Journal of Managerial Psychology, 36*(6): 505–19.

13. Supply chains and e-supply chains: the impact on flexibilisation of work and employment

Pedro Mendonça

INTRODUCTION

Supply chains have gradually become the prevailing form of industrial organisation around the world, expanding not only geographically but also in terms of the economic activities they organise (Wright & Kaine, 2015). While the growing importance of supply chains creates opportunities for firms to increase profits and flexibility, and to outsource some production to lower-cost locations, it also generates pressures on labour (Marchington et al., 2005). On the one hand, an increasing number of firms tend to shift risks and demands for flexibility across the supply chain, particularly to countries with weaker labour regulations and collective bargaining structures (Drahokoupil & Fabo, 2019). At the same time, the focus on flexible but rationalised supply chains produces pressures on firms to adopt flexible Human Resource Management (HRM) practices such as casual contracts, standardisation of tasks and processes, and the implementation of advanced technology that enables closer monitoring of workers and labour processes (Håkansson & Isidorsson, 2018), discussed in earlier chapters of this book. Consequently, jobs across supply chains may become increasingly insecure and uncertain, less skilled, and based on informalised work and employment practices (Mendonça, 2018; Mendonça et al., 2023). However, the breakout of the COVID-19 pandemic created unprecedented disruptions and new unexpected dynamics that go against the logic of the rationalised supply chain (Nikolopoulos et al., 2021). In analysing the tension between organisations seeking ever-more flexible operations to meet the demands of supply chain rationalisation and its impacts on work and employment conditions, this chapter highlights how labour is mainly seen as an exchangeable factor of production. This chapter aims to analyse the impacts of supply chain pressures within a post-pandemic context on working conditions and address the emergence of less-discussed issues in contemporary e-supply chains. This chapter goes deeper into these concerns, specifically investigating how the dynamics of the supply chain, in the aftermath of the COVID-19 pandemic, impact three key aspects that can lead to changes in the relationships between companies within a production network: job security and working time, worker skill and discretion, and informal work.

SUPPLY CHAIN CONFIGURATIONS AND THE IMPACT OF THE COVID-19 PANDEMIC

A supply chain can be defined as a series of interconnected firms, including suppliers, customers, and logistics providers, that collaborate to provide a package of goods and services to the final customer (Dicken, 2015). Supply chains and their inter-firm dynamics have become a defining feature of the structure and operation of contemporary flexible firms (Dicken, 2015). While highly coordinated and rationalised supply chains have long characterised the manufacturing and construction industries, they have now become ubiquitous in the global economy, extending to every industry and continent (Ruggie, 2013: 6). As Drahokoupil and Fabo (2019) argue, production and service provision are increasingly organised on a network and supply chain basis, and thus, no workplace exists in isolation. Consequently, the contemporary economy is characterised by intertwined supply chains, composed of organisationally and spatially separated stages.

The interest in supply chains and their impacts on work and employment relations is justified by the tendency of organisations to segment their business units through the increased use of outsourcing and offshoring, resulting in the proliferation of supply chains (Dicken, 2015). This trend is driven by three identifiable factors. The first factor is related to the incorporation of private sector management principles in the public sector, which has encouraged public sector organisations to outsource peripheral activities to specialised contractors (Drahokoupil & Fabo, 2019). For instance, hospitals and schools have outsourced activities such as security and cleaning services. The second factor is linked to organisations' increasing focus on pursuing rational and flexible strategies, resulting in subcontracting arrangements becoming increasingly common. Over the past decade, we have observed the rapid growth of segments of the economy such as platform work and gig work (Kougiannou & Mendonça, 2021). Within this trend, organisations increasingly seek to externalise (labour) risks and costs to become more flexible in adjusting to market demands. We can also observe this trend for cost-effectiveness and flexibility in high-end industries, such as car manufacturing in Sweden (Håkansson & Isidorsson, 2018). The third and final driver relates to the growth of global supply chains, also termed global value chains or global production networks (Gereffi et al., 2022), which have developed in tandem with increasing trade liberalisation and technological advancements. As a result, we can observe an international division of labour, with activities associated with raw material extraction, processing, and manufacturing being shifted to suppliers in emerging economies, while the activities associated with design, research and development, and marketing have largely been maintained by multinationals in advanced economies (Dicken, 2015). The electronics industry is a prime example of the international division of labour within global supply chains. Many multinational corporations in advanced economies design and market electronic products, while manufacturing processes are often outsourced to suppliers in emerging economies (Chan et al., 2013).

Robinson and Rainbird (2013: 97) posit that inter-firm relations are not confined to contractual agreements or ownership structures but also involve governance. Governance mechanisms and control strategies that stipulate product quality standards, quantities, delivery dates, and prices may be employed. Flecker et al. (2013) highlight two primary types of supply chain relationships. The first is the core-peripheral model, in which core production units are maintained in-house, and peripheral units are outsourced to other firms. The second is the network model, which describes the dynamic movement of production units up and down the value chain hierarchy and their relative importance within the production network. While the former may reflect a static, outdated approach, the latter offers a more flexible understanding of inter-firm competition and prominence. Coe et al. (2008: 272) use the concept of 'network' to underscore the transactional and relational nature of how goods and services are produced, distributed, and consumed.

The outbreak of COVID-19 has disrupted much of these driving forces of moving towards networked productions, particularly those that were relying on global chains of services and production. This is because many of the companies worldwide decreased dramatically (if not completely stopped) their production output due to local lockdowns. Consequently, numerous businesses ceased their orders for raw materials due to the absence of downstream demand. In certain instances, notably in emerging economies, factory employees relocated to their hometowns, which were often hundreds or even thousands of miles distant from the factories. These dual challenges caused significant disruptions as factories found themselves lacking both raw materials and labour, even when new orders started coming in (Panwar et al., 2022). Furthermore, the termination of production set off a chain reaction, resulting in a disruption in trade routes and a logistical crisis. This unfolded as numerous shipping companies scaled back the number of vessels in operation to prevent their logistics expenses from soaring (Panwar et al., 2022). To make matters worse, halted production cascaded into a trade route disruption and a logistics crisis because many shipping companies reduced the number of vessels at sea to keep their logistics costs from skyrocketing.

Outsourcing and supply chain relationships may involve distinct inter-firm control strategies, and lead firms may use a 'hands-on' or 'hands-off' approach (Drahokoupil & Fabo, 2019). The former is characterised by long-term contracts, explicit control, trust, and regular engagement between suppliers and lead firms, with a focus on enhancing the value of the product or service. This form of control is likened to the influence of headquarters on vertically integrated subsidiaries, where collaboration and trust are central to the relationship's success. Conversely, 'hands-off' control is marked by lead firms imposing measurable and auditable specifications, such as service-level agreements, product quality, or price demands, and the ability to set parameters followed by suppliers across the supply chain. This form of inter-firm governance reflects market-based relationships, where suppliers are subject to indirect pressures from client firms and must directly compete with other suppliers to remain in the supply chain. Factors such as power differentials, institutional drivers, and geographical location may influence the decision to engage in a particular form of inter-firm relationship (Drahokoupil & Fabo, 2019; Mendonça, 2018). These relationships and their influencing factors shape the employment models and working conditions found within the supply chain (Mendonça & Adăscăliţei, 2020), making them crucial to understanding the dynamics of supply chain management.

However, with the pandemic, the adoption of these relationships was challenged. In essence, the pandemic exposed vulnerabilities in global supply chains, particularly in industries heavily reliant on offshore production. Disruptions in international transportation and trade restrictions led companies to reconsider the benefits of localisation, focusing on domestic or regional supply sources to enhance flexibility and adaptability. The pandemic demonstrated the risk of relying heavily on a single supplier, or one geographic region. Companies began diversifying their supplier base to reduce vulnerability to disruptions and at the same time, inter-firm relationship became increasingly more transactional and based on dual-sourcing. For instance, as the primary supplier remains the main source, the lead firm may source secondary suppliers that serve as backup options. This strategy helps companies maintain a balance between cost-effectiveness and risk mitigation. As an example, Gereffi et al. (2022) show how countries and pharmaceuticals sourced the same medical supplies (such as vaccines or masks) from multiple suppliers in different geographical locations as a contingency strategy.

THE IMPACT OF THE FISSURED AND FLEXIBLE WORKPLACE ON WORKING CONDITIONS AND EMPLOYMENT RELATIONS IN A POST-PANDEMIC CONTEXT

Weil (2014) posits that the workplace has experienced a 'fissuring' as a result of changes in the structure of production and service provision. This has led to the emergence of more segmented and atomised organisations in the form of supply chains. After the breakout of COVID-19 and to better respond to future uncertain environments, organisations further shifted their focus from being large, rigid conglomerates of production and service units involving factories, distribution centres, and logistics, to being fractioned entities that concentrate on their core activities while contracting out peripheral ones (Nikolopoulos et al., 2021). In effect, employers in some sectors have adopted business and HR strategies that shift the boundary of the firm inwards, reducing the number of workers under direct control and increasing the number of flexible workers (Weil, 2014), in order to meet the increased consumer demand in the post-pandemic context. Consequently, in this post-pandemic context, organisations are increasingly meeting their demand for labour through franchise arrangements, outsourcing, and subcontracting. Outsourcing firms and subcontractors often use agency workers, apply zero hour contracts, and employ migrant labour either casually or informally (Adăscăliței et al., 2022).

Different supply chain structures result in a range of interlinked processes that impact production requirements, firm decision-making, and the labour process (Hoque et al., 2011). In a post-pandemic context, researchers and policymakers have suggested that the new economic environment around supply chains has generated favourable conditions for new and better employment opportunities (Kano et al., 2022). These arguments are underpinned by the suggestion that HRM can bring 'mutual gains' for firms and workers, such as high productivity and high job quality/well-being (Guest, 2017). Although in a first instance the pandemic has triggered in some locations mass unemployment, rising inequality, or exposure to the virus due to poor working conditions (Dobbins et al., 2023; Gavin et al., 2022), researchers have argued that uncertain environments may be a catalyst for achieving better working conditions. Research indicates that the social changes triggered by crises present a chance for multinational companies to engage more strategically with local stakeholders. This involvement can lead to contributions to recovery initiatives, consequently enhancing their legitimacy and solidifying their acceptance within the local market (Mithani, 2017). For instance, during the COVID-19 pandemic, some multinational companies in the retail sector faced scrutiny for their treatment of frontline workers. In response to public pressure and the need to maintain a healthy workforce, these companies improved working conditions by providing personal protective equipment, implementing safety protocols, and offering hazard pay (Unison, 2020). This was particularly evident in the gig economy and the food delivery segment, where workers were briefed extensively on how to protect themselves from unnecessary social contact (Howson et al., 2022). However, a substantial body of research suggests that as organisations increasingly shift their focus towards networked modes of production, it brings about a transformation in the dynamics of production. This transformation exerts downward pressures on companies, ultimately resulting in diminished job quality and employment opportunities (Wright & Kaine, 2015). In a post-pandemic context, Hadjisolomou and Simone (2021) show how the tension between cost-saving mechanisms and the need to be prepared for any uncertain context was detrimental for workers' job security, working hours, and ultimately the development of skills. In the hospitality and tourism industry, lockdowns and travel restrictions led to a massive downturn in business. Many hotels, restaurants, and travel agencies had to lay off or furlough a significant portion of their workforce, resulting in widespread unemployment and financial hardship for employees (Chen & Chen, 2021). Similarly, the airline industry experienced a sharp decline in demand for air travel. As a result, airlines were forced to implement massive layoffs and salary cuts, impacting the job security and income of thousands of employees (Sobieralski, 2020).

In a post pandemic context, the existence of transactional arrangements characterised by highly dependent suppliers on lead firms is likely to intensify problems of insecurity and disposability of labour, particularly in countries with weak employment laws and collective bargaining institutions (Khaled & Ansar, 2023). This has been evident in several recent prominent international cases. For instance, the case of Bangladesh apparel workers is an evident case of arbitrary dismissal just weeks after the COVID-19 pandemic outbreak. Recent reports argue that although workers have begun to return to the factories, the poor and precarious working conditions remain and are exacerbated by increasing inequality and lack of power (Brown, 2021).

A number of scholars have identified a tension between the growing emphasis on flexibility across supply chains and its impact on the standard permanent employment contract, leading to an increase in non-standard forms of work such as subcontracting, dependent self-employment, and agency-based employment (Mendonça et al., 2023). In contemporary supply chains in a post-pandemic context, firms and managers have capitalised on new technologies and the availability of insecure employment to exert greater control over the workplace (Gereffi et al., 2022; Mendonça & Adăscăliței, 2020). For instance, the platform economy, with particular focus on the food delivery segment, has increased exponentially during and after the pandemic

(Polkowska, 2021). This is because technology is becoming a key mechanism employed by dominant firms to remotely monitor the labour process, as discussed in earlier chapters of this book. New information and communication technology (ICT) is used not only to monitor and predict production and consumption patterns in supply chains but also to control workers who increasingly undertake their work remotely (Skountridaki et al., 2020).

These arguments underscore the role of markets in mediating relationships between supply chains and workplaces, and the consequences for employment and working conditions. This chapter delves further into these issues, examining specifically how supply chain dynamics, together with the COVID-19 pandemic, affect three areas that are susceptible to shifting firm relations within a production network: job security and working time, worker skill and discretion, and informal work.

THE IMPACT OF SUPPLY CHAIN ON THE EMPLOYMENT RELATIONSHIP: CONTRACTS AND WORKING TIME

Gereffi et al. (2022) argue that variations in inter-firm dynamics directly impact how management uses contractual flexibility to adjust to supply chain requirements. On the one hand, inter-firm relationships characterised by a hands-on approach, where trust and long-term relationships are prioritised, can encourage long-term and stable jobs within the supplier organisation. Firms that focus on quality products and rely on a highly skilled and trained labour force may promote long-term standard employment contracts to preserve essential skills and knowledge required for a relational inter-firm arrangement (Marchington et al., 2005). However, relational supply chain relationships require high levels of trust and collaboration, which can be challenging to maintain, particularly in contexts with a lack of institutional support and skilled workers (Marchington et al., 2005).

The COVID-19 pandemic came to challenge these established inter-firm relationships disrupting traditional models and prompting a revaluation of supply chain strategies. One significant aspect of this transformation relates to the tension between cost-saving practices and maintaining the business profitability, and the capacity to deal with future uncertainties (Gereffi et al., 2022). This tension is arguably challenging for maintaining secure employment contracts and stable and predictable working time patterns.

Pre-pandemic tightly managed supply chains that prioritised HR practices aimed at matching labour costs to production demands in order to increase the end-value of goods (Caroli et al., 2010; Flecker et al., 2013; Kalleberg, 2003). For example, Price (2016) shows how suppliers help large companies save costs and achieve flexibility by employing labour on non-standard contracts through temporary agency firms. Non-standard employment contracts may therefore be utilised to cope with volatility in production and consumption demand or to directly match labour costs to production demand (Flecker & Meil, 2010). However, in a post-pandemic context, the increasingly volatile nature of supply chains during the pandemic has intensified uncertainties in employment contracts. The unpredictability of supply chain disruptions, such as lockdowns, transport issues, and raw material shortages, which often lead to production stoppages, have resulted in sudden layoffs or non-renewal of short-term contracts (Sharma et al., 2022). In a post-pandemic era, we are seeing a time of ultra-flexibility with workers being ever-more exposed to the vagaries of the market (Dobbins et al., 2023). This is particularly evident in the rise of the gig economy where the risk of uncertainty is passed directly to the worker through self-employment arrangements. As companies seek cost-effectiveness and on-demand labour, they engage workers on short-term or project-based contracts. Delivery drivers, freelance professionals, and temporary workers have become integral to supply chains (Mendonça et al., 2023).

In terms of working time patterns, pre-pandemic trends were already showing a tendency for production planning disruptions with increasing cost pressures being cascaded on to suppliers throughout the chain. The need to cope with such demands, coupled with pressures for cost control, was leading employers to adopt non-standard hours and shifts that change working time schedules, typically at short notice (Caroli et al., 2010; Wood, 2016). For instance, Hadjisolomou et al. (2017) illustrate how flexi-workers in the retail sector are contractually obligated to accept changes in working time schedules or calls for work at very short notice in order for the employer to meet customer flow and save costs. However, with the COVID-19 pandemic, the irregular patterns in demand and disruptions caused in globalised chains, flexible working time has become increasingly central for companies to adjust to unpredictable demand periods (Sharma et al., 2022). This is resulting in increased reliance on 24/7 production to meet unpredictable demand periods. Overtime and unexpected changes in working time patterns have been the solution found by organisations to cope with such unpredictable demands, leading to extended and irregular working hours. For instance, after the pandemic and lockdowns there has been a widespread call for the right to disconnect from work amid what has been called an 'overtime epidemic' (Jones & Bano, 2021). Extended and irregular working hours pose risks of fatigue and burnout among workers, affecting their physical and mental well-being. For those on short-term contracts, the expectation to work irregular hours may be intensified, amplifying stress and job dissatisfaction (Gavin et al., 2022).

Adding to the prevalence of unpredictable and extended working hours, in the aftermath of the pandemic, the gig economy has seen unprecedented growth, becoming deeply embedded in the fabric of supply chain operations.

The gig economy, in the way it is based on the self-employment model and piece-rate pay system, has been identified as a key disruptive mechanism for working time patterns. Characterised by short-term and on-demand tasks, it lacks the consistency seen in traditional employment and gig workers often find it challenging to predict their working hours accurately (Mendonça & Kougiannou, 2023). This unpredictability creates challenges for workers in planning their personal lives, making it difficult to schedule other commitments or maintain a work-life balance. At the same time, the gig economy pressures workers to be always available for work as companies typically link pay directly to the time spent working or the number of tasks completed. This creates a situation where workers may feel compelled to work continuously to maximise their earnings (Mendonça & Kougiannou, 2023). The direct correlation between work time and pay incentivises gig workers to take on as many tasks as possible and essentially be always available for work. This pressure to constantly work, without clearly defined working hours, is argued to lead to burnout and fatigue.

THE IMPACT OF SUPPLY CHAIN ON SKILL DEVELOPMENT IN A POST-PANDEMIC CONTEXT

Indeed, an overlapping concern between employment, working conditions, and supply chain literature is the influence of the latter on firms' ability to foster skill development (Gereffi et al., 2022; Sharma et al., 2022). However, little research has focused on how inter-firm relations impact skill development dynamics particularly in the post-pandemic context.

Recent research, particularly evaluating the potential impacts of the COVID-19 pandemic, argue that the novel demands created by an unprecedented context would push companies to develop workers' skills to deal with the new sets of challenges created by the pandemic as well as to cope with potential future crisis (Kano et al., 2022). As the pandemic highlighted the importance of skilled and adaptable workers, companies in different industries required quick adjustments to production processes, such as healthcare and manufacturing of essential goods. This adaptation process arguably relies heavily on workers' expertise and discretion to adapt to changing conditions. It was then predicted that training and upskilling was to become essential to ensure workers could perform new tasks effectively (Gereffi et al., 2022).

Documented by critical studies, the trend in pre-pandemic context was that the pressures on firms to standardise and routinise tasks to achieve performance targets diminished workers' capacity to utilise their skills and make decisions. For example, Mullholland and Stewart (2014) illustrated that as the labour process is divided into many smaller, simpler tasks, allowing tighter and more precise managerial control, worker autonomy and discretion are reduced to a minimum. This means that the need for skilled workers is replaced by work intensification. As research emerges evaluating the impact of the pandemic in supply chain and skills development, we can see that the pandemic has accentuated earlier deskilling trends. Amid economic uncertainties and cost-cutting measures triggered by supply chain disruptions, some companies may reduce their investments in employee training programmes. For instance, Hadjisolomou and Simone (2021) show that in response to the urgency of overcoming supply chain challenges, line managers involved in retail prioritised immediate operational needs at the expense of investing time and resources in the workforce (such as training and skill development). In addition, companies may be hesitant to invest time and effort in developing new skills due to the volatile post-pandemic supply chain environment and the immanency of further job losses. Optimistic accounts argue shifts in skill requirement may result in upskilling. For instance, many companies during and after COVID-19 moved to remote or hybrid work and studies implied that workers would have to learn new skills by engaging with online forums, amending work documents, undertaking online meetings, sharing resources, and making the argument online (Li et al., 2020). However, the rapid changes in supply chain dynamics and workplace environments may result in companies not providing adequate training support to help existing employees acquire these new skills (Mallet et al., 2020). Moreover, as noted in Chapter 3, as technology advances and algorithmic management increasingly becomes a tool to control employees, we may see a paradox where remote work is highly monitored. Although employees may experience less direct human control, companies will invest in technology-enhanced control mechanisms which will reduce workers' discretion and ability to utilise their skills.

Therefore, on the one hand, firms involved in relational supply chains are arguably required to increase skills through the sharing of technical and managerial knowledge so that quality standards can be maintained. On the other hand, the transactional inter-firm relations that are highly focused on cost-effectiveness are being pressurised to standardise and routinise job tasks in order to get more efficient and predictable production, which results in lower skill levels required in the workplace.

THE RISE OF E-SUPPLY CHAINS AND THE CREATION OF ULTRA-FLEXIBLE WORK

Another important aspect of the shift within supply chain configuration in a post-pandemic context lies in the increasing mediation and control through new technological apparatus, such as digital platforms and algorithmic management (see details in Chapter 3). Although the question of how digital platforms are used to manage and control operations across supply chains is relatively new, there are already some important contributions to the debate. The elaboration of this link is a key step in understanding current work and employment restructuring because as Coe and Yang (2021: 308) argue, '[platform and supply chain literature] can be used synergistically to better understand the distinctive ways in which certain industries are being dramatically and rapidly restructured by the expanding scale and size of platforms. Ultimately, both are concerned with the processes through which the market power of lead firms is produced.' Platforms and their algorithmic management have been identified as intermediators and enabling more rationalised forms of transaction as they facilitate matchmaking between supply and demand. Studies on the integration of digital platforms and supply chains have focused on the interactions between different user groups (customers and suppliers) and the platforms (McIntyre et al., 2021). This involves key mechanisms of platform governance, the nature of transactions and pricing, and the extent to which platforms are open or closed. In this way, a digital platform and its digital applications (apps) intermediate between customers who pay for work performed by an employee, worker, or contractor and the producer, with the platform retaining a percentage of the exchange (Aloisi & De Stefano, 2022). In this sense, the platform creates the relationship between customer, labour (i.e., the contractor), and producer by programming the required performance of specific tasks and charges a fee for this intermediation (Mendonça et al., 2023). It does so by creating and regulating a relationship between the different actors involved in the supply chain, that is, producer, contractor (or worker), consumer and the platform itself. Cennamo et al. (2018) add to this debate in highlighting the role of the platforms' technological complexity for the relationships between different actors in the platform ecosystem.

Recent contributions have been key in providing building-blocks for the understanding of how supply chains integrate digital technologies to coordinate and structure production and value creation. For instance, Sturgeon (2021) has identified three key business strategies related to how new digital technologies affect supply chain governance: modularity, open innovation, and platforms. The concept of modularity involves breaking down supply chain processes into interchangeable components, facilitated by advanced data analytics and communication technologies. Open innovation emphasises collaborative value creation with external partners, enabled by digital platforms that foster transparency and trust. Platforms, as intermediaries, connect supply chain players, with digital technologies enhancing real-time visibility and coordination. Together, these strategies signify a transformative shift in supply chain governance, emphasising adaptability, collaboration, and responsiveness in the digital era (Sturgeon, 2021). At the sectoral level, researchers have also contributed to the understanding of how digitalisation facilitates industrial restructuring and fragmentation. Thun and Sturgeon (2019) address the recent trajectory of the mobile phone industry and highlight the rising relevance of platforms for supply chain governance. At the same time, the authors highlight the role that the introduction of these technologies (such as platforms) have in the blurring of organisational boundaries. In essence, the increasing capacity lead firms have in directly monitoring and controlling other organisations' activity results in further integration between firms (Mendonça & Adăscăliţei, 2020), and at the same time blurs boundaries between one and another organisation (Thun & Sturgeon, 2019). In another sector, disruptive supply chain innovators, purveyors of 'platform capitalism', such as Deliveroo and Uber argue that they are not traditional businesses built on the production of goods or the supply of services but rather an intermediary that brings potential buyers and sellers together (Mendonça et al., 2023). Platform companies take advantage of 'flexibilised' labour markets to engage couriers in their supply chain as self-employed independent contractors and, in this way, cut labour costs by circumventing the imposition of employer on-costs such as national insurance contributions, holiday and sick pay, as well as health and safety regulations (Aloisi & De Stefano, 2022).

Some supply chain researchers have argued that mutual data exchange and digital integration of operations results in closer and longer-term and more balanced power supply chain relationships (Butollo et al., 2022; Coe & Yang, 2021). For instance, by exchanging data on demand forecasts and production schedules, the automotive manufacturer and its suppliers can align their operations more effectively. This mutual understanding reduces uncertainties, minimises the risk of overstock or shortages, and enhances overall supply chain efficiency. However, critical studies have challenged this notion by arguing that the introduction of digital platforms and algorithmic management in the supply chain may result in the centralisation of power by lead firms (Vallas & Schor, 2020). This may be particularly present in supply chains where lead firms are able to establish the parameters and terms of exchange across the supply chain. The introduction of digital platforms is said to accentuate this power imbalance as lead firms are able to fully control the data and the supply chain entry and exit requirements, forcing suppliers and business partners to agree and to incur on most risks associated with the business (López et al., 2022). For instance, lead firms operating digital platforms set stringent entry and exit requirements for suppliers and business partners. In the case of Amazon, third-party sellers on its marketplace must adhere to specific terms and conditions, ranging from fulfilment standards to pricing policies. This control allows Amazon to maintain a standardised and consistent customer experience (Rikap, 2022).

Focusing on the impact of digital supply chain integration on labour processes, studies from labour process tradition have highlighted that building digitally integrated supply chains entails heightened control and monitoring over the labour process and worker performance across the various stages of the supply chain. As a result, digital supply chain integration tends to result in standardisation of tasks and operations, workflow optimisation, and tight monitoring of worker performance (Mendonça & Adăscăliței, 2020). By examining labour process transformations linked to the introduction of digital platforms and algorithmic management onto supply chains, research studies found labour processes in warehouses, factories, and logistics becoming ever-more standardised, rationalised, and intensified. Labour process changes under digital supply chain dynamics have been argued to represent a form of 'Digital Taylorism', whereby the platforms and algorithms assume a central role in managing the labour process and worker performance (Fuchs et al., 2021). One central argument in this context lies in the increasing transfer of labour process control from the workplace to the technologically driven supply chain (Mendonça & Adăscăliței, 2020). The mediation of supply chains by algorithms and platforms seeking ever-more cost-efficient and flexible operations results in pressures for the labour process to become increasingly standardised, fragmented, and tightly monitored (López et al., 2022). As a result, workers experience an ultra-flexible work environment, with the absence of employment relationship, with no fixed hours of work, and skills are atomised to undertake the minutest of the tasks. For instance, as a prominent e-commerce platform, Amazon extensively leverages technologically driven supply chain dynamics to achieve cost-efficient and adaptable operations. This transformation is characterised by several key aspects. Firstly, the introduction of algorithmic management has resulted in the standardisation and rationalisation of labour processes within Amazon's warehouses. Workflows are meticulously designed and optimised for efficiency, with algorithms dictating optimal methods for tasks such as picking, packing, and shipping. Secondly, algorithmic management plays a pivotal role in intensifying labour processes, subjecting workers to stringent performance targets monitored by algorithms, thereby tightly coupling productivity with technological directives. The implications of this transformation are significant. Worker precarity is exacerbated by the ultra-flexible work environment and task-specific training, prompting scrutiny of Amazon's labour practices for their impact on employee well-being. Additionally, constant algorithmic surveillance affects worker autonomy, creating a highly monitored work environment where algorithms track and evaluate performance metrics, influencing day-to-day activities and shaping the overall labour process (Briken & Taylor, 2018).

REGULATING EMPLOYMENT STANDARDS IN SUPPLY CHAINS

Scholars and policymakers have stressed the significance of regulation in ensuring that competitive interactions within supply chains do not result in negative impacts on work and employment standards. The literature typically distinguishes between two forms of regulation: private and multistakeholder. Private regulation relies on voluntary adherence to supplier conduct codes and is typically monitored unilaterally by the lead firm, whereas multistakeholder regulation involves formal assessment and oversight from regulatory bodies and/or unions. Private regulation, based on unitarist principles and voluntary standards, has been criticised for being ineffective and even functioning as a marketing tool to gain consumer compliance. Critics also note the limitations of such an approach in protecting work and labour standards (Donaghey et al., 2014).

In contrast, multistakeholder approaches, involving independent actors, are generally considered more effective for improving labour standards across supply chains, with the International Labour Organization being a notable example. Although only a few global framework agreements have been established, these agreements tend to be negotiated by unions with lead firms to provide a reference point for conditions for suppliers and subcontractors to adhere to (Donaghey et al., 2014). However, studies show that even when such agreements are present, lead firms tend not to enforce them in the absence of strong local unions and national regulatory institutions (Davies et al., 2011).

Moreover, trade unions have been identified as key actors in encouraging and compelling lead firms to adopt labour-friendly supply chain practices to minimise risks arising from poor management practices at the supplier level (Drahokoupil & Fabo, 2019). For instance, trade unions have actively advocated for improved working conditions and safety standards within garment factories. Following tragic incidents like the Rana Plaza collapse in Bangladesh in 2013, trade unions have pushed lead firms to prioritise factory safety, enforce building standards, and invest in facilities that ensure the well-being of workers (Siddiqi, 2016). However, supply chain pressures and weak membership coverage make it difficult for unions to convince lead firms to improve conditions among suppliers. Successful union campaigns in the UK have managed to overcome these challenges by identifying their strategic position in the supply chain and creating alliances with and beyond the workplace. For example, Mendonça and Adăscăliței (2020) demonstrate that a local union in the whisky industry in Scotland strategically used health and safety standards as a platform to improve working conditions. The authors show that trade unions can successfully defend workers' employment rights by exploiting the opportunities provided by the architecture of the supply chain and taking advantage of supply chain 'choke points'. The case study presented by Mendonça and Adăscăliței (2020) illustrates that trade unions can successfully assert coalitions with other organisations across supply chains. The union's successful attempt to reframe poor health and safety standards as an industry issue rather than restricting it to their workplace provided the opportunity for workers to enhance their bargaining power and to promote multi-sited governance compromises. Therefore, the union compensated for the lack of institutional support with an inclusive strategy (Doellgast et al., 2018) that framed health and safety issues as a sectoral rather than workplace issue.

In contemporary discussions on global supply chains, consumer mobilisation has been recognised as a key force in labour rights campaigns, as consumers leverage their influence to compel lead firms to adopt ethical practices (Saeed & Kersten, 2019). However, limitations exist; these strategies are most effective against large and renowned firms, may not yield sustained regulatory outcomes, and could result in firms relocating operations without addressing root issues. To overcome these challenges, I advocate for a synergy between consumer and trade union campaigns. Trade unions, with their expertise and capacity for sustained advocacy, can complement consumer-driven initiatives, ensuring enduring regulatory pressure, collaborative oversight, and advocacy for systemic changes within the industry. This collaborative approach addresses the shortcomings of consumer-driven activism, offering a more comprehensive and sustained framework for addressing labour issues in the complex dynamics of global supply chains.

CONCLUSION

This chapter provides a conceptual analysis of the power dynamics operating through supply chain configurations and how these shape and constrain firm behaviour to create pressures on work and employment. It has engaged in trends pre- and post-pandemic and how these affect flexible work practices in terms of employment and experienced working conditions. Research on supply chain and flexibility often shows that labour is weakened in various dimensions: employment is being fragmented by organisational and workplace fissuring; employment is becoming less secure and working hours are becoming ever-more uncertain by increasing organisational needs to rapidly adjust to market demands; jobs are becoming less skilled by increasing standardisation and atomisation of the labour process so that companies can better monitor and evaluate performance across supply chains; fragmentation of the workforce supports a divide and rule strategy that further weakens labour power and agency; and lastly, informal work is enabled by technological advancements together with permissive regulatory and procedural apparatus.

Given the discussion above, in the post-pandemic context it is likely that future trends in supply chain dynamics will continue to reinforce the power imbalances and challenges faced by labour. The ongoing trends of employment fragmentation, increased job insecurity, uncertain working hours, and the standardisation of labour processes are anticipated to persist. The pressure on companies to rapidly adapt to market demands may intensify, exacerbating the precarious nature of work. The use of technology for monitoring and evaluating performance across supply chains is expected to expand, contributing to further job standardisation and atomisation. Additionally, the divide and rule strategy, facilitated by the fragmentation of the workforce, may persist as a means to weaken labour power and agency. Informal work, aided by technological advancements and permissive regulatory frameworks, may continue to grow.

Studies show that labour and work organisation are central to the articulation between firms as well as to the creation of value within the complex context of supply chain and inter-firm dynamics (Drahokoupil & Fabo, 2019). This supports the conceptualisation in the organisational pursuit of flexibility embedded in supply chain dynamics as having direct impact on work and employment conditions. Firstly, the cost efficiency coupled with production demand volatility (flexibility) tend to push suppliers across the supply chain to adopt increasingly flexible working practices. Consequently, workers within rationalised supply chains tend to experience lower levels of job security, as well as heightened pressure to accept non-standard working hours, unexpected calls for overtime, and shift extensions (Mendonça & Adăscăliţei, 2020; Wood, 2016). In addition, the drive towards reliability and predictability within the supply chain is argued to result in task standardisation and implementation of monitoring technology. Technologically driven changes to work organisation when introduced are used to ensure further inter-firm integration and more reliable supply chains, free of disruption. However, this may impact workers' skill utilisation and discretion. On the one hand, new technology can become integral to more direct and longer-term relations between lead firms and suppliers, as it enables easier monitoring of suppliers' key performance metrics (and service-level agreements); but rather than enhancing workers' skill to increase inter-firm coordination, the governance relationship may introduce technology to achieve supply chain targets more reliably, leading to a more automated work context and making worker skill irrelevant. Therefore, supply chain dynamics, organisational behaviour and its labour outcomes cannot be dissociated.

REFERENCES

Adăscăliței, D., Heyes, J. & Mendonça, P. (2022). The intensification of work in Europe: A multilevel analysis. *British Journal of Industrial Relations*, 60(2): 324–47.

Aloisi, A. & De Stefano, V. (2022). Your *Boss Is an Algorithm: Artificial Intelligence, Platform Work and Labour*. Oxford: Bloomsbury Publishing.

Briken, K. & Taylor, P. (2018). Fulfilling the 'British way': Beyond constrained choice – Amazon workers' lived experiences of workfare. *Industrial Relations Journal*, 49(5–6): 438–58.

Brown, G.D. (2021). Women garment workers face huge inequities in global supply chain factories made worse by COVID-19. *NEW SOLUTIONS: A Journal of Environmental and Occupational Health Policy*, 31(2): 113–24.

Butollo, F., Gereffi, G., Yang, C. & Krzywdzinski, M. (2022). Digital transformation and value chains: Introduction. *Global Networks*, 22(4): 585–94.

Caroli, E., Gautié, J., Lloyd, C., Lamanthe, A. & James, S. (2010). Delivering flexibility: Contrasting patterns in the French and the UK food processing industry. *British Journal of Industrial Relations*, 48(2): 284–309.

Cennamo, C., Ozalp, H. & Kretschmer, T. (2018). Platform architecture and quality trade-offs of multihoming complements. *Information Systems Research*, 29(2): 461–78.

Chan, J., Pun, N. & Selden, M. (2013). The politics of global production: Apple, Foxconn and China's new working class. *New Technology, Work and Employment*, 28(2): 100–15.

Chen, C.C. & Chen, M.H. (2021). Well-being and career change intention: COVID-19's impact on unemployed and furloughed hospitality workers. *International Journal of Contemporary Hospitality Management*, 33(8): 2500–20.

Coe, N.M. & Yang, C. (2021). Mobile gaming production networks, platform business groups, and the market power of China's Tencent. *Annals of the American Association of Geographers*, 112: 307–30.

Coe, N.M., Dicken. P. & Hess. M. (2008). Global production networks: Realizing the potential. *Journal of Economic Geography*, 8(3): 271–95.

Davies, S., Hammer, N., Williams, G, et al. (2011). Labour standards and capacity in global subcontracting chains: Evidence from a construction MNC. *Industrial Relations Journal*, 42(2): 124–38.

Dicken, P. (2015). *Global Shift: Mapping the Changing Contours of the World Economy*. London: Sage Publications.

Dobbins, T., Johnstone, S., Kahancová, M., Lamare, J.R. & Wilkinson, A. (2023). Comparative impacts of the COVID-19 pandemic on work and employment – why industrial relations institutions matter. *Industrial Relations: A Journal of Economy and Society*, 62(2): 115–25.

Doellgast, V., Lillie, N. & Pulignano, V. (2018). From dualization to solidarity: Halting the cycle of precarity. In Doellgast, V., Lillie, N. & Pulignano, V. (eds), *Reconstructing Solidarity: Labour Unions, Precarious Work, and the Politics of Institutional Change in Europe* (pp. 1–58). Oxford: Oxford University Press.

Donaghey, J., Reinecke, J., Niforou, C. et al. (2014). From employment relations to consumption relations: Balancing labour governance in global supply chains. *Human Resource Management*, 53(2): 229–52.

Drahokoupil, J. & Fabo, B. (2019). *Outsourcing, Offshoring and the Deconstruction of Employment: New and Old Challenges* (pp. 33–61). Springer International Publishing.

Flecker, J. & Meil, P. (2010). Organisational restructuring and emerging service value chains: Implications for work and employment. *Work, Employment and Society*, 24(4): 680–98.

Flecker, J., Haidinger, B. & Schönauer, A. (2013). Divide and serve: The labour process in service value chains and networks. *Competition & Change*, 17(1): 6–23.

Fuchs, M., Dannenberg, P. & Wiedemann, C. (2021). Big tech and labour resistance at Amazon. *Science as Culture*, 31(1): 29–43. doi:0.1080/09505431.2021.1937095.

Gavin, M., Poorhosseinzadeh, M. & Arrowsmith, J. (2022). The transformation of work and employment relations: COVID-19 and beyond. *Labour and Industry*, 32(1): 1–9.

Gereffi, G., Pananond, P. & Pedersen, T. (2022). Resilience decoded: The role of firms, global value chains, and the state in COVID-19 medical supplies. *California Management Review*, 64(2): 46–70.

Guest, D. (2017). Human resource management and employee well-being: Towards a new analytic framework. *Human Resource Management Journal*, 27(1): 22–38.

Hadjisolomou, A. & Simone, S. (2021). Profit over people? Evaluating morality on the front line during the COVID-19 crisis: A front-line service manager's confession and regrets. *Work, Employment and Society*, 35(2): 396–405.

Hadjisolomou, A., Newsome, K. & Cunningham, I. (2017). (De) regulation of working time, employer capture, and 'forced availability': A comparison between the UK and Cyprus food retail sector. *The International Journal of Human Resource Management*, 28(21): 3047–64.

Håkansson, K. & Isidorsson, T. (2018). Job quality for temporary agency workers and client organisation employees at a Swedish manufacturing plant. In *Job Quality in an Era of Flexibility* (pp. 177–99). London: Routledge.

Hoque, K., Kirkpatrick, I., Lonsdale, C. & Ruyter, A. (2011). Outsourcing the procurement of agency workers: The impact of vendor managed services in English social care. *Work, Employment & Society*, 25(3): 522–39.

Howson, K., Ustek-spilda, F., Bertolini, A. et al. (2022). Stripping back the mask: Working conditions on digital labour platforms during the COVID-19 pandemic. *International Labour Review*, 161(3): 413–40.

Jones, P. & Bano, N. (2021). The right to disconnect. Available at: https://autonomy.work/wp-content/uploads/2021/08/the-right-to-disconnect-AutonomyFINAL.pdf. Accessed 14 October 2023.

Kalleberg, A. (2003). Flexible firms and labour market segmentation: Effects of workplace restructuring on jobs and workers. *Work and Occupations*, 30(2): 154–75.

Kano, L., Narula, R. & Surdu, I. (2022). Global value chain resilience: Understanding the impact of managerial governance adaptations. *California Management Review*, 64(2): 24–45.

Khaled, A. & Ansar, A. (2023). Bangladesh's ready-made garments sector rebound: Revisiting gendered labor precarity and dependency. *Asian Journal of Comparative Politics*, 20578911231170208.

Kougiannou, N.K. & Mendonça, P. (2021). Breaking the managerial silencing of worker voice in platform capitalism: The rise of a food courier network. *British Journal of Management*, 32(3): 744–59.

Li, J., Ghosh, R. & Nachmias, S. (2020). In a time of COVID-19 pandemic, stay healthy, connected, productive, and learning: words from the editorial team of HRDI. *Human Resource Development International*, 23(3): 199–207.

López, T., Riedler, T., Köhnen, H. & Fütterer, M. (2022). Digital value chain restructuring and labour process transformations in the fast-fashion sector: Evidence from the value chains of Zara & H&M. *Global Networks*, 22(4): 684–700.

Mallett, O., Marks, A. & Skountridaki, L. (2020). Where does work belong anymore? The implications of intensive homebased working. *Gender in Management: An International Journal*, 35(7/8): 657–65.

Marchington, M., Grimshaw, D., Rubery, J. & Willmott, H. (2005). *Fragmenting Work. Blurring Organisational Boundaries and Disordering Hierarchies*. Oxford: Oxford University Press.

McIntyre, D., Srinivasan, A., Afuah, A., Gawer, A. & Kretschmer, T. (2021). Multisided platforms as new organizational forms. *Academy of Management Perspectives*, 35(4): 566–83.

Mendonça, P. (2018). Job quality, flexibility and obstacles to collective agency. In *Job Quality in an Era of Flexibility* (pp. 160–76). London: Routledge.

Mendonça, P. & Adăscăliţei, D. (2020). Trade union power resources within the supply chain: Marketisation, marginalisation, mobilisation. *Work, Employment and Society*, 34(6): 1062–78.

Mendonça, P., & Kougiannou, N.K. (2023). Disconnecting labour: The impact of intraplatform algorithmic changes on the labour process and workers' capacity to organise collectively. *New Technology, Work and Employment*, 38(1): 1–20.

Mendonça, P., Kougiannou, N.K. & Clark, I., (2023). Informalization in gig food delivery in the UK: The case of hyper-flexible and precarious work. *Industrial Relations: A Journal of Economy and Society*, 62(1): 60–77.

Mithani, M.A. (2017). Liability of foreignness, natural disasters, and corporate philanthropy. *Journal of International Business Studies*, 48: 941–63.

Mulholland, K. & Stewart, P. (2014). Workers in food distribution: Global commodity chains and lean logistics. *New Political Economy*, 19(4): 534–58.

Nikolopoulos, K., Punia, S., Schäfers, A., Tsinopoulos, C. & Vasilakis, C. (2021). Forecasting and planning during a pandemic: COVID-19 growth rates, supply chain disruptions, and governmental decisions. *European Journal of Operational Research*, 290(1): 99–115.

Panwar, R., Pinkse, J. & De Marchi, V. (2022). The future of global supply chains in a post-COVID-19 world. *California Management Review*, 64(2): 5–23.

Price, R. (2016). Controlling routine front line service workers: An Australian retail supermarket case. *Work, Employment and Society*, 30(6): 915–31.

Polkowska, D. (2021). Platform work during the COVID-19 pandemic: A case study of Glovo couriers in Poland. *European Societies*, 23(suppl.): 321–S331.

Rikap, C. (2022). Amazon: A story of accumulation through intellectual rentiership and predation. *Competition & Change*, 26(3–4): 436–66.

Robinson P. & Rainbird H. (2013). International supply chains and the labour process. *Competition & Change*, 17(1): 91–107.

Ruggie, J.G. (2013). *Just Business: Multinational Corporations and Human Rights*. New York: W.W Norton & Co.

Saeed, M. & Kersten, W. (2019). Drivers of sustainable supply chain management: Identification and classification. *Sustainability*, 11(4): 1137.

Sharma, M., Luthra, S., Joshi, S. & Kumar, A. (2022). Developing a framework for enhancing survivability of sustainable supply chains during and post-COVID-19 pandemic. *International Journal of Logistics Research and Applications*, 25(4–5): 433–53.

Siddiqi, D. (2016) Before Rana Plaza: Towards a history of labour organizing in Bangladesh's garment industry. In *Labour in the Clothing Industry in the Asia Pacific* (pp. 78–97). London: Routledge.

Skountridaki, L., Zschomler, D., Marks, A. & Mallett, O. (2020). Organisational support for the work-life balance of home-based workers. *The Work-Life Balance Bulletin*, 4(2): 16–22.

Sobieralski, J. (2020). COVID-19 and airline employment: Insights from historical uncertainty shocks to the industry. *Transportation Research Interdisciplinary Perspectives*, 5: 100123.

Sturgeon, T.J. (2021) Upgrading strategies for the digital economy. *Global Strategy Journal*, 11(1): 34–57.

Thun, E. & Sturgeon, T. (2019). When global technology meets local standards: Reassessing China's mobile telecom policy in the age of platform innovation. In Rawski, T. & Brandt, L. (eds), *Policy, Regulation and Innovation in China's Electricity and Telecom Industries* (pp. 177–220). Cambridge: Cambridge University Press.

Unison. (2020). Lack of protective equipment for health and social care staff is 'a crisis within a crisis'. Available at: https://www.unison.org.uk/news/article/2020/04/lack -protective -equipment -health -social -care -staff -crisis -within -crisis/. Accessed 20 September 2023.

Vallas, S. & Schor, J.B. (2020). What do platforms do? Understanding the gig economy. *Annual Review of Sociology*, 46: 273–94.

Weil, D. (2014). *The Fissured Workplace*. Cambridge, MA: Harvard University Press.

Wood, A. (2016). Flexible scheduling, degradation of job quality and barriers to collective voice. *Human Relations*, 69(10): 1989–2010.

Wright, C. & Kaine, S. (2015). Supply chains, production networks and the employment relationship. *Journal of Industrial Relations*, 57(4): 483–501.

14. Innovation, technology and the changing world of work

Peter Holland, Nadia K. Kougiannou and Chris Brewster

In 2019, Holland and Brewster penned a chapter in a Routledge book about not predicting the future. The central narrative was that the acceleration of work and life, while not uniform across the world, was invariable in the same direction – intensifying. Two months later, the pandemic hit, and everything stopped – or did it? As the traditional mode of commuting to work for most knowledge workers in Advanced Market Economies (AMEs) came to a halt initially, the existing yet underutilised technological advancements became pivotal. This led many individuals to transition into what has now evolved into a widely recognised work terminology: working from home (WFH). This trend has persisted beyond the pandemic, shaping the emergence of a new normal – the hybrid model.

The transformation in work and employment dynamics stemmed from the convergence of flexible work structures and innovative technological advancements, as highlighted by the central themes of this book's title. This convergence sparked an accelerated shift in how we work following the initial disruption caused by the pandemic and its subsequent waves globally. In the current context, as we write this post-pandemic, our aim has been to encapsulate some of these transformative changes within the pages of this book. During the course of writing this book, notable acceleration has continued, particularly evident in advancements related to artificial intelligence (AI) and robotics. While this book addresses their relevance within the gig economy context, the expanding discourse on their influence on the landscape of work and employment might warrant exploration in a separate publication.

We structured the book into four major parts in an effort to encapsulate a comprehensive overview of substantial changes and offer a contextual understanding of the evolving landscape. It is important to acknowledge that the contemporary flexible work patterns we discuss have been under development and scrutiny for several decades. In Part I, the focus was context. After the editors' synopsis, Kougiannou and Mendonça discussed the evolving work landscape, examining its challenges to traditional assumptions regarding work's location, mode, performance, and nature. They concur that the pandemic has hastened these transformations, particularly in remote work, non-traditional work arrangements, and automation. Within the framework of technology and innovation themes, their argument emphasises the substantial growth of the gig economy and its workforce. They foresee continued turbulence in work patterns and practices with the introduction of novel and disruptive forms of flexible work patterns. They emphasise a crucial aspect, echoing Kelliher's point, which highlights the dark side of the newfound flexibility within the gig economy. This flexibility redefines the work relationship for workers, often depriving them of the benefits and protections typically granted to traditional employees. Consequently, this scenario can lead to a race to the bottom, fostering substandard working conditions and a lack of regulation. Kougiannou and Mendonça term this as 'hyper-flexibility', advocating for regulations within the platform economy.

In the third chapter of this section, Kelliher notes, flexible working arrangements have become increasingly prevalent globally in the past four decades, influenced by factors such as advancements in technology, innovation, global integration, more intense competition, and changing workforce attitudes to work. Kelliher importantly notes that flexibility has become an umbrella term for multiple work arrangements, extensively researched. An analysis of this research enables an understanding of the benefits to specific stakeholders, as well as the 'darker side' of flexible working, such as the trade-off between employment security for flexibility. What she observes is that the pandemic has served as a catalyst in perpetuating the discussion around flexibility, with the experiences gained during this time likely to persist in shaping the perspectives of both workers and managers regarding flexible work arrangements. Consequently, it becomes crucial for researchers and policymakers to actively monitor these ongoing developments.

In the book's second part, we explore the complexities surrounding time, place, and space to grasp the evolving array of flexible work patterns highlighted in the first part. Wheatley critically assesses authentic and faux flexibility. While acknowledging technology's role in augmenting time flexibility and the pandemic's influence in fostering hybrid work models, Wheatley emphasises that this shift isn't universal across all job types. He asserts that in the flexibility discourse, managerial and professional occupations often emerge as the winners due to their bargaining power, contrasting starkly with lower-skilled jobs, where what might seem like flexibility could actually be encapsulated in the insecurity of zero-hour contracts or perceived flexibility within gig work. Wheatley underscores the paradox of apparent autonomous control in such contexts, where actual control remains with management either directly or through (AI) algorithms. This dynamic plays out in a scenario where work becomes pervasive, occurring anytime and anywhere. Nonetheless,

Wheatley remains optimistic, suggesting that by reducing micro-management and adopting job redesign approaches, positive avenues for flexibility can be attained for all parties involved.

Bučiūnienė and colleagues, in exploring the place of work through the evolution of telework, provide an understanding of the drivers and barriers to this form of work. As with the narrative throughout this book, the pandemic significantly shifted perceptions surrounding telework. Despite studies indicating enhanced productivity and improved work-life balance associated with telework, the management's lingering concern revolves around production paranoia. This stems from their reluctance to relinquish 19th-century management practices rooted in physical surveillance, instead of favouring a trust-based approach that prioritises productivity as a paramount metric. A theme supported by Calvo. Bučiūnienė and colleagues argue that the pandemic has irreversibly altered people's habits and elevated their expectations for flexible work opportunities, further accelerating the shift towards flexible work patterns. Much like Wheatley, they highlight job design as a pivotal aspect in monitoring employee performance.

Finally, Garcés et al. conclude this part with a focus on innovation in a changing world. The authors call for the post-pandemic period to be an opportunity to relaunch social dialogue on several aspects, including the maintenance of jobs and secure worker income. While, they note, there are political and economic factors that will mark the agenda. Exploring this from a European perspective, the authors argue that the pandemic may have functioned as a stimulus for European social cohesion. Providing a voice to social stakeholders and strengthening them as sources of legitimate representation helps pool efforts that can be essential in cohesive societies. The authors note that the protection afforded to those in the labour market during the pandemic, making certain rules more flexible, helped protect the most vulnerable. As will be noted, a theme of regulation runs through these chapters.

Part III is a deliberate thought-provoking section focusing on the impact of the changes described in this book on traditional aspects of the work environment. Kougiannou and Holland explore the impact of the changing landscape of work through the lens of workplace communication, specifically employee voice and silence. With the rapid acceleration of hybrid and remote work through the widespread adoption of smart technology, they note that the shift to remote work may also have unintended consequences on organisational communication structures. They investigate the potential fragmentation of voice systems, shedding light on the adverse aspects of these changes. Their exploration unveils the possibility for management to exploit these evolving work patterns by constructing a unitarist voice system. In this scenario, management exercises control over the message, themes, and narrative by dominating the communication systems. They argue that these issues are emerging within a context where new voice systems are lacking development in this virtual space.

The darker aspect of flexibility is continued in Tham and colleagues' review of electronic monitoring and surveillance (EMS) in the evolving virtual workplace. Examining the emerging research on the rapid surge in EMS during the pandemic, which has led to the autonomy-flexibility paradox outlined in Part II, reveals that higher flexibility levels result in increased and broader forms of control. Moreover, the blurring of boundaries between work and home in remote and flexible arrangements raises valid concerns about the breach of privacy. This issue is exacerbated by the lack of clear legal frameworks governing electronic tracking, monitoring, and work surveillance in many countries. These emerging issues demand immediate attention in the management of these new work approaches.

This part concludes with Forsyth's analysis of the role and future of trade unions in this rapidly changing work environment. His analysis raises concerns about the future trajectory of trade unions. Similar to earlier chapters in this part, Forsyth highlights a noticeable power shift favouring management, underscored by several prominent case studies. His primary conclusions emphasise the imperative for unions to adapt through technology, appealing to younger and marginalised workers. Echoing Kougiannou and Mendonça's perspective, Forsyth stresses the necessity of exerting pressure on governments to establish supportive regulatory systems that amplify union representation as the voice of the workforce. Aligning with the core theme of this book, Forsyth argues for the continued relevance of unions as a defence against employer power in the hyper-flexible contemporary workplace. Here, he underscores how AI and other technologies have transformed into new tools for employee surveillance, performance management, and discipline.

The final part explores the broader topics and challenges of the emerging workplace in terms of learning development, employability, disadvantages, and supply chains. Anderson concludes that advancements in technological capabilities, alongside the swiftly evolving work landscape, hold the potential to unsettle established labour markets. This assertion leads her to advocate for a re-examination of the foundational assumptions guiding learning, development, and employability. The primary takeaway from Anderson's analysis is the imperative, at a macro level, to reassess education and training systems. This re-evaluation aims to cultivate the requisite levels of skill and proficiency demanded by an increasingly uncertain labour market, necessitating a fundamental overhaul. This aligns with Anderson's proposition of a necessary paradigm shift in assumptions concerning the purpose of workplace learning. Specifically, this shift is vital in response to heightened global competition, supporting organisational agility, and fostering responsiveness.

Building on this theme, Meacham and Chhim's argument explores the intricate dynamics of flexibility in the labour market, particularly its role as an entryway for marginalised individuals. They underscore the crucial point that while flexibility appears to offer an opportunity for workforce participation among marginalised groups, there's a need to revisit the discussion about the negative dimensions of flexible work. They specifically emphasise two critical issues within this domain. The first centres around the challenge of work identification, highlighting that in certain flexible work arrangements, individuals might face difficulties in establishing a consistent or clear professional identity. The second concern pertains to the potential for exploitation within flexible work structures. Contrary to the perceived flexibility, these arrangements might actually manifest as more rigid or exploitative, subjecting individuals to precarious conditions such as unpredictable schedules, inadequate compensation, or limited job security. This exploitation, often disguised under the guise of flexibility, can actually constrain individuals' choices and opportunities rather than empower them as initially presumed.

The final chapter in this part by Mendonça explores the effect of international supply chain issues on work. As with the role of unions, Mendonça highlights the power dynamics operating through supply chains shaping work and employment and illustrates that supply chain use of flexibility often weakens and fragments employment, making it a less secure variable. Work is being de-skilled with a fragmentation of the workforce, highlighting a divide-and-rule strategy by management that further weakens labour power and agency. Mendonça suggests that future trends in supply chains will continue to reinforce the power imbalances and challenges faced by labour as market demands intensify, exacerbating the precarious nature of work.

Mendonça's concluding remark highlights the omnipresent impact of technology on the landscape of work and employment, which has entrenched itself deeply in modern society. It reinforces the realisation that predicting the future of work and employment is challenging, characterized by volatility, uncertainty, complexity, and ambiguity (VUCA). This acknowledgement indicates a paradigm shift wherein the traditional methods of foreseeing work patterns may not hold true in this evolving landscape. However, amid this uncertainty, there exists an opportunity for innovation and creative adaptation in the realm of work, as emphasised throughout this book. Recognising this potential highlights the adaptability and resilience of individuals and organisations in responding to the challenges posed by the VUCA nature of the future of work.

Nevertheless, as illuminated in our exploration, there is also a parallel acknowledgement of the darker aspects emerging within these evolving contours of the work landscape. The recognition of these darker aspects within the changing landscape of work serves as a crucial reminder of the complexity inherent in these transformations. While innovation and adaptability are pivotal for progress, it's equally imperative to acknowledge the potential downsides that can accompany rapid changes. The evolving contours of the work landscape have brought to light various challenges. For instance, as organisations strive for enhanced flexibility and technological integration, there's a risk of inadvertently perpetuating inequities. This might manifest as the exacerbation of disparities in access to opportunities, unequal treatment of different workforce segments, or the creation of a two-tier system where some workers benefit while others face intensified challenges or exploitation. Moreover, the constant pursuit of efficiency and optimisation might inadvertently overlook the well-being of individuals within the workforce. Recognising these potential adverse effects underscores the need for a balanced approach. It's not just about embracing change but doing so responsibly. This calls for proactive measures that prioritise the fair treatment of workers within these shifting dynamics. Organisations and policymakers alike need to implement strategies that ensure fairness, inclusivity, and sustainability in the evolving work landscape. This proactive stance might involve developing and enforcing policies that safeguard against exploitation, fostering inclusive work cultures that value diversity and well-being, and creating mechanisms for continuous evaluation and adjustment to mitigate any unintended negative consequences of rapid changes. Ultimately, the goal is to foster a work environment that not only embraces innovation and adaptability but also upholds ethical standards, respects individual well-being, and strives for equity and sustainability amid the evolving contours of the work landscape.

Index